Managing the Windows NT Registry

Managing the Windows NT Registry
by Paul Robichaux

Copyright © 1998 O'Reilly & Associates, Inc. All rights reserved.
Printed in the United States of America.

Published by O'Reilly & Associates, Inc., 101 Morris Street, Sebastopol, CA 95472.

Editor: Robert Denn

Production Editor: Clairemarie Fisher O'Leary

Printing History:

April 1998: First Edition.

This book is printed on acid-free paper with 85% recycled content, 15% post-consumer waste. O'Reilly & Associates is committed to using paper with the highest recycled content available consistent with high quality.

ISBN: 1-56592-378-2

Table of Contents

Preface

Keys and Values and Classes, Oh My!

The Registry scares people. Practically every Win95 or NT user or administrator has some horror story of the damage done to a machine by careless Registry editing. Microsoft doesn't try to discourage this perception, either; the MS Knowledge Base and documentation is liberally peppered with warnings about the dire consequences of screwing something up if you make a mistake.

While making a mistaken Registry edit can indeed send your machine to Blue Screen Of Death territory quick as a wink, there's no reason to be afraid of the Registry any more than you'd be afraid of a chainsaw, your car, or a high-speed lathe. If you know how to safely handle any of those inanimate objects, you can do much more work with them than you could do manually.

This book will teach you how to safely use the Registry; how to administer, back up, and recover NT machines' Registry data, both locally and over the network; and how to use the Registry editing tools Microsoft supplies, and when you should—and should not—do so.

Who's This Book For?

This book is for anyone running Windows NT, particularly people responsible for administering NT machines or providing technical or help desk support. It's also for programmers who are familiar with the Win95 Registry and its workings but are making the move to the similar-looking but internally different NT world.

To get the most out of this book, you should be familiar with the NT user interface; you should know how to right-click, run programs, and so on. Some background as an NT administrator would be useful, but it's not required.

How This Book Is Organized

The book is organized into ten chapters:

Chapter 1, *A Gentle Introduction to the NT Registry*, locates the Registry in the evolution of Windows systems. After a historical discussion of INI files and their traditional role as the repositories of configuration information, the chapter offers an apologia for the Registry, its philosophy and its advantages.

Chapter 2, *NT Registry Nuts and Bolts*, discusses the keys, subkeys, values, and hives that comprise the Registry structure.

Chapter 3, *In Case of Emergency*, provides the compendium of caution. The major topics of discussion include the creation of emergency repair disks and strategies for effectively backing up and restoring the Registry.

Chapter 4, *Using RegEdit*, is a complete guide to the original Registry editor.

Chapter 5, *Using RegEdt32*, is a similar guide to Microsoft's 32-bit Registry editor.

Chapter 6, *Using the System Policy Editor*, explains the roles of system policies and the management of them with POLEDIT.

Chapter 7, *Programming with the Registry*, presents the Registry API and follows up with sections on how to administer the Registry with programs implemented in C++, Perl, and Visual Basic.

Chapter 8, *Administering the NT Registry*, covers a number of vital topics, including user accounts, INI file mapping, remote access, security, and a number of Resource Kit utilties.

Chapter 9, *Registry Tweaks*, is a collection of tips and tricks you can use to bring your own system's Registry under control.

Chapter 10, *The Registry Documented*, is a snapshot of the Registry keys created by the Windows NT system. It is supplemented by the online Registry documentation you can find at *http://oreilly.windows.com/registry*.

Conventions in this Book

Throughout this book, we've used the following typographic conventions:

`Constant width`
>   indicates a language construct such as a data type, a data structure, or a code example. Text in constant width also indicates Registry key and value names. In syntax statements, `*constant width italic*` denotes placeholder elements for which the user must provide actual parameters. **Constant**

width **bold** in examples indicates text that the user enters into the computer.

Italic

in text represents filenames, URLs, function names, variable names, utilities, and function names. Italic is also used to highlight the first mention of key terms.

Registry path names can get long and unwieldy. To save space, we've used the following abbreviations for the top-level keys:

```
HKCR   HKEY_CLASSES_ROOT
HKCU   HKEY_CURRENT_USER
HKLM   HKEY_LOCAL_MACHINE
HKU    HKEY_USERS
HKCC   HKEY_CURRENT_CONFIG
HKDD   HKEY_DYN_DATA
```

We'd Like Your Feedback!

We have tested and verified all of the information in this book to the best of our ability, but you may find that features have changed (or even that we have made mistakes!). Please let us know about any errors you find, as well as your suggestions for future editions, by writing:

O'Reilly & Associates, Inc.
101 Morris Street
Sebastopol, CA 95472
1-800-998-9938 (in the U.S. or Canada)
1-707-829-0515 (international/local)
1-707-829-0104 (FAX)

You can also send us messages electronically. To be put on the mailing list or request a catalog, send email to:

nuts@oreilly.com

To ask technical questions or comment on the book, send email to:

bookquestions@oreilly.com

Acknowledgments

Books don't write themselves; they are the end product of a long cycle of blood, sweat, toil, and tears powered by many people who are often invisible to the reader. I'll mention them in reverse order, starting with the professional yet pleasant production team at O'Reilly & Associates. Robert Romano did an excellent job of converting my weird-looking diagrams into attractive illustrations, and Edie Freedman gets the credit for the orangutan on the cover. Clairemarie Fisher O'Leary copyedited and managed the production of the book. Seth Maislin created the index, and Mary Anne Weeks Mayo, Ellie Maden, and Jane Ellin provided quality assurance. If it weren't for these editors, artists, and general book-fixers, you'd be holding a stack of inkjet-printed 8.5"x11" pages in your hands instead of an actual book. Erik Ray is the primary author of the CGIs that make the book's companion web site tick.

Before the production team got their hands and keyboards on the book, a group of technical reviewers pored over every page, looking for mistakes, clumsy explanations, and other obstacles. If you find a mistake, it's my fault; if you don't, they get the credit. My thanks to the reviewers: Sean K. Daily, an MCSE and contributing editor for *Windows NT Magazine*, Lori Hufford of Enterprise Software Solutions, Inc., Rajeev Nagar of NT Core Services, and Andy Oram and Eric Pearce of O'Reilly.

Before *that*, I actually had to write the book. I am fortunate to have two bosses, Larry and Janie Layten of LJL Enterprises, who encourage my writing, even when it has nothing to do with my nominal job description. I also would like to recognize John Johnson, Martin Liversage, Donald MacLean, Hermann Tse (with whom I used to regularly argue about OLE at Intergraph), Michael Seamans, Darren Tidwell, Bryan Wilkerson, Chris Williams, and other readers of the NT Security mailing list who contributed Registry tweaks to flesh out Chapter 9.

I would be remiss if I didn't mention that this book was entirely written on an Apple Power Macintosh 8100, which serves as my primary writing machine. In fact, I even wrote the code in Chapter 7 on the Mac using Metrowerks CodeWarrior, then tested and debugged it on a "real" PC running NT 4 and 5. I use NT every day and love it, but I'm a more productive writer with the Mac—go figure.

Throughout the writing and production of this book, I was privileged to work with Robert Denn, the editor of O'Reilly's NT book line. He provided a great deal of useful direction while I was writing, and I appreciate his help. I wouldn't have written this book if it weren't for my agent, David Rogelberg of StudioB. He got tired of me complaining that I wanted to write an "O'Reilly book," so he went out and found me one.

Finally, my wife Arlene and toddler David were heroically patient and supportive of me. In fact, David threw a fit while at our local public library; his grandmother was trying to get him away from one of the public-access Win95 machines, and David loudly protested "But I have to finish writing my *book!*" My love and thanks go to them both.

In this chapter:
- *A Brief History of the Registry*
- *What Does the Registry Do?*
- *Advantages Offered By the Registry*
- *Registry Zen*

1

A Gentle Introduction to the NT Registry

The Windows NT Registry plays a key role in making NT work. It serves as a central data repository, and it's involved in everything you do with NT-based computers, from the initial boot sequence to logging in and running applications and services. For such an important component, though, there is surprisingly little documentation that explains how the Registry works, what's in it, and what it's good for. Even seasoned NT administrators admit to being a little unsure of the Registry's inner workings.

Part of the Registry's mystery comes from the fact that its data is stored in a special format that can be read only with the tools and API routines Microsoft provides; part of it comes from the strict warnings against Registry tampering plastered on page after page of NT-related documentation, books, and web pages. However, since the Registry's an integral part of NT, you have to be comfortable using, repairing, and modifying it if you want to administer systems running NT. The overall goal of this book is to demystify the Registry's workings and help you understand when, how, and why NT services, applications, and operating system components use it so you'll be better able to administer the machines under your care.

A Brief History of the Registry

Before I plunge into the nuts and bolts of working with the Registry, let me set the stage by explaining how the Registry gained its starring role in Windows NT. Besides being good preparation for amazing your friends with computer-industry trivia, the Registry's path to fame illustrates some of its strengths and weaknesses.

In the beginning, of course, there was no Registry. MS-DOS applications were responsible for keeping track of any persistent settings they supported in their own configuration files. The operating system had its own set of configuration files, the most famous of which are *config.sys* and *autoexec.bat*, for controlling hardware and operating system settings.

At first blush, this approach may seem reasonable. After all, applications' settings are generally private, and they don't usually affect other programs. Most components of MS-DOS itself weren't configurable anyway, so there was little need (or demand) for a better configuration mechanism. If the configuration or settings data for a single application was lost or corrupted, restoring it was reasonably simple and could be done without affecting anything else on the computer.

Windows 3.0

Windows 3.0 improved on the MS-DOS approach by introducing the idea of a single, system-wide set of preference and settings data for the operating system. In addition to DOS's configuration files, Windows 3.0 itself added four *initialization files* (*progman.ini*, *control.ini*, *win.ini*, and *system.ini*) that contained information about the system's hardware configuration, device drivers, and application settings. These files quickly became known as *INI files*, after their extension.

Microsoft chose a simple ASCII format for INI files; not only did this ease the task of writing programs to use these files, but it also made it possible for end users to inspect and change their contents. One of the important features Microsoft wanted to deliver in Windows 3.0 was Macintosh-like customization; users wanted to be able to set their own color schemes, fonts, desktop backgrounds, and so on. By default, the Windows File Manager included a file mapping so that double-clicking an INI file would open it in the Notepad text editor, as shown in Figure 1-1.

In addition to storing Windows' settings in INI files, Microsoft provided a set of API routines (often called the *private profile API*) that gave programmers a way to create their own initialization files. The theory was that application programmers could use INI files to store private settings that were specific to their applications. Settings that could be shared between applications—for example, lists of which fonts were installed on a computer—were supposed to live in the system's INI files, while application-specific settings would go in the application's private INI files. Application programmers enthusiastically embraced this idea, and before long most applications used INI files for their private settings.

However, INI files weren't perfect; in fact, they suffered from some fairly serious weaknesses:

They were easily editable
> An old quote from the Unix *fortune* program says that you can make software foolproof, but you can't make it damn-fool proof. INI files quickly provided a

```
[Encryption]
Card=LJL_ENT
Card=LJL_FORT
;Card=LJL_DES
EntrustEncryptionAlgorithm=CAST
BypassProfileSelection=1
;DontIncludePlainTextFileIfSigning=0
Default Per=0
Receipt=0
Crypt Mode=SIGN
Card=LJL_Fort
OverWrite=1
SaveOpenMessagesInTheClear=No
Update=1
Timeout=0
SendAsSingleAttachment=1
DontIncludePlainTextIfSigning=0
DontUUencodeAttachments=0

[Directories]
ADDRESSBOOK=C:\MS-ARMOR\ENTRUST.DIR
;ADDRESSBOOK=C:\MS-ARMOR\KEYCACHE.DIR
;Tracer=DebugLog.txt
MultiCryptoPrefs=C:\MS-ARMOR\mprefs.txt
PLUGINS=C:\MS-ARMOR\plugins\
FORTCACH=C:\MS-ARMOR\FORTCACH\
```

Figure 1-1. Simple INI file

concrete example of this old saw; because INI files were editable, users felt free to edit them. This flexibility did make it easy for users to customize their environments or make necessary changes; it also made it much easier for a user to break a single application, an entire service (like printing or file sharing), or Windows itself by making an accidental or ill-informed change to an INI file.

They were easy to break

INI files provided a one-way link between a program and its settings; they weren't flexible enough to account for changes in the machine's configuration or environment. For example, many presentation graphics programs would build a list of available fonts during their installation process. If you later added—or, worse, removed—fonts, the presentation package might or might not notice the changes, meaning that you either couldn't use newly installed fonts or could crash while trying to use fonts the application thought were still available. This lack of flexibility was partly due to the fact that Windows didn't have any way to get notification when something on the computer was changed; without these alerts, there was no way to tell when INI file data needed to be updated.

They led to Balkanization

Microsoft didn't provide any explicit guidelines covering where INI files should be stored or what should go in them; in the absence of these rules, application programmers felt free to put INI files in various locations. Some used the Windows directory itself, while others stored their INI files in the same directory as the application or in some other seemingly logical location. To compound the problem, some applications put their private data directly into *win.ini*, while others kept their own private copies of things like font lists and printer settings that were explicitly supposed to be shared between applications.

They had implementation limits

INI files had to be smaller than 64Kb in length; in addition, the Windows profile API calls would blissfully ignore all but the first instance of settings with the same name within one section. An even more serious limit was that INI files were inseparably bound to the original PC concept of "one user, one machine"; there was no way to easily move settings around so that users who needed to use different computers could keep their preferred settings.

The First Registry: Windows 3.1

Windows 3.1 added several new features that improved interapplication integration and ease of use. Chief among them were two new technologies, Object Linking and Embedding (OLE) and drag-and-drop. Both of these features required an up-to-date, correct database of program locations and capabilities. For example, object embedding could only work if the source and destination applications had some way to communicate exactly what type of data was being embedded, and the File Manager required access to a database of mappings to associate files with the applications that created them.

To provide this oracle, Windows 3.1 included the first Windows *registration database,* which quickly became known as the Registry. This Registry offered solutions to several of the problems posed by INI files:

The Registry provided a single place for storing data

Instead of segregating data into separate INI files, both system and application-specific configuration data could be stored in the Registry. In the original Windows 3.1 implementation, all Registry data was stored in a single file named *reg.dat.* Keeping system and application settings in one place reduced both the number and complexity of INI files; in addition, having a one-stop system for storing preferences and setting data made it possible to better share information like font lists between different applications.

The Registry wasn't as easy to edit

INI files were plain text, so it was easy to edit them. This was both a blessing and a curse; users could make changes when necessary, but they were often prone to making unnecessary or instability-causing changes. The data in *reg.dat* was stored using an undocumented binary format, and the only way users could edit it was with the Windows 3.1 Registry editor. Windows 3.1 also introduced the first version of the Registry access API, thus making it possible for programmers to read and write Registry data directly from their programs.

The Registry had a clearly defined hierarchical structure

The structure of INI files was haphazard at best: sections could appear in any order within the file, and values could appear anywhere in the section. There was no good way to group related settings, especially when they might appear in different files!

However, the Windows 3.1 Registry still wasn't perfect. It only supported a single hierarchy, and the *reg.dat* file was still subject to the 64Kb size limitation that hampered INI files. In addition, Windows 3.1 itself didn't improve on the problem of synchronizing the Registry's contents with the state of software, fonts, and other items actually loaded on the computer, so there was no guarantee that the Registry, the INI files, and the actual software loaded on the computer would stay in synch. Finally, the 3.1 Registry didn't offer any solution to the problem of allowing users' settings to move with them to different computers on a network, or even allowing more than one user to keep settings on a single machine.

Despite these shortcomings, the Windows 3.1 Registry introduced several features that carried over into its successors. First and foremost is the concept of the Registry's hierarchy, which looks much like the structure of a Windows directory tree. In a file system, the topmost item is a disk drive, which can contain any number of files and folders. Each folder can in turn contain nested subfolders or files, and you can uniquely identify any object on the disk by constructing a full pathname that points to it; for example, *c:\users\paul\proposal.doc* and *c:\program files\ eudora\attach\proposal.doc* are different files, even though they share the same name. The topmost item in the Registry's structure (corresponding to a disk drive in a file system) is a *root key*. All other keys in the Registry are children of one of the root keys (although Windows 3.1 only supported one root key, named HKEY_ CLASSES_ROOT). Each key can contain either *values* (the Registry equivalent of a data file) or nested *subkeys*. Just as with files and folders, you can uniquely identify a Registry key by building a full path to it.

In addition to providing a hierarchy for keys, the Windows 3.1 Registry introduced the idea that keys had names and values. The key's name (for example, DisableServerThread) can be combined with the full path to the key to identify it (as in HKEY_LOCAL_MACHINE\System\CurrentControlSet\Control\ Print\DisableServerThread). The value for the key holds whatever data belongs to the key; the actual contents vary from key to key.

Windows NT 3.1, 3.5, and 3.51

Windows NT was introduced in 1993 as Microsoft's industrial-strength operating system. It was expressly designed to compete with Unix workstations and servers; since these machines easily supported multiple users who could take turns using a single computer, shared workspaces, and network-wide configuration sharing, Microsoft decided that NT would need to do all of these as well. To accomplish these goals, NT would need a more flexible and capable Registry than the one in Windows 3.1, so they kept the basic concepts but changed both the implementation and capabilities to match NT's requirements.

As I've noted before, the NT Registry is key to everything NT does—from the time the machine boots until you shut it down, applications, drivers, and services depend on the data they get from the Registry to do their jobs. Since the Registry was going to be ubiquitous, some implementation changes were needed. First to go was the old 64Kb limit; NT Registry files can grow as large as needed. Instead of using a single file, NT's Registry data is split up into a number of files, but they all appear as a single set of keys. To handle the variety of data that needed to be stored, Microsoft added several additional root keys (see Chapter 2, *NT Registry Nuts and Bolts*, for details on these keys). In addition, a great deal of effort went into optimizing the Registry-handling code to keep Registry performance from being a system-wide bottleneck.

NT's security model could easily take up a book on its own, but I'll boil it down to its bare essence: every object in an NT machine has a unique security ID, is owned by someone, and can have its own access control list (ACL) that determines who can read, modify, and remove the object. Under NT, anything can be an object: files, devices, the Win32 subsystem, and Registry keys are just four prominent examples. The Registry itself is an object, as are all its keys; this means that each root key or subkey can have an ACL associated with it, so it's possible to grant very fine-grained control over which users and system components can read and modify keys.

NT also provided tools that could remotely access the Registry on one computer from another; for example, a system administrator can use his machine to view and modify the Registry on any machine to which he has administrator access. This makes it easier for administrators to troubleshoot and fix Registry-related problems, since they can often make an initial diagnosis without leaving their desks.

Microsoft strongly encouraged developers writing NT software to use the Registry instead of INI files. They set a fairly good example by making most NT system components and applications use the Registry themselves; as an added incentive, they provided a special facility that lets older Windows 3.x programs automatically use the Registry instead of an INI file by creating a copy of the INI file in the Registry.

To top off these changes, NT 3.1 included a brand-new, 32-bit Registry editor, *RegEdt32* (see Figure 1-2). Each root key appears in its own child window; in addition to showing keys in a familiar tree format, *RegEdt32* adds commands for connecting to remote computers' registries, viewing and changing access controls on keys, and exporting and importing Registry entries. (All of these commands will be explained in Chapter 5, *Using RegEdt32.*)

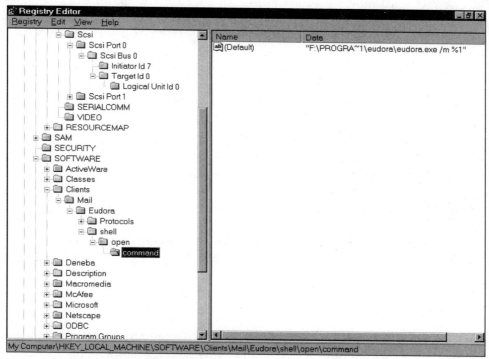

Figure 1-2. RegEdt32, the NT Registry editor

NT 3.5 and 3.51 didn't make any fundamental changes to the Registry's implementation or behavior; they did, however, add new keys to the Registry to support their new features. Different versions of NT have different sets of Registry keys; for example, some keys that were part of the 3.51 Registry aren't used in 4.0; conversely, 4.0 adds a number of new keys that weren't present (and won't be recognized by) NT 3.51.

Windows NT 4.0

NT 4.0 combined the underpinnings of NT 3.51 with the Win95 user interface; given this heritage, it's not surprising that NT 4.0 has a large number of Registry keys with names identical to Win95 keys. The primary Registry-related change between NT 4.0 and its predecessors is the addition of two new Registry keys. In NT 4.0, a single machine may have several hardware profiles that reflect different configurations; for example, a laptop computer running NT might have one profile that includes drivers for devices in a docking station (for use when it's docked) and another, with different drivers, for when it's on the road. HKEY_CURRENT_CONFIG provides access to the current hardware and driver configuration, but what's *in* that configuration depends on which hardware profile the user chooses during the boot process. HKEY_CURRENT_CONFIG was included in NT 4.0 so that Win95 applications that use it would be able to run under NT 4.0. HKEY_DYN_DATA provides a root key for information that's generated on demand, like Performance Monitor counter data. This dynamic data isn't stored in the Registry, but applications can access it locally or remotely by using the standard Registry API calls.

In addition to these changes, NT 4.0 fully integrates the Win95 concept of *system policies*. These policies control what users may and may not do on their machines; for example, a policy can specify that users can use the *Run* command in the Start menu and that they can't move icons around on the desktop. These policies can apply to individual users or computers, members of defined groups, or all machines or users in an NT domain. Policies are actually implemented as Registry settings; the System Policy Editor (shown in Figure 1-3) provides a friendlier (and safer!) alternative to the Registry editor for building and distributing system policies to one or many computers in a domain or workgroup.

Windows 95

Even though Win95 actually came between NT 3.51 and NT 4.0, I've saved it for last because it's so similar to the NT 4.0 Registry. Both support multiple root keys, and both store their data in several different files instead of Windows 3.1's single file. The Win95 Registry is also tightly integrated with—and heavily used by—all components of the OS. However, the underlying implementation is very different between the two; in fact, there's no Microsoft-supported way to migrate data between the two systems' Registries or share data between them. The basic ideas remain the same, though. Win95 has the same set of root keys from NT 3.51, plus two new ones: HKEY_CURRENT_CONFIG and HKEY_DYN_DATA. The overall organization of the two Registries is similar. The Win95 Registry doesn't support NT-style security (though you can enable remote access), but it does support hardware and user profiles in much the same way. See the Nutshell Handbook *Inside*

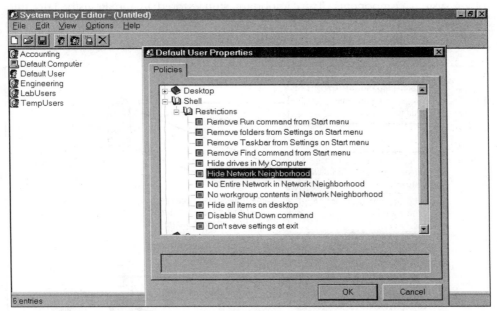

Figure 1-3. SPE for managing small- or large-scale policies

the Windows 95 Registry, by Ron Petrusha (O'Reilly & Associates, 1996) for a complete dissertation on the guts of Win95's Registry implementation.

What Does the Registry Do?

The concept of a central repository that holds all the system's configuration data may strike you as a boon (since it keeps applications and services from scattering their settings in hundreds of small files buried in odd locations) or a danger (since it provides a single point of failure.) The truth is somewhere in between these extremes. The Registry provides a neat, tidy way for applications, device drivers, and kernel services to record configuration data. That data can be used by, and easily shared between, the original owner or by other system components. At the same time, if the Registry is damaged, the effects can range from not being able to use a single application to not being able to boot NT at all. (Chapter 3, *In Case of Emergency,* details the backup and recovery tools you can use to keep this single point of failure from causing you trouble.)

It Holds Lots of Important Stuff

The chief role of the Registry in NT is as a repository for settings data. In this role, it acts as a sort of super-librarian; system components can look for the data they need in the Registry and use what they find to control how they interact with other system components. The "important stuff" stored in the Registry falls into five separate categories; each category's data is gathered during a particular stage of the boot process, as shown in Figure 1-4.

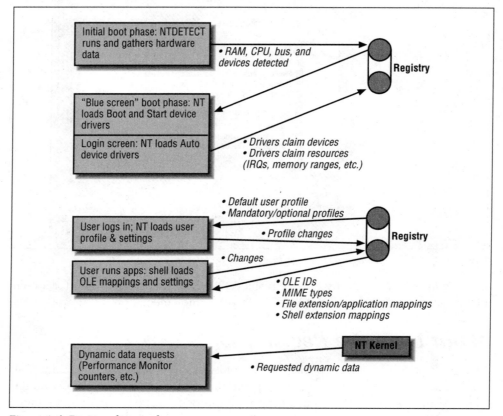

Figure 1-4. Registry data exchange

Hardware configuration data

As part of the NT boot loader's normal execution, it runs a program called *ntdetect;** as its name implies, *ntdetect* figures out what hardware exists on the computer. This configuration data is basically an inventory of five things:

- The number, kind, and type of system processors
- The amount of system physical RAM
- The types of I/O ports available

---

* When NT runs on RISC hardware (MIPS, PowerPC, or Alpha, though NT 4.0 only supports the latter two), the ARC firmware handles hardware detection; *ntdetect* is only for x86-based machines.

- The bus types (PCI, EISA, ISA, VLBus, etc.) the system has installed
- The devices found on those system's buses

Once all this information has been gathered, *ntdetect* stores it in memory and maps it to the Registry's HKEY_LOCAL_MACHINE\HARDWARE subtree so that the NT kernel and device drivers will have access to it. No hardware configuration information is written to disk, since at the time the kernel loads it the needed drivers won't have been loaded yet! Because knowing the low-level details of the hardware is critical to the kernel, this detection phase has to happen first. Hardware configuration data is strictly read-only; no system components are allowed to change keys in this section of the Registry once their values have been established. As you might expect, this is part of the reason why NT 4.0 doesn't fully support plug-and-play.

Driver parameters and settings

After the hardware detection phase, the NT boot loader loads the NT kernel, which handles the difficult work of finding the right driver for each device installed in the computer. The kernel can load device drivers in three different places. Drivers that are set to load during the boot phase load immediately after the kernel. These drivers are typically low-level drivers that provide basic services to other drivers, like the NT PCMCIA card and IDE disk drivers. Once those drivers have loaded, the famous NT "blue screen" appears; in addition to the other things happening during this boot phase, the kernel will also load any drivers whose load state is set to "system." These drivers, which are usually mid-level components like the CD-ROM driver, usually require the presence of one or more boot drivers like the IDE, SCSI, or ATAPI drivers. Once NT has booted into its GUI, the logon dialog will appear and the kernel will begin loading any drivers marked as "automatic." Automatic drivers can be loaded as the result of some system action (the remote access service, or RAS, drivers are automatically loaded when you start or receive a RAS connection) or automatically as part of the GUI startup.

No matter where it falls in the boot process, each driver makes heavy use of the Registry during its initialization. As each driver loads, the kernel uses the Registry for three things. First, the kernel's driver loader walks through the hardware configuration inventory to figure out which driver to load for each device. Second, once NT identifies the right driver for a device, the driver starts; as part of its startup, the driver will claim the device it "owns" by marking it as owned in the Registry. Finally, the driver reserves whatever machine resources it needs; for example, the generic SoundBlaster16 driver provided as part of NT 4.0 will attempt to reserve an IRQ, port address, and DMA block to talk to the sound card. Which values it requests depends on the hardware configuration information gathered by *ntdetect*. Once the driver has staked out the device and resources it needs, the Registry will reflect the driver's reservations so other drivers that load later in the boot sequence won't try to seize them. Each of these steps uses a separate sub-tree under `HKEY_LOCAL_MACHINE\HARDWARE`; see the specific subkey mappings in Chapter 2 for complete details on which subkeys correspond to each phase.

Dynamic data

Actually, no dynamic data is stored in the Registry at all! Instead, the NT kernel intercepts requests for subkeys of the `HKEY_DYN_DATA` key and returns the requested data directly. Because the data for this key is assembled on demand and not written to disk, `HKEY_DYN_DATA` doesn't show up in the Registry editor. This is less of a problem than it might seem, since that data isn't of any use to you directly anyway. The NT Performance Monitor (and, of course, kernel components) can get to it when needed.

User profiles and user-specific settings

From its inception, NT supported the idea that more than one person could use a single computer. Each user on an NT machine (whether it's a workstation or a server) has her own *profile* that controls when, how, and whether she can log on, what scripts or programs are executed at logon time, and what she can do once logged on. In addition, the user's profile stores the contents of her Start menu, the appearance of the desktop, and other look-and-feel settings. This profile's actually a composite of the data from several different subkeys in the Registry, including security account manager (SAM) data for the user, plus a number of settings scattered around in different places in the Registry. To users, however, it looks like it's all one seamless collection of data—your workspace magically reappears when you log onto any computer in your domain.

In earlier versions of NT, these profiles were only usable on one machine—you and your officemate could share a PC in your office, but if you had to go down the hall to use another machine your profile wasn't available, and you'd be stuck with an unfamiliar workspace. To solve this problem, NT 4.0 included support for two new types of profiles: *roaming* and *mandatory* profiles. In many environments (like college computing labs or workstation clusters in an engineering office), it makes sense for a user's settings to be kept on a central server and downloaded to whatever machine the user actually logs onto. This makes it possible for a user to sit down at any machine, not just the one at her desk, and go right to work. Roaming profiles make this possible; when you log onto a machine in a domain that uses roaming profiles, your profile will be fetched from the server and cached in the local machine's Registry. Mandatory profiles work the same way, but with a twist: by using the System Policy Editor, system administrators can restrict what changes you can make to the profile, and if you do make any changes, they won't be stored back on the central server. In practice, this means that administrators can build profiles that configure users' workspaces a certain way and don't allow users to change them—a great help for environments where lots of people need to share machines.

OLE, ActiveX, and COM

Windows 3.0 introduced the concept that a file's extension could be used to automatically figure out which program was used to create it. Adding these *file associations* to the Windows File Manager meant that Windows users could double-click on a data file to launch the application that created it and open the file.* In Windows 3.0, these associations were kept in the *win.ini* file, but in Windows 3.1 and later, they're stored in the Registry instead. Windows 95 and NT 4.0 extend the concept of associations to include information about the kind of data stored in the file, too; this is especially useful for figuring out what to do with data downloaded by a web browser.

Windows 3.1 also marked the debut of Object Linking and Embedding, or OLE. OLE was designed to allow users to build compound documents that contained several different types of data. For example, you could create a Word document and embed an Excel chart and an Imagineer Technical† mechanical drawing in it, then edit either of the embedded objects without leaving Word using what Microsoft called *in-place activation* (IPA). IPA required a large amount of new information to work; to start with, there had to be a list of all the types of data that could be embedded in a document, plus some way to figure out which program to run when the user wanted to create a particular kind of data object. The original Windows 3.1 Registry only had one root key, HKEY_CLASSES_ROOT; its purpose in life was to store the data that OLE needed to function.

In 1993, Microsoft started touting the Component Object Model, or COM, as the wave of the future. (The combination of COM and OLE has since been retitled ActiveX; you've probably heard of *that* by now.) The basic idea behind COM is that developers can break their software down into lots of little, independent objects that communicate with each other via COM interfaces.‡ As with OLE, though, COM requires still more new data to make it work. Each type of object has to have its own unique ID so the system can tell them all apart; in addition, the system has to somehow keep track of which interface methods a particular

---

* This is of course only one of the many Macintosh features that Microsoft "adopted" as part of the Windows GUI. While reading the rest of this book, see how many others you can spot.

† Imagineer Technical® is a little-known but very cool 2D drafting and technical illustration package from Intergraph. I used to work on its OLE support code, so I still have a soft spot for it.

‡ If you *really* want more details, try *Inside OLE* by Kraig Brockschmidt (Microsoft Press, 1994) for 1400 pages or so of hard-core OLE. Not recommended for the faint of heart.

object supports (especially since COM objects can pass commands back and forth). ActiveX controls, which can be embedded in web pages, Office documents, and other kinds of documents have the same requirements—the system has to be able to turn the unique class ID into the name of the program it should run to create, draw, or edit the object. All this data (and more besides) lives under the HKEY_CLASSES_ROOT subtree.

Application settings

So far, I've only talked about how the operating system uses the Registry. Applications can use it too, and most well-written Win32 applications do. The proliferation of INI files in Windows 3.x was bad for users, but it was every bit as bad for most software vendors—imagine trying to troubleshoot a customer's problem when your product's settings are intertwined with settings for every other program on that user's computer! The Registry offered a neat solution to this problem, with the twin benefits of better performance and some tamper-resistance thrown in as *lagniappe.**

Microsoft's guidelines (which may be, and frequently are, freely ignored) say that third-party programs should install program-specific settings in the HKEY_LOCAL_ MACHINE\SOFTWARE\<VendorName> subtree. For example, Netscape's products keep their settings under HKEY_LOCAL_MACHINE\SOFTWARE\Netscape. This key is for settings that pertain to the program itself, not the user's configuration settings for that program. User-specific settings go under the user's key in HKEY_ USERS. This is a subtle but important distinction. As you can see in Figure 1-5, the settings under the Netscape Navigator key in each of the Registry root keys are quite different. HKEY_LOCAL_MACHINE\SOFTWARE\Netscape\Netscape Navigator\4.04 (en) stores information about where different components of Navigator are installed, while the corresponding entry under HKEY_CURRENT_USER\ SOFTWARE\Netscape has settings that apply only to my configuration, like where my personal bookmark file is stored.

Applications and system components can store any data they want in the Registry: configuration settings for hardware or software, user preferences, paths to shared components, licensing information, and so on. Most "modern" Win32 applications tend to keep *all* their settings in Registry values. For example, the Office 95 and Office 97 suites use the Registry to store information about each user's preferences for which toolbars are displayed, whether the Office Assistant appears, and so on. Netscape and Microsoft's web browsers both keep their user profile data in the Registry too.

---

* *Lagniappe* is a Cajun French word meaning "something thrown in for free as part of a deal." For example, "Mais, I bought dat houn dog from Pierre and he t'rew in 10 pound of shrimp for lagniappe."

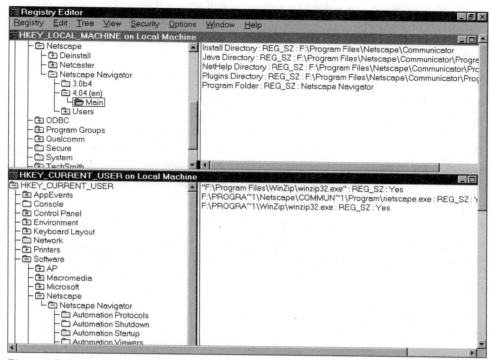

Figure 1-5. User versus application settings

Of course, applications can freely use any of the other types of data stored in the Registry. For example, an image-retouching program can use the Registry to get the I/O address of the port to which the user has connected her digital camera, or a web page editor might use it to fetch a list of all the ActiveX objects a user can embed in a page he's designing. For the most part, though, well-behaved applications will read but not modify keys that aren't theirs.

Advantages Offered By the Registry

The Registry offers a number of significant benefits to programmers, users, and administrators. These benefits stem from the characteristics I just described.

It Keeps Everything Tidy

Instead of the dozens (or even hundreds) of separate INI files typically found on a Windows 3.1 machine, NT machines usually only have a few—and those typically belong to 16-bit legacy applications that can't use the Registry. NT itself uses the Registry for its configuration data, as do almost all 32-bit applications for Win95 and NT. There's more to tidiness than just the reduction in clutter that comes from eliminating INI files, though. Centralizing where configuration information is stored makes it easier for administrators to back up, restore, and secure the data.

It Provides Security

Access control for the Registry comes in two sizes. First, you can set individual workstations or servers to disallow any remote Registry connections at all. While this is secure, it also makes it impossible to use the System Policy Editor to set and inspect policies on that machine. A better and more fine-grained solution is to use NT's built-in access control lists. As I mentioned earlier, each Registry key, from the root keys on down, can have its own individual set of access permissions in the form of ACLs that apply to the keys.

Each entry in an ACL actually has two parts: a permission (as shown in Table 1-1) and the account or group name that holds the permission. ACL permissions are usually written like this, with the holder first and the permission following:

```
Everyone:Read
paul:Full Control
Engineering:Full Control
```

Table 1-1. Registry Access Permissions

Permission	What it allows
Read	Read-only access to a specific key, its subkeys, and their values (includes Query Value and Enumerate Subkeys)
Query Value	Getting the data or contents of a specific key's value
Set Value	Changing the value of a specific key
Create Subkey	Creating a new subkey under the key that holds this permission; the new subkey will inherit the parent's permissions unless they're explicitly changed
Enumerate Subkeys	Traversing all subkeys of a specific key and getting their full path names
Notify	Getting or setting auditing notifications
Create Link	Creating a symbolic link (like a shortcut or a Unix symlink) that points to another key in the Registry
Delete	Removing the specified key, its subkeys, and all associated values
Write DAC	Changing the Discretionary Access Control (DAC), or permissions, on the specified key
Write Owner	Changing the owner associated with the specified key
Read Control	Reading the access control list for the key
Full Control	All of the above rights; Full Control allows the holder to do literally anything to the keys with that permission

Any account or group that is listed in the ACL will have the matching permission; any group or account that's *not* in the ACL will have *no* access. This gives you precise control over Registry access, since anyone you don't explicitly include in an ACL won't have any access.

In addition to whatever accounts you've got defined on your workstation or domain, you can use the built-in NT accounts and groups. In particular, you'll see the Everyone account* used to grant read access to most keys in the Registry, while the Administrators and Domain Admins groups usually have Full Control access to all keys. Since many NT software installers require write access to the `HKEY_LOCAL_MACHINE\Software` and `HKEY_CURRENT_USER\SOFTWARE` subkeys, you'll often see them tagged with `Everyone:Full Control`. It's also worth mentioning the SYSTEM account name; SYSTEM refers to processes and services owned by the kernel, so it's usually used to grant Full Control access to many of the keys in `HKEY_LOCAL_MACHINE`.

Besides their access controls, Registry keys also have owners; for example, the Administrators group owns the `HKEY_LOCAL_MACHINE\HARDWARE` subkey. You can restrict access to parts of the Registry by changing their ownership to a single account to which you control access; since any account that's not in an ACL won't have any access, everyone except the owner will be locked out.

As an additional security feature, NT allows you to create an audit trail of access to, and operations on, the Registry. When you enable auditing for a key, you specify two things:

What actions you want audited
    You can create an audit trail of the success or failure (or both) of all of the permissions in Table 1-1 except Read, Full Control, and Write Owner.

Which accounts will be audited
    The accounts you specify will generate audit trail entries when they attempt one of the actions you specify.

The auditing data is written to NT's system event log, where you can view it with the Event Viewer application or parse it with programs or scripts you've written.

It Allows Remote Management

Every computer running NT has a Registry. If you're supporting more than one NT machine on a network, you'll be happy to know that the Registry supports network inspection *and* modification. This capability, which is built into *RegEdit* and *RegEdt32*, allows you to troubleshoot and fix some types of Registry prob-

---

* Everyone's not really an account; it's a special token that matches *any* account in the SAM database, but you can use it anywhere in NT that you could specify a "real" account. NT 4.0 SP3 also includes the new Authenticated Users token, which is similar.

lems on network machines from your desktop. In addition, network Registry access makes it possible to automatically inspect the Registry of every machine on your network—a valuable way to gather statistical ("how many of our machines are still running Netscape Navigator 2.x?") or configuration ("what machines have *impala.oreilly.com* as one of their DNS servers?") data.

NT's system policies require network access to the Registry; there are also a number of useful administrative tools and utilities that build on network Registry access. For example, the *ERDisk* product from MWC (*http://www.ntsecurity.com/*) allows you to build an Emergency Repair Disk (ERD) for a machine across the network; in fact, you can automatically build updated ERDs for all the machines on your network every night if you like. (*ERDisk* is described in detail in Chapter 3.) Microsoft's System Management Server (SMS) product makes heavy use of network Registry access, as does NT 5's Microsoft Management Console.

Registry Zen

Even if you're accustomed to using Windows NT and Windows 95, the Registry may sometimes seem like a New Orleans graveyard at midnight, full of strange shadows, half-glimpsed terrors, and legendary tales of misfortune. In this vein, I want to digress a little to talk about the philosophy behind the Registry, as well as the Zen of editing and using it.

First of all comes the obligatory scare tactic. Microsoft's documentation contains many warnings about the dire consequences that can result from editing the Registry if you aren't careful and knowledgeable. Instead of repeating these warnings, I'll offer one of my own, but just once, so you won't have to keep seeing it over and over.

WARNING   The Registry is a key component of Windows NT. If you remove a necessary key or change a key's value to an out-of-range value, some programs will repair the damage automatically, but others will fail spectacularly. Microsoft's Registry editors immediately make changes, so there's no backing out if you make a mistake. Please don't edit the Registry on your production machines until you've read Chapter 3, which explains how to recover from a damaged Registry.

You can think of the Registry like one of those self-service storage warehouses that have popped up across North America like sheet-metal mushrooms. If you've never seen one, let me briefly digress: these warehouses, which usually have catchy names like "Public Storage" or "U-Store-It," are fenced compounds filled with long, low metal buildings. These buildings are segmented into individual garages. When you rent a space, you get the magic code that opens the outer gate, and you use your own lock to secure the unit you've rented. Once you've rented it, the space is yours to use as you wish (though you're not supposed to live in them or keep anything illegal or dangerous there).

Just like the local U-Store-It, every tenant of the Registry has its own individual space, where it can store anything under the sun. Access to that space is controlled both by the operating system and the tenant who created the keys. Also like the real-world equivalent, the landlord takes no responsibility for protecting what's in individual spaces—that's up to the renter (or application). That's where the analogy stops, though. In Windows NT, Registry keys fall into three basic groups:

Keys you don't need to edit directly

> Keys in this group have some other way to set their value; most control panels are nothing more than pretty interfaces that make it easy for you to change settings in the Registry without using a Registry editor. The Explorer's file types dialog box is another good example; all it does is display, and allow you to change, data in the HKEY_CLASSES_ROOT tree.

Keys you must edit directly

> In the grand Microsoft tradition, the NT Registry is chock-full of keys whose values can't be edited anywhere else. For example, you can control how often NT domain controllers synchronize their user account databases, and how much bandwidth they may use to do so, with the HKEY_LOCAL_ MACHINE\System\CurrentControlSet\Services\Netlogon\Parameters\ ReplicationGovernor parameter. Microsoft documented this parameter in the MS Knowledge Base, but the only way to change its value is via the Registry editor. There are also a fairly impressive number of "secret" features that you can only enable or disable by adding, or removing, entries in the Registry.

Keys you should leave alone altogether

> Just because you *can* edit a key in the Registry doesn't mean you *should*. Many of NT's subsystems, particularly device drivers, are intended to be self-tuning; they continually adjust their settings based on the system's workload. If you directly adjust a setting behind its owner's back, your reward can be anything from reduced performance to an unbootable machine.

2

In this chapter:
- *How the Registry Is Structured*
- *What Goes in the Registry*
- *Getting Data In and Out*

NT Registry Nuts and Bolts

Chapter 1, *A Gentle Introduction to the NT Registry,* was just that: it was an introduction, and it was gentle. Now it's time to get down to business and focus on how the Registry actually works. In this chapter, you'll learn how the Registry is organized, both logically and physically, and how data gets into and out of it.

How the Registry Is Structured

Since the Registry is such an important part of Windows NT, understanding how it's put together is crucial to learning how to use, modify, and protect the data it contains. Let's start by examining the basic structures and concepts that underlie the Registry; once you understand how these pieces fit together, we can move on to the data that actually lives in the Registry.

The Basics

You may find it helpful to think of the Registry like a filesystem; their organizations are similar in many respects. Both have a well-defined hierarchical structure, and they both support the concept of nesting items within other items. Files are identified by names and paths; likewise, every key in the Registry is identified by a full path that identifies exactly where to find it. Since the Registry can be shared and accessed over a network, this full path can optionally include a computer name, which works as it would for a file share. The data within a file can be interpreted by applications that understand that file type; so it is with Registry keys, whose values can be understood and used by applications, kernel services, and other Registry clients.

Root keys

Root keys are like disk volumes: they sit at the root of a hierarchy and aren't contained or "owned" by any other item in the hierarchy. Windows Explorer groups all local disks together under "My Computer," and the Win95 *RegEdit* app does the same for Registry keys, but these groupings are fake, since the disks and root keys are actually logically separate entities. The groupings just provide a convenience for users. The six root keys that make up NT's Registry (see the section "The Big Six" later in this chapter) are logically independent of one another; to reinforce this idea, the NT-specific Registry editor, *RegEdt32*, shows each root key in an individual window.

In NT 4.0, there are six root keys: HKEY_CURRENT_USER, HKEY_LOCAL_MACHINE, HKEY_CURRENT_CONFIG, HKEY_DYN_DATA, HKEY_USERS, and HKEY_CLASSES_ ROOT. Earlier versions of NT don't have HKEY_CURRENT_CONFIG or HKEY_DYN_ DATA, and Win95 doesn't have HKEY_USERS.

Subkeys

Any key in the Registry may have subkeys. Just as folders are contained inside other folders, these subkeys can in turn hold other subkeys, and so on down the line. (Throughout the rest of the book, I'll call a subkey's parent a *parent* key.) Naturally, the root keys all have subkeys, but no parent keys; any other key, though, can have both parents and subkeys.

A subkey can have values of its own, or it can be a placeholder for subkeys that contain values themselves. For example, HKEY_CURRENT_USER\Software has subkeys, but it doesn't have any values attached to it. By contrast, HKEY_ CURRENT_USER\Software\Netscape\Netscape Navigator is a subkey too, but it has several values of its own in addition to those of its subkeys. For example, the Netscape Navigator key has subkeys named Bookmark List, Mail, and Security, among others. The Bookmark List key in turn has a value named File Location. If you talk about the value named HKEY_CURRENT_USER\Soft-ware\Netscape\Netscape Navigator\Bookmark List\File Location, then you've completely described the path to a particular value. Leave off File Loca-tion, and you're talking about a subkey.

Values

Speaking of values, now would be a good time to mention that any Registry key can have zero or more values attached to it. These values normally have three components:

- A *name*, which identifies them both to NT and you. Just like files, there can be many Registry values with the same name, but each key can only have one value with a particular name. The combination of the value's name and the path used to reach it must be unique. This means that it's okay to have values named Stuff under both HKEY_CURRENT_USER\Software\SomeVendor\AProduct and HKEY_CURRENT_USER\Software\BigCompetitor\AnotherProduct, but neither of those keys may have more than one value named Stuff.

- A *data type*, which tells the Registry and its clients what kind of data the value represents. The "Major Data Types" and "Minor Data Types" sections later in this chapter elaborate on the available types for Registry data.

- Some *contents*,* which are subject to any limitations imposed by the value's type. In Windows NT, the contents must be smaller than 64K of data. As a practical matter, 2Kb is about the point beyond which performance starts to suffer. In reality, most keys are much smaller—a few dozen bytes at most.

As with most other statements that include the word "normally," there's an exception to this three-part rule: Registry keys can have a single value with *no* name. The Microsoft editing tools will show this value with a name of (Default) or <No Name>; applications can still reach it by querying the key it's attached to.

The combination of these components makes it possible for Registry clients (including editors, applications, and NT itself) to locate specific values, figure out what kind of data they contain, and get that data for whatever purpose necessary.

Hives

Hives aren't just for beekeepers any more;† in the Registry world, a hive is a portion of the Registry tree structure from any subkey under a root key on down. For example, the SOFTWARE hive contains HKEY_LOCAL_MACHINE\Software and all of its subkeys, and their subkeys, and *their* subkeys, on down to the values attached to the "deepest" subkey.

Hives are significant because each hive corresponds to a disk file that contains the hive's data. Instead of INI files, these hive files are the actual on-disk location for the system's crucial configuration data. Consequently, they're what you need to back up and restore (you'll learn how to do this in Chapter 3, *In Case of Emergency*). NT supports seven hives: .DEFAULT, HARDWARE, SAM, SECURITY, SOFTWARE, SYSTEM, and one for the currently logged-in console user. You'll learn what each hive is for and where its corresponding file is stored in the section titled

---

* The contents are just the value's value.

† The best explanation I've heard for this term (courtesy of Sean Daily) is that the term "hives" was used by Microsoft developers for the files that comprise the Registry because the files contained important data essential to NT's operation, data that is compartmentalized into keys, subkeys, values, and data (the "honey" of NT's configuration).

"Hives and Files" later in this chapter. In the meantime, if you look at `HKEY_LOCAL_MACHINE\SYSTEM\Control\CurrentControlSet\hivelist`, you can get a sneak preview of the list of supported hives.

Links

The Windows NT shell and filesystem support shortcuts. (You might be familiar with aliases or symbolic links, the Mac and Unix equivalents.) All a shortcut does is point to something else; for example, the "Inbox" icon on your desktop is actually a shortcut to Microsoft Exchange.* When you double-click it, NT can resolve the shortcut to find the thing it points to and run that instead.

The Registry equivalent of a shortcut is called a link. These links provide alternate paths and names for Registry subkeys. For example, the entire `HKEY_CURRENT_USER` root key is a link to the current user's subkey under the `HKEY_USERS` root. Since links can be built dynamically, it's easy to construct a link whose destination varies depending on some condition or other. NT uses these links internally in a number of places; `HKEY_LOCAL_MACHINE\System\Controls\CurrentControlSet` is a link whose origin depends on which set of device drivers, hardware components, and system software is currently active.

Registry road map

Figure 2-1 shows a road map of the root keys and their major hives. As you can see, several keys and subkeys are actually links to areas in different root keys. You may find it helpful to refer back to this figure as we plunge forward into discussing the six root keys themselves.

The Big Six

The root keys are, well, the root of the Registry's hierarchy. In the Windows 3.1 Registry, there was only one root key; in Windows NT 3.1 there were four, but Windows 95 and NT 4.0 both have the same set of six. These keys form the foundation upon which all of the Registry's capabilities rest; they provide a logical structure for grouping related items, and each of them plays a role in providing configuration data to clients and kernel components.

---

* Or Outlook, or Outlook Express, or Windows Messaging: it depends.

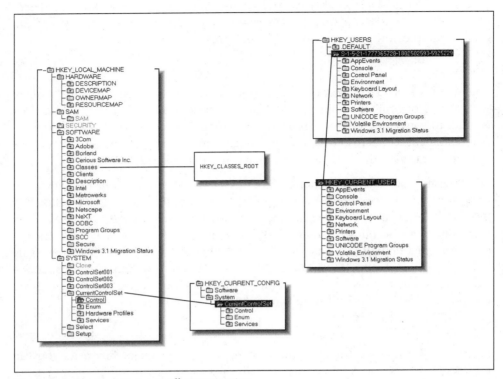

Figure 2-1. The Registry's overall organization

NOTE   You'll notice that all the names start with odd nonwords like HKEY and REG. Microsoft uses a system called Hungarian notation for naming variables; in this scheme, the name of every variable, data type, or constant starts with a short code that identifies the type of data it is. This notation carried over into the Registry's design. HKEY is actually a handle to a key, which seems reasonable for the root keys.

HKEY_LOCAL_MACHINE

HKEY_LOCAL_MACHINE (abbreviated HKLM) is the king of the Registry. Its job is to consolidate and store all of the system-wide configuration data for a particular computer. HKLM includes the hardware configuration data without which NT couldn't even boot. Besides that, it also holds settings for the computer's network connections, security configuration, device driver settings, and more.

There are five major subkeys under HKLM, each of which plays a critical role in keeping NT running. They're enumerated in the section "Major Subkeys of HKLM" later in the chapter. As you may have noticed in Figure 2-1, some of the other root keys and their subkeys are actually links to subkeys of HKLM; that's another reason why this root key is so important. For example, HKEY_CLASSES_ROOT is actually a link to HKLM\SOFTWARE\Classes.

HKEY_USERS

HKEY_USERS (also known as just plain old HKU) contains all the profile and environment settings for users on the local machine. These settings comprise all the per-user controls controllable by the System Policy Editor (see Chapter 6, *Using the System Policy Editor*, for more on SPE), plus user-specific environment variables, as well as user-specific software settings. At a minimum, there will be two subkeys in HKU. The first, .Default, contains a default group of settings (surprise!) that are applied when someone whose profile isn't already in HKU logs in; the second will be for the built-in Administrator account.

Each subkey of HKU is named by its security ID, or SID, a long string of digits that uniquely identifies every system object, process, user, and computer on an NT network. Once an object is created, its SID never changes—but its name can, so NT uses the SID to keep track of user account profiles to keep them working when you change your account name from FredSmith to "The Administrator Formerly Known As FredSmith."* For a more concrete example, the SID for my account on my desktop machine is S-1-5-21-1944135612-1199777195-24521265-500,† so on that desktop machine, HKU has subkeys for my account, the default account (named .DEFAULT), and a test account.

When you create local accounts on a machine running NT (Workstation or Server), their profiles will be stored under HKU when they first log on from that machine's console. When that logon takes place, NT copies the standard profile from HKU\.Default and creates a new subkey under HKU, named with the account's SID. Until an account logs on interactively, no profile will exist. This might seem odd until you remember that network logons (like the ones used to access a file server's shares or printers) don't create or use any of the profile information.

NT supports three types of profiles: *normal, mandatory*, and *roaming*. Normal profiles are just that: plain, unadorned, ordinary groups of settings that live on a single machine. If you have a normal profile on one machine, it won't follow you to another machine, and you may change or modify it as you wish. A mandatory profile is one that can't be changed by the end user. As an administrator, you'll

---

* I wanted to include that odd-looking symbol used by the Artist Formerly Known as Prince but, strangely, it's not anywhere on my keyboard.

† And you thought it was hard to spell "Robichaux"!

probably find it useful to specify unchangeable profile settings for your users and computers. Roaming profiles follow users from machine to machine: they live on the domain controller and are downloaded to a machine when a user logs in. You can combine them, too: you can have normal or mandatory roaming profiles.

For domain accounts,* the workings are a little different. Let's say you're administering an NT domain named *ADMIN* that has a few dozen workstations in it. You add a new account for Catbert, your new VP of human resources.† There are three possible scenarios:

Catbert doesn't have a mandatory or roaming profile
> The first time he logs onto any machine in the *ADMIN* domain, that machine will create a new profile for him, using the SID of his domain account. The new profile will be based on the contents of *that machine's* HKU\.DEFAULT key. Changes made to his profile on one machine won't be visible on any other machine.

Catbert has a roaming profile
> The first time he logs onto a domain machine, that machine will attempt to fetch Catbert's roaming profile from the primary domain controller (PDC). If he's ever logged on to any other machine, and if the PDC is available, the logon machine will make a local copy of Catbert's profile under HKU; if not, it will make a new profile based on that machine's default and use it instead. On subsequent logons, NT will compare the locally cached profile with the one stored on the PDC; if they're different, Catbert gets to choose which profile he wants the machine to honor. Any changes he makes to his profile on one machine will be mirrored back to the PDC, and they'll appear on other machines when he logs into them.

Catbert has a mandatory profile
> Mandatory profiles *must* be used. When setting up an account, the domain admin will specify which mandatory profile Catbert's account will use. When Catbert logs onto a domain machine for the first time, NT will get that profile from the PDC and use it. If the PDC can't deliver the profile for some reason, Catbert's logon attempt will fail. If Catbert makes changes to the profile, they won't be mirrored back to the PDC.

At this point, you might be wondering what's under the individual subkeys of HKU, since each user on an NT machine has her own subkey, which stores her set-

---

* Domain accounts can be used anywhere within an NT domain, while local accounts are available only on a single machine. If this doesn't make sense, see Chapters 14, 15, and 16 of my *Windows NT Server 4 Administrator's Guide* (Prima, 1996), available at fine bookstores everywhere.

† If you don't read the *Dilbert* comic strip: a) you should and b) you won't get this joke.

tings independently of everyone else's. Instead of answering that directly, let's see what lives in `HKEY_CURRENT_USER`.

Profiles Demystified

When you create a user profile, you assign it using the Profile button of the User Properties dialog in the User Manager or User Manager for Domains. Once you specify the UNC path to the profile, NT will automatically download—and upload—the profile so the user has a consistent environment. If you don't explicitly provide a profile for a user account, that account will use the default profile from *%systemroot%\profiles\Default User*. This, then, is the profile you should edit if you want to change what profile-free users will end up seeing.

The best way to build a default profile for your users is to create a special account for profile editing. Log on as that account and modify the profile to your liking, then log off and back on as Administrator. Once you do that, you can use the Copy To... button on the User Profiles tab of the System control panel to copy the profile account's profile to whatever share you specified in the User Manager. The next time a user with a profile logs in, her workstation will get an updated copy of the profile.

To specify that a profile should be mandatory, name it *ntuser.man*. You still have to modify each user's account in the User Manager so that it points to the mandatory profile, but once you do NT will faithfully download and apply it when a user logs in, but changes made on the local workstation won't be propagated back to the original profile as they would with regular profiles.

HKEY_CURRENT_USER

Surprise! `HKEY_CURRENT_USER` (better known as `HKCU`) is actually a link to the currently logged-in user's subkey in `HKU`. Using a link was a smart decision on Microsoft's part; the link allows applications to look up things they need without needing to obtain the current user's SID first. When faced with the choice of finding data in `HKCU\Software\KoolStuff\AnApplication` or the mysterious-looking `HKU\S-1-5-21-1944135612-1199777195-24521265-500\Software\KoolStuff\AnApplication`, the choice is pretty clear.

Microsoft's guidelines specify that applications should put *their* settings into `HKLM` and *users'* settings into `HKCU`. The idea is that settings that apply to all users on a machine go in that machine's key, while settings that users may—and probably will—change should be stored somewhere else. `HKCU` provides this mechanism; as an added bonus, a collection of subkeys under `HKCU` can be used as an individual user profile, and it's easy to store, load, or remove settings on a per-user basis. In fact, when NT loads a profile it actually copies data from the stored profile into HKCU.

HKEY_CLASSES_ROOT

HKEY_CLASSES_ROOT (better known as HKCR) made its debut in Windows 3.1 and has been around ever since. It serves as a giant lookup table that maps file extensions to the applications that own them. The NT shell components (the desktop interface, Windows Explorer, the File Manager, and Internet Explorer 4.x) all make heavy use of HKCR, as do OLE container and server applications and ActiveX-capable software.

HKCR works because each registered file type or OLE class has two subkeys associated with it. File extensions are registered under their own name; for example, Microsoft registers HKCR\.doc, HKCR\.xls, and HKCR\.ppt (among others) as keys for MS Office document types. The file extension key's value specifies the default file type to associate with the extension. For example, the default value of HKCR\.doc is WordPad.Document.1, since WordPad comes with the standard NT installation.

Besides the associated name, the file extension's key can contain a subkey called ShellNew. The NT shell uses this subkey's value to figure out how to create a new instance of that file type when the user requests it. In addition to ShellNew, the file extension key can contain one or more document type keys that tie the extension to particular document types. This allows a single extension like *.doc* or *.bmp* to be shared by several applications on the same machine. Each of these document type keys will contain a ShellNew key.

The file extension key tells the shell what type corresponds to a document, but so what? The Windows 3.1 File Manager could do that too. In order to support OLE embedding and linking, HKCR has some additional tricks that center on the file type key. This key's name will match the default value of an extension key—when you install WordPad, you'll get a new key named HKCR\WordPad.Document.1, which matches the file type specified in HKCR\.doc. Its structure looks like this:

- The CLSID key specifies the globally unique class ID of this particular OLE object type. NT, and thus OLE and ActiveX clients and servers, use these class IDs to figure out what type of object to create when you create a new embedded or linked object.

- The DefaultIcon key's value tells the NT shell where to find the icon for the file type. This is usually the name of the executable that created the file; the value must also include the integer ID of the icon to use, since the executable can contain many different icons.

- `Protocol` stores information that OLE needs to support embedding, linking, and in-place editing, including which OLE verbs (open, in-place activate, deactivate, etc.) the object supports. OLE containers use this data to decide which commands to pass on to embedded or linked objects.

- `Shell` holds subkeys that list the types of operations that can be done on the file type from the shell. In the case of WordPad, there are three: `Shell\Open`, `Shell\Print`, and `Shell\PrintTo`. Each of these has a `Command` subkey that contains the actual command line the shell can use to carry out the associated action. When you select a file in Explorer and open, print, or right-click on it, Explorer will look up the file's type in the Registry, then look for a subkey of `Shell` for that file and the requested command. For example, if you double-click a Microsoft Word 97 document, Explorer will look for `HKCR\Word.Document\Shell\Open\Command` and execute the command it finds there.

HKEY_DYN_DATA

`HKEY_DYN_DATA`, or `HKDD` for short, was originally introduced in Win95. It provides a central clearinghouse for dynamic data that is rebuilt anew each time the OS starts. In Win95, it stores performance data that the Performance Monitor can extract, plus a list of virtual device drivers (the list of which VxDs are installed can potentially change at every boot).

Under NT 4.0 and later (it's not present in NT 3.x), `HKDD` stores performance data only. "Stores" is perhaps a misnomer; none of the data in `HKDD` is ever written to disk. Instead, when an application requests a subkey value for any of `HKDD`'s subkeys, the NT kernel gathers up the appropriate dynamic data, makes a fake subkey under `HKDD`, and passes it back to the requester. Since the data doesn't exist until it's requested, you could even argue that it's not stored in memory.

There's another catch, too: alone among the Big Six, `HKDD` doesn't appear in the NT Registry editor. (It does appear in *RegEdit*, though.) You can't directly enumerate or expand `HKDD`, either, as you can in Win95; only kernel clients can get or set values for keys under `HKDD`, making it pretty worthless to most of us.

NOTE	NT 3.1, 3.5, and 3.51 supported a Registry root key that worked much like `HKDD`. Called `HKEY_PERFORMANCE_DATA`, it was mostly used by NT's Performance Monitor application and by some internal services. It still exists for backward compatibility, but (like `HKDD`) you still can't access it directly.

HKEY_CURRENT_CONFIG

HKEY_CURRENT_CONFIG, abbreviated HKCC, is the one-stop shopping center for data about the computer's current hardware configuration. When NT 4.0 boots, you can choose a hardware profile that reflects your current hardware setup; when you choose a profile, it's stored in the key that HKCC actually links to, HKLM\ SYSTEM\CurrentControlSet\Hardware Profiles\Current. Like HKDD, HKCC is new in NT 4.0; it's not present on NT 3.51 machines.

NOTE   Now that you've made it through one and a half chapters, it's time to start using the conventional abbreviations for the root keys. From now on, I'll refer to root keys with the abbreviations given above, even when they're in paths. Get used to reading HKCU\Software\ Microsoft... instead of the fully spelled out version.

Hives and Files

The Registry appears to be a single monolithic blob of data, but it's not. Instead, it's made up of several hives. Each hive is a separate file or memory block that contains a Registry subtree. The NT kernel knits these individual hives together into a single seamless block; when your application (or any other) queries the Registry, it doesn't have to be concerned with which physical hive the desired key lives in.

NT maintains a list of which hives exist on a particular machine in HKLM\SYSTEM\ Control\CurrentControlSet\hivelist; this key normally contains seven entries, as shown in Table 2-1. Each entry's value contains the full disk path to the corresponding hive file. Interestingly, these paths aren't specified with drive letters; instead, they use paths that are based on the hierarchy of loaded device drivers. At the time NT's kernel loads, the driver hierarchy can be set up, but drive letters can't. The SOFTWARE hive for a machine that boots off the first partition on a SCSI disk with ID 0 looks like this:

    \Device\Harddisk0\Partition1\WINNT\System32\Config\Software

The first half of the path (*Device\Harddisk0\Partition1*) tells NT where to find the disk volume itself (it can either be FAT or NTFS); the second part, *WINNT\ System32\Config\Software*, points to the hive file itself. NT keeps its hives in the *System32\Config* subdirectory of the NT install directory.

This table contains a few surprises. First, let's start with the HARDWARE key. It doesn't have a permanent hive because its data is never stored on disk—but there's an entry for it in the hive list anyway. There's undoubtedly a good reason for this, but no one outside Microsoft knows what it is. Next is the *SID* hive. It's

Table 2-1. Hives and Files

Hive name	Hive file	Corresponding Registry key
.DEFAULT	DEFAULT	HKU\.DEFAULT
HARDWARE	None	HKLM\HARDWARE
SOFTWARE	Software	HKLM\SOFTWARE
SAM	SAM	HKLM\SECURITY\SAM
SYSTEM	System	HKLM\SYSTEM
SECURITY	Security	HKLM\SECURITY
SID	It depends	HKU\SID

not really named that; *SID* is just a placeholder for the SID of the user currently logged into the console. This hive actually points to the user's profile, which can be stored anywhere on the machine but is usually in the *Profiles* subdirectory of the NT system directory. For example, when I'm logged into my desktop PC, the hivelist entry for my SID points to ...*Profiles\Paul\ntuser.dat*. The exact value of this hive's entry will depend on whether the user has an existing profile, whether it can roam, and whether it's mandatory.

By now, you might be wondering why these files exist as separate entities at all. The answer is twofold. The first reason is that splitting the Registry data into the groupings shown in Table 2-1 provides a clean separation between different types of data. The user's profile data (for example) should go in its own hive, since it doesn't have anything to do with the hardware, software, or security configuration of the machine. Likewise, the SAM database goes in its own hive because it doesn't belong just to the local machine—for servers that are part of a domain, the SAM hive holds the *domain* SAM, too. As a bonus, dividing the Registry into several components makes it possible to restore whole sections of the Registry without affecting others. The hive contents were chosen with this in mind; as you'll see in the section "All About Emergency Repair Disks" in Chapter 3, the ability to restore only *part* of the Registry can be invaluable.

Access Controls and Security

NT implements access control and security for the Registry in four overlapping bands. The specifics of how you actually use these settings are discussed in other parts of the book, but it's helpful to understand them at a high level before you move on to implementing them.

Control via Registry APIs

The simplest and least effective control is via a key that Microsoft provided, first in Win95 and then in NT 4.0, which administrators can use to disallow Registry editing on a machine. The good news is that this key, HKCU\Software\

`Microsoft\Windows\CurrentVersion\Policies\System\DisableRegistry-Tools`, exists. The bad news is that this key doesn't actually do anything! Microsoft's Registry editors will check the key and refuse to run if it exists; however, there's no enforcement of this method, so third-party Registry editors can, and do, ignore this value with no penalty.

Worse still, users can clear this flag themselves if they have access (and permission) to use the System Policy Editor. Don't depend on this flag to keep any but the least sophisticated users out of your Registry; even though it's not much help, it's still worth setting.

Remote-access control

The next step up the security ladder is to restrict who can attach to and modify your Registry remotely. By default, NT machines grant remote read access to their Registries. This stands in sharp contrast to Win95, where you have to manually install the Remote Registry Access service on clients whose Registries you want to edit remotely. Depending on the account permissions you have, you may even be able to make changes to other systems' Registries; however, you may disallow it manually as described in the section "Fixing Registry Security ACLs" in Chapter 8, *Administering the NT Registry*.

NT security controls

NT Registry keys all have access controls and permissions attached to them. Unfortunately, by default, in NT 4.0 prior to Service Pack 3, most keys in the Registry had Everyone:Full Control as their permissions. This led to a security exploit popularly known as the "RedButton" or "MWC" exploit, where an untrusted program could attach to and modify Registries on network machines where the exploiter had no Administrator access. SP3 fixes this problem; in addition, the section "Fixing Registry Security ACLs" in Chapter 8 explains how to set adequate NT access controls on your Registry keys.

As an additional safety measure, you can—and should—set up auditing events so you can log changes to the Registry on critical machines. There's a fine line between doing this too much and not enough; there are guidelines in Chapter 8 as well.

System Key Security (SKS)

Microsoft has frequently (and not always fairly) been criticized for leaving security holes in its products. In particular, an exploit was reported in mid-1997 that took advantage of the fact that NT 4.0 and earlier stored some account passwords—those for services—in the Registry. Even though the passwords were obfuscated, having them there represented a security risk, since an attacker could, in theory, grab the hive files and figure out the passwords.

To fix this, Microsoft introduced a new feature called System Key Security, or SKS, in Service Pack 3 for NT 4.0. SKS encrypts a portion of the Registry (mainly the SAM and SECURITY subkeys of HKLM) using the CryptoAPI cryptographic services. As a practical matter, this makes it statistically *very* unlikely that someone will be able to get useful information out of your Registry unless the attacker knows or can steal the key used to encrypt it. You can choose your own password (which then must be entered when you boot the machine), or you can have the system generate and store a password. Either way, without that password, the SAM data stored in the Registry is useless. It's important to note that SKS doesn't keep people from browsing the Registry or opening keys with the programming interfaces; instead, it keeps the data from being read.

Once you turn on SKS, it can't be turned off. If you want to turn on SKS, complete instructions are given in the section titled "Encrypting HKLM\SAM with SYS-KEY" in Chapter 8.

Major Data Types

The NT Registry can directly store and manipulate 11 different types of data: seven major and four minor. This doesn't seem like very many at first, but remember that applications can use the seven fundamental types to store whatever kind of data they want. Only the application knows what the data actually means, and NT doesn't care; it will happily store and retrieve whatever data you pass it as long as you specify one of the following types for it.

REG_DWORD

REG_DWORD (the DWORD is Hungarian notation for a double word, or two 16-bit words—so it's a 32-bit value) is probably the most common data type in the Registry. A REG_DWORD value can hold any integer up to 2^{32}. Even though this provides a range of more than four billion possible values, many Registry keys use REG_ DWORD to stand in for Boolean* values—you'll see a lot of keys whose values can either be 1 or 0. In other cases, the value represents a quantity of something, like the percentage of time that a replication request can echo on the network or the number of seconds allowed between replication attempts. The hard part is knowing *what* the value represents, since without that there's no way to intelligently decide whether it needs to be changed. Chapter 9, *Registry Tweaks*, will point out

---

* "Boolean" comes from George Boole, the mathematician who first described formal systems for working with problems whose solutions could only be expressed in terms of truth or falsehood. This makes a good trivia question for springing on coworkers.

Service Packs Versus Hotfixes

Microsoft often issues bug fixes and enhancements for its operating system products. These changes come in two flavors. *Service packs* include a large number of fixes, plus occasional enhancements. While there's no fixed schedule, they usually appear at least every six months, and sometimes more often. As I write this, it's been 11 months since NT 4.0 shipped and there have been three service packs released for it. These updates are usually referred to as SPs, and when used with a number (i.e., SP3) you can tell what SP is being discussed.

SPs are cumulative; if you install NT 4.0 SP3, it includes all the patches and fixes included in SP1 and SP2. You can use the NT system utility *hotfixes.exe* to get a quick indication of which SPs are installed on a particular machine; you can also find the same data yourself in `HKLM\Software\Microsoft\ Windows NT\CurrentVersion\CSDVersion`.

Unlike SPs, hotfixes are intended to fix one or two critical problems. For example, the IIS 3.0 denial-of-service attacks that brought down Microsoft's web site several times in 1997 quickly led to the release of a hotfix that repaired that specific problem. In their hurry to get hotfixes out the door, Microsoft doesn't always do complete tests on them before release—if you install a hotfix that fixes a problem you're not having, you may end up with new problems caused by the hotfix itself!

Regrettably, some SPs have been released without adequate testing as well. My best advice to you is this: install a new SP on one or two machines so you can see how it does before rolling it out across your network. If Microsoft releases a hotfix for a problem you're experiencing, get it and install it. If it's a security-related hotfix, get it and install it even if you're not having the problem. Otherwise, leave it alone.

---

some of the most significant or interesting Registry keys, and others are documented in Microsoft's knowledge base (*http://www.microsoft.com/kb*) and in the *REGENTRY.HLP* file included with the Windows NT Server resource kit.

There is one other stumbling block: the NT Registry editors default to showing `REG_DWORD` values in hexadecimal, not decimal, and you have to use hex values when you're setting them unless you tell the editor you're entering decimal or binary values. This isn't too surprising, since the Registry stores values internally as hex bytes, but it can be annoying to have to set Registry values for things like replication timers: "Start with the time, which is 2 days, 4 hours, 30 minutes— that's 189,000 seconds, which is, ah, 0x2d620 hex."[*]

---

[*] Yes, I *did* do that by hand—proof of a misspent youth.

REG_SZ

In Hungarian notation, *S* means "string" and *Z* means "terminated with a zero byte at the end." Put them together and you get the REG_SZ value, which stores fixed-length strings by tacking on a zero at the end of the string. This extra zero is usually called the string's *terminator*. The simple string "NT" actually takes up three bytes when stored as a REG_SZ: two bytes for its contents, and one for the terminator. The terminator is mostly invisible to you (unless you write programs to manipulate Registry values in C or C++); the Registry editing tools you'll usually use take care of adding, removing, and storing the terminator as appropriate.

After REG_DWORD, REG_SZ is probably the second most common Registry data type. Strings are pretty versatile; they can be used to store human-readable names, file paths, version numbers, and lots of other useful tidbits. These strings can contain Unicode characters, which means that they're not limited to the ASCII character set. If you ever have occasion to edit the Registry on a machine running the Japanese, Korean, or Chinese versions of NT, be prepared to see non-English characters aplenty.

REG_MULTI_SZ

Sometimes it's useful to store a group of related strings as a single block. For example, since a single PC can have more than one video BIOS, NT stores the identification strings for each video BIOS it finds in HKLM\HARDWARE\DESCRIP-TION\SYSTEM\VideoBiosVersion. To support this aggregation, NT has a special data type called REG_MULTI_SZ—a fancy name for what is essentially a collection of several Unicode strings. Programs that use REG_MULTI_SZ values get the strings as a block and can add to or remove from the block at will. Of course, you can edit the strings too, using the editor provided as part of *RegEdt32*; see Figure 2-2.

REG_EXPAND_SZ

As part of what passes for its system scripting language, NT provides a number of system-defined variables. You may already know that these variables can be used in *.BAT* files, the System control panel's Environment tab, and directly from NT's command line, but they can also be used within Registry values of type REG_EXPAND_SZ. For example, the *%SystemRoot%* environment variable points to the root directory of the NT installation (it's usually *C:\WINNT* or something similar). If a Registry key has type REG_EXPAND_SZ and a value of %SystemRoot%\Media, any caller who retrieves the value can expand the embedded variable to its true value. You might think, based on the name, that the Registry would expand the embedded variable itself; sadly, this isn't the case. You have to do it yourself, as

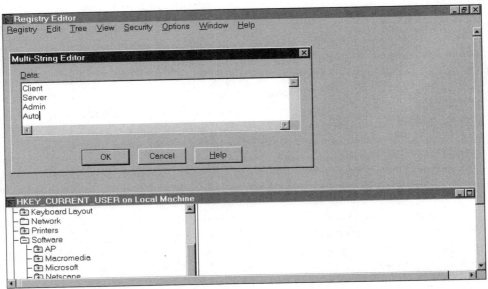

Figure 2-2. The multiple-string editor in RegEdt32

you'll see in Chapter 7, *Programming with the Registry*. In fact, this type is identical to REG_SZ.

REG_BINARY

Programmers often use binary representations directly. For example, using a mask of binary digits is a convenient way to represent features or flags that may or may not be set; each bit in the flag data can represent a separate on-off flag, making it possible to pack 32 independent flags into a single DWORD. Of course, it's often useful to store arbitrary binary data—pictures, cryptographic keys, encrypted passwords, and so on—in a binary format. The NT Registry editor supports storing and editing binary values with the REG_BINARY type. Binary data is totally raw; there are no terminators, string expansion, or anything else to interfere with the data's content. What you put in is what comes back out. Figure 2-3 shows the binary value editor; you'll learn more about how to use it in Chapter 5, *Using RegEdt32*.

REG_LINK

In the section "Links" earlier in this chapter, you learned that the NT Registry supports links that tie one subtree to another, much in the same way that we can figure out that "Charles Windsor" and "Prince Charles" are actually the same person. These links have their own data type, REG_LINK, which actually looks just like a REG_SZ. Let's say you have an intranet application that stores its configuration

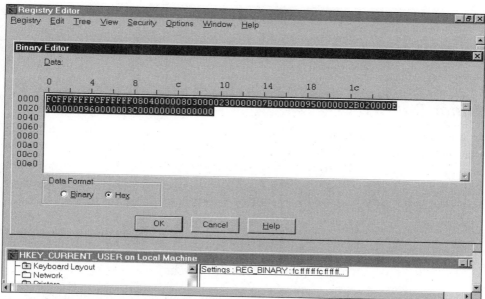

Figure 2-3. The binary value editor in RegEdt32

information in HKLM\Software\BigCorp\NiftyApp*version*, where *version* is the application's version number. If you wanted to be able to read the application's settings without regard to what version was installed, you could create a new key named HKLM\Software\BigCorp\NiftyApp\CurrentVersion and make it a REG_LINK; its link value would be HKLM\Software\BigCorp\NiftyApp*version*. To reach the application's communications settings, you could always refer to HKLM\Software\BigCorp\NiftyApp\CurrentVersion\CommSettings, no matter what the actual value of *version* is; the Registry API routines will automatically resolve the link and take you to the correct destination of HKLM\Software\BigCorp\NiftyApp*version*\CommSettings.

As a more immediate example, consider HKCU. Software written for NT must be aware that there can be several different user accounts on a single machine, each with its own unique security ID. Win95 apps may be aware of these accounts too, but the Win95 Registry doesn't have security IDs—making it impossible for a Win95 app to find the current user's settings when run under Windows NT. Enter HKCU, which is a link that NT builds at logon time. Instead of having to know what the current user's security ID is, and how to resolve that to a name, the application can just look for settings under HKCU.

NOTE   You can't create a new REG_LINK value from within *RegEdit* or
              RegEdt32. You can use the Registry API calls described in Chapter 7
              to create these types if you need to; most often, though, you won't.

Minor Data Types

In addition to the data types presented above, NT supports four additional types
that are less frequently used but still worth discussing. The first two, REG_NONE
and REG_DWORD_BIG_ENDIAN, aren't used very often, but they're available if you
need them. The remaining two are reserved for NT's use; *RegEdt32* can display
them but won't let you change any of their values.

NOTE   The NT Registry editors won't let you create new values using any
              of the types described in this section, though you can use the Regis-
              try programming APIs to create REG_NONE and REG_DWORD_*_
              ENDIAN values. If you try creating new values or keys using the
              resource types, however, NT's security won't let you put them in
              HKLM\HARDWARE, where they belong. You can create them else-
              where, but NT will ignore them.

REG_NONE

REG_NONE is a nice antidote to the more complicated data types featured in this
chapter—it's just a big zero. It's used to indicate the presence of a value only;
since REG_NONE doesn't store any values, you can't use it to retrieve or store data
in a key, but you can see whether the key is there or not. This is useful in some
limited situations where the existence or absence of a key indicates something
important, but it's a much better idea to use actual value types, and REG_NONE is
rare.

REG_DWORD_BIG_ENDIAN

It's an often-forgotten fact that NT was designed to work well on other types of
CPUs besides the ubiquitous Intel x86. At one point, NT actually ran on five different CPU families: Intergraph's Clipper, the MIPS CPU family, DEC Alphas, the
Apple/IBM/Motorola PowerPC chip, and the x86. Not all of these platforms order
their bytes in the same way, though. "Big-endian" platforms put the most significant byte of a quantity in the lowest address, while "little-endian" platforms put
the least significant byte at the low address. Figure 2-4 shows how the hex number 12345678 is represented with both kinds of endianness.

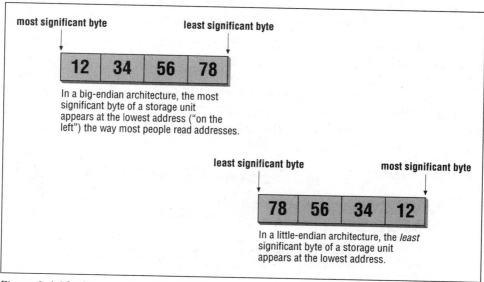

Figure 2-4. The hex number "12345678" in big- and little-endian form

To mix data between little- and big-endian machines, one end or the other will have to swap the byte ordering. Even though NT was originally designed for little-endian machines (the x86 and MIPS), Microsoft realized that it might be desirable to run it on big-endian platforms someday. In aid of that goal, they gave us REG_ DWORD_BIG_ENDIAN, which is rarely if ever seen on little-endian machines. It stores DWORD values in big-endian order, without translating them back to little-endian order on little-endian machines. Unless you're running NT on a PowerPC or Alpha, you probably won't ever see any values of this type in your Registry.

NOTE   There's also a REG_DWORD_LITTLE_ENDIAN type, but you won't ever see it on little-endian machines—it's only there so big-endian machines have a way to store little-endian data. NT automatically converts big- or little-endian data to the correct representation when you query a key's value and tell the Registry you're storing it as an ordinary DWORD.

REG_FULL_RESOURCE_DESCRIPTOR

Computers have finite resources; in particular, Intel-based PCs suffer from a limited number of IRQs and direct-memory access (DMA) address ranges. Someone has to be in charge of allocating this finite supply of goodies to requesters; in NT, it's the hardware abstraction layer (HAL), which loads as part of the boot process, that provides this necessary service. The resource arbitration's goal is (if at all possible) to keep two or more devices from fighting over the same resource.

To make this work, NT stores information about what resources are available in **HKLM\HARDWARE**; this information's gathered at boot time and stored in RAM, which is then mapped to Registry keys. Completely describing a resource requires quite a bit of data, and NT aggregates all the data for a resource into a resource descriptor. The **REG_FULL_RESOURCE_DESCRIPTOR** data type consolidates this data, as shown in Figure 2-5. (These fields may look familiar to you, since Microsoft's *WinMSD* diagnostic tool uses a similar format.)

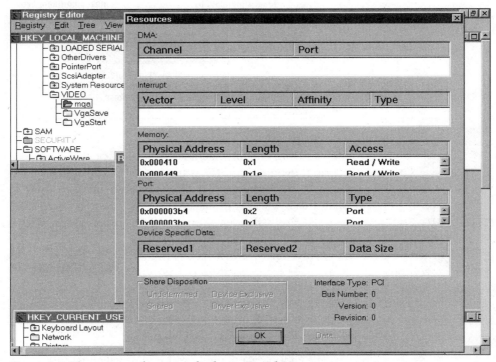

Figure 2-5. The resource descriptor display in RegEdt32

REG_RESOURCE_LIST

Even though the number of resources on a particular computer is finite, it can still be large. Instead of scattering many values of type **REG_FULL_RESOURCE_ DESCRIPTOR** around, the Registry offers **REG_RESOURCE_LIST**, a type designed to group related resource descriptors into a single unit. Figure 2-6 shows a sample of *RegEdt32*'s display for this data type.

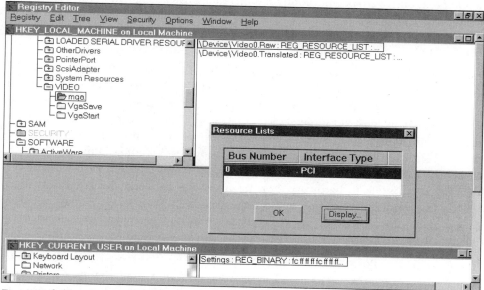

Figure 2-6. The resource list viewer in RegEdt32

What Goes in the Registry

No two snowflakes are alike. It's not quite true to say that no two Registries are alike, but they can vary significantly from machine to machine. There's a standard set of keys that NT uses, but even this standard set varies somewhat, depending on whether the computer's running NT Workstation or NT Server, what optional components are installed, and how the machine's network connection is configured.

The Registry database (fully described in Chapter 10, *The Registry Documented*) explains what individual keys are for, but using that database to grasp what's important is like trying to build a watch out of a bag full of parts—it's much better to examine a working watch and see how its parts relate. To provide a working watch for your entertainment,* this section will examine the most important subkeys of the root keys described earlier in this chapter.

Major Subkeys of HKLM

HKLM's purpose is to encapsulate all of the important configuration data for the local machine. It doesn't contain any information about other machines on the net-

---

* If you're not entertained, please send me better jokes for the Second Edition.

work or about user-specific configuration data; instead, it's nothing but settings for the machine where it's stored. HKLM has four important subkeys.

HARDWARE

All of the keys and subkeys of HKLM\HARDWARE are generated by NT at boot time and exist only in memory; they aren't stored on disk. This may seem odd, but when you consider NT's boot process it makes more sense. The NT boot loader (*NTLDR.COM*) is loaded by the standard DOS boot mechanism. When it executes, it loads and starts the NT kernel. The kernel in turn must first start up NT's Hardware Abstraction Layer, or HAL; the HAL provides a buffer between the gory details of hardware resources and the neatly structured system of device drivers that NT uses to talk to hardware. For this approach to work, the HAL must register the hardware it finds—but at the time it finds those devices, it may not have found any disks to register the data on! Keeping the hardware keys in memory nicely solves this problem.

There are four major subkeys of HKLM\HARDWARE. For the most part, your interaction with them will be very limited, especially since you can't change them. All of the information you might gain by manually inspecting these subkeys is more easily available in NT's diagnostic program, *WINMSD.EXE*. Having said that, though, here they are:

DESCRIPTION

> This subkey keeps track of which hardware devices are present. During NT's boot phase, the hardware detection software creates entries under this key for every hardware device it can find. Note that it keeps track of ports, not devices on those ports—it will find a parallel printer port, but doesn't check to see what's attached to it. Disk controllers are an exception to this rule.

DEVICEMAP

> DEVICEMAP links the list of which devices are present and the drivers that make them available to the system. Each driver starts up and attempts to take control of whatever device it controls. If the driver succeeds, it registers its ownership of the device in DEVICEMAP. This isn't much different from the human process of registering car titles at the county courthouse.

OWNERMAP

> This subkey ties bus devices to particular system buses. Many machines support multiple buses; e.g., PCI, ISA, EISA, or VLBus controllers can all coexist in a single machine. OWNERMAP registers which installed cards are attached to which buses.

RESOURCEMAP

> As its name strongly suggests, RESOURCEMAP provides a map of what resources are available. To be more specific, it lists the IRQs, DMA port

addresses, and bus controller slots supported by the hardware. Drivers choose from this list to reserve the resources they need; as they successfully claim hardware, they register which resources they're using here so other drivers won't try to use them too.

SECURITY

The `SECURITY` subkey holds two important collections of data. First off, it caches the local copy of the Security Account Manager database in `HKLM\SECURITY\SAM`. This database is the foundation of all of NT's access control. Besides ACLs for every object that has permissions assigned to it, this subkey contains a roster of local and domain accounts and groups, since the ACLs grant permissions to groups and users. This subkey actually maps to a separate hive, and its data is normally readable only by NT kernel services that have the appropriate "need to know." The SAM data has been kept here since Windows NT 3.1 first shipped.

NT 4.0 adds the capability to use user and group policies. These policies also live in subkeys of `HKLM\SECURITY`. These policies control what users can and cannot do on the machine, ranging from small things like changing the desktop wallpaper to big things like rebooting servers or editing the Registry. The data in the SAM is encrypted, so you can't directly access or modify it. Instead, you'll need to use the System Policy Editor (as described in Chapter 6) to set profiles, which NT will then automatically load into this subkey when they're needed.

Not even the Administrator account has permission to open these subkeys. Even if you change the ownership rights on `SECURITY` or its hive so that your account can open it, you'll find that the data there is encrypted. Even if you manage to decrypt it, the data is in an undocumented format that probably won't do you any good. Don't despair, though: there are functions in the Win32 API that you can use to create, read, and change security descriptors, permissions, and policies.

NOTE   The `HKLM\SAM` subkey just points to `HKLM\SECURITY\SAM`; it's provided as a convenience for parts of the kernel that need access to the SAM data.

SOFTWARE

Applications and system components store their settings under subkeys of `SOFTWARE`. By convention, programs that keep things here are supposed to create subkeys using the program and/or vendor name, then put their settings underneath. `HKLM\SOFTWARE\TechSmith\Snagit32` thus contains settings for TechSmith's SnagIt/32 screen capture utility. Most NT system components keep their system-wide settings under `HKLM\SOFTWARE\Microsoft\`*ComponentName*. Settings that only belong to a single user are stored elsewhere. The exact contents of this sub-key will vary from machine to machine, depending on what software's installed. My best estimate is that about 80% of the time you spend viewing or editing the Registry will be spent in various subkeys of HKLM\SOFTWARE.

In particular, HKLM\Software\Microsoft\Windows NT holds most NT-specific software configuration settings. In addition, there's a counterpart key named HKLM\Software\Microsoft\Windows that provides an equivalent to the Win95 key with the same name. The NT shell (which, of course, is based on the Win95 shell's code) makes heavy use of this key for tracking where applications are installed and how they can be uninstalled when needed.

SYSTEM

The SYSTEM subkey contains a potpourri of critical data. If HKLM is the most important part of the Registry, SYSTEM is its most important subkey. It has four major subkeys that merit further discussion:

- The DISK subkey contains information stored by NT's Disk Administrator application—which drives have which drive letters, whether any drives are part of stripe or mirror sets, and so on. This information can later be used to help regenerate damaged disks or rebuild stripe and mirror sets if something goes *boom*. If you haven't run Disk Administrator on a machine, this subkey won't exist.

- Subkeys for each *control set*. A control set is nothing more than a group of driver settings, hardware profile settings, and Registry entries: one control set is loaded every time NT boots. Since you can change drivers, hardware pro-files, and other control set elements, NT creates one control set subkey under HKLM\SYSTEM for each control set it sees. At a minimum, there will be two sets: one that you last used to boot, and one that was the last one that suc-cessfully booted. This "last known good" set can be a lifesaver when things go wrong, as you'll see in Chapter 3. When you change control set settings, NT will create a new control set; the sets are named with a sequence number; ControlSet001 is first, followed by ControlSet002, ControlSet003, and so on.

- The Select subkey remembers which control sets exist on the machine, which one was the last known good set, and which one was the last to cause a failed boot.

- The Setup subkey is NT's way of detecting whether it's in the middle of installation. When you install NT, it goes through a multi-step installation pro-cess; once the first step completes, the machine actually boots into a "light" version of NT so *ntdetect* can do its work and get the hardware mapped out. If this phase fails, the machine is in limbo—NT's not completely installed, but its boot loader is. The NT boot loader checks the value of `HKLM\Setup` to see whether setup was running when the machine was last booted; if so, it restarts the setup process.

SYSTEM\CurrentControlSet

`CurrentControlSet` is a link to whatever control set was used to boot the machine; system services, control panels, and well-behaved applications use this link instead of using a particular `ControlSetXXX` key, since it may move or even be deleted without the application's knowledge. The structure of `CurrentControlSet` is thus identical to any of the `ControlSetXXX` keys; for convenience, I'll describe it since that's the actual subtree that NT will use while running:

- `Control` holds NT's static configuration information. Among other things, sub-keys of `Control` contain information about the time zone the machine's in (`TimeZoneInformation`), what directories contain NT and its system files (`Windows`), and what the computer's network name is (`ComputerName`). These data are all static; NT loads them at startup; though they can be changed, the changes won't normally take effect until the next time NT boots.

- `Enum` contains information about the hardware devices found in the system during the boot phase. It has two subkeys: `HTREE` and `ROOT`. `HTREE` contains subkeys for the devices that were actually found, while `ROOT` contains sub-keys for all the devices that have installed drivers.

- By contrast with `Control`, `Services` holds configuration parameters for all of NT's services and kernel drivers. In a basic NT Server or NT Workstation installation, there are about 35 different subkeys of `Services`, one for almost every installed service. When you add services, they typically add their own keys here as well.

- `Hardware Profiles` holds the hardware profile settings that appear in `HKCC`. At a minimum, there will be two entries under this key: `Current` holds the current profile, and `0001` holds the default profile. If you define multiple profiles, they'll get new sequence numbers: `0002` is the second profile you define, `0003` the third, and so on. Each profile's key in turn contains its own copy of the `CurrentControlSet` key that matches the profile.

Major Subkeys of HKCU

The user profiles stored under `HKCU` are actually made up of data from ten major subkeys. Since the values under these keys control most of the environment and desktop settings that NT lets you customize, it's worth examining each of these subkeys to see what it's for.

AppEvents

The `AppEvents` subkey stores the mappings between system events (new mail arrived, window maximized, Windows logout, and so on) and sounds. You set these mappings with the Sound control panel; in addition to the system events, applications can define their own events (Visual C++ defines "compilation done"). When one of the listed events occurs, NT can look in `HKCU\AppEvents` and play the appropriate sound.

Console

`Console` stores the console window properties you set with the Console control panel or the "Command Line" Properties dialog available from the console window itself. When you change the default command-line window's size, position, buffer size, or font, those changes are stored here.

Control Panel

`Control Panel` doesn't directly store anything; instead, it's a placeholder for the system's control panels. Each control panel that wants to store persistent settings *on a per-user basis* can create its own subkey under `HKU\Control Panel` and use it however it wants. Control panels that manage system-wide settings, like the Network and System panels, store their settings in subkeys of `HKLM`.

Environment

`Environment` holds the user-defined environment variables set in the Environment tab of the System control panel. System-wide environment variables are kept in `HKLM\System\CurrentControlSet\Control\Session Manager\Environment`.* Interestingly, when you make changes to the user environment variables, the changes don't take effect until you log off and back on, but changes to the system's environment variables take effect immediately (though applications that use environment settings may need to be restarted to pick up the changes).

Keyboard Layout

`Keyboard Layout` retains the user's preferred keyboard layout. If you're used to using the standard U.S. English layout you may not know that, like the Mac, NT supports international keyboards whose layouts are different than the standard QWERTY. For example, the standard French keyboard's upper row starts with AZERTY. NT needs to know the physical layout of the keyboard so it can map keystrokes to the appropriate character codes.

---

* Okay, you caught me; they're *really* kept in `HKLM\System\ControlSetXXX`.

Network

Settings that apply to network hardware are stored under HKLM, as are network settings that apply to all users on the machine. By contrast, Network stores user-specific network settings, notably drive mappings that the user has made with the "reconnect at logon" option set. For each persistent mapping, NT will create a new subkey under Network, using the mapped drive letter as the subkey name. The subkey's values will indicate the network transport used to reach the server, the server name, and the name the user used to connect to the server. This information allows NT to re-establish mappings once the user logs in.

Printers

The Printers key has two major subkeys. Settings stores the user's default print settings, including the name of the default printer and whatever page setup parameters the user has set. Connections contains one subkey for each installed printer to which the current user can print. If no printers have been defined, this key will either be empty or missing, since NT creates it the first time a printer's created. Once a printer's been defined, a new subkey named after the print server and printer (for example, ARMORY,HP5M Postscript) will appear under Connections. The new subkey's values store the name of the printer driver DLL used with the printer and the name of the print server (if any) that shares the printer to other users.

Software

Software, like Control Panel, is a placeholder for a set of subkeys. The exact list of subkeys varies, since any software vendor can create program-specific keys. Applications are supposed to use HKCU\Software for user-specific settings (like the location of private mail folders) and keep their system-wide settings in HKLM\Software; however, many applications don't have any system-wide settings, so they keep everything under HKCU\Software.

Other

UNICODE Program Groups holds program group settings from previous versions of NT installed on the machine. This key will always be present, but on machines that have never had a pre-4.0 version of NT it'll be empty. On machines that have been upgraded from NT 3.x to NT 4.0, it will contain information about the defined user and system Program Manager groups, but the key's main purpose under NT 4.0 is as a placeholder for backward compatibility.

The Volatile Environment key stores per-user environment settings that change between logon sessions. The only key that NT 4.0 routinely creates here is LogonServer, which points to the computer that validated the user's logon.

On systems that were upgraded from Windows 3.x, there will be a `Windows 3.1 Migration Status` subkey under `HKCU`; this subkey stores the contents of the original *REG.INI* file, as well as assorted settings from other INI files. NT can automatically map INI files to sections in the Registry, making it possible for 16-bit applications to automatically use the Registry without being rewritten. (For more information on building your own mappings, see the section "Using Initialization File Mapping" in Chapter 8.)

Major Subkeys of HKCC

`HKCC` was originally introduced in Windows 95, and it appeared in NT 4.0 strictly to allow Win95 applications that use `HKCC` to run under NT. NT supports the concept of multiple hardware profiles; a profile is just a small set of Registry keys that define the hardware available to the computer. The most often-cited example for which hardware profiles are useful is that of a laptop. Let's say you buy a fancy laptop and a docking station, then install NT on it. You can use the laptop in three different configurations:

- At your office, plugged into the docking station. You want to use your docking station's display adapter and Ethernet card, and you have access to DNS, DHCP, and WINS servers for your intranet.

- On the road, with a PC Card modem to give you dial-up access to your intranet. In this mode, you need drivers for the modem and Dial-Up Networking, and you need to use different settings for all your network software.

- In the field, where you have no net access (well, you could use a satellite phone, but at $6/minute let's just stick with the "no access" plan).

Each of these configurations can be stored as a unique hardware profile; when you boot NT, you can tell it which one to use, and NT will load the appropriate drivers and settings. All the machine's hardware profiles are stored in the `Hardware Profiles` subkey of control sets under the `HKLM\System` tree. More importantly, system components and applications that are savvy enough to know about `HKCC` can query it to see what kind of hardware you currently have installed.

`HKCC` contains two subkeys: `Software` and `System\CurrentControlSet`. These are sufficient to store the individual profile settings; as you learned earlier in the chapter, `CurrentControlSet` actually stores driver settings. In addition, `HKCC` only stores the settings that are different from the default. If you use a profile that adds devices not present in the default profile, they'll be added in `HKCC` and merged with the default set.

What About the Other Root Keys?

At this point, you might be wondering why this chapter doesn't discuss the major subkeys of HKCR, HKDD, and HKU. The real reason is that none of these root keys has any particularly interesting subkeys under them! HKDD is opaque and can't be browsed; HKCR has many subkeys, each of which has the same format and similar contents. Finally, HKU's structure and contents are described earlier in this chapter in the section titled "Major Subkeys of HKCU." The subkeys discussed in that section are the real meat of the Registry; for more details on individual subkeys not covered here, see Chapter 10.

Getting Data In and Out

There are several ways to move data into and out of the Registry; which one you use depends on what you're trying to accomplish and the amount of time you're willing to spend. Each of them will be covered in more detail in later chapters.

First of all, you can make direct calls to the Win32 Registry API routines. At bottom, this is what all the other methods will eventually do; NT's security and the undocumented internal format of the hive files ensure that the only way to load data is to use these routines. The basic process is fairly simple: you start by opening a key or subkey by its name. Once you've done so, you can do things to that key or its subkeys: you can query its value, create new subkeys beneath it, or even ask about its security settings. You can continue to use that particular key until you're all done with it, at which time you must close it again. Here's a small sample that shows these steps in action; it gets the computer's network name and uses it to print a welcome message. You'll learn more about programming for the Registry in C (as in this example) in the section titled "Programming with C/C++" in Chapter 7.

```
// Hello, World! for the Registry: gets this machine's name and prints
// it out.
#include <windows.h>
#include <winreg.h>
#include <stdio.h>

void SayHello(void)
{
    unsigned char lpName[MAX_PATH] = "";
    DWORDnNameLen = MAX_PATH;
    HKEY hkResult, hStartKey = HKEY_LOCAL_MACHINE;
    LONG nResult = ERROR_SUCCESS;

    nResult = RegOpenKeyEx(hStartKey,
            "SYSTEM\\CurrentControlSet\\Control\\ComputerName",
            0L, KEY_READ, &hkResult);
    if (ERROR_SUCCESS == nResult)
```

```
        {
                nResult = RegQueryValueEx(hkResult, "ActiveComputerName", 0, 0,
                                          lpName, &nNameLen);
                if (ERROR_SUCCESS == nResult)
                        printf("Hello, world, from %s!", lpName);
        }
        RegCloseKey(hkResult);
}
```

The next step up the evolutionary ladder of Registry access is to use a library or language that removes you from direct contact with the Registry API routines. Depending on your needs and inclinations, there are several ways to accomplish this end:

- If you're using Visual Basic or Delphi, you can use a third-party library like SomarSoft's *RegEdit** (available from *http://www.somarsoft.com/*) or Desaware's Registry Control for Visual Basic (*http://www.desaware.com/*). These libraries typically wrap several API calls into one, so you can more easily perform the typical find-query-close cycle by making a single call. The Desaware control is covered at length in Chapter 7 of the Nutshell Handbook *Inside the Windows 95 Registry*, by Ron Petrusha (O'Reilly & Associates, 1996).

- The Win32 version of the Perl programming language includes a number of features that ease access to Registry data from Perl programs. Besides wrapping the find-query-close cycle for you, they make it easy to enumerate and search keys and quickly put the results into associative arrays. You'll see how to harness these features in the section titled "Programming with Perl" in Chapter 7. For a complete treatment of Win32 Perl, see the Nutshell Handbook *Learning Perl on Win32 Systems* by Randal L. Schwartz, Erik Olson, and Tom Christiansen (O'Reilly & Associates, 1997).

- The Windows NT Resource Kit includes a tool called *REGINI.EXE* that allows you to load text files of settings into the Registry. This is a handy and fast way to take a predefined set of data and jam it into the Registry; best of all, you can easily use *REGINI* to automate the process of loading Registry data into many different machines.

The final layer of Registry editing and spelunking revolves around using Registry editors. In addition to *RegEdt32* and *RegEdit*, there are a number of freeware and shareware alternatives floating around.

---

* Don't confuse this with the *RegEdit* application.

3

In Case of Emergency

By now, you've probably gotten the impression that working with the Registry is serious business. *How* serious it can be may not become apparent until the first time one of your NT machines stops working because of a problem with the Registry. This stoppage may be slight—say, Microsoft Office stops working—or it may be profound, resulting in the Blue Screen of Death or a lockup before the logon dialog appears.

Either way, this chapter will teach you two things: how to prepare for that eventuality, and how to recover from it smoothly when it does happen. If you're wondering why this chapter is here instead of further back in the book, the reason is simple. It's a very good idea for you to know how to restore your Registry *before* you learn how to edit it.

Don't Panic!

Scaring people is often a good way to get their attention. For example, you may have had to suffer through intentionally vivid films of auto accidents in drivers' education class; the rationale behind this kind of shock treatment is to blast the viewer out of his comfortable "it won't happen to me" mindset. This tactic is often effective, but, when exaggerated, it can backfire.

Instead, ask yourself a question. "Self, what would happen if my NT machines' Registries were abducted by aliens?" Just think: all your hardware, and the data it contains, gone in a heartbeat. Sure, it's easy to disregard the risk of hardware failure, fire, theft, or Registry corruption—that won't happen to *you*—but aliens? Look what happened to Elvis.*

---

* He's alive, you know.

Instead of panicking and running out into the streets like people do in alien-invasion movies, wouldn't it be nice if you could lean back in your chair and smile, knowing that your Registry data could easily be restored without breaking a sweat? There's nothing like that state of calmness that comes from having a known good backup of your critical data, and that's why I encourage you to read, and heed, the material in the rest of the chapter. Don't panic, but don't fall asleep, either.

Safety Strategies

The first step towards effectively preparing yourself to handle Registry problems is to adopt some strategies to safeguard your data. There are a number of fascinating books about the minutiae of planning for disaster recovery, but this isn't one of them, so I'll leave it to you to find out about off-site backups, fire suppression, and the other facets of preparing to deal with catastrophic failures. If you want to read more on this subject, see Jody Leber's *Windows NT Backup and Restore* (O'Reilly & Associates, 1998). Instead, I'll present two simple concepts that will save your bacon if you implement them. While they're targeted at helping you recover from Registry failures, you can also apply them to other situations that might render your NT machines (or any others, really) unusable or unavailable.

Make Backups

The cardinal rule of data protection is *don't depend on a single copy of your data!* Of course, this rule is usually observed in the breach. You'd probably be surprised at the number of experienced NT administrators who make sure to back up data on all machines on the network, then forget to back up their own personal workstation! As you'll see below in "Backing Up the Registry...," there are several ways to accomplish the desired result of duplicating the Registry's contents. Whichever you choose, though, the following four principles will make sure your backup strategy works for you, instead of leading you into a false sense of security.

Make regular backups

If you only back up data at irregular intervals, you run the risk of losing an indeterminate amount of data. Ask yourself this: if you had to reload your Registry tomorrow from the most recent backup, how recent would it be? Would it reflect all the configuration and user account changes you've made since that last backup? (Hint: as often as the Registry's contents change, the most likely answer is probably a rueful "no.")

Only you know how frequently your Registry data changes—so only you know how often to back it up. Remember that every change to the domain

SAM database—including adding or removing accounts, changing the default profile, changing account policies in the User Manager, or modifying any of your domain's local or global groups—is actually a change to the Registry. On top of these changes, installing or removing any NT component can cause changes, as can installing or removing applications.

However often things change, establish a consistent schedule and stick to it. As you'll see in the section "Using the ERDisk utility" later in this chapter, you can even automate your Registry-only backups to occur nightly with very little effort.

You'll probably be able to schedule Registry backups in parallel with other scheduled maintenance actions. I know of several sites that schedule software installations and account database changes twice weekly; that night, they back up the new changes. At worst, they lose no more than the previous update's changes.

Make sure your backup software is working

There aren't many feelings that compare to the despair of trying to reload data from a backup and finding that the data is missing or unusable. Oops. To prevent this, you should make a regular habit of inspecting the data that is actually sitting on your backup media. Make sure that the backups contain everything that should have been backed up, and that the modification and update times are reasonable.

If you're using conventional backup software, you can check to make sure the files named in the section "But What Needs Backing Up?" later in this chapter are actually making the backup list. If you're building an emergency repair disk (ERD), you can check the timestamps on the files to make sure they correspond to your expectations; if you're using a tool like *ERDisk*, you can also check its log files.

As a practice measure, one day when you're feeling brave go out and find a scratch machine somewhere on your network. Back up its Registry using your preferred method, then intentionally damage it and see whether you can restore it. *Be sure not to do this on a production machine*—but be sure to do it. Experience is the best reassurance, and if you're comfortable with the process of restoring a damaged Registry you'll be much less stressed when the time comes to do it for real.

Don't leave anyone out

Your backup plan needs to include every machine that's important. At a minimum, make sure you're backing up all your NT servers, especially the primary and backup domain controllers. If you have special-purpose servers running software like Microsoft Exchange Server, Lotus Notes or Domino servers, or Netscape's server products, make sure you include them as well, since server products like these often make exceptionally heavy use of the Registry for their own settings.

User workstations present a slightly different kettle of fish. If every user has her own workstation, you probably need to back them all up. If all users share a pool of workstations, and your network is set up to use profiles, you may be able to slip by without backing up the Registry data of pool machines. If one crashes, you'll have to reload whatever software was on the machine to restore its installation entries in the Registry, but the user account and profile data will transparently be restored by NT as users log in.

Keep an up-to-date repair disk

Even if you make regular backups, you still need to keep your ERD up to date. While the ERD is a subset of the full Registry's contents, it contains the most important data: the SAM account database and most of HKLM. In addition, you can use NT's setup utility to repair the Registry with the ERD, so you can repair the Registry even if your machine won't boot directly into NT. This can be a lifesaver, as illustrated in the following true story.

I bought a new Dell computer. It came preinstalled with Windows 95, which I don't like. I promptly installed Windows NT on it, then went to Dell's web site and downloaded what Dell claimed were the correct drivers for the built-in Crystal Labs audio hardware. After installing the drivers, my machine would hang as soon as it got to the GUI phase of the NT boot sequence. Since the device driver's load flag was set to "Auto," I couldn't turn it off manually, since it loaded before I had a chance to log in. Solution: whip out the fresh ERD I had made before installing the driver, reload the appropriate hives, and reboot. No problem! (Dell's driver wasn't the right one, but the one from Crystal Labs didn't work either. I ended up using NT's generic SoundBlaster16 drivers. Go figure.)

Of course, for the repair disk to be most useful, the data that gets copied onto it needs to be kept up-to-date as well. Since applications and the system update the Registry as needed, you don't have to do much to keep everything current. One notable exception is NT's Disk Administrator (*diskadmin.exe*) utility, which stores information about your machine's disk configuration under HKLM\SYSTEM\Disk. For the best chances of successful recovery, the copy of HKLM\SYSTEM\Disk on the ERD must match the actual disk configuration. The best way to ensure that this is so is to re-run Disk Administrator whenever your disk setup changes, then immediately create a new ERD.* Of course, you should keep making ERDs on your regular schedule.

---

* You can also save the disk configuration from within Disk Administrator via the Partition ➤ Configuration ➤ Save menu command.

> NOTE   The *RDISK* utility (which you'll learn how to use later in this chap-
> ter) displays a message telling you not to depend on ERDs as a
> backup tool. This is good advice—an ERD should be part of your
> backup plan, not a substitute for one.

This leads me to another general principle: make backups when things change.
For example, one network administrator I know instituted a strict policy of updating ERDs and Registry backups before installing prerelease or beta versions of any
Web browser. To her delight, this strategy saved her a significant amount of trouble when the browser's installers misbehaved and damaged the Registry.

Be Prudent

"Fools rush in where angels fear to tread." When Alexander Pope said so in 1711,
he wasn't talking about Windows NT, but his words apply, in spades, to working
with the NT Registry, since it represents a potential single point of failure that can
render your whole machine unusable if you make a mistake while editing it.

The best defense against this sort of mistake is simple: abstinence! However, it's
not always possible to avoid editing the Registry yourself; some settings and
parameters aren't editable anywhere else. Here's how you can exercise maximum
prudence to guard yourself against Registry mishaps:

Practice random acts of self-restraint

A wise man once said that computers allow people to make mistakes faster
than any invention other than handguns and tequila; you should keep that
thought in mind whenever the temptation to edit the Registry enters your
mind. *Don't* change a value just to see what it will do when changed; if you
want to know what a particular key does, look it up in Chapter 10, *The Registry Documented,* instead of tweaking it to see what breaks.

In the same vein, don't remove keys or their values unless you've previously
uninstalled the software that uses those values. You may be certain that no
one needs the data in `HKLM\Software\SomeVendor\SurfWriter`, but it's
generally not wise to test your certainty by arbitrarily whacking the whole subkey to see what happens. Instead, you can use the *REGCLEAN* utility (provided with Microsoft's Developer Studio, Visual Basic, and Visual C++ products, or at *ftp://ftp.microsoft.com/softlib/mslfiles/regcln41.exe*) to automatically
clear out any superfluous entries.

WARNING	As of this writing, *REGCLEAN* is at version 4.1. This version crashes under NT 4.0, particularly under NT 4.0 SP3. The flaw is serious enough that Microsoft has stopped distributing *REGCLEAN* 4.1. If you have it, *don't* use it on an NT 4.0 machine. If you don't have it, avoid it until Microsoft fixes the bugs.

Practice safe security

Of course, self-restraint is a virtue, but so is good security. You can think of it as a way to help others have self-restraint when it comes to your data. Make sure you follow the suggestions for choosing appropriate Registry permissions and auditing settings in Chapter 8, *Administering the NT Registry*.

In particular, if you choose to enable *SYSKEY* protection (as described in "Encrypting HKLM\SAM with SYSKEY" in Chapter 8), make sure you pay careful attention to the description of what you must do to restore a *SYSKEY*-protected Registry.

Use the scientific method

Sometimes there actually are good reasons for editing Registry values. Microsoft's Knowledge Base (*http://www.microsoft.com/kb*) is chock-full of articles that explain how to tweak normally invisible NT parameters like replication frequency and whether the printer browse thread is active. These settings are often worth changing for security, performance, or bandwidth-related reasons; however, it can be hard to tell whether making the changes will work well for you or not.

If possible, set aside a machine or two on your network for experimenting with these sorts of seemingly necessary changes. Doing so gives you a safe area to make changes, then study their effects, without compromising any of your production machines. If the changes have the desired effect, you can always add them to more machines when it's convenient; if, by chance, they turn out to be detrimental, you don't have a long list of user or server machines to go fix.

Consider buying better tools

Neither of the Registry editors provided with NT support an "undo" function, and neither of them log what changes were made during an editing session. While word processor, CAD, spreadsheet, and other "productivity" applications have had both of these features for years, they haven't made the leap into Microsoft's OS development group.

There's good news and bad news to report. First the good news: there are other third-party editors that allow you to undo changes at any time, even if you've already applied them. The bad news: they cost money. Consider

Symantec's Norton Utilities for NT (available from *http://www.symantec.com/*). For its US$100 or so purchase cost, you get a Registry editor that combines many of the features included in *RegEdit* and *RegEdt32* with a robust undo capability. If that's too rich for your blood, you can instead use the shareware *RegView95* application (available from *http://www.xnet.com/~vchiu/ regview.shtml*), which runs fine under NT and offers its own undo facility.

All About Emergency Repair Disks

The very phrase "emergency repair disk" sounds ominous, like something the crew aboard the *Mir* space station might keep close at hand. In fact, the ERD (as it's usually called) is a terrific insurance policy that can protect you from a number of potential Registry mishaps, up to and including losing the password to your Administrator account. However, ERDs won't do you any good unless you keep them up to date; you must also be careful to keep close physical control over them, since they contain a good bit of sensitive data that could potentially make it easier to compromise a machine.

What Is an ERD?

An ERD is nothing more than a FAT-formatted* floppy containing a subset of data from several Registry hives. When you create an ERD, you're actually making a backup copy of the Registry's most essential data in a form that NT can directly use to replace damaged or missing keys. The ERD also keeps copies of additional useful data:

- The configuration files that NT uses for running DOS and Win16 programs (*autoexec.nt* and *config.nt*).

- A copy of the current setup log file, *setup.log*. This file tracks the list of files installed during NT's setup phase, including a checksum; this log file enables setup, repair, service pack, and hotfix installers to know whether they're replacing the right files or not.

- The default user profile for the machine, normally stored in *ntuser.dat*.

The ERD contains copies of the *SAM*, *SECURITY*, *DEFAULT*, *SOFTWARE*, and *SYSTEM* hives; because this data (especially the SAM database) is specific to a particular machine, you can only use an ERD on the machine it was built with. To be more exact, if you use an ERD from one machine on another, portions of the target machine's Registry will be summarily replaced with the ERD contents; in the case of the SAM database, this can render the machine unusable.

---

* Because the ERD is a FAT filesystem (as it must be, since it's a floppy), it doesn't have any access controls. Be sure to safeguard your ERDs as sensitive material.

When you build an ERD, you're making a snapshot of the Registry's contents at that point in time. Any changes you make after building the ERD won't be preserved, which is why it's so important to keep your ERDs up to date. For example, if you make an ERD for a machine, then change its Administrator account password, the ERD will contain the old password. If you ever use the ERD, you'll find the password set back to its old value—which you may no longer remember!

WARNING   By default, the ERD will contain the *original* SAM created when NT is installed. You *must* use the /s switch (see the section "Using the RDISK utility" later in this chapter) to force *RDISK* to back up the *current* SAM data instead.

Files on the ERD are compressed, so you can't directly modify or view them; however, they're ordinary files, so you can back them up, archive them, or copy them to other media if you'd like (in fact, that's what the *ERDisk* program discussed in the following sections does).

What ERDs Can and Can't Do

The ERD can restore data for any of the hives it has backed up: *SAM, SECURITY, DEFAULT, SOFTWARE,* and *SYSTEM.* It restores data on a wholesale basis, so the entire contents of a hive will be replaced with the ERD's copy. When running the repair application that applies the ERD's data, you can choose which portions to replace, but not which individual values you want to update. Furthermore, the ERD requires that you be able to boot into NT's setup application; if you're using the ERD because you can't boot into NT, you'll need a bootable CD-ROM or another operating system you can boot into and run NT's setup utility.

Applying an ERD takes all the data in that section of the Registry back to *status quo ante*: all changes you've made since the ERD was created will be lost. As long as you keep your ERDs reasonably up-to-date, this shouldn't be a problem, especially since many applications and components are now smart enough to recognize when their Registry entries are missing and will recreate them when needed.

As useful as the ERD is, it's not magical. First of all, it can't restore what's not on it—you must keep your ERDs up to date if you want them to be available to you at crunch time. Secondly, it doesn't store anything in HKU (or HKCU, for that matter), so it doesn't preserve user-specific settings. It also doesn't restore all of HKLM\ SOFTWARE, so be alert to the fact that application installations and user preferences in your Registry won't be preserved by the ERD.

How to Make an ERD

Making an ERD is pretty simple; all you need is a floppy disk and a copy of the *RDISK* utility, which is fortunately included with NT. If you want to do fancy things like scheduling ERD updates or building ERDs for machines on your network, you can use the *ERDisk* utility, a commercial product from Midwestern Computers (*http://www.ntsecurity.com/*).

Using the RDISK utility

RDISK.EXE is a fairly simple application to use; its main window is shown in Figure 3-1. As you can see, there are only two useful things you can do with RDISK; each of the four buttons in the window controls a single function of the utility. The Help and Exit buttons do what you'd expect, so I won't discuss them here.

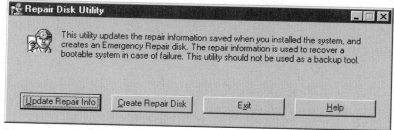

Figure 3-1. The RDISK utility

The Update Repair Info button does just that: it makes a private copy of the data described earlier and stores it on your hard disk. NT's setup utility can use this data to try to repair some parts of a damaged installation without having an ERD available. When the update is complete, you'll see the dialog shown in Figure 3-2, which allows you to create an ERD immediately or defer it until later.

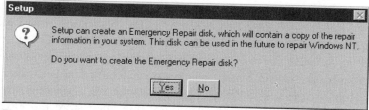

Figure 3-2. Generating an ERD with RDISK

Clicking Yes in this dialog will generate an ERD, while clicking No will (as you'd expect) do nothing. You may notice that the dialog shown in Figure 3-2 is titled Setup—there's a good reason for it, namely that NT's setup executable uses the same dialog to ask if you want to build an ERD during installation. It's a good idea to build an ERD when you install NT on a machine, then file it away in a safe place so you can use it if the Administrator account password for the machine is ever lost or forgotten. This works because the original ERD will contain whatever Administrator password you chose during the NT install process.

You can also kick off *RDISK* with two switches. /s has exactly the same effect as starting *RDISK* and clicking "Update Repair Info"; it copies the contents of the security and SAM hives to the floppy. If you instead use the /s- switch, that starts *RDISK* and copies the repair files into the *REPAIR* subdirectory *without* prompting you to insert a floppy disk. This latter switch is extremely useful for automating or scheduling Registry backups.

You actually create an ERD with the Create Repair Disk command, or by choosing Yes in the dialog presented after you use the Update Repair Info button. *RDISK* will ask you to insert a formatted floppy (but not without warning you that its contents will be erased). Once you've inserted the floppy and clicked OK, *RDISK* will create an ERD by copying the system's copy of the repair files to the floppy. When the ERD's done building, you can pop out the floppy and put it in a safe place.

WARNING   If you use the /s switch, the ERD will contain a complete copy of the source machine's SAM and security data. This data is much sought after, since it can be run through a password cracker like *l0phtcrack* and used to find weak passwords, that can then be used to enter your system. Treat ERDs as sensitive material and keep them away from public scrutiny.

Using the ERDisk utility

The ERD is a great idea, but how well will it work on networks with many computers? If you've spent more than a day or two as a sysadmin, then you know that not all users will take the time to update their own ERDs, but sitting down in front of every machine in a medium- to large-size network to update its ERD just isn't viable. MWC (at *http://www.ntsecurity.com/*) has a solution to this problem; their *ERDisk* utility allows you to run a process on one machine that makes an ERD for another machine across the network. You can batch up a list of many machines, and *ERDisk* will build ERDs for them one by one, then store the ERD files in a location you specify. *ERDisk* is available as a 30-day demo; the full product costs a reasonable US$49.

The main screen for *ERDisk* is shown in Figure 3-3. The list at the top of the window shows which machines *ERDisk* will attempt to build ERDs for; the rest of the buttons and controls in the window perform operations on this list or the machines in it.

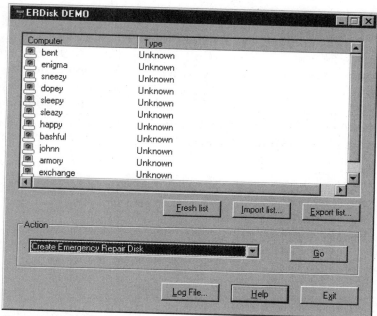

Figure 3-3. ERDisk's interface

An *ERDisk* backup set can have one or many machines in it—the program doesn't care. This gives you flexibility to back up your entire network at once or split the load up into several smaller sets. There are only four steps to building a set of ERDs with *ERDisk*, two of which are optional.

The first step, of course, is to tell *ERDisk* what machines to back up. The three buttons beneath the machine list allow you to manage the set of machines to be backed up:

- The "Fresh list" button builds a list of all the machines visible on your network. Any machine that appears in a standard browse list (as in the Network Neighborhood or the Map Network Drive dialog in Explorer) will appear in the list. When you start *ERDisk* for the first time it will automatically gather a list of machines from the network, but it won't regenerate the list until you click the Fresh List button.

- The "Import list..." button reads a text file of computer names. *ERDisk* will helpfully ignore anything after the first space in the list, so you can embed comments in the list, like this:

```
ARMORY      every Monday, Wednesday, and Friday
ENIGMA      boss' machine; make sure it goes daily
PURPLE      1st and 15th
HQ          every day
```

- Once you've created a list (either with the "Fresh list" button or by importing an existing list), you can re-export it to a text file with the "Export list" button. After prompting you for a filename, *ERDisk* will save the list of machines into a text file that you can edit to your heart's content, then re-import with the "Import list..." button. Since there are no built-in editing facilities, this export-edit-import cycle is the only way for you to make changes to the list of machines that *ERDisk* will back up from within the program itself. (It's worth mentioning that the list is stored in HKLM\SOFTWARE\MWC\ERDisk, along with the other settings you're about to learn about.)

NOTE   You can start *ERDisk* with the name of a file to import; if you do, it's the same as starting the program and using the "Import list..." button. For example,

```
erdisk accounting.imp
```

will start the program and import the *accounting.imp* file for use as a backup set.

You actually select machines to make ERDs from by clicking machines in the list; you can use the standard Windows modifier keys while clicking to support continuous ranges, individual machines, or groups. Once you've selected a set of machines to be backed up, the next (and optional) step is to set the backup session's options. There are only two options you can change: where the ERD files are stored and how long *ERDisk* waits before deciding that an ERD creation session has timed out. By default, *ERDisk* supplies values that it uses for these; the timeout is set to 1200 seconds (that's 20 minutes for those of us with second-handless watches), and the default storage location is a directory named *%COMPUTERNAME%* under *ERDisk*'s installation directory. Of course, there won't be an actual directory named *%COMPUTERNAME%*; instead, *ERDisk* will create a new subdirectory for each machine, using its name. For the machines in Figure 3-3, you'd end up with subdirectories named *ENIGMA*, *ARMORY*, and so on in *c:\tools\regtools\erdisk*.

Of course, you can modify these settings. To do so, use the Action combo box to select the "Create Emergency Repair Disk..." option. Notice the ellipsis at the end of the option name? *ERDisk* is confusing in that regard. If you want to use the defaults, you'd select the "Create Emergency Repair Disk" option with no ellipsis; to change the defaults to something else, you use the option with the ellipsis. When you successfully choose the option with the ellipsis, you'll see the dialog shown in Figure 3-4; once you change the settings, *ERDisk* preserves them for future use by storing them in its own Registry key.

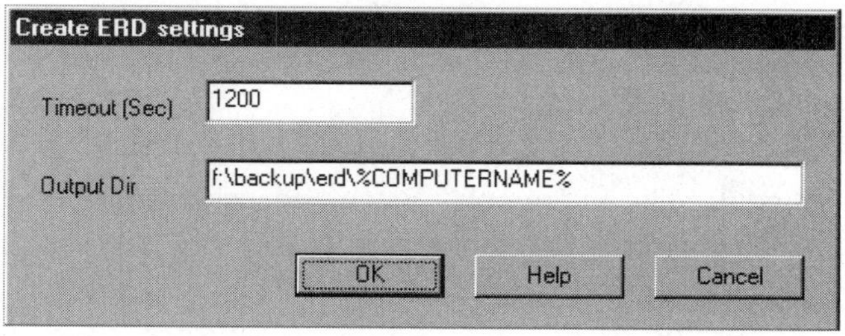

Figure 3-4. ERDisk output directory and timeout settings

The third step (like the second, it's optional) is to tell *ERDisk* what to log and how to log it. Since the whole point behind ERDs is to have an emergency disk ready when you need it, I strongly recommend turning on *ERDisk*'s logging so you'll know whether your ERDs are being properly created for all the machines you've specified. You reach the logging options dialog by using the Log File... button in the main ERDisk window; the dialog itself is shown in Figure 3-5. You can choose whether to log all operations, failed operations only, or nothing at all; at a minimum, you should choose to log all errors. (Of course, you also need to periodically review the logs, but log review is probably already a part of your regular administration schedule, right?)

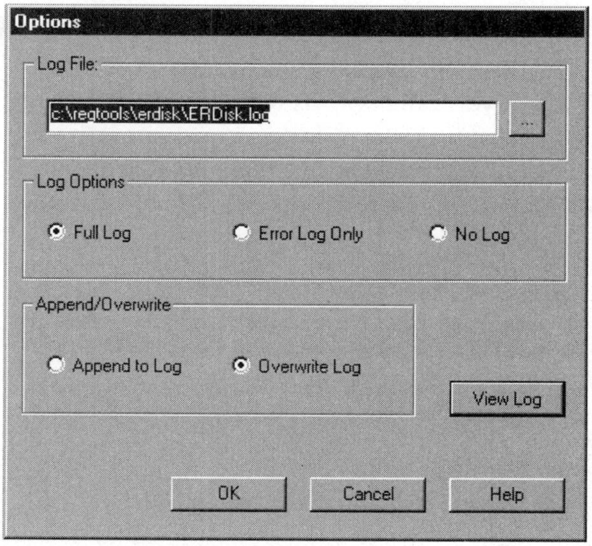

Figure 3-5. ERDisk log dialog

The fourth and final step is to actually let *ERDisk* build the ERDs. If you run the program manually, the Go button will present a confirmation dialog showing you what machines will have ERDs built. Once you confirm this dialog, the program will start gathering ERD data for the machines in your list, then building and saving ERD files for each machine, one at a time. However, you can also run *ERDisk* with the /s switch, which tells it to keep quiet and get all of its configuration data from HKLM\SOFTWARE\MWC\ERDisk. With /s, it's possible to use NT's command scheduler (or a third-party scheduler like Intergraph's Batch Services or any of the free *cron* implementations) to schedule an ERD session. For example, typing this:

```
at 0430 M,W,F c:\regtools\erdisk /s
```

at an NT command line schedules an early-morning ERD collection run every Monday, Wednesday, and Friday. Since /s tells *ERDisk* to be silent, you'll only find out about errors from log files, so make sure you have logging enabled to use this option.

In either case, it's worth mentioning how *ERDisk* actually works. When you create an ERD for a remote machine, *ERDisk* pushes a small program it calls the "ERD agent" to the remote machine and runs it—so the account you run *ERDisk* from must have Administrator access to all target machines, or this step will fail. Once the agent's installed, it runs *RDISK* on the remote machine, but forces it to save the ERD files back to the directory you've specified. When the agent is finished (whether it failed or succeeded), *ERDisk* removes it from the remote machine and proceeds to the next one.

How to Apply an ERD

An ERD won't do you any good unless you can apply its data to a machine when needed. Depending on what's wrong with the machine you're trying to repair, you may be able to boot it or not. Which repair tack you take depends on whether or not you can boot into NT and log on with an account that has Administrator privileges.

Using RegEdt32

There's one caveat I need to share before we start talking turkey: ERD floppies (and the files created by *ERDisk*) are compressed using Microsoft's standard compression tool. You've undoubtedly seen files whose extension ended with an underscore, like those on the NT distribution CD. These files are compressed with Microsoft's tool, as are the ERD files. To manually restore data from these files, you'll need a copy of *EXPAND.EXE*, Microsoft's utility for expanding these compressed files. You probably have a copy sitting around somewhere on your disk, or perhaps on one of your Microsoft-product CDs. Make sure you have it handy before starting a manual ERD restore. In fact, make sure you have a recent copy of *EXPAND.EXE*—older versions can't handle NT 4.0's compression format.

If you can successfully boot NT and log into a privileged account, restoring data from an ERD is easy to do with *RegEdt32*. First, you'll have to find the ERD hive file you want to restore from and uncompress it. *EXPAND.EXE* takes two arguments: the source file name and its destination name. Since hive files don't have extensions, you shouldn't specify one for the output name. Here's an example:

```
expand default._ default-save.
```

Next, launch *RegEdt32*. Depending on what you're trying to restore, now is when you'll have to make some choices. If you want to reload data that was accidentally deleted, or that you need to refer to, *without overwriting an existing hive*, you can load the ERD hive into a new subkey of HKLM or HKU by using the Registry ➤ Load Hive... command. If you want to load the ERD data and replace the existing hive, you'll need to use the Registry ➤ Restore... command. Both these commands are documented more fully in the section "Using RegEdt32 and RegEdit" of the section "Restoring a Backed-Up Registry..." later in this chapter.

Using NT's setup application

Sometimes your only hope of restoring a downed machine is to restore all or part of the Registry from an ERD by using NT's setup program. This last-chance restoration is the original reason for the ERD, and there are times (like my Dell horror story mentioned earlier) when nothing else will do the trick.

This scheme works because of the way NT's setup process works. NT's installer proceeds in three separate phases. In the first phase, NT copies just enough of the NT kernel and its support drivers and infrastructure to your hard disk. It then reboots into NT, using the newly made skeleton copy of NT, and proceeds with the "blue screen" portion of the setup process. It's at this point that you can tell Setup that you're repairing an existing NT installation. If you're not doing a repair, the third phase begins after another reboot; that's the familiar Windows GUI portion of the installation.

To get the ball rolling, you'll need to get NT setup started. If you have the original boot floppies and CD, you can use them; otherwise, if you have Windows 3.1, DOS, or Windows 95 installed (with appropriate CD drivers), you can boot it and run the setup program from the CD. Once you've done so, the first install phase will complete, then your machine will reboot. When it does, you'll have the opportunity to tell Setup whether you want to repair an existing installation (you do) or perform a complete installation. When you select the repair option, the setup installer will ask you which hives you want to restore (*SYSTEM, SECURITY, SOFTWARE, DEFAULT,* and *USERS* are your choices). Once you've chosen, you'll be prompted to provide the ERD and the saved hives will be restored; after the restoration's complete, you can reboot.

Backing Up the Registry...

You probably remember from the "Hives and Files" section of Chapter 2, *NT Registry Nuts and Bolts*, that each hive of the Registry is stored in a separate file. While it might seem reasonable to assume that you could just back up these files as though they were Word documents or some other innocuous file, the harsh reality is that you can't. The NT kernel always keeps the Registry data files open, so ordinary backup software won't be able to back them up. However, there are ways to successfully duplicate the files for safekeeping; we'll explore three ways in the remainder of this section.

But What Needs Backing Up?

In Chapter 2 you learned that the Registry's made up of several hives, which are actually files that live on your disk. They're normally stored in the *System32\Config* subdirectory of your NT system volume; you can always find the correct location by examining the value of HKLM\SYSTEM\Control\CurrentControlSet\ hivelist.

If you change to your NT system directory and get a directory listing, you'll see five files whose names match the hives listed in Table 2-1: *DEFAULT, SAM, SECURITY, SOFTWARE*, and *SYSTEM*. (The other two hives, *SID* and *HARDWARE*, aren't stored here.) The hive files themselves don't have extensions on them, but there are other files with the same names that do have extensions. Files whose names end in *.LOG* contain log and auditing information for the corresponding hive, while files with the *.SAV* extension keep backup copies of Registry transactions so a hive can be automatically restored if the system crashes. Finally, there's one file with its own unique extension: *SYSTEM.ALT* contains a transaction log of the *SYSTEM* hive. If the computer crashes, NT's boot loader can automatically replace the *SYSTEM* hive with *SYSTEM.ALT* if the latter has more current data.

You can back up any or all of them; however, as long as you're going to the trouble of backing them up at all you should back them all up. Special note to the curious: you can't rename, move, or delete these files while NT is running, since the kernel owns them and is holding them open for exclusive access—other applications that try to modify the files cause a sharing violation when they try.

The Old-Fashioned Way

In the days before NT, backing up Windows' configuration files was simple. You could just boot into DOS without starting Windows, then do whatever you needed to do. In fact, the "boot-edit system files-reboot-run Windows" routine is familiar to most Windows users, not just heavy-duty administrators. Windows 95 modified this tactic a bit; not only could you boot directly into DOS, you could use the built-in "safe mode" to tweak configuration files before rebooting.

NT doesn't have a safe mode, but booting into another operating system (DOS, Windows, Linux, OS/2, or whatever else you have installed) will still allow you to copy your files. There are four basic things you'll need to do a manual backup of your Registry files; which ones you use will depend on your system configuration:

- If you want to back up your Registry to a backup device, you'll need appropriate drivers for it (whether you're using a tape drive of some sort or a removable-media drive like a Zip, Jaz, SyJet, or similar).

- If you don't already have another bootable operating system installed on your machine, you'll need a DOS, Linux, or OS/2 boot disk that includes a command shell.

- If your NT system partition uses the NTFS file system, you'll need a copy of Mark Russinovich's *NTFSDOS* driver, which gives DOS, Windows 3.1, and Win95 read-only access to NTFS volumes. There are similar drivers for Linux (available from *http://www.informatik.hu-berlin.de/~loewis/ntfs/*).

- You'll need some kind of compression utility (unless you're booting into Win95, *don't* depend on *WinZip32*, which won't run under DOS or Windows 3.x). You need this because the uncompressed hive files can be several megabytes in size, so you won't be able to store them on a floppy without compressing them.

NOTE   You can't use an NT boot floppy to accomplish this task if your boot partition is NTFS; even though the floppy contains its own copy of the NT boot loader and kernel, it will use the configuration settings in the Registry on your "normal" system volume. You can use a separate boot disk if it contains a complete NT installation, like it would if you installed NT onto a Zip or Jaz removable disk and booted from it.

Once you've gathered all these things, you're ready to proceed. The first step in making a backup is to determine whether you can boot from another OS on your disk. If you can't, you'll need an alternative way to boot your machine from a floppy or removable disk. Once you've arranged a bootable configuration, you must also identify what type of filesystem your NT boot and system partitions are using; that determines whether your boot disk or OS needs additional drivers.

Boot Versus System Partitions

NT allows you to separate boot and system partitions. However, Microsoft's terminology is backwards: they define the system partition as the place where the boot loader is installed and the boot partition as the place where NT's system files live! While this is undoubtedly confusing, just remember that each term means the opposite of what you'd think and you'll be fine.

If your system partition is FAT, that means that you can boot DOS, Windows, or another OS that requires a FAT boot partition—but your NT system files can still be on an NTFS partition. In fact, many NT experts recommend this setup, since NTFS offers auditing and security features that you can use to keep your system files protected, but using FAT still allows you to install and boot other operating systems.

If you don't ever need to boot from another OS, or if you're willing to use a floppy for those times when you do, you can use NTFS for your boot *and* system partitions. This setup offers maximum security; it may offer better performance and disk-space usage, depending on the size of your drive.

If your boot and system partitions are both using FAT, you don't need any special drivers (other than those you need for whatever backup device you're using). However, if your boot partition uses the NTFS filesystem, you'll need an additional driver to allow whatever OS you boot to read it. For Windows 3.1, Windows 95, or DOS, you can use the excellent (and free!) *NTFSDOS* driver, available from *http://www.ntinternals.com/ntfs13.htm*. If you're using Linux, a similar driver is available from *http://www.informatik.hu-berlin.de/~loewis/ntfs/*. These drivers provide read-only access to NTFS filesystems, without any regard for NTFS's file permissions.

Once you've accomplished these two steps, you're ready to back up the files themselves. Here's what to do:

1. Boot your computer, using whatever OS you've chosen. Get to a command prompt and change to the *System32\Config* subdirectory of your NT installation directory. Make sure you can see the hive files you want to back up.

2. If you're using a backup program, start it, point it at the hive subdirectory, and tell it which hives to back up. It should do the rest.

3. If you're not using a backup program, use your preferred compression utility to create a new archive containing the files from the *System32\Config* directory you want to back up.

4. Safeguard your backup archive, tape, or disk: it contains a complete and readable copy of your entire Registry.

You might wonder whether this approach is worth the hassle. The answer is "it depends." If you don't have a tape drive, you can't use NT Backup. Many third-party backup utilities can back up to floppies or removable disks, but not all of them are able to back up the Registry. You can always use *REGBACK* and *REGREST,* but they may not always be available when you need them. The ERD mechanism works well and is easy to use, but it has a critical defect: it doesn't back up the *entire* Registry, just what Microsoft thought were the most important parts.

Using NT Backup

Microsoft provides a backup utility, *NTBACKUP.EXE,* as part of the standard Workstation and Server installations. As with many other bundled utilities, it's not the be-all of backup tools, but it works tolerably well and it's included for free. It can back up local or network volumes (as long as they're already mounted), and it does a good job of logging errors and exceptions.

Lots of tools can do the same things as *NTBACKUP,* but unlike some other backup tools (particularly those designed for Windows 95), *NTBACKUP* has one extremely important feature: it can back up the Registry to any supported tape device.* This Registry backup captures an up-to-date copy of the Registry files *from the local machine*; if you're backing up network drives and include the Registry, you'll get the Registry of the machine that's running *NTBACKUP* along with data from whatever drives you've mapped. *NTBACKUP* does not back up Registry data from any remote machine, so don't depend on it to do so or you'll be seriously disappointed.

Figure 3-6 shows the main interface of *NTBACKUP.* The main window contains two child windows at startup. The Drives window shows a list of all mounted volumes on the current machine (including shares connected over the network), while the Tapes window shows a list of all the available tape devices. A basic backup with *NTBACKUP* only requires three simple steps:

1. Use the Drives window to select the drives and files you want backed up. Double-clicking a drive expands it into a File Manager-like window with two

---

* This is only a skeleton description of *NTBACKUP*; for more details, see *Windows NT in a Nutshell*, by Eric Pearce (O'Reilly & Associates, 1997) and *Windows NT Backup and Restore*, by Jody Leber (O'Reilly & Associates, 1998).

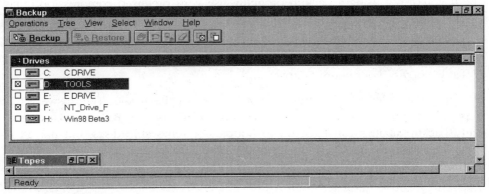

Figure 3-6. NTBACKUP

panes. The left pane contains a tree view of the folders on the disk, while the right pane contains a list of the files in the selected folder. Each item in either pane has a checkbox next to its file or folder name. If the checkbox is marked, the file or folder will be backed up; if it's cleared, it won't be. Figure 3-7 shows a sample window with some files marked.

2. Click the Backup button or use the File menu's Backup command. You'll see the dialog shown in Figure 3-8. Make sure the Backup Local Registry checkbox has an X in it, then click OK. The backup will start.

3. Go do something else while the backup runs. When it's done, put the tapes in a safe, secure place.

For best performance, you may want to run *NTBACKUP* only after stopping other applications on your computer. The Registry files will be backed up even if system components are using them; however, other files (like SQL Server databases, Office documents, or any other file) will only be backed up if they're closed. To ensure a complete backup of all of your machine's data, I recommend closing all other applications and stopping any shared services (IIS, SQL Server, Netscape FastTrack or Enterprise, and so on) whose files you want to back up.

One final note: if you're using *NTBACKUP*, make sure to turn on backup logging *and* check the log files to be sure your backups are capturing the data you expect. Not much is worse than being lulled into a false sense of security by your backup scheme, only to find it didn't back up the data you really needed! You can put the log Use the Log File field in the Backup Information dialog (see Figure 3-8) to specify where you want the log to go. If you want to make sure you see it, put it in the Administrator's desktop folder (try *%systemroot%\PRO-FILES\Administrator\Desktop*).

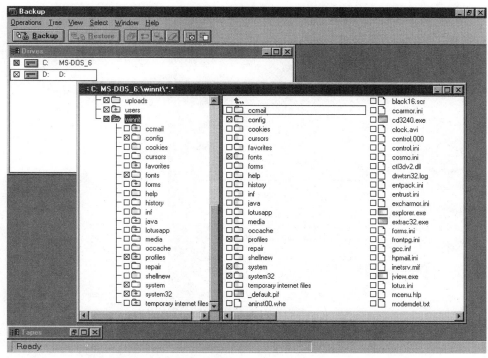

Figure 3-7. The NTBACKUP file selection window

Using REGBACK

NOTE The NT Server Resource Kit costs money, so you might wonder whether it's a necessary expense. The answer is a resounding "yes." The *REGBACK* and *REGREST* utilities *alone* can literally save you days of effort when rebuilding a trashed machine. In that light, the US$150 or so for the Resource Kit seems much more reasonable, and I recommend it highly.

The *REGBACK* utility does pretty much what its name implies: it allows you to back up all or part of the Registry. Microsoft recommends that you use *NTBACKUP* for making Registry backups if you can, but *REGBACK* is still a very useful tool in its own right, since you can use it to export parts of the Registry for storage onto media that *NTBACKUP* doesn't support, namely floppies and removable-media drives. You can also execute *REGBACK* from the command line, so you can schedule Registry backups or perform them as part of an NT batch file. For example, you can schedule a nightly Registry backup of some, or all, of your

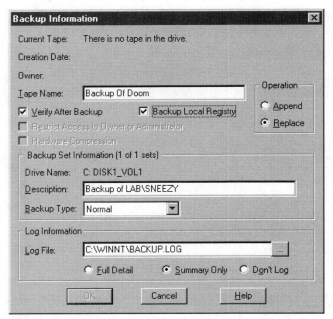

Figure 3-8. The Backup Information dialog

machines and put the backup files on a central server. In addition, *REGBACK* stores its output as uncompressed files, so you don't have to worry about having the correct decompression tool handy.

There are some caveats to using *REGBACK*, though; let's examine them before I tell you how to use it:

- The account that you use to run *REGBACK* must have the "Back up files and directories" right. NT uses this right internally to let certain accounts copy files without giving them read access; this allows a backup-only account to copy files owned by other users without being able to open them. The Administrator account has this right by default, as do any accounts that you've placed in the Backup Operators group.

- *REGBACK* will only back up the hives in the *System32\Config* directory, not any of the other files stored there. In addition, it won't back up inactive hives that you've unloaded with *RegEdt32*. However, it will warn you with an error message indicating what files it found that need to be copied manually.

- *REGBACK* isn't very flexible. If you try to back up files to a device that doesn't have enough space, it will silently fail. If the destination for your backup already has hive files in it, the backup will silently fail. *NTBACKUP* doesn't have either of these limitations.

You can run *REGBACK* in two different modes. In the first mode, every active hive in your Registry is backed up to a directory you specify, like this:

```
regback directory
```

The specified *directory* has to be on a mounted volume; you can't use UNC paths. *REGBACK* will cheerfully back up all the Registry hives it finds on your machine and warn you of any files that it didn't back up, like this:

```
C:\>regback \regsave
saving SECURITY to \regsave\SECURITY
saving SOFTWARE to \regsave\SOFTWARE
saving SYSTEM to \regsave\SYSTEM
saving .DEFAULT to \regsave\DEFAULT
saving SAM to \regsave\SAM

***Hive = \REGISTRY\USER\S-1-5-21-1944135612-1199777195-24521265-500
Stored in file \Device\Harddisk0\Partition1\WINNT\Profiles\Administrator\
            ntuser.dat
Must be backed up manually
regback <filename you choose> users S-1-5-21-1944135612-1199777195-24521265-500
```

Notice that *REGBACK* warned that it didn't copy my user account hive, but it gave me a command line that would do so—the last line of its output. This command line uses the second mode that *REGBACK* supports, one that allows you to back up a specified hive instead of the entire Registry:

```
regback output hivetype hivename
```

output

Specifies where you want the saved hive to go; can be a full or partial pathname, but cannot be a UNC path.

hivetype

REGBACK only accepts two hive types: `machine` represents `HKLM`, while `users` represents `HKU`. If you supply any other hive type, *REGBACK* will fail.

hivename

Specifies a subkey immediately beneath either `HKU` (either `.DEFAULT` or one of the SID-identified subkeys) or `HKLM` (`SOFTWARE`, `SYSTEM`, and so on). If you specify a key that's not immediately beneath either `HKLM` or `HKU`, *REGBACK* will fail.

This form of *REGBACK* will save the entire contents of the specified hive to the file you specify; there's no way to preserve individual values within a hive. If you want to back up an entire Registry, you may still prefer to use this form of the command, since you can specify the filename for each hive's output file—a valuable feature when you want to back up several machines on a network to the same directory on a server. This snippet shows the output from me telling *REG-BACK* to preserve my main subkey under HKU:

```
C:\>regback d:\regsave\paul users S-1-5-21-1944135612-1199777195-24521265-500
saving S-1-5-21-1944135612-1199777195-24521265-500 to d:\regsave\paul
```

REGBACK returns standard DOS-style error codes: 0 for success, 1 if there were files that need to be manually backed up, and 2 if something else went wrong (disk full, bad hive type, and so forth). You can use the ERRORLEVEL construct in a batch file to branch when errors occur; for example, this small batch file will attempt to back up HKLM\SOFTWARE to a central directory:

```
regback j:\save-me\enigma-software  machine  SOFTWARE
if ERRORLEVEL 1 echo "Some files weren't backed up"
if ERRORLEVEL 2 echo "An error occurred."
```

Using RegEdt32

You can do some rudimentary backup and restore tasks with nothing more than *RegEdt32*. It allows you to load previously stored hives into your Registry, then unload them later (though you can only unload hives you loaded yourself). In addition, you can export keys and hives in a format that *RegEdt32* can reload at a later time.

You can't actually save any of the predefined hives (i.e., the hives stored in *System32\Config*) from *RegEdt32*, but there's a good reason for this limitation: those hives are already saved as disk files! Remember, a hive is a disk file that contains Registry keys; since the hives *already* store the contents of the Registry's root keys, there's no point in providing a separate command in *RegEdt32* for saving a hive file. You can, however, load a hive that you got from somewhere else; see the section "Using RegEdt32 and RegEdit" in the section "Restoring a Backed-Up Registry..." later in this chapter for more details.

RegEdt32 does allow you to do something else, though; you can save any key that's not a root key into a hive file. To keep from confusing the "big" hives (which store the root keys' contents) from the files you can create, I'll call them "honeycombs" (after all, what's a hive full of? well, besides bees). When you create a honeycomb file, *RegEdt32* will take the specified key and its subkeys and store them in a file that uses the hive format. You can then move the file to any other NT machine and load it into that machine's Registry (with some caveats that I'll discuss later on).

The mechanics of doing this are simple: select the key or subkey that you want to save, then use *RegEdt32*'s **Registry ➤ Save Key** command. When the standard Save dialog appears, specify a filename; the editor will happily save your key's contents to the file (assuming you have adequate permission to read all the keys and their values). Once the save is finished, you can copy, compress, fold, spindle, and mutilate your new honeycomb file just like any other, plus you can load it into the Registry on any NT machine—either in place of or in addition to existing keys.

Using Text Files

You might think that using a plain text file to represent the Registry is crazy. While it's not the best way to make a complete copy, and it's not a very good way to make copies for restoration use, there *are* some sensible reasons to use this method. For example, if you periodically dump the contents of a Registry key (whether a root key or any subkey) to a text file, you can use a file comparison tool to highlight changes between the two files. This is an invaluable strategy when you're trying to figure out what Registry keys and values have changed due to software installation or user tinkering; it's also a winning plan for tracking what your own home-grown software does to the Registry and how that matches up with what you *wanted* it to do.

There are a number of tools for dumping Registry contents to text files. Which one you use is largely a matter of personal preference; they're all free and they all work well.

Using RegEdt32

RegEdt32 can save any Registry key (and its subtrees) as text. The output is pretty verbose, as shown in this sample from **HKLM\SOFTWARE\Netscape**:

```
Key Name:           SOFTWARE\Netscape\Netscape Navigator\4.0 (en)\Main
Class Name:         <NO CLASS>
Last Write Time:    6/24/97 - 11:26 PM
Value 0
  Name:               Install Directory
  Type:               REG_SZ
  Data:               C:\Program Files\Netscape\Communicator

Value 1
  Name:               Java Directory
  Type:               REG_SZ
  Data:               C:\Program Files\Netscape\Communicator\Program\Java

Value 2
  Name:               NetHelp Directory
  Type:               REG_SZ
  Data:               C:\Program Files\Netscape\Communicator\Program\NetHelp
```

To save a subtree, all you need to do is select the subtree (or root key) you want to save, then use *RegEdt32*'s **Registry ➤ Save Subtree As...** menu command. You'll be prompted for a file to save the data in, then *RegEdt32* will spit out the data you selected. However, it's worth noting that there's no way to import this data back into the Registry again! You can use a file comparison utility like *WinDiff* to compare two file dumps generated by *RegEdt32*, but you can't restore the Registry's contents based on a *RegEdt32* file.

Using REGDUMP

Andrew Schulman's *REGDUMP** produces similar output to that generated by *RegEdt32*, but it's more nicely formatted, as you can see from this sample:

```
Netscape Navigator
  CurrentVersion="4.0 (en)" -> ""
  4.0 (en) -> ""
    Main
      Install Directory="C:\Program Files\Netscape\Communicator"
      Java Directory="C:\Program Files\Netscape\Communicator\Program\Java
      NetHelp Directory="C:\Program Files\Netscape\Communicator\Program\NetHelp"
```

Like the output from *RegEdt32*, *REGDUMP* output is primarily useful for your reading pleasure; there's no way to take a dumped file and import it back into the Registry. However, because *REGDUMP*'s output is compact and neatly formatted, it lends itself well to use with *WinDiff*.

Using RegEdit

Alone among the utilities in this chapter, *RegEdit* can generate text dumps of the Registry that it can actually import and restore again. When you run *RegEdit*, you can use its **Registry ➤ Export Registry File...** command to produce output that looks like this:

```
[HKEY_USERS\S-1-5-21-1944135612-1199777195-24521265-500\Software\inetstp\
    Netscape Navigator\Bookmark List]
"File Location"="C:\\Program Files\\Netscape\\Navigator\\Program\\bookmark.htm"
"Start Menu With"="Entire Listing"
"Add URLs Under"="Top Level of Listing"

[HKEY_USERS\S-1-5-21-1944135612-1199777195-24521265-500\Software\inetstp\
    Netscape Navigator\Cache]
"Cache Dir"="C:\\Program Files\\Netscape\\Users\\cache"
"Disk Cache SSL"="no"
"Disk Cache Size"=dword:00001388
"Memory Cache Size"=dword:00000400
```

Note that each key is enumerated with its full path; this makes it possible for *RegEdit* to tell exactly where a key and its values belong when it reimports the exported file. Choosing the command produces the dialog shown in Figure 3-9. The controls in the "Export range" group let you export the entire Registry or just

---

* *REGDUMP* made its debut in Chapter 5 of the Nutshell Handbook *Inside the Windows 95 Registry*, by Ron Petrusha (O'Reilly & Associates, 1996).

the currently selected branch; in addition, you can edit the branch shown in the "Selected branch" field to further tighten the output's scope.

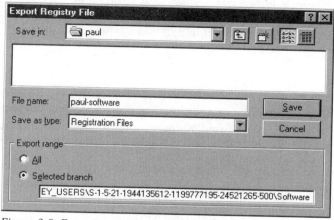

Figure 3-9. Exporting a Registry key

Restoring a Backed-Up Registry...

Now that you know how to back up your Registry, the next logical step is to learn how to restore it. You need to be comfortable enough doing this that the prospect doesn't scare you; no one looks forward to repairing a damaged Registry, but it shouldn't be frightening either—so practice until you're comfortable with the approaches described in the rest of the section.

The Old-Fashioned Way

Restoring the Registry from a manual backup isn't useful in all circumstances, since to restore the hive files you must be able to boot your machine and gain access to NT's boot partition, as described earlier in the chapter. Once you've booted your machine into DOS, Linux, or some other OS that gives you access to the partition where your hive files are stored, all you need to do is copy the backup copies over to the original hive directory. (Of course, you'll have to uncompress them first if they're compressed!) Reboot into NT, and you're done.

While this approach is appealingly simple, it has its disadvantages. Apart from requiring that you be able to boot into another OS, it has the drawback of being indiscriminate. When you restore a hive, you'll be restoring everything in the hive; this can have the unwanted consequence of removing changes you wanted to keep while fixing whatever problem originally required you to use a backup.

Using NT Backup

Restoring a Registry backup with NT's backup utility is fairly painless. It's not smart enough to check whether you're restoring to the same machine you backed up from, so you must be careful to avoid installing the wrong Registry (including the SAM database and HKLM\SECURITY subtree) on the wrong machine.

Earlier in the chapter, you saw Figure 3-6, which shows *NTBACKUP*'s user interface. To make a backup, you had to select a drive (and its subfolders and files) to back up. Guess what? To restore from a backup, you do the opposite and select a tape to use for the restoration. Here's how the process works:

1. Use the Tapes window to select the tape that contains the files you want backed up. The selection interface works just like the one shown earlier in Figure 3-7; you mark the items you want restored. You have to restore at least one item to restore the Registry. Though you can restore files to any drive, you can only restore the Registry to the drive where it normally lives.

2. Click the Restore button or use the File menu's Restore command. You'll see the dialog shown in Figure 3-10. Make sure the Restore Local Registry checkbox has an X in it, then click OK. The restore will start.

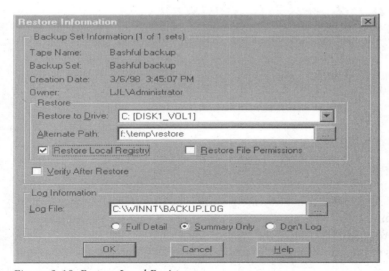

Figure 3-10. Restore Local Registry

Using REGREST

If you back up your Registry with *REGBACK*, naturally you'll use its companion, *REGREST*, to restore it. *REGREST* can only use the files created by *REGBACK*, but since they come as a pair that shouldn't be an impediment. However (like its partner) *REGREST* has some limitations you should be aware of up front.

First, and most seriously, it only runs under NT. *REGREST* actually works by repeatedly calling the `RegReplaceKey` API routine, meaning that it has to have access to the NT registry. Even though this routine exists in Win95, the Win95 version operates only on the Win95 registry. If you can't boot your machine into NT, you'll need to use an ERD to fix it, not a *REGREST* backup.

NOTE   Of course, you should plan on keeping a copy of *REGREST* on any boot disks you might use to effect a Registry repair. It's small enough to comfortably fit on an NT boot floppy.

Second, you can only run *REGREST* from accounts that have "Restore files and directories" privilege. In most cases, that means your local Administrator account, plus any accounts you've added to the Backup Operators group. (Of course, you can grant this right to any user with NT's User Manager.)

Next, *REGREST* only works with *REGBACK* files that are on the same volume as the hive files themselves; if your backup files are stored elsewhere, you'll have to move them to your NT boot volume before running *REGREST*.

Finally, you have to reboot your machine before *REGBACK*'s changes will take effect. This is sometimes an annoyance, but it's actually a safety feature: you can undo or redo restores as much as necessary, and the changes won't be permanent until you reboot.

If you can live with these four restrictions, *REGREST* is fairly easy to use. It actually operates in three individual steps:

1. It copies the original hive file to a backup directory that you specify; this allows a graceful fallback position if steps 2 or 3 fail.

2. It moves the new hive file to the hive directory; this movement requires the "Restore files and directories" privilege mentioned earlier.

3. It repeatedly calls `RegReplaceKey` to put the new hive file's contents into the Registry. (That's why it can work when the hive files are open, and it's also why you must reboot before the changes take effect.)

Like *REGBACK, REGREST* comes in two flavors. The first restores as many hives as it can find; it looks for files in the backup directory whose names match hive files in the hive directory. When it finds a match, it copies the matching file according to the three steps above. You use it like this:

```
regrest  backupDir  saveFilesDir
```

backupDir

Specifies where the files generated by *REGBACK* are stored; must be on the same volume as your NT system files.

saveFilesDir

Tells *REGREST* where to put the secondary backup files it creates. If necessary, you can copy these files back to the hive directory before rebooting to undo a restore.

REGREST will warn you if there are hives it couldn't restore automatically, or if errors occurred. Here's a sample transcript:

```
C:\>regrest \regsave \backsave
replacing SECURITY with \regsave\SECURITY
replacing SOFTWARE with \regsave\SOFTWARE
replacing SYSTEM with \regsave\SYSTEM
replacing .DEFAULT with \regsave\DEFAULT
replacing SAM with \regsave\SAM

***Hive = \REGISTRY\USER\S-1-5-21-1944135612-1199777195-24521265-500
Stored in file \Device\Harddisk0\Partition1\WINNT\Profiles\Administrator
\ntuser.dat
Must be replaced manually
regrest <newpath> <savepath> users S-1-5-21-1944135612-1199777195-24521265-500

You must reboot for changes to take effect.
```

The second form of the command allows you to manually restore one hive at a time.

```
regrest backupFileName saveFileName hiveType hiveName
```

backupFileName

Specifies which hive file (including its full path, if desired) *REGREST* should restore.

saveFileName

Tells *REGREST* what name and directory to use for the copy it makes of the existing hive file.

hiveType

Just like *REGBACK, REGREST* only accepts two hive types. Specify machine for HKLM or users for HKU. If you provide any other hive type, *REGREST* will fail.

hiveName

> Specifies a subkey immediately beneath either HKU or HKLM. If you specify any other key, *REGREST* will fail.

Using RegEdt32 and RegEdit

As you've seen in earlier sections, the two stock resource editors shipped with NT are useful when it comes time to back up your Registry data. Fortunately, they can also help you restore it should you need to.

Loading hives

You can load hives or honeycombs created with *RDISK*, *ERDisk*, or *RegEdt32* into your Registry. When you do, however, it's important to note that *RegEdt32* will create a *new* key that contains your hive or honeycomb contents; that key and the hive or honeycomb it contains will remain loaded until you explicitly unload them.

There's another wrinkle, too: *RegEdt32* will only allow you to load hives under HKU and HKLM. As a practical matter, this isn't a big deal; it just means that the hives you load will be subkeys of one of those two roots, *not* subkeys of their subkeys. If you have anything other than HKLM or HKU selected when you give the command, you'll get an error dialog telling you that you don't have permission to load the hive.

When you use the **Registry ➤ Load Hive** command, *RegEdt32* will ask you for a hive file to load. Once you've identified a file, it will ask you for the name of the key you want the loaded hive to be under. For example, if you load the .DEFAULT hive to a new key named "MyDefaults" under HKU, you'll see that HKU\ MyDefaults is now equal with HKU\.DEFAULT and HKU\sid, and it will contain whatever the original hive or honeycomb file contained.

Once a hive's loaded, you can add, remove, or change keys and values in it like any other part of the Registry; the changes will be reflected in the associated hive file.

Reloading saved keys

You can reload a previously saved key at any time using *RegEdt32*'s **Registry ➤ Restore Key...** menu command. However, this command is an accident waiting to happen. Why? Well, when you save a key, the saved key doesn't contain any path data. For example, if you save HKLM\SOFTWARE\Qualcomm\Eudora, its values and all its subkeys will be saved—but not the fact that it originally came from HKLM\SOFTWARE\Qualcomm\Eudora. This in and of itself isn't so bad, but the real danger comes when you get ready to reload the key.

When you tell *RegEdt32* to reload a key, you'll see a warning dialog (shown in Figure 3-11) telling you what's about to happen. It's not an idle warning, either; if you click Yes, the currently selected key in the Registry will have all its subkeys and values replaced by whatever's in your saved file. Not only does the saved key not go where you wanted it; it also destroys whatever happened to be underneath the key you had selected! If you accidentally load `HKLM\SOFTWARE\Qual-comm\Eudora` while you happen to have `HKCU\SOFTWARE\AppEvents` selected (to pick a fairly innocuous victim), you'll find that *RegEdt32* will happily blast your Eudora settings into the middle of NT's sound-to-event mapping list. The results are, at best, unpredictable.

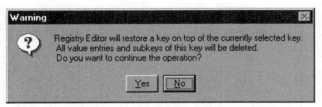

Figure 3-11. RegEdt32 overwrite warning

Of course, this problem can be worked around with a little caution: make sure you have the correct key selected when using this command. Failing that, make sure you have a reliable, up-to-date backup.

Using RegEdit files

Since the *.REG* files produced by *RegEdit* contain the full path for each exported key, they're extremely simple to use. To reimport a *REG* file, all you need to do is run *RegEdit* and use its **Registry ► Import Registry File...** command. When you do, *RegEdit* will import the file's contents without any further intervention on your part; it automatically replaces existing keys and their values with whatever's in the file, as well as adding back any keys that are in the file but not in the Registry. It will not, however, delete keys in the Registry that have been added since the *REG* file was created; you'll have to do that yourself if necessary.

4

Using RegEdit

In the first three chapters, you learned what the Registry is, how it functions, and how to safeguard it against accidental damage or loss. Now that you've absorbed this basic knowledge, the real fun starts: now you learn how to modify the Registry's contents. In later chapters, you'll learn how to use the powerful *RegEdt32* application, as well as how to write your own programs that find, store, and modify Registry data. As a departure point, though, let's start with *RegEdit*, a simple, easy-to-use tool that will help you get familiar with the mechanics of navigating and editing the Registry.

Know Your Limitations

The *RegEdit* included with NT 4.0 is a direct descendant of the first version, which shipped with Windows 3.1. That first *RegEdit* couldn't do much because there was so little in the Registry; in the intervening years, Microsoft has added a great deal of data to the Registry, but *RegEdit* itself hasn't progressed too much beyond its original capabilities. Sure, it uses the Win32 common controls, so it looks like a modern application, and it's been rewritten as a 32-bit application for Win95 and NT—but overall, it's still the flat-blade screwdriver of Registry editing tools: ubiquitous but of limited capability.

Let me start by pointing out the useful and desirable things *RegEdit* doesn't do:

- It has no undo or journaling capability, so there's no easy way to back out of an unwanted change or keep an auditable record of changes made.

- It is completely innocent of any understanding of NT's security features, so you can't view or change permissions or ownership settings for keys.

- You can only create and edit binary, string, and DWORD values; when you view other data types, they're displayed as binary data.

While this list may seem like a harsh assessment, remember how valuable a single screwdriver can be. It can be a punch, a prybar, a chisel, a spacer, a mallet (albeit a small one), and it can drive screws. Likewise, *RegEdit* can do some very valuable things: it allows you to search the Registry for a value or key, and these searches can be local or remote. It provides a nicely unified display of all the root keys, allowing you to quickly browse and compare values in different roots. Finally, its limited functionality makes it easy to understand and use.

Learning the RegEdit Interface

I have a weakness for power tools—the more powerful, the better! One thing I've learned is that it's a good idea to spend some time getting accustomed to a new tool before starting a real project with it. This break-in period helps me get familiar with how the tool works, teaches me how it feels as I use it to saw, drill, or whatever, and gives me some confidence that I won't screw up whatever I'm working on.

In the same vein, allow me to present the user interface for *RegEdit*; as you read through this section and its successors, you'll gain an understanding of how *RegEdit* looks, feels, and works, but the best way to cement that knowledge is to launch it and experiment: practice moving around, searching for things, and exploring the Registry. Even after you've mastered the skills needed to administer the Registry, you'll still find *RegEdit*'s search abilities to be quite useful in your everyday administration.

Don't I Know You from Somewhere?

If you've ever used Explorer (or even the old-style Windows File Manager), you'll feel instantly comfortable with *RegEdit*'s interface (shown in Figure 4-1). The application's window is divided vertically; the left-hand pane (which I'll call the *key pane* from now on) shows a tree representing the Registry's hierarchy, while the right-hand side (the *value pane*) shows the values associated with whatever key is selected in the key pane. You can adjust the relative widths of the two panes by dragging the gray bar that divides them.

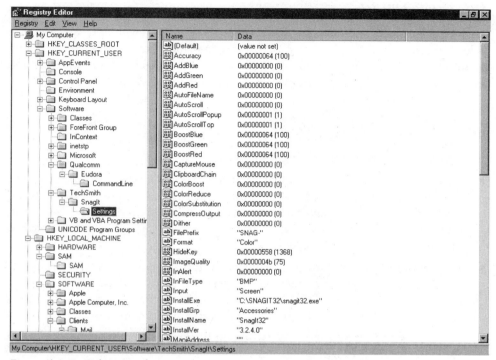

Figure 4-1. RegEdit's interface

The value pane is further subdivided into two columns: the first, known as the name column, shows the value's name, while the second (the data column) shows the value's actual contents. You can change the width of these columns by clicking and dragging the divider bar in the header at the top of the value pane.

By default, *RegEdit's* main window includes a status bar across its bottom margin; when the status bar is visible, the full path of the currently selected key will appear there. This provides a quick reference if you need to make a note of a particular key (perhaps to search for it in the Registry database, discussed more fully in Chapter 10, *The Registry Documented*).

When you first start *RegEdit*, the root keys (HKLM, HKCU, HKU, HKDD, HKCR, and HKCC) appear directly under the My Computer icon. As with Explorer, you can expand or collapse individual keys by clicking the small icon next to the key in the left pane; as you move around, clicking at will, the tree will grow and shrink to reveal the keys you're interested in.

Interface Trivia

As with most other system administration tools provided with NT, *RegEdit* provides a View menu. For the most part, the commands here are of little use and seem to have been added for parity with the User Manager, WINS Manager, and so on. Nevertheless, in the spirit of completeness, let me briefly describe the commands that live there:

- *Status Bar* controls *RegEdit*'s bottom-of-the-window status bar. When checked, you'll see the status bar. By default, this option is turned on, and it's useful, so I recommend leaving it that way.

- *Split* activates the vertical bar that segments *RegEdit*'s window; once you use the Split command, moving your mouse left or right (or using the left and right arrow keys) will move the bar with it. Why this is included is beyond me (though it *does* let you repartition the window when you don't have a mouse).

- *Refresh* is the only worthwhile command in this menu. *RegEdit* will update its display to reflect any changes you make in the Registry from within *RegEdit*, but it won't notice updates that occur because of other programs. For example, if you're testing a Perl script you've written to do something to the Registry, it would be nice to see the changes immediately. To force an update, you can use the Refresh command (or F5, its key equivalent). You can also use the Refresh command to quickly update the display when you're browsing the Registry of a remote computer.

"Just Browsing, Thanks"

The first thing you should learn to do with *RegEdit* is to browse around the Registry and see what's there. The Explorer-style interface makes the Registry's data very "discoverable"; that's a fancy way of saying that you can start off with a high-level view, then see as much or as little detail as you like as you become more comfortable with the Registry's structure.

Navigating with the Keyboard

RegEdit follows the standard Windows conventions for keyboard navigation—not surprising when you consider that the key pane itself is built with the standard Windows 95 tree-list control. When an item is selected, it will be highlighted using the standard system highlight color, and you can maneuver about by using the keys shown in Table 4-1.

Table 4-1. Navigational Keys for RegEdit

Key	When used in...	Action
Tab	Key or value panes	Switches focus between the key and value panes
Return	Value pane	Opens selected item for editing
Up/down arrows	Key or value panes	Moves focus to the next or previous item in the current pane
Left/right arrows	Key pane	If selected item has subkeys, expands (left arrow) or collapses (right arrow) it; if not, moves to next or previous item
Left/right arrows	Value pane	Scrolls the value pane left or right
PgUp/PgDn	Key or value panes	Moves up or down one pane's worth of data without changing focus
Home and End	Key or value panes	Moves to top or bottom of pane's contents
Backspace	Key or value panes	Returns the focus to "My Computer" in the key pane
Keypad *	Key pane	Expands all subkeys of the currently selected key
Keypad -	Key pane	Collapses the selected subkey

Using the Context Menu

Windows 95 brought the concept of a "context menu" to the Windows world. The basic idea is that by clicking the right mouse button* you can get a pop-up menu of commands or actions that are specific to the object you clicked on. For example, the context menu in Borland C++ has choices like "Toggle breakpoint" and "Browse symbol," while the corresponding menu for Netscape's Communicator features items like "Open link in new window" and "Save image to disk."

RegEdit has these context menus, too. There are three separate context menus that you can summon; the commands in each menu duplicate commands that are already present in the application's menu bar:

- Right-clicking a key in the key pane pops up a menu with six commands:

    — *Expand/Collapse* (which one appears depends on whether the key's already expanded or collapsed) will open or close the selected key. This command is dimmed if the key has no subkeys

    — *New* allows you to create a new key or value

    — *Find* opens the find dialog

---

* Or the left one, if you're using a left-handed mouse setup.

— *Delete* deletes the selected key and all its subkeys

— *Rename* allows you to change the key's name without removing and rein-serting it

— *Copy Key Name* copies the current key's full path to the Clipboard

- Right-clicking a value name in the name column of the value pane displays a smaller menu with three commands. The *Modify* command opens a dialog that allows you to edit the value; the *Delete* and *Rename* commands are the same as those in the key pane's context menu.

- Right-clicking anywhere else in the value pane displays a single command, *New*.

Connecting to Other Machines' Registries

RegEdit allows you to connect to the Registry of any NT machine on your network. Of course, there are two caveats: you must have permission to do so, and the remote machine must be configured to allow remote Registry access. You can also browse Win95 machines if they've got the Remote Registry Access service installed.

From within *RegEdit*, you connect to other machines with the **Registry ➤ Connect Network Registry**... command. When you do, you'll see a small dialog that prompts you for a computer name to attach to. This dialog also contains a Browse button; clicking it will display a network browser window (similar to the one in Windows Explorer) that allows you to poke around your LAN to find the machine you want to connect to. Once you've identified the machine you want to reach, *RegEdit* will open its Registry and display its root keys in the key pane. Your local machine's root keys are under the My Computer icon; other machines' keys will appear under folder icons with their names, as shown in Figure 4-2.

While you're connected to a remote computer's Registry, you can browse keys subject to whatever permission the remote Registry's owner has imposed. Depending on those same permissions, you may be able to modify, create, or remove keys; before doing so, of course, you should make sure that you have both a good backup of the target machine *and* permission from its owner.

Because *RegEdit* doesn't dynamically update the Registry, you'll quickly become practiced at the skill of using the **View ➤ Refresh** command (or the F5 key, its accelerator) to force *RegEdit* to update the portion of the Registry you're viewing.

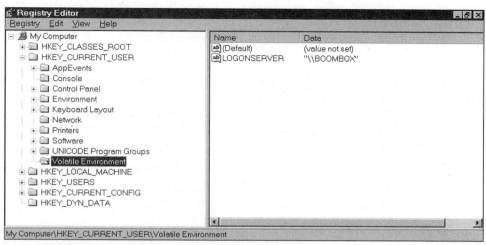

Figure 4-2. Remote Registries and local Registries

WARNING   *RegEdit* often fails to allow access to the various root keys of remote
Registries even when they are displayed (whereas *RegEdt32* works
flawlessly and consistently well). There doesn't seem to be any pattern to the failures. If you have trouble connecting with *RegEdit*
then try *RegEdt32* instead.

Finally, when you're done with your Registry connection, you'll need to close it—
knowing how to put away toys is a prerequisite skill for kindergarteners and system administrators! The **Registry ➤ Disconnect Network Registry** command will do
the job, allowing you to choose from a list of machines you're connected to.

Searching for Keys and Values

One of *RegEdit*'s best features is its ability to search the Registry for a particular
key or value. For example, let's say that you want to find where the Dial-Up Networking (DUN) service stores its list of phonebook entries. You could go to
Microsoft's Knowledge Base and look it up, or you could search the Registry database on the Web—but the fastest way to find your answer is to use *RegEdit*'s
search function to look for entries whose contents match the name of one of your
phonebook entries.

There are a few things you'll need to know about how searches work. Searches
are case-insensitive, so you don't have to pay attention to proper capitalization.
By default, searches are substring searches, not literal searches. Searching always
starts with the "first" root key, so in *RegEdit*'s case that means that all searches

have to plow through HKCR first. Finally, the search process only accepts ASCII text, and it only looks in string values. That makes it impossible to find all the values whose DWORD value is 0x220, or to find data stored in values of type REG_BINARY.

You activate the Find command with the **Edit➤Find** menu command. When you do, you'll see the dialog shown in Figure 4-3. Finding values is pretty straightforward: if you want to search the entire Registry, just type your search string into the "Find what" field and click the Find Next button. Of course, you can be more selective by using the four checkboxes in the Find dialog:

- The "Look at Keys" checkbox (on by default) tells *RegEdit* to look for the specified string in the names of keys. Searching for "software" would thus find HKLM\SOFTWARE, HKCU\Software, HKU\.DEFAULT\Software, and perhaps other keys whose names contain "software" in some form or other.

- The "Look at Values" checkbox (on by default) instructs *RegEdit* to search for your string in the names of values, too; searching for "User" with this checkbox set might find HKCR\DAO.User, HKLM\Software\SMIME\Users, and HKCU.

- The "Look at Data" checkbox (on by default) enables *RegEdit* to actually look within values' data for the specified string. Searching for "System" will turn up a treasure trove of string values that contain the search string.

- The "Match whole string only" checkbox (off by default) constrains *RegEdit* to reporting only those items that match exactly. Searching for "User" with this option off will find both HKCR\DAO.User and HKLM\Software\SMIME\Users; turning the option on won't find either, but would match HKLM\Software\LJL\CurrentVersion\User.

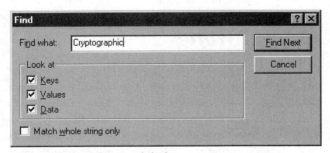

Figure 4-3. RegEdit's Find dialog

While the search is proceeding, you'll see a progress dialog. That's perhaps a misnomer, since it doesn't actually indicate the search's progress—it gives you a Cancel button, though. *RegEdit*'s searching performance is poor, so don't be alarmed if searches seem to take a long time.

As with many other programs that include search capability, *RegEdit* provides a convenient shortcut for finding the next item that matches your search target. To find the next match, use the **Edit➤Find Next** command or its accelerator key, F3. When you do, *RegEdit* will find the next match; if it can't find any more matches, it will display a dialog telling you that no more matches exist.

Printing Registry Contents

If you want to print all or part of the Registry, you're in luck: *RegEdit* can produce a printout that contains the full path, subkeys, and values of the key you select. The **Registry➤Print...** command allows you to print the entire Registry or any subset of it, using the dialog shown in Figure 4-4.

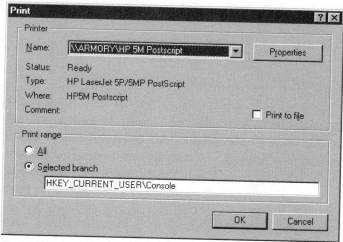

Figure 4-4. RegEdit's Print dialog

The "Print range" group gives you a convenient way to filter the keys that you print. Selecting the All radio button will (as you'd expect) print the entire Registry. I don't recommend doing this unless you have a very fast printer with a very large paper tray. The "Selected branch" button is a better alternative; with it, you can choose a single subkey to be printed.

RegEdit's printed output is pretty rudimentary; it doesn't have any way to print page headers or footers, and its output isn't indented or otherwise formatted to make it more readable. For quick reference, you may find it more useful to export a portion of the Registry (as described in the section "Exporting Registry Data" later in this chapter), then print it using your favorite text editor.

Working with Keys and Values

By now, you probably have a good feel for the Registry's structure. Once you're comfortable navigating the Registry with *RegEdit*, it's time to move on to the mechanics of working on keys and values in the Registry. *RegEdit* has a complete suite of commands for creating, modifying, deleting, and renaming keys and values. However, it doesn't have a safety net, so be sure to limit your initial experimentation with editing to changes you can back out if necessary—and don't forget the backup strategies you learned in Chapter 3, *In Case of Emergency*.

WARNING   Even though it was mentioned before, it bears repeating: there's no convenient way to undo changes you make when editing the Registry with *RegEdit*. Make sure you've developed and are executing a Registry backup strategy. If you're not, please go back and read Chapter 3 before you start editing anything.

Now is also a good time to mention a few things that *RegEdit* can't do. Chief among them is the fact that it can't directly edit or create values that aren't of one of the three types it supports: DWORD, binary, and string. You *can* create or edit values of these other types, but you have to do so by viewing and editing the hex bytes that make up the binary version of the data—not a task to undertake lightly! If you do create new values, they'll be shown as REG_BINARY instead of their true types. This limitation makes it harder to edit REG_MULTI_SZ or REG_EXPAND_SZ values, which are fairly common; you also can't create or modify the more obscure data types discussed in the section "Minor Data Types" in Chapter 2, *NT Registry Nuts and Bolts*. As a practical matter, this isn't a huge hindrance, since most Registry values use one of the three types that *RegEdit* supports.

A Word About the Clipboard

RegEdit would have been a much better application if it had full Clipboard support, thus allowing you to cut, copy, and paste keys and subkeys, especially when you're viewing more than one machine's Registry from a single instance of *RegEdit*. Though it doesn't explicitly have much Clipboard support, you can still manage to exchange names and values through the Clipboard if you keep in mind the available ways to do it.

Let's start with key names: to copy a key's name to the clipboard, you can use the **Edit ➤ Copy Key Name** command, *RegEdit*'s only Clipboard command. This command copies the key's full path, including the root key, to the Clipboard as a text string, ready for use elsewhere. When renaming a key, for example, you can paste a name into the Rename dialog instead of typing it.

Likewise, it's possible (though not through the menu) to copy a value's name or value. To accomplish this, you'll have to open up the editing dialog for the value whose name or value you're interested in, either by double-clicking it or using the **Edit ➤ Modify** command. When the edit dialog appears, you can use the mouse to select either the name or the value, then issue the appropriate Windows shortcut to copy, cut, or paste the value.

Modifying Values

The most common use for *RegEdit* is to modify existing values. Many of the settings NT stores in the Registry are accessible through the Control Panel, but others aren't, and applications often keep private settings that occasionally require adjustment.

You can modify a value by double-clicking its entry in the value pane, by selecting it and using the **Edit ➤ Modify** command, or by selecting Modify from the right-button context menu. What happens next depends on the value type that you're modifying. However, in all cases, once you click OK in the editing dialog, the change is made, and there's no way to undo it other than changing back the value by hand or restoring from a backup. Note that most applications won't notice changes to a Registry value if they're made once the application is running; you'll usually have to quit and restart the application before the changes take effect.

Modifying a string value

The Edit String dialog (pictured in Figure 4-5) is pretty simple; it displays the selected value's name and data. You can select and copy the value name, but you can't change it. You can change the value's data using the "Value data" field; like the name field, this field supports the Windows cut, copy, and paste keyboard shortcuts, so you can quickly paste in values from elsewhere. You'll see this dialog when you select a value whose type is REG_SZ or REG_EXPAND_SZ.

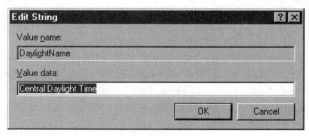

Figure 4-5. The Edit String dialog

Modifying a DWORD value

When you edit a REG_DWORD value, you'll see the dialog shown in Figure 4-6. Like the Edit String dialog, you can copy text from the "Value name" field, and you can copy, paste, or cut text in the "Value data" field itself. The two radio buttons in the Base group give you the ability to specify a DWORD value in either decimal or hex; if you choose hex, you don't need to add a leading 0x to the value you provide.

WARNING   It's a very, very good idea to always double-check the value you
             enter to make sure it matches the setting of the Base radio buttons.
             If you're entering a value in hex, make sure the Hexadecimal but-
             ton's selected. If the base you select and the data you enter don't
             match, the change you make may not have the expected effect.

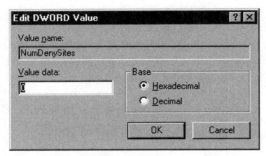

Figure 4-6. DWORD edit dialog

Modifying a binary value

The Edit Binary Value dialog appears whenever you edit something that's not a DWORD, a REG_SZ, or a REG_EXPAND_SZ. Specifically, when you edit a REG_BINARY, a REG_MULTI_SZ, or either of the resource types described in Chapter 2, you'll see a dialog like the one shown in Figure 4-7. Like its predecessors, you can copy text from this dialog's Value name field; however, the Value data field's behavior is a bit different.

Instead of holding plain text or a single binary value, the Edit Binary Value dialog's Value data field displays as much data as the value holds. Some binary values are a single byte; others, like the one pictured here, can be hundreds of bytes long. *RegEdit* doesn't care; it displays whatever data is stored for the value. The offset column shows the offset, in hex, at which each block of data starts. The hex display area shows the value's data as blocks of 8 hex bytes per line, and the ASCII display area shows the printable representation (if any) of the corresponding line's hex data.

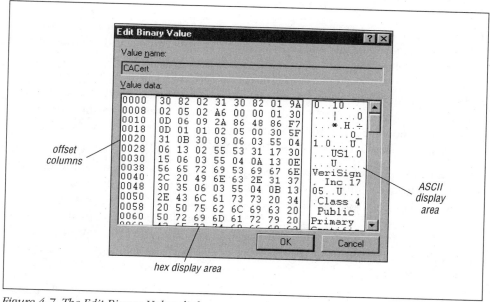

Figure 4-7. The Edit Binary Value dialog

As with the string and DWORD dialogs, you can cut, copy, and paste text in the Value data field. You can also insert or replace text by highlighting the text you want to modify, just like in a word processor. There's one important difference, though: what you type will be interpreted according to where you clicked to select text. If you click on the hex area, whatever you type will be taken as hex (only the digits 0-9 and letters A-F are acceptable input, though). If you click in the ASCII display area, what you type will be interpreted as ASCII text.

What this means is that you have to be careful. Let's say you want to change part of the value shown in the figure: you want to change the part that says "1705" to say "1999."* If you select the text in the ASCII area and type "1999," you'll get the change you expect. If, instead, you select the corresponding range of bytes in the hex display area and type "1999," *RegEdit* will change the first two bytes, 0x31 and 0x37, to what you typed: 0x19 and 0x99. Not exactly what you had in mind!

You can insert data, too; just position the insertion point where you want the new data to go and start typing. This is particularly useful for adding strings to a REG_MULTI_SZ value; you still have to make sure to add the hex 0x00 byte that indicates the end of each string. (Better still, use *RegEdt32*, which offers a built-in editor for REG_MULTI_SZ strings.)

---

* This change makes no sense. Don't do it. It's shown here for instructional purposes only.

Adding New Keys or Values

For the most part, you will probably have little use for the commands that let you add values and keys. This is because of the way applications and components use the Registry—they look for data in predetermined locations, and if you add new data that they don't expect to find, they'll ignore it. I call this the "hide in plain sight" effect. Think of it like this: if you leave your FedEx delivery person a note taped to your front door asking them to leave your package on the front porch, they will. If, however, you hide the note under your doormat, they won't look for it, won't find it, and won't do what you wanted. So it is with NT.

However (and you knew this was coming, right?), Microsoft didn't add these commands just to make *RegEdit* look more impressive. There are good reasons to add values and keys; it's just that the circumstances that lead to these reasons are relatively rare. First of all, if you're a software developer, you may need to use *RegEdit* to add keys and values that you use in your own program. The industry trend has been to have installers take care of any Registry changes that need to be made, but before the installer is written sometimes you have to do it by hand.

The second, and probably more common, reason is that Microsoft often adds options or functions to NT system software that are only accessible by adding *new* keys to the Registry. These options may be documented in Microsoft's knowledge base (*http://www.microsoft.com/kb/*), but they may remain undocumented until Microsoft feels like revealing their presence. Here's an example: in NT (server or workstation), creating a shared printer also creates a thread that periodically announces the printer's existence. This generates unnecessary network traffic, and Microsoft provided a way to turn it off. You have to add a new value named `DisableServerThread` to `HKLM\SYSTEM\CurrentControlSet\Control\Print`; while it's documented in the knowledge base, it requires you to make a change to the Registry—which brings us to the mechanics of doing so in *RegEdit*.

Third-party manufacturers often take this same approach and put hidden tuning or diagnostic settings into their software or device drivers. These settings can only be activated by adding keys or values with a name known to the software.

The **Edit ➤ New** command can create new keys or values; it's actually a submenu with four commands in it: New Key, String Value, DWORD Value, and Binary Value. These commands all work in a similar way:

1. Select the key under which you want to create a new key or value.

2. Choose the appropriate command from the menu bar or the context menu.

3. *RegEdit* will create the requested object and give it a temporary name, which you may edit in place. When you create a new key, it gets an empty value:

(Default). Similarly, new string and binary values are empty when created, and new DWORD values have an initial value zero. Figure 4-8 shows the results of some (injudicious) experimentation on my (backup) computer.*

4. If you're creating a value, you can now use the **Edit ► Modify** command to actually assign a real value to the newly created object.

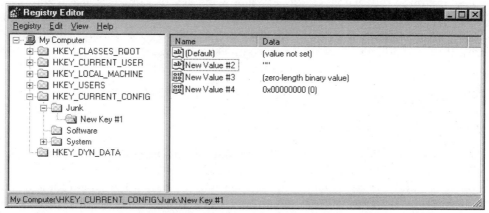

Figure 4-8. New keys and default contents

If you're ready to try out your newfound powers, look no further than Chapter 9, *Registry Tweaks*—it contains a list of the most-frequently-sought-after Registry modifications.

Deleting Keys or Values

There are times when you may need to remove data from the Registry. For example, even commercial products that include "uninstall" programs may not completely clean up all the Registry entries they've made. However, of all the potential ways to damage your Registry, this is the one I most often see people have problems with. Why? Two reasons: there's no way to undo mistaken deletions from within *RegEdit* or *RegEdt32*, and some deletions don't cause problems until the next reboot. I strongly recommend (again) that you have a current Registry backup on hand before deleting any key that you didn't create yourself.

Having said that, on to the instructions. *RegEdit* will let you delete any key except the root keys, and any value except the (Default) value some keys have. You can delete keys and values in two ways: by selecting them (using the mouse or keyboard) and using the **Edit ► Delete** command (or its shortcut, the Del key) or by

---

* Surely you don't think I'd experiment on my *production* machine, do you?

clicking the right mouse button over the target item and using the context menu's Delete command.

When you delete a key, *RegEdit* displays a confirmation dialog that asks you whether you *really* want to delete the selected item. However, in a major *faux pas*, the dialog doesn't tell you which key you're deleting! Before clicking the "Yes" button in this dialog, closely examine what key or value is selected and confirm that what's selected is what you actually wanted to delete. Once you confirm the deletion, *RegEdit* will delete the selected key, all its subkeys, and all their values. If you accidentally delete a major key like HKLM\SOFTWARE, you're in for big trouble unless you have that backup handy.

Be very, very careful when deleting keys *or* values. End of sermon.

Renaming Keys or Values

You can rename keys and values with the **Edit ➤ Rename** command, which works equally well on keys or values. Select the item you want to rename and give the command, and the item's name will change into an editable text field into which you can type or paste. Hit the Return key when you're done, or the ESC key to cancel your changes.

A cautionary note: just because you *can* rename keys and values doesn't mean that doing so is a good idea. System components and applications *always* look for values with specific names, and they expect to see them in specific locations. If you change the key or value name for an important parameter, the software that uses it won't be able to find it; depending on how robust the software is, you may not notice any difference, or your machine may crash. The best heuristic I can recommend is never to rename any keys that belong to NT itself and to avoid renaming keys whenever possible.

Exporting and Importing Data

One of *RegEdit*'s unique features is its ability to store Registry data in a human-readable format, then import data in that same format to repair or recreate existing data, or even create new keys and values. Better still, you can create your own files, so you can automate Registry changes needed for your particular network or computing environment. You can also store multiple sets of Registry data and switch between them as needed; this is often useful for system administrators who need to develop their own management tools.

What's in a .REG File?

The *.REG* file format is simple to understand. Fortunately, that makes it simple for programs to parse, too; in Chapter 7, *Programming with the Registry,* you'll see some Perl scripts that manipulate *.REG* files. In the meantime, let's examine the format that *RegEdit* uses so you'll be able to make sense of it when you see it.

Here's a snippet gleaned from my desktop machine's Registry:

```
REGEDIT4

[HKEY_LOCAL_MACHINE\SYSTEM\CurrentControlSet\Services\Browser]
"Type"=dword:00000020
"Start"=dword:00000002
"ErrorControl"=dword:00000001
"ImagePath"=hex(2):25,53,79,73,74,65,6d,52,6f,6f,74,25,5c,53,79,73, \
    74,65,6d,33,32,5c,73,65,72,76,69,63,65,73,2e,65,78,65,00
"DisplayName"="Computer Browser"
"DependOnService"=hex(7):4c,61,6e,6d,61,6e,57,6f,72,6b,73,74,61,74,69, \
    6f,6e,00,4c,61,6e,6d,61,6e,53,65,72,76,65,72,00,4c,6d,48,6f,73,74, \
    73,00,00
"DependOnGroup"=hex(7):00
"ObjectName"="LocalSystem"

[HKEY_LOCAL_MACHINE\SYSTEM\CurrentControlSet\Services\Browser\Linkage]

[HKEY_LOCAL_MACHINE\SYSTEM\CurrentControlSet\Services\Browser\Linkage\Disabled]

[HKEY_LOCAL_MACHINE\SYSTEM\CurrentControlSet\Services\Browser\Parameters]
"MaintainServerList"="Auto"
"IsDomainMaster"="FALSE"
```

The first line in the file identifies the file as a *.REG* file. If this string's present, *RegEdit* will attempt to interpret the rest of the file as a set of keys and values; if it's not present, *RegEdit* will complain that the file you're importing isn't really a *.REG* file.

The next interesting line identifies the full path to a key. In this case, the key is `HKLM\SYSTEM\CurrentControlSet\Services\Browser`. There are two noteworthy things about this key path: it's enclosed in square brackets (which *RegEdit* looks for as delimiters), and the root key is spelled out: `HKEY_LOCAL_MACHINE` instead of the more convenient `HKLM`.

The remaining lines for this key specify its values as name/value pairs. The general syntax looks like this:

```
"name"=[type:]  ["] value ["]
```

Each value has a name. Keys can have a special value whose name is empty; *RegEdit* displays this value with a name of (Default), but in *.REG* files the special name @ takes its place. The name must always be in double quotes to accommodate the fact that Registry value names can contain spaces.

Next comes the optional data type specifier. The specifier's necessary to preserve all the details of the values; even though *RegEdit* can only directly edit binary, DWORD, and string values, its export and import commands must correctly preserve the entire state of the keys and values they're operating on. When the value is a standard REG_SZ string, *RegEdit* will omit the type specifier; otherwise, it will use the values shown in Table 4-2. Note that if a type specifier's used, the colon that follows it is required.

Table 4-2. .REG File Data Type Specifiers

Registry Type	.REG Type
REG_BINARY	hex
REG_DWORD	dword
REG_EXPAND_SZ	hex(2)
REG_FULL_RESOURCE_DESCRIPTOR	hex(9)
REG_MULTI_SZ	hex(7)
REG_RESOURCE_LIST	hex(8)
REG_SZ	none

The value's actual value is the next item in the name/value definition. Standard REG_SZ strings are easy to identify, since they're always between double-quotes. DWORD values are written as 32-bit hex numbers, including leading zeros but without any kind of type identifier (like the "0x" prefix that *RegEdt32* uses). The other data types are all represented as a comma-delimited list of hex bytes, as you can see in the example above. Since all these data types can be of arbitrary length, the actual number of bytes can vary from value to value. *RegEdit* allows you to use the backslash character as a line continuation character; when present at the end of a line, the backslash indicates that the following line should be considered part of the current line.

Blank lines aren't significant to *RegEdit*; however, if no value definitions follow a key definition, that key will be created without any values, as with Browser\ Linkage and Browser\Linkage\Disabled in the example above.

Exporting Registry Data

You can export any key and its subkeys, from the root keys on down. When you export a key, all the data necessary to recreate it is stored in a *.REG* file that you can archive, print, or edit like any other. You can also reimport the file; as you learned in Chapter 3, this capability gives you a useful way to back up and restore individual keys within the Registry.

The **Registry ➤ Export Registry File...** command actually does the exporting; when you invoke it, you'll see the dialog shown in Figure 4-9. If you have selected a key in the key pane, the Selected branch radio button will be selected, and the currently active key will appear in the associated text field. If you'd rather export the entire Registry, you can use the All radio button to do so.

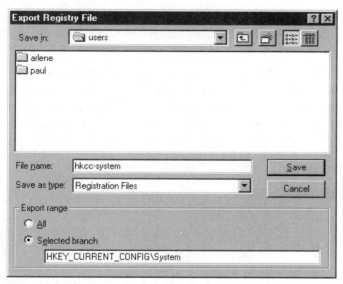

Figure 4-9. The Export dialog

Once you've supplied a filename and chosen exactly what you want to export, *RegEdit* will write out the selected data to your file, using the format described earlier in the section "What's in a .REG File?"

Importing Registry Data

Once you've exported a *.REG* file, or created one by hand, *RegEdit* allows you to load it back into the Registry. As you read in the preceding section, the *.REG* file contains enough information for *RegEdit* to load key and value data from the file and place it in the proper location in the Registry. However, the program's indiscriminate; once you tell it to load a file, it will happily blast the entire file's contents into your Registry, with no further opportunity for you to limit the scope of its replacements.

When you select the **Registry ➤ Import Registry File...** command, *RegEdit* will display the standard Open File dialog so you can choose a file. If you select a file that's not in *.REG* format, you'll get an error dialog telling you that the file you chose can't be loaded. If, however, the file is in valid format, *RegEdit* will import it, displaying a progress dialog to tell you how far along it's gotten. There's no way to cancel or interrupt the loading process from within the program. Forcing *RegEdit* to quit during an import operation (by using the Task Manager, *PVIEW*, or other tools) can leave your Registry looking like the front yards of your local college's Fraternity Row after a football game—don't do it.

Once the import operation's finished, you'll see a confirmation dialog that tells you that *RegEdit* did in fact import the entire file; it also includes the path name of the imported file so you'll know exactly what file got imported (just in case you've forgotten).

One caveat: when you import data with a *.REG* file, *RegEdit* will add any keys that are in the *.REG* file but not in the Registry, and it will change the value of any keys that appear in both places. It will *not* remove keys that are in the Registry but not in the *.REG* file, so you cannot use *RegEdit* to clean out an accidentally added key or remove keys that have been added since the time the *.REG* file was created.

Creating Your Own .REG Files

Even though *RegEdit* can generate *.REG* files, there's no reason why you can't generate your own files; in fact, this is a handy strategy when you need to make the same set of Registry changes on more than one machine. You can create a *.REG* file, test it and tweak it on a single machine until you're satisfied that it does what you want, then import it using *RegEdit* on each machine you want to modify.

A concrete example

Windows NT Server includes the Services for Macintosh (SFM) package, which lets an NT server serve NTFS volumes to Mac clients. To the Mac, these SFM volumes look just like native Mac disks, and they preserve the Mac-style file type and creator information needed to associate files with the applications that created them. Unfortunately, NTFS doesn't support these type and creator codes; instead, SFM keeps a table that translates PC-style file extensions to the corresponding type and creator codes. This enables PC and Mac users to both recognize files with names like *chapter04.doc* as Microsoft Word files.

Microsoft helpfully provides a default set of type/extension mappings with SFM. That's the good news; the bad news is that it doesn't include many of the most useful file types.* Even if it did, the exact mix of file types you want to use will

---

* Of course, it already has type information for Microsoft's Office applications.

depend on what programs your users are running. SFM provides a dialog for associating types and extensions, but it's a tedious task at best. *RegEdit* provides an ideal solution: once you have a set of file extensions built on one server, you can easily replicate it to other SFM servers by importing a *.REG* file. In fact, you can easily do this with new servers in your domain, too, making it easy to maintain and upgrade your file services without undue effort on your part.

Safely experimenting with .REG files

One especially handy use for these files is to let you fine-tune your *.REG* files without endangering the rest of your Registry. You accomplish this by building a file that contains the values and keys you want to modify, but puts them beneath a different key than the original. For example, if you're writing a *.REG* file that you want to apply to `HKLM\Software\Netscape\Netscape Navigator`, you can safely fiddle around with your *.REG* file without fear by following these steps:

1. Export the key you're going to modify using *RegEdit*'s export facility. You'll end up with a *.REG* file that will duplicate the existing key's contents when reloaded.

2. Make a note of the path that contains the keys you're modifying. For example, if you're modifying keys that live under the `HKLM\Software\Microsoft\ Windows NT\CurrentVersion\IniFileMapping` tree, your *.REG* file will contain code that looks like this:

```
[HKEY_LOCAL_MACHINE\SOFTWARE\Microsoft\Windows NT\
    CurrentVersion\IniFileMapping\Clock.ini]
@="#USR:Software\\Microsoft\\Clock"
```

3. Use a text editor to change all instances of the key's path to a new, unused value. For example, you might change from `HKLM\Software\Microsoft\ Windows NT\CurrentVersion\IniFileMapping` to `HKLM\Software\ Microsoft\Windows NT\Testing\IniFileMapping`. Of course, you must use one of the root keys as the base, but you are otherwise free to improvise a path, since *RegEdit* will create any keys or subkeys that need to be created to complete the import.

4. Load the new *.REG* file; its contents will appear under the key you've specified.

You can now edit the *.REG* file to your heart's content; when you're satisfied with the changes it makes, you can reverse step 3 to put the original key path back in place so the changes will go where you want them to, then use, distribute, or store the *.REG* file however you'd like.

Why does this work? Applications and system components look for Registry data in a particular path. If the data isn't in that precise location, the using application won't find them. This is akin to what would happen if your postman put your incoming snail-mail under your doormat: it would be delivered, but when you checked your mailbox, you wouldn't find your mail. Likewise, if you take the Browser service's settings from `HKLM\System\CurrentControlSet\Services\Browser` and copy them to `HKLM\Software\TestBrowser`, you'll still be able to see your changes—but the system component they're intended for won't.

WARNING   This approach won't help you tell whether the changes you're making are appropriate or will do what you want; it will only help you
ensure that the changes go where you intended them to and that
nothing extraneous was added or deleted.

RegEdit Command-Line Options

Even though I've been talking about using *RegEdit* as a standard Windows application, it also supports several command-line options that let you use it to import and export Registry data from scripts, batch files, or the NT command line. Both of these switches run *RegEdit* as a background process. The export process is quiet; the import process will display a completion dialog, just as it does when you use the **Registry ➤ Import Registry File...** command.

Exporting Data

You tell *RegEdit* to export data with the /e command-line switch. The command looks like this:

```
regedit  /e targetFile  [registryPath]
```

targetFile
Specifies where *RegEdit* should write its data; you can specify any path, filename, and extension you like so long as it's not a UNC path

registryPath
This optional parameter tells *RegEdit* what to export. If you omit it, the entire Registry will be exported; if you specify a key, that key and all its subkeys will be exported. The path must be a complete path, including a root key, and you must spell out the name of the root key.

If you wanted to dump the contents of `HKLM\Software\metrowerks` to a file named *warrior.reg*, you could do it like this:

```
regedit /e c:\dist\hklm\warrior.reg HKEY_LOCAL_MACHINE\SOFTWARE\metrowerks
```

Importing Data

The simplest way to import data using *RegEdit* is to specify the name of the file you want imported on the command line, like this:

```
regedit warrior.reg
```

RegEdit will happily import the file's entire contents and present a confirmation dialog when done. Alternatively, you can force *RegEdit* to replace the entire contents of the Registry with a *.REG* file. *RegEdit* won't replace the keys that are dynamically built (like HKLM\HARDWARE and HKDD), but everything else is fair game—make sure the file you're loading has a complete set of Registry contents *and* that you have a current backup. To invoke this mode, use the /c switch, like this:

```
regedit /c whole-enchilada.reg
```

When you use the /c switch, you may get an odd dialog accusing you of tampering with the product type (see Figure 4-10). Windows NT 4.0 keeps a pair of threads running in the background; these threads do nothing more than watch HKLM\System\Setup\SystemPrefix and HKLM\System\CurrentControlSet\ Control\ProductOptions\ProductType for changes and reverse any changes that occur. When you reload the entire Registry, the threads notice and present the warning dialog because they're not smart enough to tell that the value isn't any different—just that someone tried to change it. (For more information on these threads and why they're there, see Andrew Schulman's article at *ftp:// ftp.ora.com/pub/examples/windows/win95.update/ntnodiff.html*.)

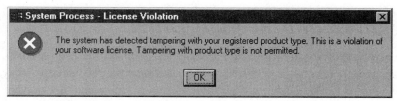

Figure 4-10. Alert you may possibly trigger with the /c switch

5

Using RegEdt32

In Chapter 4, *Using RegEdit,* you learned how to use the *RegEdit* utility to browse, search, and edit the Registry. *RegEdit* ships with both Windows 95 and Windows NT; however, NT also includes *RegEdt32,* a more powerful Registry editor that fully supports NT's security and auditing features. In this chapter, you'll learn how to use *RegEdt32* to view, edit, create, and delete data in the Registry.

How RegEdt32 and RegEdit Differ

Since *RegEdit* was originally written for Win95, it doesn't support the full capabilities of NT's Registry; in particular, it doesn't have any support for NT's security features. While this may make *RegEdit* look like the computer equivalent of a tricycle when compared to *RegEdt32,* this isn't really accurate. A better comparison is between a bicycle and a car. Each has its uses; sometimes a bicycle is the best, cheapest, most enjoyable, or fastest way to reach your destination—but it's not a good way to bring home a new baby from the hospital or take six friends out to dinner.

So it is with the two Registry editors. *RegEdt32* has a number of features that *RegEdit* doesn't, but it also has some unique limitations:

- *RegEdit* can search keys and values, while *RegEdt32* can only search key names. You'll quickly become comfortable with firing up *RegEdit* to find the value you're looking for, then editing it as needed in *RegEdt32.*

- *RegEdt32* fully supports NT's security features; it allows you to view and set ownership, permissions, and auditing controls for root keys and their subkeys.

- *RegEdt32* can load and save keys in binary format; in addition, it can import these saved keys as self-contained hives, making it easy to transfer data from machine to machine.

- *RegEdt32* supports many more display options, and its interface allows you to view as many or as few root keys as you're interested in, each in its own window.

The two are similar in many respects, too; both allow you to view and edit Registry data on other computers, and both allow you to edit different data types with an appropriate editor (though *RegEdt32* supports more of NT's Registry data types than does *RegEdit*).

Learning the RegEdt32 Interface

Where *RegEdit*'s interface is like that of Windows Explorer, *RegEdt32* has an interface very similar to the original Windows 3.1/NT File Manager. This likeness is partly due to heritage; *RegEdt32* was first delivered with NT 3.1 back in 1993, and hasn't been rewritten to take advantage of the user-interface enhancements included with Win95 and NT 4.0.

Figure 5-1 shows *RegEdt32* in action. Each root key has its own document window; these windows are independent of one another and can be moved, tiled, resized, and arranged however you wish. You cannot, however, close individual root key windows for the keys on your own machine, but you can minimize them to keep them out of the way, or you can use the **Registry ➤ Close** command to close *all* the root windows.

Each root key window is further divided into two panes: the tree pane, which is similar to *RegEdit*'s key pane, is on the left and shows a tree structure representing the hierarchy of keys under that root. The data pane is on the right; it displays all values for whatever key is selected in the tree pane. Between the two panes is a standard Windows splitter control, which allows you to adjust the relative width of the two panes. In a welcome departure from *RegEdit*, the tree and data panes both have horizontal scrollbars, thus making it easier to view long values without having to resort to trickery.

RegEdit wouldn't automatically update its display as keys and values changed; however, *RegEdt32* gives you a choice. In "automatic update" mode, *RegEdt32* periodically refreshes its display, but this is time-consuming and sometimes unnecessary. You can turn this mode off, in which case *RegEdt32* will act like *RegEdit*: it won't automatically update values that have been changed by other applications or system components.

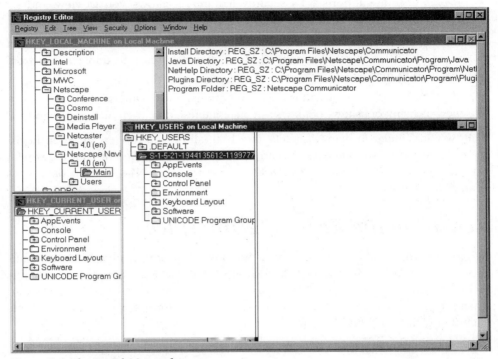

Figure 5-1. The RegEdt32 interface

Manipulating Windows

When you start *RegEdt32* for the first time, all five root key windows will appear, stacked diagonally across the *RegEdt32* root window area. (Yes, five: even though HKDD is a legitimate root key, *RegEdt32* doesn't know about it, doesn't display it, and won't allow you to open it.) You can manually move the windows around however you like; the Window menu also offers you several commands for quickly arranging windows the way you want them:

- The Cascade command (Shift+F5) arranges all the open root key windows in a diagonal pattern; the first window snugs up immediately beneath the menu bar, and the others are offset down and to the right so that all their title bars are visible. The currently active window will end up at the bottom-right corner of the stack.

- The Tile command (Shift+F4) sizes and positions the open windows so that all of them are equally sized and visible simultaneously.

- The Arrange Icons command neatly aligns any minimized windows along the bottom margin of the application window.

Besides these commands, *RegEdt32* also includes the root key windows in the Window menu; each of the five windows has its own entry, and you can jump to any one by selecting it from the menu. If you have additional root keys on other computers open, they'll be displayed too; if you have more than nine open root key windows, the **Window ➤ More Windows...** command appears, making available a dialog from which you can choose any open window.

There's one more useful window command, but it's not in the Window menu: **Registry ➤ Close**. The individual root key windows don't have the standard "close" icon in their title bar, and the tool stripe pop-up menu doesn't have a close command on it either. However, **Registry ➤ Close** can close your windows in two ways. If you select it while the active window is for a root key on your local machine, all the root key windows for your machine will close, and you'll have to use the **Registry ➤ Open Local** command to reopen it.* If you select **Registry ➤ Close** when the active window is displaying a root key from another machine, that window only will be closed. When you close the last window to another machine's Registry, *RegEdt32* will disconnect from the remote machine altogether.

Controlling What You See

RegEdt32 includes a View menu that gives you some degree of control over the way data are displayed in the root key windows. The commands in this menu affect only the frontmost window, with one exception (the Refresh All command).

- By default, *RegEdt32* shows both the tree and data panes. This corresponds to the View menu's first command, Tree and Data. If you prefer, you can use the Tree Only or Data Only commands to limit the display to whatever you're interested in looking at. The current setting will be marked with a checkmark.

- The **View ➤ Split** command activates the vertical window splitter bar that separates the tree and data panes. Once you issue the Split command, you can drag the splitter left or right just by moving your mouse left or right or using the left and right arrow keys. Of course, this duplicates what you could do by clicking and dragging the splitter bar itself (that little black square at the bottom of the splitter).

---

* Oddly, every time you use the command, *RegEdt32* opens up a new set of local root key windows. Do it three times, and you've suddenly grown 15 new root key windows! This appears to be a bug (at least, I can't imagine why it would be a feature).

- *RegEdt32* normally displays data in its native format; for example, DWORD values are shown as hex numbers, REG_SZ values are shown as strings, and so on. The **View ➤ Display Binary Data** command lets you override this behavior and force *RegEdt32* to show everything as though it were binary data (it actually appears as a string of hex digits, not in true binary).

- *RegEdt32* may or may not automatically refresh its display to reflect any added, deleted, or changed keys or values, depending on your preference. If you've told *RegEdt32* not to automatically update the display, you must manually ask for updates when you want them. There are two ways to do so. The first way is to ask *RegEdt32* to update its display of *all* open root keys with the **View ➤ Refresh All** command or its accelerator, Shift+F6. As its name suggests, this command tells *RegEdt32* to update every root key window for local *and* remote machines. For those times when you only care about what's displayed in the frontmost window, the **View ➤ Refresh Active** command (or its accelerator, F6) will do just that, updating only the values and keys in the currently active root key window.

The View menu also sports a Find Key command, which we'll discuss in the section "Searching for Keys" a bit later.

Setting Session Options

RegEdt32 lumps a number of useful settings into its Options menu; these settings give you additional control over how *RegEdt32* behaves. The first one worth mentioning is actually the last command in the menu: Save Settings on Exit. When this command is checked (as it is by default), *RegEdt32* will remember the settings of all the other options in the menu, as well as the positions, sizes, and minimized/maximized states of all the root key windows. *RegEdt32* stores this information in HKCU\SOFTWARE\Microsoft\RegEdt32\Settings. The other **Options** menu commands are a mixed bag:

- You can choose the font face and size used to draw the root key windows and their contents with the **Options ➤ Font...** command. This is a boon for both high- and low-resolution displays, since you can find a comfortable point size that allows you to read the tree and data panes without squinting.

- The Auto Refresh command controls whether *RegEdt32* automatically updates its tree and data panes to keep them in sync with the actual contents of the Registry. If this command is enabled, *RegEdt32* will periodically update all open root key windows. This takes a small, but noticeable, amount of time; the time required will be more noticeable if you have root keys on remote machines open over a slow network link. If you turn Auto Refresh off, you can still use the manual refresh commands in the View menu to force

RegEdt32 to update itself when you think it's necessary. However, Auto Refresh is convenient and works fine as long as you don't mind the occasional pause.

- Read Only Mode is, sadly, *not* turned on by default. When it is on, *RegEdt32* won't let you change anything in the Registry. You can look at keys and values as much as you'd like, but you won't be able to add or delete keys or add, edit, or delete values. Whenever you open a value to edit it, *RegEdt32* will present a polite dialog telling you that this mode's enabled and that your changes won't be saved.

  When setting up a new installation, I always make sure to run *RegEdt32*, make sure "Save Settings On Exit" is checked, and turn on Read Only Mode. Savvy users can always turn it off; in the meantime, it's useful protection against the curious but unschooled. It can also keep you from making mistakes on your *own* machine, so I recommend turning it on there as well.

- The **Options ➤ Confirm On Delete** command is another potential bacon-saver, which probably explains why it's turned on by default. When it's on, *RegEdt32* will warn you with a confirmation dialog when you try to remove a value or key; this last-ditch "are you sure?" step has saved many an administrator from accidentally removing something unintended. For your own health and safety, please leave this option turned on.

Browsing with RegEdt32

RegEdt32's interface isn't as "discoverable" as *RegEdit*; that's just a fancy way of saying that it's not as easy to just jump in and start poking around. However, this doesn't mean that using *RegEdt32* is hard—just a little unfamiliar if you're not an old File Manager hand.

Since each root key appears in its own independent window, your browsing sessions will usually focus on the subkeys of one particular root key. One nice thing about having each root key in a separate window is that it makes it easy to compare Registry values on different machines, as shown in Figure 5-2. Since you can minimize, resize, and position each window independently, it's easy to put off the ones you're not interested in at the moment, then recall them later when you need them.*

---

* Of course, since HKCU and HKCR are really links to subkeys of HKU and HKLM respectively, you can get all you need by leaving HKU and HKLM open and hiding the rest.

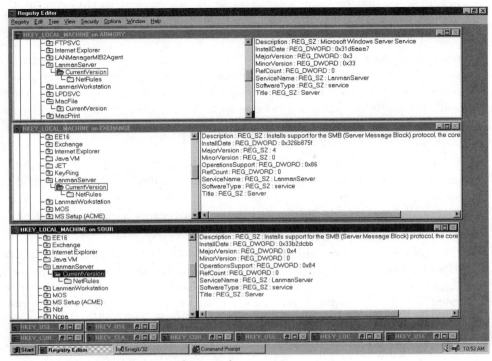

Figure 5-2. Arranging your RegEdt32 windows

Navigating with the Keyboard

If you've used the keyboard to navigate around the Windows 3.1 File Manager, you'll feel right at home doing the same in *RegEdt32*. Table 5-1 shows the key navigation commands that you can use to move around. The last four entries in the table are actually accelerators for commands in the Tree menu.

Table 5-1. Navigational Keys for RegEdt32

Key	When used in...	Action
Tab	Tree or data panes	Switches focus between the key and value panes
Return	Tree pane	Expands currently selected key, but not its sub-keys
Return	Data pane	Opens selected item for editing
Up/down arrows	Tree or data panes	Moves focus to the next or previous item in the current pane
Left/right arrows	Tree or data panes	Scrolls the active pane left or right if it has scrollbars; does nothing otherwise

Table 5-1. Navigational Keys for RegEdt32 (continued)

Key	When used in…	Action
PgUp/PgDn	Tree or data panes	Moves up or down one pane's worth of data without changing focus
Home and End	Tree or data panes	Moves to top or bottom of pane's contents
Backspace	Tree or data panes	Returns the focus to "My Computer" in the key pane
Keypad +	Tree or data panes	Expands the currently selected key, but not its subkeys
Keypad *	Tree or data panes	Expands all subkeys of the currently selected key
Ctrl+ keypad *	Tree or data panes	Expands the entire tree; may take a few seconds
Keypad -	Tree pane	Collapses the selected key and all its subkeys

Remote Registry Editing

RegEdt32 originated the concept of remotely editing another machine's Registry. This is invaluable for administrators, since it gives you the ability to peek into the Registry of a misconfigured or broken machine from the comfort of your office. As with most magic powers, this ability to edit the Registry from afar has some associated constraints and requirements.

First of all, you must have sufficient privilege to see the Registry on the remote machine. By default, NT Workstation machines will allow anyone to connect to their Registries, as will NT Server version 3.51 and earlier. NT Server 4.0 turns remote access off. This privilege, which is discussed in the section "Limiting Remote Registry Access" in Chapter 8, *Administering the NT Registry*, lets you view HKU and HKLM on the remote machine, but that's all—if you want to see the contents of HKCR, HKCC, or HKCU, you'll have to look in the appropriate section of the two keys you *can* see.[*]

Next, you must be able to modify the Registry on the remote machine. Let's say you're logged into a machine where your account has Administrator privileges. If you use *RegEdt32* to open the Registry of another machine on your network where your account doesn't have Administrator access, you'll see that machine's HKLM and HKU entries but you won't be able to open them! This also holds true when your machine and/or the target are members of an NT domain: to change data on the remote machine, you must have Administrator access *on the remote machine.*

---

[*] HKDD is, of course, not visible either; this isn't surprising since you can't see it in *RegEdt32* at all.

RegEdt32 doesn't buffer or cache any Registry data from whatever remote machines you're connected to, and it won't automatically update windows containing remote machines' root keys. This means that your display can quickly lose sync with the target machine's Registry; make sure to refresh the display as needed.

Connecting to Remote Computers

You actually connect to remote machines' Registries with the **Registry ➤ Select Computer** command, which displays the standard Select Computer dialog shown in Figure 5-3. Neither *RegEdt32* nor NT makes any attempt to restrict the list of machines displayed to NT machines, so the list may contain machines whose Registries you can't edit—including Win95, Windows 3.11, and even Unix machines running the Samba file server package! If you try to connect to a machine that doesn't support remote Registry editing, *RegEdt32* will tell you that it couldn't connect to the remote machine.

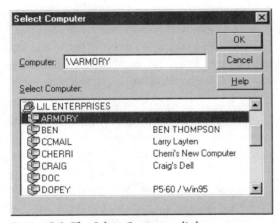

Figure 5-3. The Select Computer dialog

Once you've successfully selected and connected to a remote machine, its HKU and HKLM keys will appear in new windows within the *RegEdt32* frame window. Assuming that you have the right permissions, you can browse, edit, export, and otherwise modify the Registry on the remote machine as much as you'd like. You may freely close root key windows that point to remote machines; when you close the last window to a machine, *RegEdt32* closes the Registry connection to that machine as well.

Searching for Keys

RegEdt32's search capability is much less capable than *RegEdit*'s, but it's better than nothing. Where *RegEdit* can search key names, value names, and value contents, *RegEdt32* can only search key names. This is still useful, however, since most of the available documentation covering Registry keys gives you the key names even when value names and contents aren't specified.

When you search the Registry with *RegEdt32*, the search starts at whatever key you currently have selected and proceeds until one of two things happens: a match is found or the search hits the end of the Registry. In the former case, *RegEdt32* will highlight the matching key; in the latter, it will display a dialog telling you that no more instances of the search string could be found.

You get to *RegEdt32*'s Find dialog with the **View ➤ Find Key** menu command; the dialog itself is shown in Figure 5-4. It looks, and works, very much like the Find dialogs of other applications you've probably used before: Notepad, Wordpad, and Microsoft's Office suite. Here's what its controls do:

- You specify the key name you want to find by typing all or part of it into the "Find what" field. You may also use the standard Windows keyboard shortcuts to cut, copy, or paste Clipboard text into this field.

- The "Match whole word only" and "Match case" checkboxes control how *RegEdt32* compares the search string you type against the Registry data. By default, both these checkboxes are off.

- The Up and Down radio buttons control the direction in which *RegEdt32* searches: Up searches from the selected key to the root key of the active window, while Down searches from the selected key to the last subkey of the last key of the active root.

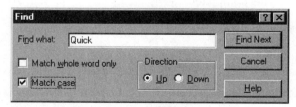

Figure 5-4. RegEdt32's Find dialog

Each time *RegEdt32* finds a match, it will highlight the matching key in the tree pane of the active root key window; you can then use the Find Next button to search for the next instance, or the Cancel button to stop looking.

Saving and Loading Registry Keys

RegEdt32 allows you to dump Registry data into ordinary files that you can back
up or use on other machines. You can save data in binary and text formats, and
you can reload binary data when you need it again. The text format has the
advantage of being human-readable, but the binary format is more efficient and is
the only one *RegEdt32* can import. (For more details on using this capability to
back up your Registry, see Chapter 3, *In Case of Emergency.*)

RegEdt32 normally deals with the hive files stored in *System32\Config*. However,
you can also create your own files that contain just the keys and values you want.
Once you've created such a file, you can load it back to its original location or
anywhere else in the Registry; you can also use the file on another machine's Registry.

Saving Keys

To create a binary file of Registry data, just select the key or subkey that you want
to save, then use *RegEdt32's* **Registry ➤ Save Key** command. When the standard
Save dialog appears, specify a file name, and *RegEdt32* will store the selected
key's contents to the file (as long as you have adequate permission to read the
key, its subkeys, and their values). The completed file is an ordinary NT file, so
you can copy it to floppy, email it, or handle it just like any other kind of document.

There's no way to combine more than one key in a file unless they have a common parent. If you want to capture web browser settings from your local
machine, you could save `HKLM\Software\Microsoft` and `HKLM\Software\`
`Netscape` in two separate files, or you could save `HKLM\Software` and get them
both—plus a lot of other unrelated stuff.

Restoring Keys

Once you've saved a key, restoring it is fairly straightforward. Select the location
where you want the key to appear when loaded, then use the **Registry ➤ Restore
Key...** command. *RegEdt32* will load the saved key as a subkey of the currently

selected key. For example, if you select `HKLM\Software\Qualcomm\Eudora` and load a file, the saved file's contents will appear under `Eudora`. Be careful with this command; the saved key file doesn't contain any information about the key's path, so *RegEdt32* can't warn you that you're restoring a key in the wrong place.

When the new key's loaded, it actually replaces *all* subkeys and values of the selected key. Before anything actually gets replaced, you'll see a warning dialog asking you to confirm that you want to wipe out all the existing subkeys and values of the selected key. Unfortunately, though, the dialog doesn't tell you *which* key is about to be affected, so make sure you double-check the selected key to ensure it's the one you meant to restore over.

Loading Saved Keys as Hives

When you load a key with **Registry ➤ Restore Key...**, it overwrites whatever was there before. You can also load a saved key as a new hive without overwriting any existing data. When you do this, the loaded key is mapped into the Registry the same way as the standard system hives are, and it remains loaded until you manually unload it. This function gives you an easy way to add a copy of a user account, since you can just grab `HKU\`*`sid`* from one machine and load it as a hive under `HKU` on another.

You may load a saved key as a hive under `HKU` or `HKLM`, but not any other root key. If you have `HKU` or `HKLM` selected, *RegEdt32* will enable the **Registry ➤ Load Hive...** command; it will be disabled otherwise. When you load a key as a hive with this command, the saved key will be loaded as a subkey of whichever root you loaded it into. For example, if you select `HKU` and load a file whose top-level key is `ExplodingStuff`, the new hive will appear as `HKU\ExplodingStuff`.

Once a saved key's been loaded as a hive, you can modify its keys and values like any other key; the changes will be reflected in the saved key file, which remains loaded and available until you explicitly unload it with the **Registry ➤ Unload Hive** command.

Saving as Text

RegEdt32 also allows you to save a key and its values to a text file with the **Registry ➤ Save Subtree As...** command. The formatting is identical to what appears when you print a key. If you need to search the Registry for a particular value (as opposed to a key name, which *RegEdt32* can do) your options are to use *RegEdit* or to save the root key you want to search to a text file and search it yourself. Apart from that, this command isn't very useful.

Providing an Improvised Clipboard

There's one major feature that *RegEdt32* and *RegEdit* both lack: a real set of Clipboard operations. It would really be handy to be able to copy a Registry key from one location and paste it in another, especially since both programs let you open the Registries of other machines on the network.

While *RegEdt32* doesn't directly provide Clipboard support, you can get the same effect with the **Registry ➤ Save Key...** and **Registry ➤ Restore Key...** commands. Let's say you're setting up a batch of new laptop machines running NT for your company's sales force.* They're all on the network, but you want to set up each laptop's Remote Access Service (RAS) phonebook entries so that they're all the same. Here's one way to accomplish your goal:

1. Set up one laptop so that its RAS dialing options and phone book settings are configured the way you want them. Let's call this machine the source machine.

2. Copy the source machine's phonebook file (*%systemroot%\system32\ras\rasphone.pbk*) to the corresponding place on each of the target machines.

3. Run *RegEdt32* on a machine (the source machine will do, or you can use your desktop machine). Open the source machine's Registry and select HKCU\ Software\Microsoft\RAS Phonebook, then use the **Registry ➤ Save Key...** command to save the data to a file.

4. Open the Registry of each machine you need to modify, then use **Registry ➤ Restore Key...** to load your saved file into HKU\.DEFAULT\Software\Microsoft\RAS Phonebook. Now any new user account created on that machine will inherit the RAS phonebook settings. If you instead want to apply the phonebook settings to another account, feel free. In fact, as long as you have administrative rights on the machine, you can add the phonebook settings to *all* the accounts under HKU.

A True Story

Now it's time for an anecdote. While writing this chapter, I ran into a problem. The shareware screen capture software I use to grab figures for my writing (the excellent SnagIt/32 from TechSmith; *http://www.techsmith.com/*) is installed under my account on a machine named *enigma*. When I'm logged in to that machine, SnagIt can find its registration key and settings data in HKCU\Software\TechSmith\SnagIt\Settings, and it's happy. However, for some of the figures, I

---

* If you've ever tried running NT on a laptop, you may find this to be a contrived example; however, NT 4.0 is much better about power management than NT 3.51, and NT 5.0 should be better still.

needed to log into a different domain—so SnagIt could no longer see its settings data, since I wasn't logged in as the same user! To make things worse, I couldn't find the piece of paper with my registration code, and I was in a hurry.

Solution: use *RegEdt32*. I logged onto *enigma*, saved the SnagIt settings key by selecting HKCU\Software\TechSmith\SnagIt\Settings and using the **Registry ➤ Save Key** command, and logged out. I then logged into my domain account, selected HKCU\Software\TechSmith\SnagIt, used the **Registry ➤ Restore Key** command to restore the file I'd just saved, and ran SnagIt again. Problem solved! A few short minutes later, I'd captured all the necessary images and was back on schedule.

Printing Registry Contents

RegEdt32 includes a rudimentary printing function. When you select a key and use the **Registry ➤ Print Subtree** command, you'll get a hardcopy version of that key's subkeys and values that looks like this example:

```
Key Name:          SOFTWARE\Netscape\Netscape Navigator\Users\paul
Class Name:        <NO CLASS>
Last Write Time:   6/29/97 - 7:07 PM
Value 0
  Name:            DirRoot
  Type:            REG_SZ
  Data:            C:\Program Files\Netscape\Users
```

RegEdt32 will print everything below the key you've selected, so if you select HKLM\SOFTWARE for printing (as I foolishly did while writing this section) expect to wait a while for the completed output. The formatting and indentation help make the printout slightly more readable, but you'll probably find it more worthwhile to save the keys you're interested in as text with the **Registry ➤ Save Subtree As...** command, then print that text file with your favorite editor.

The related **Registry ➤ Printer Setup** command allows you to set characteristics for the printout, including what printer, paper size, and print orientation to use.

Editing Keys and Values

RegEdt32 is a more powerful and flexible Registry editor than *RegEdit*. However, the two are roughly equivalent when it comes to adding and deleting keys and values—since the underlying functionality of the Registry is identical, it makes sense that their workings should be identical as well. (Just a reminder: don't edit things unless you're sure they need editing. End of sermon.)

Viewing Values as Binary Data

By default, *RegEdt32* shows each value as its native type. Sometimes, though, it can be useful to see a Registry value in raw form, without any kind of interpretation or formatting. Since hive files are always open, you can't use a standard file or hex editor to look at the file's contents; instead, *RegEdt32* gives you a way to get a hex dump of any value in the Registry. The **View ➤ Display Binary Data** command takes the selected value's contents and displays it in hex, as shown in Figure 5-5.

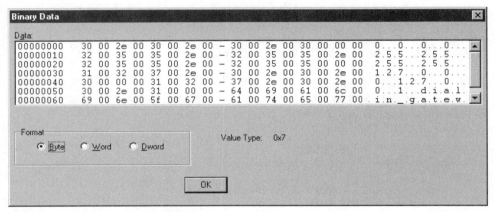

Figure 5-5. The Binary Data dialog

The radio buttons in the Format group let you control how *RegEdt32* presents the data. The default setting, Byte, shows the data as individual bytes; as a bonus, the rightmost section of the dialog shows the byte representations of the data, making this setting particularly useful for viewing strings. The Word and Dword buttons show the same data, but grouped as words or DWORDs respectively. These settings are most useful for viewing binary or DWORD values.

Modifying Values

Once you've selected a value in the data pane, you can modify it by double-clicking it, pressing the Enter key, or using the commands on the Edit menu: Binary, String, DWORD, and Multistring.* Each data type has its own editing dialog; while they all basically work the same way, some have subtle differences or additional controls.

---

* You may notice the lack of editing tools for REG_FULL_RESOURCE_DESCRIPTOR and REG_RESOURCE_
LIST. Microsoft doesn't want you editing those types, since they're only used in HKLM\HARDWARE.

Modifying a string value

The String Editor dialog, shown in Figure 5-6, is arguably the simplest of all the data editors in *RegEdt32*. The current string value is shown in the String field; you can type or paste any data you'd like into the field. When you click OK, your changes will be stored as the new contents for the value you're editing.

Figure 5-6. String editing

This string editor works for REG_EXPAND_SZ and plain old REG_SZ strings; there's a separate editor (discussed below) for REG_MULTI_SZ values.

Modifying a DWORD value

If strings are the simplest type of value to modify, DWORD runs a close second. The DWORD Editor dialog is shown in Figure 5-7; like the String Editor, it offers you a field in which you type the desired new value. The three radio buttons in the Radix group allow you to specify what number base you're using. The default is Hex, so you can enter quantities like "FF00" and "a29d" without any prefix or suffix. If you prefer, you can use the Binary and Decimal buttons to select base-2 or base-10 instead.

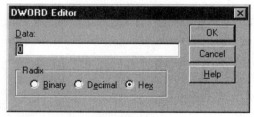

Figure 5-7. The DWORD editor

If you edit a big- or little-endian DWORD, this same editing dialog will appear; *RegEdt32* takes care of converting between the format stored in the Registry and whatever the native format is for the computer whose Registry you're editing. This automatic conversion means you don't have to worry about whether the data you're providing is in the right format for the CPU you're using to run NT.

Modifying a multiple-string value

The Registry stores multiple-string values as a concatenation of all the individual strings, separated by null characters (hex 0x00). While you can edit these multi-string blocks as binary data, remembering where to put the null character that terminates each individual string gets to be tedious pretty quickly. *RegEdt32* offers a better solution in the form of the Multi-String Editor dialog (see Figure 5-8).

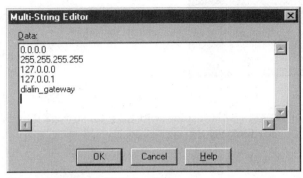

Figure 5-8. The Multi-String Editor

You may enter as many (or as few) strings as you like in this dialog's Data field. Each string's treated as an individual entity; when you hit Return at the end of a line, *RegEdt32* takes that as a signal to move to the next line and start another string. As with the other editors, you can use the standard Windows keyboard shortcuts to cut, copy, and paste text into this dialog.

Modifying a binary value

Many of the Registry's most important values are stored as raw binary data. This can pose a problem when you need to change (or undo a change!) their contents. After all, strings and numbers are easy to edit, but binary data can be a little tougher. *RegEdt32* includes a binary editor that makes it easier to inspect and change binary values when the need arises. The Binary Editor itself, shown in Figure 5-9, is fairly straightforward.

The column of digits on the left side of the edit field shows the offset of that line's data from the beginning of the data block. For example, the row labeled "0020" indicates that the first byte on that line starts 32 bytes (or hex 0x20) from the start of the data item. Likewise, the scale across the top of the edit field shows the offset within the line. The 44th byte in Figure 5-9 is at offset 0x2c from the beginning of the block; to find it, you'd first use the left column to find the row labeled "0020", then read across to "c" to find the correct byte.

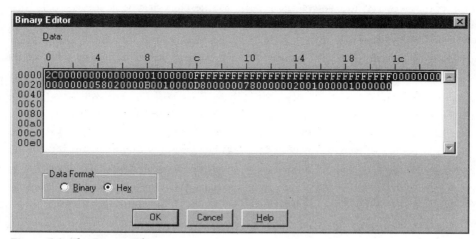

Figure 5-9. The Binary Editor

The Binary and Hex radio buttons control how *RegEdt32* actually displays the data. When you change from one mode to another, the contents of the edit field will change, as will the horizontal and vertical scales.

The edit field itself shows the value's contents. *RegEdt32* treats the data there as text, so you can insert, remove, cut, copy, and paste in this field as much as you'd like. If you hit a key that's not legal (for example, "2" while editing binary data, or "J" in hex mode) *RegEdt32* will ignore it. If you enter data that represents an odd number of bytes, *RegEdt32* will warn you with a dialog, then pad the data with zeroes until it's the proper length.

One final caveat: unlike Windows 95, NT stores its strings in Unicode format. That means that each character in a string actually takes up *two* bytes of storage space. When you edit an ordinary ASCII string using the binary editor, you'll see that every other byte is zero: that's because ASCII strings only need one byte of the two reserved for each character. Don't fool with the zero bytes, or you risk turning your strings from ASCII to a weird hybrid of ASCII, Japanese, Cyrillic, and maybe even Pinyin Chinese.

Modifying a value of a different type

RegEdt32 is helpful enough to remember, and store, a data type for every value in the Registry. However, you're free to ignore that data and edit a value as though its type were different. You've already seen one example of how this works: the **View ▸ Display Binary Data** command lets you inspect the contents of any type of value as though it were a REG_BINARY value.

When you have a value selected, if you double-click it you'll see its data displayed in whatever editor is appropriate. If instead you use the **Binary**, **String**, **DWORD**, or **Multistring** commands in the **Edit** menu, you can open any value's data as any of those types. For example, if you open a string as binary data, you'll see a display like the one shown in Figure 5-9.

While this is a useful trick, be careful. It's easy to corrupt data when editing it with an editor that has no knowledge of the data's native format. The safest course of action is to use the native format editor whenever possible; if you need to tweak a value without using its native format, I'd recommend using the binary editor instead.

Adding New Keys or Values

Like *RegEdit*, *RegEdt32* allows you to add new keys and values. The same cautions discussed in "Adding New Keys or Values" in Chapter 4 apply here too; for the most part, you won't need to add new keys unless you're adding one of the famous Microsoft hidden keys that are sometimes needed to activate (or deactivate) a particular feature.

Adding new keys

When you add a new key, it has to be a subkey of one of the existing root keys, and you must have appropriate access to that subkey. You tell *RegEdt32* where you want the new key by selecting a key in the tree pane of any root key window; the new key will be created immediately *beneath* the selected key. There's no way to relocate a key once it's in place, so make sure you put it in the right location the first time.

Once you've picked out a good spot for your key, you can use the **Edit ➤ Add Key** command to actually create the new key. When you do, you'll see the dialog shown in Figure 5-10. You specify the key name by typing it into the Key Name field (big surprise, right?), and you may optionally specify a data class for the default value (the one that shows up as "<No Name>") with the Class field. When you click the OK button, *RegEdt32* will add the new key in the selected location.

Adding new values

Adding a new value is a three-step process. The first, and arguably hardest, step is to select the key to which you want to add the new value. This is important, since *RegEdt32* doesn't give you a good way to move a value from one key to another. Be sure to visually confirm that the key you want the new value on is actually the one that's highlighted.

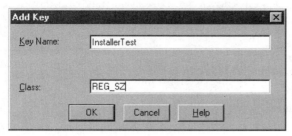

Figure 5-10. The Add Key dialog

The second step (once you've selected the desired key) is to use the **Edit ➤ Add Value...** command, which displays the dialog shown in Figure 5-11. You use this dialog to supply a name and type for the new value: the name goes in the Value Name field, of course, while the Data Type combo box allows you to choose any one of the data types that *RegEdt32* supports (REG_SZ, REG_EXPAND_SZ, REG_DWORD, REG_MULTI_SZ, and REG_BINARY).

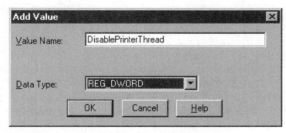

Figure 5-11. The Add Value dialog

The third and final step is to actually give the value some contents. You'll use the dialogs shown earlier in the section "Modifying Values"; which dialog pops up in this third step depends on the type of data you selected in the second step. Once you enter a value into the appropriate editor dialog, *RegEdt32* will add the new value and store it permanently in the Registry. At any prior point, you can cancel the operation without actually adding the new value.

Deleting Keys and Values

Contrary to what you might think, deleting data from the Registry is required somewhat more often than adding it. The biggest reason for deleting keys or values is to remove traces of applications or system components whose uninstallers are nonexistent or (more commonly) too poorly written to fully reverse whatever the original installation program did. Of course, sometimes it's necessary to undo something you've done yourself; for example, if you add one of the magic

Microsoft keys sprinkled throughout their knowledge base, you may one day find it necessary to remove it again.

WARNING   You may remember the **Options ➤ Confirm on Delete** command dis-
              cussed earlier in the section "Setting Session Options." I strongly
              recommend leaving this option turned on, as it can save you from
              accidentally deleting something you would rather have kept.

Whether you're deleting a key or a value, the basic procedure is the same: high-light the key or value you want to remove, then either hit the DEL key or use the **Edit ➤ Delete** command. If you have the **Options ➤ Confirm on Delete** option turned on, you'll see a confirmation dialog asking you if you *really* want to remove the selected key or value; if you say "Yes," *RegEdt32* will delete the item, just like you requested.

When you delete a key, *RegEdt32* also deletes all of its subkeys and their values, so be sure to visually confirm that the key you want to delete is actually the one that's highlighted. The confirmation dialog unfortunately doesn't tell you what key or value is about to bite the dust, so it's up to you to double-check.

Registry Security

The Registry's hierarchical arrangement looks suspiciously like that of a file system in more ways than one. Like NTFS files, directories, and volumes, Registry keys can have attached attributes that control who owns them, who may read, write, and change them, and what events should be logged for further scrutiny.

In particular, every key has an access control list, or ACL, associated with it. This ACL authorizes certain accounts to have certain types of access to the key. The ACL's permissions (which are also called ACEs, for *access control entries*) apply to the object that holds the ACL and its children, if any. Even though NT uses the same permission names for all types of objects, the semantics of Registry permissions are a bit different from those of filesystem or object permissions. Table 5-2 shows the nine basic permission types that can be attached to Registry keys.

Table 5-2. Registry Access Permissions

Permission	What it allows
Query Value	Getting the contents of a specific key's value: for example, the value Paul Robichaux of the `HKLM\SOFTWARE\SMAIL\Users` key
Set Value	Changing the contents of a specific key's value

Table 5-2. Registry Access Permissions (continued)

Permission	What it allows
Create Subkey	Creating a new subkey of the specified key; the new subkey will inherit the parent's permissions, but they may be explicitly changed later
Enumerate Subkeys	Traversing all subkeys of a specific key and getting their full path names
Notify	Receiving or setting auditing notifications
Create Link	Creating a symbolic link (like a shortcut or a Unix symlink) that points to another key in the registry
Delete	Removing the specified key, its subkeys, and all associated values
Write DAC	Changing the Discretionary Access Control (DAC) permissions attached to the specified key
Read Control	Allows the permission holder to read the access control list for the key

Besides these basic DACs, there are three additional composite DACs; these composites grant combinations of two or more of the rights listed in Table 5-2. For example, the Full Control composite grants all nine of the rights listed above, but Full Control only uses a single ACL entry to work its magic. Table 5-3 shows the composite DACs and the rights they include.

Table 5-3. Composite DACs

Permission	What it allows
Read	Read-only access to a specific key, its subkeys, and their values (actually includes Query Value and Enumerate Subkeys)
Write Owner	Changing the owner associated with the specified key
Full Control	All of the above rights; Full Control allows the holder to do literally anything to the keys with that permission

---

WARNING   NT 3.51 and NT 4.0 share a serious security weakness: by default, most keys in the Registry are set to Everyone:Full Control access. This is unnecessarily permissive. Microsoft finally fixed this in NT 4.0 SP3, which has been called "security pack 3" by more than one magazine writer. If you haven't already, apply SP3, then run David LeBlanc's excellent *everyone2user* utility, available from the ISS web site at *http://www.iss.net/*.

Setting Registry Permissions

RegEdt32 allows you to give a unique set of permissions to any key in the Registry. Since most of the data in the Registry belongs to system components, you must use this feature carefully; if you change permissions on a key so that the application that needs it can't get to it, you may destabilize your system.

Your gateway to key permissions is the **Security ➤ Permissions...** command, which displays the Registry Key Permissions dialog (see Figure 5-12). To use it, select a key in any root key window, then give the command. When the dialog opens, it shows you which key you've selected and which account owns it (you can't change either of them from the dialog, however). The controls in the dialog give you access to the permission settings for the key.

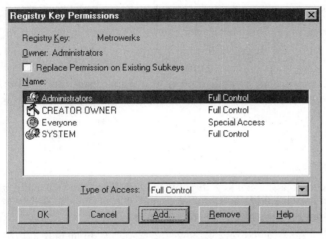

Figure 5-12. Registry Key Permissions dialog

- The "Replace Permission on Existing Subkeys" checkbox tells *RegEdt32* whether to apply the permission changes you specify to all subkeys of the current key or not. When subkeys are created, they inherit the parent key's access controls; however, by the time you change the parent key's access controls the subkeys may have different controls in place. Use this option only when you intend to override any access controls that have been applied to subkeys.

- The Name field lists the current access controls in force on the key. Each line in the list shows an account name and the DAC granted to that account. The standard DACs are listed in Tables 5-2 and 5-3; if you see an account with "Special Access" in the DAC column, that just means it has a combination of DACs for which NT has no synonym.

Any account that is valid on a machine may have access controls assigned. For machines that are members of an NT domain, domain accounts and groups may be assigned permissions. On all NT machines, there are also several built-in account proxies (like CREATOR OWNER, which represents whichever account originally created an object) that may have DACs attached.

- The Type of Access combo box lets you change the DACs for any account in the Name list. Changes you make will be immediately reflected in the list, but won't be applied until you click OK.

- The Add... button allows you to use NT's standard "Add Users and Groups" dialog (see Figure 5-13) to add new accounts to the ACL. The accounts you add from this dialog will appear in the Name list with Full Control as the default DAC; make sure you change this to avoid opening a security hole.

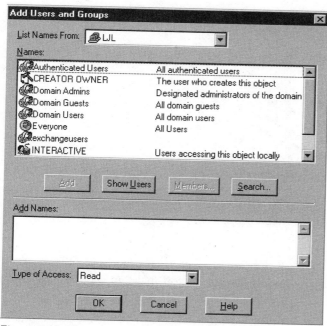

Figure 5-13. The Add Users and Groups dialog

Auditing Registry Key Activity

Auditing allows you to keep a trail of evidence that you can use to identify problems and pin their start down to an exact time. NT's auditing facility lets you audit specified actions taken by specified accounts. For example, you can audit any attempt to change security policy by any accounts, or you could audit failed attempts to log on by a single account. This combination of specifying who and what makes auditing pretty flexible.

Enabling auditing on an NT machine

While auditing is useful, it also takes time; by default, NT leaves system auditing turned off. Before you can audit Registry access (or anything else), you'll have to enable auditing on the machine you want audited.

You do this with the User Manager or User Manager for Domains,* yet another of the standard administrative utilities that NT includes to simplify your job. Here's how to enable auditing on a single server or workstation:

1. Run User Manager on the target machine. To change auditing control settings, you'll have to be logged in with an account that has Administrator privilege on the target machine.

2. Use the **Policies ➤ Audit...** menu command to display the Audit Policy dialog, shown in Figure 5-14.

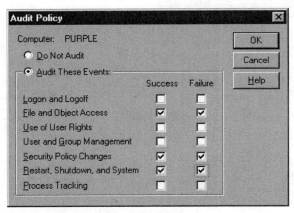

Figure 5-14. The Audit Policy dialog

3. Make sure the "Audit These Events" radio button is turned on; otherwise, NT will still happily refuse any auditing requests you make in other applications, including *RegEdt32*.

4. Use the checkboxes to select which classes of events you want to audit. For Registry access auditing, make sure the "File and Object Access" checkboxes are marked. You may also want to enable other types of auditing, but they're not strictly necessary.

5. Click OK, then exit the User Manager.

---

* Which one you use depends on whether you have domains or not; fortunately, they're very similar, so I'll treat them here as identical.

Once you take these steps on a machine, you won't have to do them again; auditing on that machine will remain enabled unless you manually turn it off using the same procedure. You do, however, have to execute these steps on every machine for which you want to enable auditing. Once you've done so, you can actually turn on auditing for the Registry.

Telling RegEdt32 what to audit

The Registry Key Auditing dialog, shown in Figure 5-15, appears when you choose the **Security ➤ Auditing...** menu command.

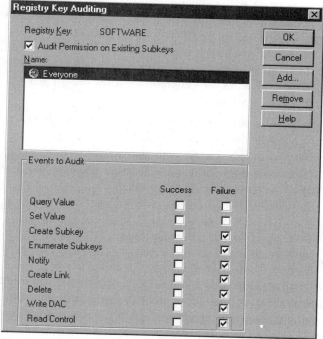

Figure 5-15. The Registry Key Auditing dialog

This dialog can be a little confusing at first, so a look at what its controls do will demystify it some:

- The "Registry Key" field shows you what subkey you've selected, but it doesn't tell you what root that subkey belongs to. You may need to move the entire Registry Key Auditing dialog around to make sure you're auditing the key you intended to audit.

- The "Audit Permission on Existing Subkeys" checkbox tells *RegEdt32* whether you want the audit changes you specify to apply to all subkeys under the selected key, or just the selected key. If you audit all subkeys of a large root key like HKLM, your performance will suffer; sometimes, though, this type of shotgun auditing is necessary so you can see which keys are being changed when you don't know in advance which ones you *need* to audit.

- The "Name" list shows which accounts will be audited. You can think of this list like the FBI's Most Wanted list: names on this list are the ones scrutinized, while other names are ignored. The Add... and Remove buttons let you change the members of this list using an interface like the one shown in Figure 5-13. In addition to actual user accounts, you can audit the built-in accounts like *Everyone*, *INTERACTIVE*, and *SYSTEM*.

- The two columns of checkboxes in the "Events to Audit" group are the meat of this dialog, since they control what actions are logged for the specified accounts. Each of the DACs listed earlier in Table 5-2 may be audited. When you check a DAC's Success checkbox, the system will create an audit record any time an account on the Name list succeeds in using that DAC. Conversely, the Failure checkbox causes NT to generate an audit record when a listed account tries to use the DAC and fails.

  For example, let's say you add the account *peanut* to the audit list for HKLM\ Software\Microsoft, then check Success for Create Subkey and Failure for Write DAC. Once you save those settings, NT will generate an audit record whenever *peanut* succeeds in creating a new subkey under the selected key or fails while trying to change the DACs for an ACL entry.

As you'd expect, the OK and Cancel buttons allow you to preserve or discard changes you make in this dialog.

Reviewing the audit records

Once you've told *RegEdt32* what to audit, you'll still need a way to see the audit entries that have been generated. If you're accustomed to administering Unix machines, you're probably familiar with the *syslog* service. NT has a similar feature; it keeps an event log that applications and system components may write to. The NT event log is actually three separate logs: one for system data, one for application-generated data, and one for security data. Auditing messages (no matter their source) go into the security log.

To view these log messages, you'll need to use Microsoft's Event Viewer application. A complete discussion of how to use the Event Viewer is way outside the scope of this book, but the basic process is simple enough to boil down into a few concise steps:

1. Launch the Event Viewer (*eventvwr.exe*). There's a shortcut to it in the Start menu, too; look under **Programs ➤ Administrative Tools (Common) ➤ Event Viewer** to find it.

2. When Event Viewer opens, you'll see a window like the one shown in Figure 5-16. Use the **Log ➤ Security** command to display the security log.

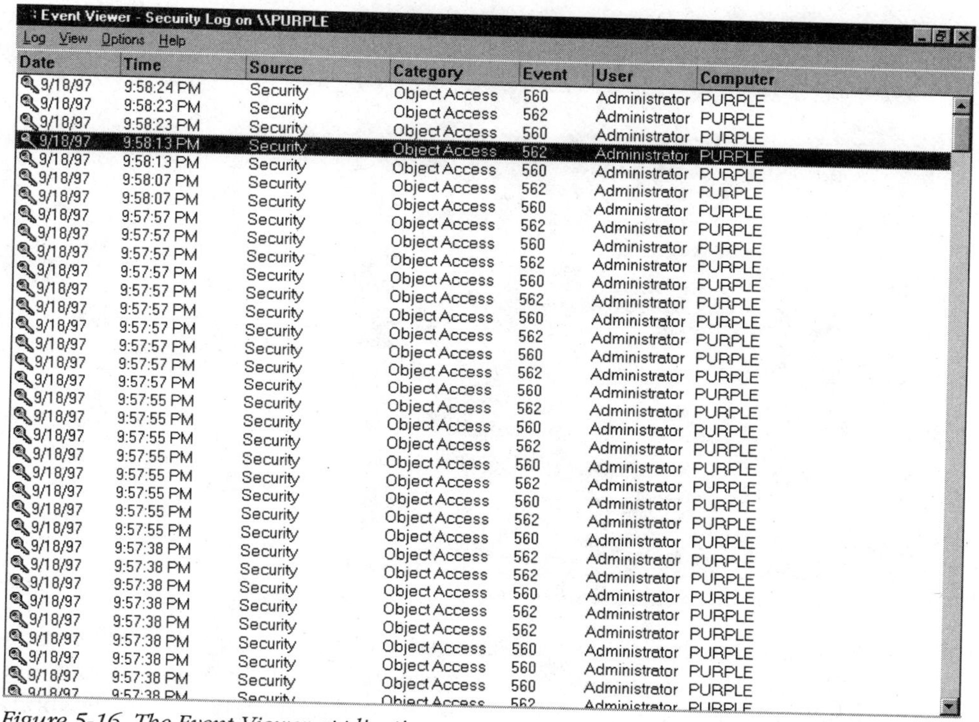

Figure 5-16. The Event Viewer application

3. Event Viewer will show you a passel of events (the exact number depends on how big the event log is). You can sort, filter, and view events using the commands in the View menu; if there's a particular event you're interested in, you can double-click it or use the **View ➤ Details...** command to get the dialog shown in Figure 5-17, which gives all the pertinent event details in one place.

Setting Key Ownership

Like every other object in NT's world, each Registry key has an owner. As with Unix, NT allows the owner to control access to objects it owns to a certain extent; the superuser or Administrator account can always take ownership of an object and change its permissions when necessary. NT does, however, provide a standard auditing mechanism that logs all manually initiated changes of ownership, so you'll always have an audit trail that shows you when someone's taken over one of your objects.

When you use this command, you're telling *RegEdt32* to change the owner of the currently selected key *and all its subkeys* to the current account. This blanket

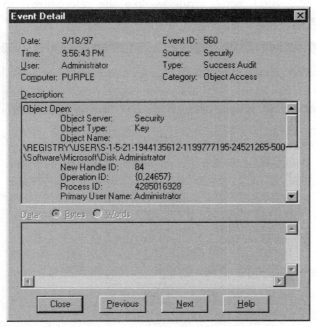

Figure 5-17. Registry audit event detail display

change of ownership can lead to unexpected behavior, since many NT components assume they'll always have unrestricted access to all subkeys of HKLM and many subkeys of HKCU and HKCR. However, it's usually a good idea to set appropriate ownership of HKU's subkeys, as well as those subkeys of HKLM that are safe to reset. The best way to set ownership is with a utility like David LeBlanc's *everyone2user*, which is discussed in the section "Fixing Registry Security ACLs" in Chapter 8.

If you insist on doing it manually, *RegEdt32* allows you to take ownership of Registry keys with the **Security ▶ Owner...** command. The Owner dialog, pictured in Figure 5-18, shows you what key is selected and which account owns it. The Take Ownership button changes the key's (and its subkeys') ownership to whatever account you're logged in as, while the Close button cancels the command without changing anything. Of course, if you don't have Administrator privileges you can't take ownership of any key you don't already own.

Figure 5-18. The Owner display

6

Using the System Policy Editor

All About NT Policies

Windows NT supports grouping users into groups and domains; you can assign users to a particular group or domain, then grant (or deny) them permission to use certain system resources based on their membership. For example, you could create a group of users in the accounting department and grant that group access to the printer in the department conference room, without having to grant access to users from outside the department. For a complete explanation of managing users, groups, and domains, see *Essential Windows NT System Administration,* by Æleen Frisch (O'Reilly & Associates, 1997).

Besides applying access controls so that users and groups gain or lose access to individual files, shares, servers, and printers, NT 3.1 offered a set of features that you could customize on a per-machine or per-user basis. As you might guess, these settings were just keys in the Registry; an example is the warning notice that you can add to NT's logon process by adding two new values to HKLM\SOFT-WARE\Microsoft\Windows NT\CurrentVersion\Winlogon. Even though these settings were present, there were two serious flaws that made them more difficult than necessary to use:

They weren't organized well

Even though there were a large number of customizable settings in NT 3.1, 3.5, and 3.51, there was little in the way of organized documentation, and related settings weren't grouped together in any meaningful way.

They were too hard to use

None of the adjustable settings were difficult to configure in and of themselves, but trying to add a logon warning to one machine is much easier than trying to do so for an entire network of several thousand machines. To compound the problem, savvy users could change the settings (assuming they had appropriate privileges).

Microsoft addressed these flaws in the NT 3.51 Resource Kit with the introduction of the idea of *system policies*. These policies were nothing more than groups of settings: one group that controlled the appearance of the desktop, one that controlled what programs users could run, and so on. However, the key innovation was a mechanism for distributing policies to all computers in a domain. This made it possible for an administrator to write policies for individual users, groups of users, and individual machines, then let NT take care of the actual work of distributing the policies to each machine in the domain and applying them.*

What's a Policy?

A policy is nothing more than a group of related settings whose values you specify. Each policy typically has a name, like "Shell Restrictions," and they're arranged in a hierarchy like Registry keys or disk files and folders. You use policies to enforce access controls on what users may do; for example, there are policies that allow you to restrict what applications users may run, whether they can change the desktop pattern, or what resources appear in the Network Neighborhood.

Categories contain one or more policies

Each user, group, or computer policy is actually made up of several policy *categories*. For example, the default template provided with NT provides categories like "Control Panel" and "Windows NT Shell." Each category in turn contains individual policies like "Restrict access to desktop" or "Hide Settings tab." This usage can be a little confusing: a user policy can contain several categories, each of which can contain several policies. I'll use the term "policy" to mean the policies that live in a category and "user policy" to mean the policy settings applied to a user, group, or computer.

Policies are made of parts

Policies are made up of *parts*. Each part represents one aspect of a policy, like "don't allow users to use the **Start ▶ Run...** command" or "here's a list of applications that the user may run." Parts got their name from the fact that each part of a policy will have a control associated with it in the *POLEDIT* policy properties dialog. Parts have values, and these controls allow you to set them. The permissible

---

* Windows 95 has system policies, too, though some of its policy elements live in different keys than their NT equivalents.

set of values for a part depends on what the part controls. Some parts need numeric values, while others accept lists of programs or true/false values.

A single policy may consist of one part or many. Each part within a policy corresponds to a value stored somewhere in the Registry. When you enable a policy, what you're really doing is telling NT to apply some particular value to each part in that policy; that in turn forces certain values in the Registry (each of which corresponds to a single part) to have particular values as well. You'll see some more concrete examples later in the chapter.

How are policies defined?

Policy definitions are built using *policy templates*. These templates are nothing more than text files that tell *POLEDIT* what to display in its interface and how to convert the user's settings into a *.POL* file

When you install NT Server, you get three policy files in *%systemroot%\INF*: *WINNT.ADM*, *COMMON.ADM*, and *WINDOWS.ADM*. These standard files cover most of the things you can restrict or constrain with policies. However, it's possible for third parties to write policy templates that add new policy definitions for other software. The most widely known examples are Microsoft's Office 97 policy templates, which are available with the *Office 97 Resource Kit*. These templates let you restrict Office 97-specific settings, like which hosts appear in the FTP dialog within Word 97. Other vendors have produced policy template files, and you can even create your own (as described in "Creating Your Own Policy Templates" later in this chapter) to control applications that don't ship with their own templates.

The template files use a simple language to specify which keys and values are affected by the policy and its parts. When you create a template, you're really giving *POLEDIT* instructions on what to display and how to build a *.POL* file based on the user's policy settings; the system policy downloader will apply that file's changes without regard to what they are.

TIP   Simac Software makes a product called Policy Template Editor (see *http://www.tools4nt.com/*). It's a specialized tool, but it works very well and is much easier than editing template files by hand.

User versus machine policies

NT allows you to build policies that apply to computers, individual users, or groups of users. Computer policies apply to all users on a machine; they're stored in each machine's HKLM root key, and they remain in effect no matter what user logs on to the machine. By contrast, user and group policies apply only to the user or group named as the target, and they are automatically downloaded and installed onto each machine the user logs into.

Here's an example. Let's say you have four machines in your domain: *titan, min-uteman, atlas,* and *trident.* Within this domain, you have a few dozen user accounts, but you create policies that apply to two accounts: *intern* and *visitor.* Whenever either of these accounts logs into a machine, the defined policy will "follow" them to the machine and will be stored in that machine's HKCU root key. Whenever any other user logs into a machine, the default policy settings will be in effect.

How Are Policies Stored?

Like butterflies, policies go through a number of stages between their initial cre-ation and their final emergence. Understanding where policy settings live at each stage of their lifecycle is key to understanding how to build and apply them.

The System Policy Editor stores policies as individual *.POL* files; you can think of these files as similar to Registry hives, as they contain a number of Registry key/ value pairs that are loaded into the target machine's Registry when the policy is applied. When you create a policy and save it, you're actually generating a file that tells the System Policy Editor what values to change in the policy target's Reg-istry.

Unlike the hives you can create with *RegEdt32,* these files can contain values from several different subkeys without having to hold the entire contents of their superior root key. For example, a single *.POL* file might contain values for HKLM\ SOFTWARE\Microsoft\Windows NT\CurrentVersion and HKLM\SOFTWARE\ Netscape\Netscape Navigator, without having to contain all of HKLM\SOFT-WARE as well.

When you first create a policy, it's stored wherever you choose to save it. Once you've created and saved a policy file, the next stage of its lifespan begins: distri-bution. You can manually apply a policy file to individual machines; you may also store it on a domain controller so that it will automatically be replicated to Windows 95 and NT machines in your domain. You may choose to replicate the policy to backup domain controllers if you want users to be able to log in when the primary controller is unavailable.[*] (In fact, if you want the policy to be auto-matically distributed, you *must* put it on the PDC and any BDCs that have replica-tion enabled if you want to ensure that the policy's available.)

---

[*] This scheme may change in NT 5.0, which will no longer distinguish between primary and backup domain controllers.

The final step in a policy's lifetime is the actual installation process. When a user logs into a Windows 95 or NT machine, the system checks the domain controller for an applicable policy. If there is one, a special system component called the *policy downloader** transfers the *.POL* file to the workstation and merges its contents with the appropriate Registry root key.

How Are Policies Applied?

Once the policy downloader has pulled the policy file down to the workstation, the policy's settings still have to be applied. This is accomplished by merging the policy settings into the appropriate parts of the Registry. As you'll see in more detail later in the chapter, policy parts can have three values:

On
> The part's policy is active and whatever controls are enforced by that part should be applied.

Off
> The part's policy is inactive and that part's controls should not be applied.

Leave as is
> Whatever value is currently in the Registry should be left alone.

If a part's corresponding value in the Registry matches the policy's value, no changes are made. If the part's value is "leave as is," no changes are made either. However, if the part's specified value and the Registry's contents are different, the policy value wins out, and the Registry's value is changed. These changes persist as long as the user's logged in, but—since the merge operation is really just loading a Registry hive—they disappear from the Registry when the user logs out.

Computer-specific policies are merged into HKLM, while user- or group-specific policies are merged into HKCU. It's important to remember that the policy settings are merged with the existing settings; they don't automatically overwrite the existing contents when the corresponding part is set to "leave as is." In addition, changes users make to policy-defined values under HKLM or HKCU are *not* written back to the policy! This prevents users from changing a policy setting and having the change propagate to other users. (Of course, if you're using policies, probably the first policy you'll set is the "Disable Registry editing tools" flag.)

---

* It's unlikely that you'll need to, but NT supports writing your own policy downloaders, which can supplement or replace the system's. Complete documentation for this is included in the MSDN SDK documentation.

The default policy

It's possible to assign policies to some users and computers, but not others. You might want to put restrictive policies onto machines in a shared lab area without enforcing any policies on individual users' machines, or you might want to restrict what some users can do no matter what machine they log into.

No matter what computers and accounts have policies, you can specify a default policy. This default applies to all users and computers that don't have an explicit policy defined for them. The default computer policy will be applied to all computers in a domain, and the default user policy will be applied to all domain users. By convention, these default profiles are saved in a file named *NTconfig.pol* (for NT systems) or *config.pol* (for Win95 systems).

The initial default policy supplied with NT just sets all policy parts to their "leave as is" state, meaning that the policy doesn't change anything. You may edit the default policy and save it back to its original file name; whatever changes you make will be applied as defaults from that point onward.

NOTE   Default policies apply to *every* user, including administrators! If you create a restrictive default policy, it will apply to local and domain administrator accounts unless you create less-restrictive group or user accounts for your fellow admins.

Applying computer and user policies

When you create computer-specific policies, they're stored in the *.POL* file as groups of settings, one for each computer. To revive our earlier example, if you define policies for *titan* and *trident*, there will be keys with the same name in the policy file. When the policy downloader retrieves the policy file, it decides to apply it, or not, based on two rules. First, if there's a key in the policy file with the same name as the computer, that policy's part values are merged into HKLM. If no such key exists, but there is a key named `.default`, that default key is applied. If neither condition is true, no changes are made. A computer-specific policy will always override the default: in fact, the default policy won't even be examined if there's a policy whose name matches the computer's.

User policies are applied using the same two rules: if there's a policy whose name matches the user who's logging in, it is applied. If not, the `.default` entry is used if it exists; otherwise, no changes are made.

Applying group policies

The rules used to decide whether or not to apply a user or computer policy are very simple; however, the rules for applying group policies are a little more complicated. There are only two rules to know. The first, and most important, rule is this: a named user policy always trumps any group policies. For example, a policy for a user named *bob* will override policies for any groups of which *bob* is a member; it will also override the default group policy.

The second rule to remember is that group policies are additive. If a user who's in more than one group logs in, the system will use the *group priority* to decide which policies to apply first. You set the group priority from within the System Policy Editor (as you'll see later in "Setting group policy priorities"). The lowest-priority group policy is applied first; its part settings are applied to the logged-in user's HKCU root key. The next lowest-priority group policy is evaluated next, and so on, until the highest-priority policy is applied. This approach means that if you put conflicting part values into two group policies, any user who's in both groups will end up with the part value of whichever policy is evaluated last.

Let's say you have two groups in your domain for executives and engineers. Your boss is an executive, but has an engineering degree, so you put her in both groups. If the "Don't allow users to play Solitaire" policy is set to "on" for executives and "off" for engineers, your boss's ability to play Solitaire hinges on the priority you assign to the two groups: the highest-priority setting will triumph.

Introducing the System Policy Editor

You create and edit system policies with the System Policy Editor (*poledit.exe*), which is normally only installed when you install NT Server. It can be run from NT Workstation, though, if you can legally obtain it from an NT Server installation. Don't confuse the NT System Policy Editor with the Windows 95 version: if you want to create policies that Win95 clients can use, you must use the Win95 editor, and the same is true for the NT version.[*]

If you don't have System Policy Editor installed, you can quickly install it (along with the User Manager for Domains, Server Manager, the Services for Macintosh Manager, and several others) by running the *setup.bat* file in the *clients\servtools\ winnt* directory of your NT Server CD. Once you've completed the installation, you'll have access to the *poledit.exe* executable, which up until now I've been calling the System Policy Editor.

---

[*] Actually, you can use the NT policy editor under Win95 with no ill effect, as long as you use the right *.ADM* files.

Learning the System Policy Editor Interface

When you use *RegEdt32* or *RegEdit*, you can definitely tell that you're using software that predates NT 4.0; although both use the 4.0 look-and-feel, they're indisputably different than other pieces of 4.0-specific software like the Windows NT Explorer or the system shell. *POLEDIT*, on the other hand, has an interface very similar to the shell, making it immediately familiar.

The main window for *POLEDIT* is shown in Figure 6-1. In the figure, each computer, user, or group policy is represented by a large icon. Double-clicking one of these icons opens the associated policy, and policies may be created or deleted from this view as well.

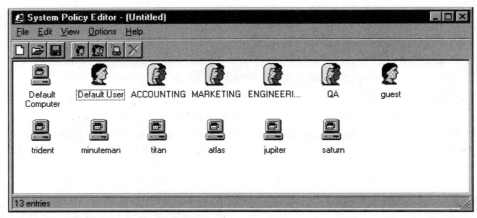

Figure 6-1. The System Policy Editor interface

Controlling what you see

The View menu allows you to change *POLEDIT*'s display in a number of ways, all of which are similar to commands in the NT shell or other NT administrative tools.

The first two commands in the menu are window dressing: the **View ➤ Toolbar** command controls the state of *POLEDIT*'s toolbar. The toolbar is visible when this command is checked (the default) and invisible when it's not. Like *RegEdit*, *POLEDIT* has a status bar that can occupy the bottom margin of the application window. The **View ➤ Status Bar** command governs whether this decorative but useless bar appears or not.

The remaining View menu commands let you change the format of the display. Unless you change it, *POLEDIT* will display policies as large icons; this default corresponds to the **View ➤ Large Icons** command. If you prefer, you can instead see policies as small icons (**View ➤ Small Icons**) or an alphabetically sorted list. For some reason, Microsoft included both the **View ➤ List** and **View ➤ Details** commands, even though they display the same information in the same format!

The settings you choose in the View menu are stored with the policy file, so when you reload a new file it will appear as it was when you last had it open.

Navigating in the policy window

As in the NT shell, you can move from item to item in *POLEDIT*'s window with the arrow, PgUp, PgDn, Home, and End keys. When a policy is selected, you can open it by double-clicking it, pressing the Enter key, or using the **Edit ➤ Properties…** command.

Managing Policies with POLEDIT

For the most part, creating policies with *POLEDIT* is simple and straightforward. Even though what you're really doing is editing the Registry on one or many machines, the interface lends itself to quickly making needed changes and saving them for later application.

The basic sequence of operations needed to apply policies is pretty simple; there are only six steps:

1. Attach whatever policy templates you want to use *before* creating any policies.

2. Decide which users, groups, and computers you want to enforce policies on.

3. Create a new policy file to contain your policies, then create enough user, group, and computer policies to satisfy your list from step 2. Alternatively, you may open the Registry of a single machine (including the local machine) to make changes to that machine only.

4. Create a "relaxed" policy for your administrative-level users that incorporates only those items from step 3 that you want to enforce on your admins.

5. Edit each individual policy to reflect the settings you want the policies to enforce.

6. Save the policy file in the appropriate location so that policy downloaders can find it.

Attaching Policy Templates

POLEDIT supports attaching an arbitrary number of policy templates. Templates you attach add their policies to the policy properties dialog; once you attach a template, its policies will be available whenever you create new policies. This argues in favor of attaching policy templates to *POLEDIT before* creating any policies; that way, whatever templates you attach will contribute to the policies you create without adding the extra work of going back and revising previously built policies.

When you first start *POLEDIT,* it will automatically attach the two NT-specific policy templates, *COMMON.ADM* and *WINNT.ADM.* You may attach other templates using the **Options ➤ Policy Template...** command, which displays the dialog shown in Figure 6-2.

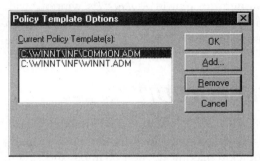

Figure 6-2. The Policy Template Options dialog

The Current Policy Template(s) list shows which templates are currently attached; you can use the Add... and Remove buttons to change this list's contents. Once you're satisfied with your changes, you can click OK to preserve the attachments or Cancel to dismiss the dialog without changing anything.

One final note: *POLEDIT* won't let you attach or detach policy templates while you have a policy file or Registry open; this restriction prevents you from accidentally overwriting an open policy with a new template's contents.

Creating Policies

After you've attached the appropriate policy templates, you're ready to start creating new policies. One of the nice things about *POLEDIT* is that it lets you make changes, store them, and make more changes without immediately affecting the Registry. Like most other document-oriented applications, changes you make to the currently open policy won't take effect until you save the policy document in the appropriate place.

Creating a new policy file

When you start *POLEDIT,* it will open with a new policy file named *Untitled.* However, at any time you may create a new, empty policy with the **File ➤ New Policy** command. As its name implies, it opens a new document named *Untitled* with no policy data in it; you're then free to add user, computer, and group policies.

Creating a new user policy

You create new user policies with the **Edit ➤ Add User...** command. This command produces a dialog (see Figure 6-3) that you use to name the new policy. The "Browse" button opens the standard NT Add User dialog, so you can browse the list of local and domain user accounts to choose a user.

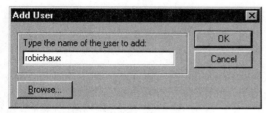

Figure 6-3. The Add User dialog

The name you enter in the "Type the name of the user to add" field is the name the policy downloader will use when trying to find a user's policy. If you're creating a policy for a user whose account is named *oreilly*, the policy won't be applied if it's named anything other than *oreilly*. Be careful to ensure that you get the right user name for the user you want the policy applied to; this is especially important on large networks where there might be several users with similar account names.

Creating a new computer policy

You create policies for individual computers in much the same way as you do those for users; the **Edit ➤ New Computer...** command displays a dialog identical to the one shown above in Figure 6-3 save for its use of the word "computer" instead of "user." In this dialog, however, the Browse button displays the NT network browser that you're familiar with from the Network Neighborhood and the Windows NT Explorer.

The same caveat about names applies to computer accounts, too; if you're trying to apply a policy to a machine named *titan* but type in *titian* instead, the policy won't take effect as you expect it to.

Creating a new group policy

Like computer and user policies, creating group policies is very straightforward: you use the **Edit ➤ New Group...** command to display the New Group dialog, then supply the name of the group to which the new policy belongs. You may apply policies to local or global groups within a domain, as well as groups that are strictly local to a single machine. As with computer and user policies, supplying the correct name is critical to getting the policy behavior you expect.

TIP   Since the Default User policy will apply to every user on the
                 machine *including the Administrator account*, it's a good idea to
                 create a group policy for the Administrators and Domain Admins
                 group. Leave these policies as is (that is, leave the checkboxes for
                 all parts in their default state) so that the policy won't impose any
                 new controls on the Administrator.

Editing Policies

Creating new policies is very easy, mostly because just creating the policy doesn't
do anything! All of the policy templates that Microsoft provides use the "leave as
is" setting. This means that if you create a bunch of new policies and don't edit
them, no changes will be enforced. This approach satisfies the Principle of Least
Astonishment ("when forced to make decisions on its own, your software should
always do whatever will least surprise the user"), but it means that you still have
some work to do once your policies are created.

NOTE   Remember that policy changes don't take effect until you save the
                 policy file in the proper location. Even after that's done, user and
                 group policies don't take effect until the next time the user logs in;
                 machine policies won't go into action until the next time any user
                 logs in.

Setting user, group, and computer policy options

Once you've created user policies for all the users, groups, and computers you
want to control, the next step is to set appropriate values for each individual part
within the categories and policies for each user. Each user policy has a properties
dialog; this dialog displays all the categories, policies, and parts for that user policy.

You can open the properties dialog for a policy in two ways: you can double-
click the icon or list item corresponding to the user policy you want to edit, or
you can select it with the mouse and use the **Edit ➤ Properties…** command. In
either case, you'll end up with the properties dialog shown in Figure 6-4.

The upper part of the properties dialog shows a tree view of the categories within
the active user policy. When you first open a user policy, the categories will all be
collapsed; you can expand or collapse individual items by clicking the small +/-
icon next to the category's name.

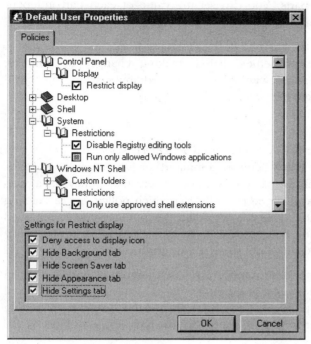

Figure 6-4. The Properties dialog

As you expand categories, you'll see checkboxes appear beneath them. Unlike normal Windows checkbox controls, these checkboxes can have three states:

- When checked, as "Restrict display" is in the figure above, the policy is active, and its settings will be applied to turn on the policy when appropriate.

- When unchecked and white (like an ordinary Windows checkbox that's not on), the policy is inactive. Its settings will be applied to turn off the policy.

- When unchecked and gray, like "Run only allowed Windows applications" in the figure above, the policy is inert. No changes will be made to a policy or its parts when its checkbox is grayed; this corresponds to the "leave as is" state I mentioned earlier.

You must pay careful attention to the wording of the policy to make sure that the effect is what you want: when the checkbox next to "Disable Registry editing tools" is on, the tools will be disabled. When it's off, that means that the tools are *not* disabled, and when it's gray that means that whatever settings are currently in effect on each target machine, group, or user will remain intact.

As you select individual policies within a category, you'll notice that the contents of the settings area at the bottom of the properties dialog will change. Some policies can have multiple parts; for example, the "Restrict display" policy shown in

Figure 6-4 has a total of five parts. You can set the value of each part independently of the others; parts may accept on/off, numeric, or list selection choices, depending on what the policy template specifies.

You can move through the properties dialog, making changes as you go; *POLEDIT* will preserve the changes within the current editing session, but they'll be lost unless you explicitly save the policy file.

Removing user policies

You can easily remove a user policy from within *POLEDIT*: select the policy you want to remove, then use the **Edit ➤ Remove** command, or just press the Del key. *POLEDIT* will ask you to confirm that you want to delete that policy; in a welcome change from *RegEdt32* and *RegEdit*, it tells you which policy you're deleting so you won't accidentally remove one you wanted to keep. Once you've removed a user policy, there's no getting it back unless you close and reload your policy file without saving changes. *POLEDIT* doesn't have an undo command.

It's worth noting that the only way to remove a policy category or part is to open the policy template file that defines it and remove it; you can't remove individual template items from a single policy, though you can use the "leave as is" setting to force the policy downloader to take no action on that part.

Policies and the clipboard

POLEDIT offers a measure of clipboard support. You can use the **Edit ➤ Copy** command to copy the contents of a user, group, or computer policy to the clipboard. However, the only place you may paste it is on top of another policy! This "feature" means that you can quickly copy a policy to several user accounts by doing the following:

1. Create one user, group, or computer policy and set it the way you want it.

2. Use **Edit ➤ Copy** to copy the policy settings.

3. Create as many user, group, or computer policies as you'll need.

4. Select all the new policies at the same time, then use the **Edit ➤ Paste** command. *POLEDIT* will ask you to confirm that you want to overwrite the existing policy settings; click Yes to paste your policy atop the existing settings, or No to cancel the paste.

Although it's not evident from the program or its documentation, you can copy from group to user policies and vice versa—select the source item, use **Edit ➤ Copy**, and paste the policy onto the user or group you want it to stick to.

Setting group policy priorities

As soon as you start creating group policies, you run the risk of a collision between two groups' mutually exclusive policies. As long as no user belongs to more than one group, you won't run into this problem; however, since Microsoft recommends putting users into groups for controlling access to network resources like file shares and printers, the odds of having one user in more than one group are pretty good.

The section "Applying group policies" earlier in this chapter explains how the policy downloader decides which group policy parts to apply and which to ignore. For this approach to work, you must do your part by specifying the priority of each group's policy. You do this with the **Options ➤ Group Priority...** command; the resulting "Group Priority" dialog appears in Figure 6-5.

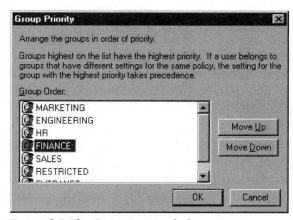

Figure 6-5. The Group Priority dialog

The initial priority order comes from the order in which you created the group policies: the first policy you create has the highest priority. You can rearrange group priorities using the Move Up and Move Down buttons; when you're happy with the ordering, you can save it by clicking OK.

Once you set a group priority ordering, it's stored as part of the policy file and is available to the policy downloader. If you change the priority ordering later, the new order will take effect every time the policy's applied at logon time.

Saving and Loading Policies

As you create and modify user policies, you'll often need to save those policies to a file and load them again later. Like most other document-oriented Windows applications, *POLEDIT* has commands in its File menu for loading and saving policy files.

The **File ➤ Open Policy...**, **File ➤ Save**, and **File ➤ Save As...** commands all work just like they do in other Windows applications. Unlike other applications, though, there's one gotcha involved with saving policy files: if you're creating policies for distribution to other Win95 or NT machines on your network, you must make sure to save the file in the right place, as described later in the section "Preventing Policy Problems."

Once you've created an initial policy, it's simple to add to or modify its user, group, or computer policies: just open the file with **File ➤ Open Policy...**, modify it as needed, and save it again. If you've configured the automatic policy distribution mechanism correctly, your policy will be applied where necessary with no further action on your part.

Creating Your Own Policy Templates

The *.ADM* policy template files that *POLEDIT* uses are just plain text files. If you open one of them up with a text editor, you'll find that the files are structured so that *POLEDIT* can figure out which categories, policies, and parts to display, where to store their values in the Registry, and what user interface controls to display so you can edit these values.

You can create your own policy templates and attach them to *POLEDIT*; for example, you could create a template that controls your standard distribution of Dial-Up Networking settings, configuration parameters for Netscape Navigator, or almost any other Registry data that lives in HKLM or HKCU. Here's a small sample of an *.ADM* file that will allow you to set the default search engine and home page that Internet Explorer uses:

```
CLASS MACHINE

CATEGORY  InternetExplorer
    KEYNAME "Software\Microsoft\Internet Explorer\Main"
    POLICY "Default search engine"
        PART  "URL of default search engine" EDITTEXT REQUIRED
            VALUENAME "Default_Search_URL"
            DEFAULT "http://www.ljl.com/intrasearch/"
        END PART
        PART  "URL of default home page" EDITTEXT REQUIRED
            VALUENAME "Default_Page_URL"
            DEFAULT "http://www.ljl.com "
        END PART

    END POLICY
END CATEGORY
```

As you can see from the sample, the format of these files is pretty structured. Let's look at what each piece of the example actually does:

- The initial CLASS MACHINE statement tells *POLEDIT* that this policy should go under HKLM. You can also use CLASS USER to specify policies that belong under HKCU.

- The CATEGORY...END CATEGORY block defines a single category of policies. In this example, we define a category named InternetExplorer; if we wanted to use spaces in the name, we'd have to enclose it in quotes. Category names can be any string, but they must be unique to a policy template file.

- The KEYNAME statement tells *POLEDIT* that all the policies and parts that belong to this category store their values under Software\Microsoft\ Internet Explorer\Main. Individual policies and parts can provide their own key names, too.

- The POLICY...END POLICY block defines a single policy for this category. Categories may contain any number of policies, each of which may have one or more parts. Each policy has a name ("Default search engine" in this case) that *POLEDIT* will display when it shows the policy.

- Each PART...END PART block specifies a single part for its enclosing policy. In this example, we're defining two parts—one for the search engine default, and one for the default home page. Both are edit text controls, and both require that a value must be specified. The returned value is stored as a value named as specified by the VALUENAME keyword; the value in turn goes under whatever key was named with a previous KEYNAME statement, and we provide a default value for the user to accept or change.

  A single policy may have many PART blocks in it; each PART block defines a single component, which may be a check box, edit field, combo box, drop-down list, or numeric input field. In addition, each of these control types has a variety of optional parameters used to specify default values, increments, and settings.

Distributing Policies

Once you've created policy files that contain the access controls you want to enforce, you still have to get those policies to each machine you want to be under policy control. This process, called *policy distribution*, is probably the most complex part of the policy development process, since how you do it depends on whether you want to use policies on one machine, a few machines, or many machines.

Applying Policies to One Machine at a Time

The simplest way to apply policies is to put them on individual machines. For example, you might want to apply policies to keep transient users from making changes to the configuration of public workstations in a library, factory floor, or conference room. For this type of requirement, you don't need to blast policies to every machine on a network; a more surgical approach lets you put policies only where you really need them.

Setting policies on the local machine

POLEDIT allows you to edit the local computer's Registry using the same interface you'd use to edit policies. When you use the **File ➤ Open Registry** command, *POLEDIT* acts as if you'd opened a new policy file, but it actually loads data from the local Registry and displays it as two user policies: "Local User" and "Local Computer" instead of "Default User" and "Default Computer."

You can edit the contents of these policies as though you were editing any other policy; however, you can't create new user, group, or computer policies while the local Registry is open. As with other policy files, though, changes you make to the local Registry aren't saved until you explicitly use the **File ➤ Save** command, so using **File ➤ Open Registry** is somewhat safer than using *RegEdt32* or *RegEdit*.

Setting policies on other computers

If you want to apply policies to a single remote machine, you can use *POLEDIT*'s **File ➤ Connect...** command to open the Registry on a remote machine and set policies on it. When you use this command, the first step is to specify the name of the machine whose policies you want to edit. If you have administrative access to that machine, *POLEDIT* will connect to its Registry and show you a dialog listing all users who are logged on. Normally, this list will only have a single entry representing whoever's logged into the console, but network and service users may be listed too. Choose the user whose policy you want to edit. *POLEDIT* won't let you interactively edit the policy of a user who isn't logged on.

Once you've completed these two steps, you may edit the computer and user policies as you normally would. You can't create new user, group, or computer policies; however, before you use **File ➤ Connect...** you can attach new policy templates if you want to change the default settings that can be applied within each policy.

Applying Policies to Many Machines

Policies offer a robust, useful way to apply settings to many machines, in such a way that the end user can't change them once they're applied. This is a boon to system administrators, since with effective policies you can prevent users from changing things you don't want them to change without a great deal of effort on your part.

The primary method of distributing policies to all machines within a domain depends on the fact that an NT domain controller always has a share named *NET-LOGON*. *NETLOGON* points to the primary domain controller's *%SystemRoot%\ System32\Repl\Import\Scripts* directory, and it contains logon scripts, user profiles, and other data needed to allow local and remote logons with shared environments. *NETLOGON* can also hold policy templates, meaning that the policy downloader on each machine in the domain has easy access to the policy files *if* they were saved in the *NETLOGON* share.

Enabling automatic policy updates

If you want machines on your network to automatically download policy changes when they happen, you'll have to make a change to the policy for those machines. For most networks, that means the `Default Computer` policy, since most admins will want automatic updates everywhere; however, you may enable automatic updates on a per-machine basis.

This setting lives in the Network category under the computer policy; Figure 6-6 shows the properties dialog with the appropriate setting selected. You can use the "Update mode" combo box to choose automatic or manual updates; if you choose manual updates, you can specify a UNC path to the share where your policies will live.

It's important to understand one thing about automatic updates: when you create a new policy file for the first time, it will automatically be downloaded to every machine. If automatic updating is then turned on, each machine will receive subsequent updates. If it's not turned on, the workstations' policy downloaders won't ever download policy changes. This may lead to undesirable behavior, since your policy changes will be silently ignored while you're expecting them to be in effect!

WinNT policies

To have your NT-specific policies automatically blasted out to all machines in your domain, save your policy file as *NTconfig.pol* in the directory you specified when setting up automatic policy updates. I recommend using *NETLOGON* to store your policies so they can be automatically replicated among and between domains; however, if you've specified another directory you can use it instead. (Note that you probably won't be able to write to *PDC\NETLOGON*, but you should be able to save the file by using the full path instead.)

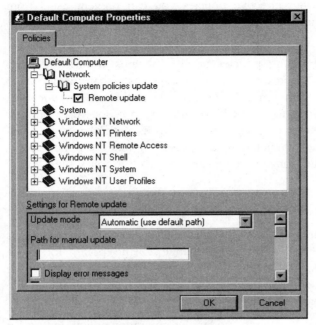

Figure 6-6. The Remote update part

WARNING   There are a series of bugs in NT 4.0, SP1, and SP2 that require you
to allow write access to the *%SystemRoot%\Profiles\Policy* directory
on all workstations where you want to support policies. Of course,
granting that access opens a security hole. If you haven't already, be
sure to upgrade your NT 4.0 machines to SP3 or later as soon as
possible.

Win95 policies

If you have a mixed network of Win95 and NT machines, you can store both
types of policies on your domain controllers so that the Win95 machines will get
automatic updates too. Save your policy file as *config.pol* in the directory you
specified when setting up automatic policy updates. If you want Win95 policies to
be automatically distributed, you must put them in *NETLOGON*; the Win95 policy
downloader isn't able to get policies from any other share.

Win95 policies also require that you turn on user profile support and install a special DLL from the Windows 95 CD. Complete details on how to do this are provided in the Win95 Resource Kit.

Supporting multiple domain controllers

If your network has more than one domain controller* (either because you have more than one domain or because you have more than one controller for backup purposes), you should use NT's directory replication service to copy your policy files to every domain controller. Since any domain controller in a network can answer logon requests, it's a good idea to duplicate your policy files to make sure they're available when a user logs in.

The simplest way to do this is to copy the policy files into the controller's *%SystemRoot%\System32\Repl\Export\Scripts* directory. As long as the directory replication service is running, NT will automatically mirror the files throughout your domains.

Preventing Policy Problems

While policies can be a great help to your administrative efforts, they can also pose some subtle pitfalls until you get them working the way you want them to. Here are some of the common problems—and solutions—you may run into while deploying policies on your network.

Make sure the files are in the right place

Perhaps the easiest policy mistake to make is putting the policy files in the wrong place. Win95 policy files must be named *config.pol*, and they must be stored in the domain's *NETLOGON* share—period! For NT policies, you must name the file *NTconfig.pol*; though you can put it in a share other than *NETLOGON*, the policy won't be used unless you specify the correct path to it when you turn on automatic updates.

Is automatic updating on?

Policies are most useful when they're always kept up to date. The NT and 95 policy downloader can automatically download and apply the appropriate set of user, group, and computer policies whenever a user logs on; to accomplish this magic, though, you have to put the policy in the right place (as described in the section you just finished reading, "Applying Policies to Many Machines"), and you must turn on automatic downloading. If your policy changes don't seem to take effect once you've made them, be sure you've enabled automatic updates as part of the computer policy for all machines you want to keep updated.

---

* Even small networks should have primary and backup controllers for NT 4.0; under NT 5.0, the primary/ backup distinction disappears but you should still maintain a second controller for redundancy.

Implement policies in all domains or none

If you're going to implement policies in one domain on your network, you may be in for a rough ride unless you implement policies on *all* domains. Why? If you have trust relationships between domains so that users from one domain can log onto another, consider this scenario:

1. You have two domains: HQ and RESEARCH. They trust each other. You've enabled system policies for all HQ users, but not for users in RESEARCH.

2. A user from HQ logs into a machine in the RESEARCH domain. Because RESEARCH gets its logon credential information from HQ, the user's logon will cause the RESEARCH machine to get a system policy update *even though policies aren't enabled in the domain!* The HQ user can still log in and get her work done.

3. When the HQ user logs out, the computer, group, and user policies downloaded at logon time are still on the machine. The next time a RESEARCH user logs onto the same machine, the policies won't be changed because RESEARCH has no policies of its own to apply.

In case it's not obvious, the solution to this potentially ugly problem is to implement policies on all your domains or none of them. It's still okay to apply policies to individual users and computers; however, if you set up group policies or policies for users who can log in to other domains, your best bet for avoiding trouble is to enable policies for all domains.

Check group membership and names

Sometimes your memory can fail you when it comes time to remember which groups a user is in. If you use group policies, make sure that all users you want to fall under those policies are actually members of the group! If there are any who aren't, you can copy the group policy and make an individual user policy out of it, or you can add them to the group.

Don't forget to double-check your group names, too; if you meant ENGINEERING but typed ENGINEERS, *POLEDIT* won't complain—but your policies won't be activated either. Worse still, they might be activated on the wrong group.

Verify which policies are in effect

If you want to see what policy is actually being applied to a user or computer, use the **File ➤ Connect…** command in *POLEDIT* to connect to the target computer. Once you do, you can open the Local Computer and Local User policies to make sure that they contain the settings you want enforced. If they don't, that's a clue that your policy distribution or downloading is amiss.

Mixing Win9x and Windows NT Policies

Many networks have a mix of Windows 95, Windows 98, and Windows NT machines. The NT policy distribution system allows you to set and distribute policies for all three operating systems, but there are some pitfalls awaiting the unwary.

The most obvious problem is that the Win 9x Registry has different keys and values from the Windows NT Registry. Even though most of the policy settings are the same, some use values that live in different places in the two different Registries. The solution for this lies in the policy template files: *COMMON.ADM* defines policy settings that are common to both systems, while *WINNT.ADM* and *WINDOWS.ADM* respectively define policies for NT and 9x systems. There's also a second Win9x-specific template file, *ADMIN.ADM*, that the Win9x policy editor uses.

The other problem—which isn't obvious from Microsoft's documentation—is that you can't create 9x system policies while running NT. You can use either the Win9x policy editor or the NT editor; whichever you choose, *you must run it under Windows 9x* to create Win9x policies. When you run *poledit.exe* under NT, you can create NT policies, but if you name an NT-created policy *config.pol* and put it on your domain controller, it won't have any effect on Win9x users. Note that this holds true even if you define your own policy templates.

To create policies for a mixed network, you must do the following:

1. Create your NT policies while running NT's policy editor.

2. Create your 9x policies while running either policy editor under Win9x. The *ADMIN.ADM* file supplied with the Win9x System Policy Editor contains some useful settings that aren't in *WINDOWS.ADM*. You can copy this file to *%systemroot%\inf* and attach it using the **Options ➤ Policy Template...** command in the NT System Policy Editor; doing so gives you the full flexibility of using multiple templates that the NT editor has but the 9x editor lacks.

3. Put your NT policies on the domain controller's *NETLOGON* share under the name *NTconfig.pol*. Likewise, put your 9x policies in the same share, but name the file *config.pol*.

What's in the Standard Policy Templates

The three primary policy templates used with Win95 and NT installations define what policy settings are available to you when building policies. Each template file contains settings that apply to HKLM and HKCU; however, in the following sections these entries are separated depending on the root key they affect.

WINNT.ADM

The *WINNT.ADM* policy template defines policy settings that are specific to Windows NT. Some entries in this template have counterparts in the Windows 95 template file. Table 6-1 shows the *WINNT.ADM* entries that apply to computer policies, while Table 6-2 shows the settings that apply to user and group policies.

COMMON.ADM

COMMON.ADM contains policy settings that are common to Windows 95 and Windows NT. Table 6-3 shows the entries that apply to computer policies, while Table 6-4 shows the settings that apply to user and group policies.

WINDOWS.ADM

The *WINDOWS.ADM* policy template defines policy settings that are specific to Windows 95. When you use System Policy Editor to edit policies for Win95 machines, this template is used to determine which policies and parts you may apply. Because the items in this policy are all Win95-specific, I've elected not to cover them here.

Table 6-1. HKLM Entries in WINNT.ADM

Category	Policy	Registry key/value	What it does	Value
Windows NT Network\Sharing	Create hidden drive shares (workstation)	System\CurrentControlSet\Services\LanManServer\Parameters\AutoShareWks	Creates *drive$* and *ADMIN$* shares on workstation	Default on (shares will be created)
	Create hidden drive shares (server)	System\CurrentControlSet\Services\LanManServer\Parameters\AutoShareServer	Creates *drive$* and *ADMIN$* shares on server	Default on (shares will be created)
Windows NT Printers	Disable browse thread on this computer	System\CurrentControlSet\Control\Print\DisableServerThread	Controls whether printer shares advertise themselves	Default off (shares will be advertised)
	Scheduler priority	System\CurrentControlSet\Control\Print\SchedulerThreadPriority	Adjusts priority of printer scheduling thread up or down	Default 0 (leave at normal priority); +1 (raise priority); -1 (lower priority)
	Beep for error enabled	System\CurrentControlSet\Control\Print\BeepEnabled	Beeps every 10 seconds when a remote print job error occurs	Default off (keep quiet and don't beep); on (Beep)
Windows NT Remote Access Service	Maximum number of unsuccessful authentication retries	System\CurrentControlSet\Services\RemoteAccess\Parameters\AuthenticateRetries	Sets the number of times a remote system can try to authenticate itself	0-10; default 2
	Maximum time limit for authentication	System\CurrentControlSet\Services\RemoteAccess\Parameters\AuthenticateTime	Sets the number of seconds allowed before an authentication times out	20-600; default 120
	Wait interval for callback	System\CurrentControlSet\Services\RemoteAccess\Parameters\CallbackTime	Sets the number of minutes to wait for a callback	2-12; default 2
	Auto Disconnect	System\CurrentControlSet\Services\RemoteAccess\Parameters\AutoDisconnect	Disconnects after X minutes of inactivity	0-65536; default 20

Table 6-1. HKLM Entries in WINNT.ADM (continued)

Category	Policy	Registry key/value	What it does	Value
Windows NT Shell	Custom shared Programs folder	Software\Microsoft\Windows\CurrentVersion\Explorer\User Shell Folders\Common Programs	Sets the path to common Programs folder for all users on this machine	Any path; can use environment variables to point to path
	Custom shared desktop icons	Software\Microsoft\Windows\CurrentVersion\Explorer\User Shell Folders\Common Desktop	Sets the path to common desktop icons for all users on this machine	Any path; can use environment variables to point to path
	Custom shared Start menu	Software\Microsoft\Windows\CurrentVersion\Explorer\User Shell Folders\Common Start Menu	Sets the path to common Start menu folder for all users on this machine	Any path; can use environment variables to point to path
	Custom shared Startup folder	Software\Microsoft\Windows\CurrentVersion\Explorer\User Shell Folders\Common Startup	Sets the path to common startup items folder for all users on this machine	Any path; can use environment variables to point to path
Windows NT System\Logon	Logon banner	Software\Microsoft\Windows NT\CurrentVersion\Winlogon\LegalNoticeCaption	Sets the text to display in logon dialog	Default "Do not attempt to log on unless you are an authorized user."
	Logon caption	Software\Microsoft\Windows NT\CurrentVersion\Winlogon\LegalNoticeCaption	Sets the caption to display for logon banner message	Default "Important Notice."
	Enable shutdown from Authentication dialog box	Software\Microsoft\Windows NT\CurrentVersion\Winlogon\ShutdownWithoutLogon	Displays "Shutdown" button in logon dialog so you can shut down without logging in	On or off; default on for NTW and off for NTS
	Do not display last logged on user name	Software\Microsoft\Windows NT\CurrentVersion\Winlogon\DontDisplayLastUserName	Hides name of previously logged in users	Off or on; default off

Table 6-1. HKLM Entries in WINNT.ADM (continued)

Category	Policy	Registry key/value	What it does	Value
Windows NT System\File System	Run logon scripts synchronously	Software\Microsoft\Windows NT\CurrentVersion\Winlogon\RunLogonScriptSync	Runs logon scripts before desktop and start menu appear	Off or on; default off
	Do not create 8.3 filenames for long filenames	System\CurrentControlSet\Control\FileSystem\NtfsDisable8dot3NameCreation	Suppresses creating 8.3 names	Off or on; default off (create names)
	Allow extended characters in 8.3 filenames	System\CurrentControlSet\Control\FileSystem\NtfsDisable8dot3NameCreation	Allows extended characters to be used in short filenames, even though some machines may not display them properly	Off or on; default off (don't allow)
	Do not update last access time	System\CurrentControlSet\Control\FileSystem\NtfsDisable8dot3NameCreation	Doesn't update NTFS "last access time" field on files that are read but not modified	Off or on; default off (do update it)
Windows NT User Profiles	Delete cached copies of roaming profiles	Software\Microsoft\Windows NT\CurrentVersion\winlogon\DeleteRoamingCache	Throws away cached profiles when users log out	Off or on; default off
	Automatically detect slow network connections	Software\Microsoft\Windows NT\CurrentVersion\winlogon\SlowLinkDetectEnabled	Automatically times network links to see whether they're slow	Off or on; default on
	Slow network connection timeout	Software\Microsoft\Windows NT\CurrentVersion\winlogon\SlowLinkTimeOut	Sets the number of milliseconds to wait before timing out on a slow link	1-20000; default 2000
	Timeout for dialog boxes	Software\Microsoft\Windows NT\CurrentVersion\winlogon\ProfileDlgTimeOut	Sets the number of seconds to wait before canceling a dialog box	0-600; default 30

Table 6-2. HKCU Entries in WINNT.ADM

Category	Policy	Registry key/value	What it does	Value
Shell\Custom Folders	Custom Programs folder	Software\Microsoft\Windows\ CurrentVersion\Explorer\ User Shell Folders\Programs	Specifies a custom "Programs" folder to be used in Explorer and the taskbar	Defaults to *%userprofile%\Start Menu\Programs*; may be any local or UNC path
	Custom Desktop folder	Software\Microsoft\Windows\ CurrentVersion\Explorer\ User Shell Folders\Desktop	Specifies a path to a custom set of desktop icons and items	Defaults to *%userprofile%\Desktop* but may be any local or UNC path
	Hide Start menu sub-folders	Software\Microsoft\Windows\ CurrentVersion\Policies\ Explorer\NoStartMenuSub-Folders	Hides the standard Start menu folders; should be set when you specify custom desktop or programs folders	By default, value doesn't exist. When it exists, 1 hides the folders and 0 leaves them alone
	Custom Startup folder	Software\Microsoft\Windows\ CurrentVersion\Explorer\ User Shell Folders\Startup	Specifies location of custom Startup folder	Defaults to *%userprofile%\Start Menu\Programs\Startup*; can be any local or UNC path
	Custom Network Neighborhood	Software\Microsoft\Windows\ CurrentVersion\Explorer\ User Shell Folders\NetHood	Specifies location of custom items for Network Neighborhood	Defaults to *%userprofile%\NetHood*, but may be any local or UNC path
Shell\Restrictions	Only use approved shell extensions	Software\Microsoft\Windows\ CurrentVersion\Policies\ Explorer\ EnforceShellExtensionSecurity	Restricts which Explorer extensions may be loaded and run to those included in this list	Doesn't exist by default; you must manually add any shell extensions you want to approve
	Hide common program groups in Start menu	Software\Microsoft\Windows\ CurrentVersion\Policies\ Explorer\ NoCommonGroups	Forces Explorer not to display any shared program groups	Doesn't exist by default. When value exists, 1 means hide groups and 0 means show them
System	Parse *autoexec.bat*	Software\Microsoft\Windows NT\CurrentVersion\Winlogon\ParseAutoexec	When on, NT will parse *autoexec.bat* when the user logs on	REG_SZ, default value of "1" forces parse; 0 means don't parse

Table 6-2. HKCU Entries in WINNT.ADM (continued)

Category	Policy	Registry key/value	What it does	Value
	Run logon scripts synchronously	Software\Microsoft\Windows NT\CurrentVersion\Winlogon\RunLogonScriptSync	When on, NT won't start the shell until the user's logon script has completed	REG_DWORD. When value is missing or set to 0, scripts are run in parallel with the shell startup. When value is 1, script executes before shell. Identical to "Run logon scripts synchronously" under HKLM; that value overrides this one

Table 6-3. HKLM Entries in COMMON.ADM

Category	Policy	Registry key/value	What it does	Value
Network Update	Remote update mode	System\CurrentControlSet\Control\Update\UpdateMode	Controls whether system policies are automatically updated or not (see "Enabling automatic policy updates" above)	0: (default) don't update 1: update automatically from DC 2: update manually from NetworkPath
	Path for manual update	System\CurrentControlSet\Control\Update\NetworkPath	Specifies UNC path from which to update policies at logon	Empty by default; may be any legal UNC path
	Display error messages	System\CurrentControlSet\Control\Update\Verbose	Toggles display of policy update error messages	When value exists, error messages are displayed
	Load balancing	System\CurrentControlSet\Control\Update\LoadBalance	Toggles load balancing of policy updates from multiple domain controllers	When value exists, load balancing occurs
System\SNMP	Communities	System\CurrentControlSet\Services\SNMP\Parameters\ValidCommunities	Displays a list of communities to which SNMP traps will be sent	Empty by default; otherwise, list of communities as individual values

Table 6-3. HKLM Entries in COMMON.ADM (continued)

Category	Policy	Registry key/value	What it does	Value
	Permitted managers	System\CurrentControlSet\Services\SNMP\Parameters\PermittedManagers	Displays a list of entities permitted to manage SNMP	Empty by default; otherwise, list of managing entities as individual values
	Traps for Public community	System\CurrentControlSet\Services\SNMP\Parameters\TrapConfiguration\Public	Displays a list of traps that may be sent to Public community	Empty by default; otherwise, list of traps as individual values
System\Run	Run	Software\Microsoft\Windows\CurrentVersion\Run	Displays a list of items to run at startup	Defaults to *systray.exe*; otherwise, list of things to run after shell starts

Table 6-4. HKCU Entries in COMMON.ADM

Category	Policy	Registry key/value	What it does	Value
Control Panel\Display	Disable Display icon	Software\Microsoft\Windows\CurrentVersion\Policies\System\NoDispCpl	Prevents user from opening Display control panel	REG_DWORD: 1 restricts control panel, 0 doesn't
	Hide Background tab	Software\Microsoft\Windows\CurrentVersion\Policies\System\NoDispBackgroundPage	Hides Background tab of Display control panel	REG_DWORD: 1 hides Background tab, 0 doesn't
	Hide Screen Saver tab	Software\Microsoft\Windows\CurrentVersion\Policies\System\NoDispScrSavPage	Hides Screen Saver tab of Display control panel so users can't change screen savers	REG_DWORD: 1 hides Screen Saver tab, 0 doesn't
	Hide Appearance tab	Software\Microsoft\Windows\CurrentVersion\Policies\System\NoDispAppearancePage	Hides Appearance tab of Display control panel	REG_DWORD: 1 hides Appearance tab, 0 doesn't

Table 6-4. HKCU Entries in COMMON.ADM (continued)

Category	Policy	Registry key/value	What it does	Value
	Hide Settings tab	Software\Microsoft\Windows\CurrentVersion\Policies\System\NoDispSettings	Hides Settings tab of Display control panel so users can't adjust display resolution or color depth	REG_DWORD: 1 hides Settings tab, 0 doesn't
Desktop\Wallpaper	Wallpaper Name	Control Panel\Desktop\Wallpaper	Controls background image used as wallpaper	REG_SZ; contains full path to specified wallpaper file
	Tile wallpaper	Control Panel\Desktop\TileWallpaper	Controls whether wallpaper is tiled or not	REG_DWORD: 0 means no tiling, 1 means tiling
Desktop\Color Scheme	Color scheme	Control Panel\Appearance\Current	Contains color settings for currently selected decor scheme	Depends on selected color scheme
Shell\Restrictions	Remove Run command from Start menu	Software\Microsoft\Windows\CurrentVersion\Policies\Explorer\NoRun	Hides Run command on Start menu so users can't run arbitrary programs	REG_DWORD: 1 hides the command, 0 doesn't
	Remove folders from Settings on Start menu	Software\Microsoft\Windows\CurrentVersion\Policies\Explorer\NoSetFolders	Hides Settings folders on Start menu	REG_DWORD: 1 hides the folders, 0 doesn't
	Remove Taskbar from Settings on Start menu	Software\Microsoft\Windows\CurrentVersion\Policies\Explorer\NoSetTaskbar	Only hides Taskbar setting folder on Start menu	REG_DWORD: 1 hides the Taskbar folder, 0 doesn't
	Remove Find command from Start menu	Software\Microsoft\Windows\CurrentVersion\Policies\Explorer\NoFind	Removes Find command from Start menu	REG_DWORD: 1 hides the command, 0 doesn't
	Hide drives in My Computer	Software\Microsoft\Windows\CurrentVersion\Policies\Explorer\NoDrives	Hides some drives in My Computer	REG_DWORD bit mask; see "Control Which Drives Are Visible Throughout The System" in Chapter 9

Table 6-4. HKCU Entries in COMMON.ADM (continued)

Category	Policy	Registry key/value	What it does	Value
	Hide Network Neighborhood	Software\Microsoft\Windows\CurrentVersion\Policies\Explorer\NoNetHood	Hides Network Neighborhood icon	REG_DWORD: 1 hides the 'hood, 0 doesn't
	No Entire Network in Network Neighborhood	Software\Microsoft\Windows\CurrentVersion\Policies\Network\NoEntireNetwork	Leaves Network Neighborhood, but removes "Entire Network" icon	REG_DWORD: 1 hides the icon, 0 doesn't
	No workgroup contents in Network Neighborhood	Software\Microsoft\Windows\CurrentVersion\Policies\Network\NoWorkgroupContents	Doesn't show contents of local workgroup in Network Neighborhood	REG_DWORD: 1 hides the workgroup, 0 doesn't
	Hide all items on desktop	Software\Microsoft\Windows\CurrentVersion\Policies\Explorer\NoDesktop	Blanks out the desktop	REG_DWORD: 1 hides the desktop, 0 doesn't
	Disable Shut Down command	Software\Microsoft\Windows\CurrentVersion\Policies\Explorer\NoClose	Stops users from shutting down their machines	REG_DWORD: 1 removes the Shut Down command, 0 doesn't
	Don't save settings at exit	Software\Microsoft\Windows\CurrentVersion\Policies\Explorer\NoSaveSettings	Forces the shell to ignore any environment changes the user makes	REG_DWORD: 0 allows changes to be saved, 1 doesn't
System\Restrictions	Disable Registry editing tools	Software\Microsoft\Windows\CurrentVersion\Policies\System\DisableRegistryTools	Tells compliant Registry editors not to run	REG_DWORD: 1 specifies that editing should be disallowed, 0 allows it
	Run only allowed Windows applications	Software\Microsoft\Windows\CurrentVersion\Policies\Explorer\RestrictRun	Specifies list of which Windows apps may be executed	When RestrictRun exists, its values specify which applications may be run

Picking the Right Policies

Which policies are appropriate for you? It depends on how your network's built, who uses it, and what they should—and shouldn't—be able to do. As you can tell from the preceding tables, the built-in policy templates offer a pretty wide range of capabilities, and you can roll your own templates to give you centralized control over almost anything whose behavior is controlled by Registry entries.

The sections below suggest which policies might be appropriate for various situations; you can pick and choose to build a set of policies that's right for you.

Policies for Anybody

Most administrators who use policies do so to prevent users from doing things they shouldn't. First on the list is probably preventing users from running unapproved applications, which you can do with the "Run only approved Windows applications" and "Remove Run command from Start menu" policies. In addition, you might want to consider using the *floplock* program from the Resource Kit to prevent user access to the floppy drives.

Most administrators hate to spend time fixing things like display resolution settings. Consequently, you may be interested in the Control Panel\Display policy category, since it allows you to prevent users from changing display settings.

Policies for a Lab Network

Many schools and universities have lab networks that students can use to do their classwork. Many companies have something similar: test labs, training classrooms, and so on. These environments share a central feature: a varying group of users have access to the machines, and they should probably be prevented from changing many of the things they might otherwise be able or tempted to modify.

In addition to restricting which applications may be run, most labs need to protect the desktop from changes. This prevents students from using their own wallpaper,* changing the desktop colors to neon green with fuschia accents, or otherwise leaving a mess for the next user. The "Control Panel\Display" and "Desktop" policies are great for this.

For labs that share a network segment with production machines, you may also find it useful to restrict what users can see over the network. The "Shell\Restrictions" category offers several ways to prevent casual network browsing, including hiding the Network Neighborhood altogether.

---

* Not that anyone would ever display an inappropriate picture as wallpaper. Heavens, no. Especially not on a public machine!

For performance reasons, you'll probably want to use the options in "Windows NT User Profiles" to control how profiles get transferred and whether slow connections are automatically flagged as such.

Policies for an "Ordinary" Office

Anything goes! The policies you set for machines in an ordinary office environment will probably vary by user, machine, and group—what's appropriate for HR may not be appropriate for engineering, and vice versa. In general, the most frequently used policy components in office networks tend to be those dealing with custom Start menu folders and security settings, like those found in "Windows NT System\Logon."

In some cases, it may be necessary or desirable to restrict display and desktop changes too, especially on public machines.

7

Programming with the Registry

So far, all the chapters in this book have taught you how, and why, to use the Registry tools that Microsoft provides as part of NT. For the most part, these tools are sufficient for everyday use; however, you may find it necessary to write your own tools from time to time.

NT provides a comprehensive set of routines that allow your programs to read, write, and modify Registry keys and values. You can also connect to remote computers' Registries, get and set security data on keys and values, and do basically everything that *RegEdt32*, *RegEdit*, and the resource kit utilities can do. This capability is a double-edged sword: you can write programs that do exactly what you want, but the burden of properly using the Registry calls is entirely on you.

The Registry API

The entire Registry API is documented in *winreg.h*, part of Microsoft's Win32 Software Development Kit (SDK). As of NT 4.0, there are 28 distinct routines in the Registry API, though most of them actually have two variants: one that works with standard one-byte ASCII strings and another that handles Unicode strings. The ASCII versions have routine names that end in "A," like *RegCreateKeyA*, while the Unicode versions end with a "W," as in *RegCreateKeyW*. Macros in *winreg.h* automatically map the correct variant to the routine name. When you call *RegCreateKey*, you'll automatically get the correct Unicode or ASCII variant depending on how your header files are set up. (Of course, in Visual Basic or Perl this distinction is moot.) The Registry stores strings in Unicode format, so when you call one of the ASCII variants, the Registry code will take care of converting one encoding to another.

API Concepts and Conventions

If you've used any other set of Win32 API routines, you'll probably find the Registry API easy to digest; if you haven't, though, a brief review of some Win32 API fundamentals will help flatten your learning curve.

Input and output parameters

Each Registry routine described below has its own unique set of parameters. These parameters give you a way to tell the API routines what you want done and how to do it; it's important to make sure that you specify them completely and correctly. If you don't, you'll likely get ERROR_INVALID_PARAMETER back as an error; it's entirely possible that instead you might get a corrupted Registry and a crashed machine.

In general, the C/C++ declarations for the Registry routines use pointers both for input and output; for example, strings are always passed as pointers (surprise!), as are outputs for things like security attributes and newly opened HKEYs. The Perl and Visual Basic declarations use the type system appropriate for the language, as you'll see in the sections that cover each language.

Registry error codes

Every Registry API routine returns an error code as its value. These codes, all of which are defined in *winerror.h*, give you an easy way to test for success or failure of an operation. Table 7-1 lists the most commonly used codes; a few routines can return other error codes as noted below, but these are the ones you're most likely to see. Your code should always test for all returned errors (not just these) and handle them properly if they should occur.

Table 7-1. Registry Error Codes

Error code	Value	Meaning
ERROR_SUCCESS	0	The requested operation succeeded.
ERROR_FILE_NOT_FOUND	2	The requested Registry key or path doesn't exist.
ERROR_ACCESS_DENIED	5	The permissions on the requested key or value don't allow you to access it.
ERROR_INVALID_HANDLE	6	The HKEY you passed in isn't a valid Registry handle.
ERROR_OUTOFMEMORY	14	There's not enough memory to read the data you requested.
ERROR_INVALID_PARAMETER	87	One or more parameters you supplied are invalid; you may have omitted values for a required parameter or supplied a bad value.
ERROR_BAD_PATHNAME	161	The path specified doesn't exist.

Table 7-1. Registry Error Codes (continued)

Error code	Value	Meaning
ERROR_LOCK_FAILED	167	The internal Registry locking mechanism failed; this is usually because you're making multiple requests of the Registry from within a single process or thread.
ERROR_MORE_DATA	234	The buffer you provided as a parameter is too small to contain all the available data.
ERROR_NO_MORE_ITEMS	259	There are no more keys or values to enumerate.
ERROR_BADKEY	1010	The key handle you provided is bad.
ERROR_BADDB	1009	The hive that holds the key or value you requested is corrupted.
ERROR_CANTOPEN	1011	The requested key or value can't be opened.
ERROR_CANTREAD	1012	The requested key or value can be opened but not read.
ERROR_CANTWRITE	1013	You can't write data to the key or value you're trying to overwrite.
ERROR_REGISTRY_RECOV-ERED	1014	One or more hive files was reconstructed.
ERROR_REGISTRY_CORRUPT	1015	Something very bad has happened to one or more hive files.
ERROR_REGISTRY_IO_FAILED	1016	NT tried to flush cached Registry data to disk but couldn't.
ERROR_NOT_REGISTRY_FILE	1017	The hive file you tried to load isn't a hive file.
ERROR_KEY_DELETED	1018	You're trying to modify a key that's been deleted.

Why some calls have names ending in "Ex"

Back in ancient times,* the original Windows 3.x API was the One True API that application developers were counseled to use. As programmers did use the API, the inertia of a large installed base made it hard for Microsoft to change the way any of the original 3.x routines worked. Instead of changing the originals, the Win32 API added new routines where necessary and gave them new names ending with *Ex.* For example, *RegOpenKey* begat *RegOpenKeyEx*, which adds an options flag and a SAM access context—both of which are specific to Win32.

In general, you should avoid using the original routines when an *Ex* equivalent exists. Most of the cool features of NT's Registry (especially those related to security) aren't available with the "classic" API; in addition, it's possible that the old-

---

* Well, all right: around 1990.

style routines will stop being supported in future Windows versions. In a few cases it may make sense to use the old-style routine anyway; I've noted these exceptions where appropriate.

NT versus Win9x

The whole point behind the Win32 API is that you can write programs that use a single API. As long as you stick with that API, your code should run on any Win32-compliant platform, whether it's Win95 on Intel, WinNT on Alpha, or WinCE on whatever CPU the HPC builder chose. You're not supposed to have to care which underlying operating system is present. While this is a wonderful theory, it sometimes breaks down in practice. For example, many of the routines described here have slightly different behavior under Windows CE;* more importantly, some routines don't work at all under Win95.

This may be too harsh an indictment; what really happens is that the routines don't fail, but they don't do what they're supposed to—they just return ERROR_ SUCCESS. This means that your code will still execute under Win9x, but it may not do what you intended it to. At present, there are only four routines that behave this way under Win9x: *RegRestoreKey, RegGetKeySecurity, RegSetKeySecurity*, and *RegNotifyChangeKeyValue*. If your application uses any of these routines, be forewarned: you won't get back the data you expect when your code is run under Win9x. Be sure to handle these cases gracefully (for example, checking whether the SECURITY_DESCRIPTOR returned by *RegGetKeySecurity* is valid before trying to use it).

New and exciting data types

One of NT's biggest advantages over Win9x is its more robust security architecture. Since the Win32 API is supposed to be common across Win9x, Windows NT, and Windows CE devices, you may have seen, and ignored, some of the NT-specific data types used in Registry API routines. These data types can be very useful, so a quick introduction will help familiarize you with these new types. (Just skip this section if you already know how to use these types.)

The Registry API makes use of many standard Windows data types like DWORD and LPSTR. However, there are six data types that are fairly unfamiliar to most programmers who haven't yet written NT-specific code. Each is used in at least one Registry call.

---

* MSDN and the Win32 SDK both document these differences, so I won't go into them here.

HKEY

> The initial letter of this type should tip you off to what it is. Microsoft uses Hungarian notation,* so the initial H means this data type is a handle to something. An HKEY is an opaque handle to a Registry key; the handle actually points to a large table of key references, so it's not a handle in the pointer-to-a-pointer sense most programmers usually use.
>
> *winreg.h* includes definitions for the standard six root keys; anywhere you can use an HKEY, you can use HKEY_LOCAL_MACHINE or one of the other predefined root key HKEYs.

REGSAM

> REGSAM is really a DWORD in disguise; its values represent the permission you're requesting when you open or create a key. Legal values are shown in Table 7-2; you can use any of them when creating or opening a key, but you should limit what you ask for to what you actually need. In most cases, that means either KEY_READ or KEY_WRITE.

Table 7-2. REGSAM Access Mask Values

Value	Meaning
KEY_ALL_ACCESS	Combination of KEY_QUERY_VALUE, KEY_ENUMERATE_SUB_KEYS, KEY_NOTIFY, KEY_CREATE_SUB_KEY, KEY_CREATE_LINK, and KEY_SET_VALUE access
KEY_CREATE_LINK	Grants permission to create a symbolic link to specified key
KEY_CREATE_SUB_KEY	Grants permission to create new subkeys
KEY_ENUMERATE_SUB_KEYS	Grants permission to enumerate subkeys of the parent key
KEY_EXECUTE	Grants permission to read subkeys and values
KEY_NOTIFY	Grants permission to request change notification on the parent key or its values
KEY_QUERY_VALUE	Grants permission to get subkey values and their contents
KEY_READ	Combination of KEY_QUERY_VALUE, KEY_ENUMERATE_SUB_KEYS, and KEY_NOTIFY access
KEY_SET_VALUE	Permission to change subkey values
KEY_WRITE	Combination of KEY_SET_VALUE and KEY_CREATE_SUB_KEY access

---

* This notation gets its name from Charles Simonyi, the Microsoft developer who invented the scheme. As you might infer from his surname, he's Hungarian. Despite the fact that it's ugly and restrictive, it has caught on in the Windows books, perhaps because Microsoft uses it exclusively in their header files and example code.

SECURITY_INFORMATION

When you're requesting or setting security information, NT requires you to specify what security information you're dealing with. The **SECURITY_INFOR-MATION** type handles this; it allows you to specify any of the four values listed in Table 7-3 when calling *RegGetKeySecurity* or *RegSetKeySecurity*.

Table 7-3. SECURITY_INFORMATION Values

Value	Meaning
OWNER_SECURITY_INFORMATION	Indicates that you want information about the owner identifier of an object
GROUP_SECURITY_INFORMATION	Indicates you're requesting information about the primary group identifier of the object; only objects connected with the POSIX subsystem will have this information
DACL_SECURITY_INFORMATION	Indicates that you want information about the discretionary ACL of the object
SACL_SECURITY_INFORMATION	Indicates that you want information on the system ACL of the object

SECURITY_DESCRIPTOR

Access control data is stored in **SECURITY_DESCRIPTOR** records. Like **HKEY**, **HWND**, and other types, a **SECURITY_DESCRIPTOR** record is opaque—there's no way to decipher exactly what it points to or contains without using the Win32 security API routines.

SECURITY_ATTRIBUTES

The **SECURITY_ATTRIBUTES** structure is used to encapsulate a security descriptor and data needed to interpret it.

```
typedef struct _SECURITY_ATTRIBUTES {
    DWORD  nLength;
    LPVOID lpSecurityDescriptor;
    BOOL   bInheritHandle;
} SECURITY_ATTRIBUTES;
```

The *nLength* member specifies the size of the security descriptor pointed to by *lpSecurityDescriptor*; the *bInheritHandle* member controls whether a child process spawned by the process that owns the **SECURITY_ATTRIBUTES** structure should inherit the security descriptor itself.

FILETIME

The **FILETIME** structure contains the access date and time for an object. Its format is a little odd:

```
typedef struct _FILETIME {
    DWORD dwLowDateTime;
    DWORD dwHighDateTime;
} FILETIME;
```

Together, the two DWORDs represent the number of 100-nanosecond intervals since 1 January 1601. I have no idea what possessed Microsoft to use this particular date as the base of their time system. Fortunately, there are a number of routines for converting between FILETIME values and more useful formats; check out *FileTimeToSystemTime* for one example.

An extremely brief example

Almost every C or C++ book includes an example based on the famous "Hello, world" example from Kernighan & Ritchie's *The C Programming Language*. Following that venerable tradition, Example 7-1 shows what a similar program that uses the Registry looks like.

Example 7-1. A Modern Variation of the Canonical "Hello, World" Program

```
#include <windows.h>
#include <winreg.h>
#include <stdio.h>

// Hello, World! for the Registry: gets this machine's name and prints
// it out.
void SayHello(void)
{
    unsigned char lpName[MAX_PATH] = "";
    DWORDnNameLen = MAX_PATH;
    HKEY hkResult, hStartKey = HKEY_LOCAL_MACHINE;
    bgv nResult = ERROR_SUCCESS;

    nResult = RegOpenKeyEx(hStartKey,
        "SYSTEM\\CurrentControlSet\\Control\\ComputerName\\ActiveComputerName",
            0L, KEY_READ, &hkResult);
    if (ERROR_SUCCESS == nResult)
    {
        nResult = RegQueryValueEx(hkResult, "ComputerName", 0, 0,
                                  lpName, &nNameLen);
        if (ERROR_SUCCESS == nResult)
            printf("Hello, world, from %s!\n", lpName);
        else
            printf("I don't even know my own name.\n");
    }
    RegCloseKey(hkResult);
}
```

This example contains code to implement the three most basic—and most common—Registry operations:

1. Opening a key whose full path you know with *RegOpenKey* or *RegOpenKeyEx*, then retaining the HKEY returned when the key is opened

2. Using that returned HKEY to get a value whose location and type you already know   (HKLM\SYSTEM\CurrentControlSet\Control\ComputerName\ ActiveComputerName in this case)

3. Doing something with the retrieved value, then closing the key you opened in step 1

Almost all programs that use the Registry involve these three steps. Of course, in addition to (or instead of) reading Registry data, you could write new data to a value, or you could enumerate a sequence of keys or values to find one that matches what you're looking for. You'll learn how to do all of these things in the following sections.

TIP   In the following sections, I'll present the API as Microsoft defined it: using C. The sections on programming with Perl and Visual Basic will contain the correct definitions for those languages.

Opening and Closing Keys

In Chapter 1, *A Gentle Introduction to the NT Registry*, I pointed out the organizational similarities between a file system and the Registry. These similarities are more than skin deep: they extend to the actual process of moving data into and out of the Registry. In general, the same rules apply when working with Registry keys and their values as with disk files.

First and foremost, you have to open a key when you want to use it, then close it when you're done. If you don't open a key, you can't get its values. If you don't close the key when done, other applications may not be able to access it, and your changes may not be written out when you'd expect them to be. The API routines that open keys require two arguments: a path to the key you want to open and an open key. This may seem like a Catch-22: how can you open a key if you must already have an open key? The answer is simple—the root keys (HKLM, HKCC, HKCU, HKU, HKDD, and HKCR) are always open, so you can use them when you open any other key.

The next similarity involves access controls and rights. If you're accustomed to NTFS, Unix, or Novell filesystems, you know that files and directories can have permissions attached to them that govern who can open, modify, delete, and move things around. Besides access control lists, or ACLs, files also have rights, which the ACLs grant. One ACL might grant Administrator the right to read or write a file, while another might deny write access to members of the Domain Users group. Registry keys have these same controls and rights; as you'll learn in Chapter 8, *Administering the NT Registry*, you can keep your Registry secure by putting ACLs on sensitive keys. When you open a Registry key, you must specify what access you want to it: read, write, enumerate, and delete are all examples. NT will check the access you request against the ACLs on the Registry key to decide whether you get access or not.

The best way to stay out of trouble when opening and closing keys is to remember to balance key openings with closings. Later in the chapter (in the section titled "Example: A Stack-Based Wrapper Class"), you'll see a C++ class, *StKey*, that automates the cleanup process. Here's a small sample:

```
{
    StKey armor(HKEY_LOCAL_MACHINE, "SOFTWARE\\LJL\\ArmorMail\\Settings");
    armor.QueryDWORDValue("Expiration", &expDate);
    if (IsExpired(expDate))
        throw(LJL_E_EVAL_EXPIRED);
    // continue on
}
```

The class constructor opens a Registry key, and its destructor closes it again. This means that you can use a key without worrying about whether it gets closed or not; whenever your code exits the local block, the key will be automatically closed. If you're not using C++, or choose not to use *StKey* or equivalent, please make sure to close any keys you open even when errors or exceptions interrupt the normal flow of control in your code.

Opening keys

When you're ready to open a key, there are two different approaches you can take. The first one is to use the *RegCreateKey* and *RegCreateKeyEx* functions, which I'll talk about in a bit. They'll automatically open the key you specify or create it if it doesn't exist. The second method, which is probably better for most applications, is to open the key with *RegOpenKeyEx* or *RegOpenKey*. Why are these calls better? They fail when you try to open a key that doesn't exist, while the *RegCreate* functions will create a new key with no values in it. Imagine that you're calling a friend named Bill on the phone. If you call and are told "Bill's not here" by the person who answers, that's the equivalent of calling *RegOpenKey* routines on a non-existent key. By contrast, calling Bill and being told "Bill's not here, but I'll change my name to Bill" is what happens when you call *RegCreate*. That may sometimes be desirable, but it shouldn't be a surprise.

The recommended way to open a key is with *RegOpenKeyEx*. You supply an open key, which may be a root key or a key you've already opened, the name of the full path to the key you want to open, and a mask describing what access you want to the newly opened key.

```
LONG RegOpenKeyEx(hKey, lpSubKey, ulOptions, samDesired, phkResult);
```

HKEY	hKey	Handle to any open key or root key
LPCTSTR	lpSubKey	Name of the subkey of *hKey* you want to open; if NULL or empty, another copy of *hKey* will be opened
DWORD	ulOptions	Reserved; must be 0
REGSAM	samDesired	Mask defining access rights you're asking for (see "REG-SAM" above for possible values, or just use either KEY_READ or KEY_WRITE)
PHKEY	phkResult	Pointer to the newly opened key; NULL if an error occurs

This code opens a key under HKLM for reading, then goes on to do some other processing (which I've omitted here). If you combine the root key and the value of *lpSubKey*, you'll see that the key being opened is HKLM\SOFTWARE\LJL\Armor-Mail\Users; if I'd already had any key in that path open (for example, HKLM\SOFTWARE\LJL) I could have shortened the subkey name accordingly.

```
DWORDresult = ERROR_SUCCESS;
HKEYfirstKey;

// try to open the user list key; if we succeed, enumerate its subkeys
result = RegOpenKeyEx(HKEY_LOCAL_MACHINE, "SOFTWARE\\LJL\\ArmorMail\\
                    Users", 0L, KEY_READ, &firstKey);
if (ERROR_SUCCESS == result)
    ...
```

If you try to open a key for access that the DACLs on the key don't allow (for example, trying to open any of the HKLM\HARDWARE subkeys for write access), you'll get *ERROR_ACCESS_DENIED* for your trouble. One of the "strongly recommended" criteria for getting the Win9x and NT 5.0 certification labels is that you should open keys with the privileges you need: don't ask for KEY_ALL_ACCESS when what you really need is KEY_READ. You should only ask for write access when you're ready to write data to the Registry; this reduces the risk that your code will accidentally damage the Registry.

If you're willing to use the default system security mask for key access, you can use the *RegOpenKey* function instead; it takes the same *hKey*, *lpSubKey*, and *phkResult* parameters as *RegOpenKeyEx*, but it doesn't accept a desired SAM mask.

```
LONG RegOpenKey(hKey, lpSubKey, phkResult);
```

HKEY	hKey	Handle to any open key or root key
LPCTSTR	lpSubKey	Name of the subkey you want opened; if NULL or empty, *RegOpenKey* will open another copy of *hKey*
PHKEY	phkResult	Pointer to the newly opened key

The only difference between *RegOpenKey* and *RegOpenKeyEx* is that the latter has two extra parameters; apart from that, they function identically. One portability warning, though: like the other Win 3.x Registry API calls, *RegOpenKey* is unsupported on Windows CE. If you're writing code that you want to be portable, stick with the . . . *Ex* functions, tempting though the old ones may be.

Closing keys

There's only one way to close a key: *RegCloseKey*. You pass in the key you want to close; if it's successfully closed, you'll get *ERROR_SUCCESS* back. Otherwise, you'll get an error that will indicate what went wrong.

```
LONG RegCloseKey (hKey);
```

You can actually call *RegCloseKey* on one of the predefined root key entries; it'll report a successful close, but it doesn't actually close the root key. This frees you from having to worry about whether the key you're trying to close is really yours or not.

When you close a key, any data you've changed in that key or its subkeys may be written to disk. On the other hand, it may not—the Registry support code may cache these changes until the next time it's convenient to flush them out to disk. Don't assume that your changes are immediately preserved as soon as you close a key; do assume that your changes are not preserved at all until you do so.

Creating Keys

You can create new keys anywhere you have permission to do so; as I pointed out in earlier chapters, you probably won't need to do so very often unless you're writing applications that use the Registry to store their parameters. Just in case, though, here's how to do it.

RegCreateKeyEx is the most powerful function for creating a key. When you ask it to create a key, it will do so, then open it. If the key already exists, it will just open it. In either case, after a successful call to *RegCreateKeyEx* you'll have an open key that may be used for all manner of things as described elsewhere in the chapter.

```
LONG RegCreateKeyEx(hKey, lpSubKey, Reserved, lpClass, dwOptions,
    samDesired,lpSecurityAttributes, phkResult, lpdwDisposition);
```

HKEY	hKey	Handle to an open key under which the new subkey will be created; applications may not create keys directly under HKLM or HKU.
LPCSTR	lpSubKey	Complete path to the new subkey you want to create; this path will be interpreted relative to *hKey*. The path name must not begin with a backslash. Any keys in the path that don't exist will be created for you.
DWORD	Reserved	Reserved; must be NULL.
LPCSTR	lpClass	Specifies the class of the key; should always be NULL.
DWORD	dwOptions	May be REG_OPTION_NON_VOLATILE (creates the key as a normal, persistent key), REG_OPTION_VOLATILE (creates the key as a volatile key that is never stored to disk), or REG_OPTION_BACKUP_RESTORE (ignores *samDesired* and attempts to open the key for backup/restore access.) The default is REG_OPTION_NON_VOLATILE.
REGSAM	samDesired	Contains an access mask specifying what access you want to the new key; see Table 7-2 for a complete list.
LPSECURITY_ ATTRIBUTES	lpSecurityAt- tributes	Points to a SECURITY_ATTRIBUTES structure that controls whether child processes and threads may access this key. Leave this NULL to turn off inheritance.
PHKEY	phkResult	Pointer to HKEY containing the newly opened key.
LPDWORD	lpdwDisposition	Points to a DWORD that indicates what happened; it will be set to REG_CREATED_ NEW_KEY if the requested key had to be created, or REG_OPENED_EXISTING_KEY if the key was merely opened.

When you open an existing key, *RegCreateKeyEx* ignores the *lpClass*, *dwOptions*, and *lpSecurityAttributes* parameters, since their values are determined by the existing key.

Once you successfully call *RegCreateKeyEx*, you're guaranteed to have an open key that you can use to add values or subkeys. Of course, a newly created key won't have any of either item, but an existing key that *RegCreateKeyEx* opened might indeed—be sure to check *lpdwDisposition* if you need to know whether the key was created or just opened.

You can also use the less-flexible *RegCreateKey*, but (in a rare agreement) neither Microsoft nor I recommend it. It lacks a way to specify what access or security attributes you want to apply to the key, meaning that it may fail unexpectedly when trying to open an existing key that has an ACL applied to it. In addition, it doesn't tell you whether it created a key or opened it.

```
LONG RegCreateKey(hKey, lpSubKey, phkResult);
```

HKEY	hKey	Handle to an open key under which the new sub-key will be created; applications may not create keys directly under HKLM or HKU
LPCSTR	lpSubKey	Full path of key you want to create; any components that don't exist will be created
PHKEY	phkResult	Pointer to HKEY containing newly opened key

Getting Information About Keys

Every key has a great deal of information associated with it, even if it's not immediately obvious. When you use one of the Registry editing tools, you see a neatly tree-structured view of what's beneath each root key, but the system maintains a lot more data beneath the surface so that it can efficiently access keys and values and give them back to requesting programs.

RegQueryInfoKey gives you access to a total of 11 different pieces of data for any key in the Registry. Typically you'd use it to find out how many subkeys or values exist so you can efficiently enumerate through them (more on that in the next section). *RegQueryInfoKey* looks like the following:

```
LONG RegQueryInfoKey(hKey, lpClass, lpcbClass, lpReserved, lpcSubKeys,
    lpcbMaxSubKeyLen, lpcbMaxClassLen, lpcValues, lpcbMaxValueNameLen,
    lpcbMaxValueLen, lpcbSecurityDescriptor, lpftLastWriteTime);
```

HKEY	hKey	Handle to any open key or root key.
LPTSTR	lpClass	Points to a buffer that receives the key's class name. May be NULL if you don't want the class name back.
LPDWORD	lpcbClass	Points to a DWORD containing the length of the class name passed back in *lpClass*. May be NULL if *lpClass* is also NULL; if one is NULL but the other isn't, you'll get ERROR_ INVALID_PARAMETER back.
LPDWORD	lpReserved	Reserved; must always be NULL.
LPDWORD	lpcSubKeys	Points to a DWORD that receives the number of subkeys of *hKey*.
LPDWORD	lpcbMaxSubKeyLen	Points to a DWORD that holds the length (not including the terminating NULL) of the longest subkey name under *hKey*.

LPDWORD	lpcbMaxClassLen	Points to a DWORD that holds the length, not including the terminating NULL, of the longest class name of any key under *hKey*.
LPDWORD	lpcValues	Points to a DWORD that holds the number of values attached to *hKey*.
LPDWORD	lpcbMaxValueNameLen	Points to a DWORD that receives the length of the longest value name. This is useful when using *RegEnumValue*.
LPDWORD	lpcbMaxValueLen	Points to a DWORD that receives the length of the longest value contents. This is also useful when using *RegEnumValue*.
LPDWORD	lpcbSecurityDescriptor	Points to a DWORD that receives the size of the security descriptor associated with this key. Security descriptors can vary in size, so it's helpful to know how big a particular key's descriptor is before calling *RegGetKeySecurity*.
PFILETIME	lpftLastWriteTime	Points to a FILETIME structure (see "New and exciting data types" above) that will be filled in with the date and time that any subkey or value of *hKey* was modified.

Any of the parameters except *hKey* can be NULL; if you specify NULL for a parameter, that data isn't returned. Here's a small routine that gets the number of values attached to any open Registry key; notice that it passes NULL for everything except *lpcValue*:

```
DWORD GetKeyValueCount(HKEY inKey)
// Gets the count of values attached to a particular key. Returns
// the value count (which may be 0) or -1 if an error occurs.
{
    DWORD valCount = 0;
    DWORD result = ERROR_SUCCESS;

    result = RegQueryInfoKey (inKey,
                            NULL, NULL,    // class & class size
                            NULL,          // reserved
                            NULL,          // # of subkeys
                            NULL,          // subkey length
                            NULL,          // class length
                            &valCount,     // # of values
                            NULL, NULL, NULL, NULL);
    if (ERROR_SUCCESS != result)
        valCount = -1;
    return valCount;
}
```

It's worth making special mention of *lpcSubKeys*, *lpcValues*, *lpcbMaxValueNameLen*, and *lpcbMaxValueLen*. These four parameters make it easier to efficiently enumerate keys and values. Knowing how many items there are makes it possible to enumerate any subset of a key's values, and knowing the maximum name and content lengths means you can allocate a buffer that's just the right size, instead of too big or too small, to hold the data returned by the enumeration.

Enumerating Keys and Values

It's often necessary to do some kind of processing over every key or value under a particular subkey. This *enumeration* is nothing more than an iterative loop that starts with the first key or value of interest, then proceeds on, continuing until it has processed every key or value. For example, you could enumerate the subkeys of HKU to find out the SIDs of every installed local account on a machine; armed with that information, you could look up the account names to build a list of users who have profiles on the machine.

The enumeration API routines treat a key's subkeys or values as an ordered list of N values, numbered from 1 to N. You pass an index value to the API routines to indicate which key or value you want; the corresponding key or value will be returned. For values, there's an extra wrinkle: keys can have a default value, which always appears as item 0 in the enumeration list. (You'll see how this works in the section "Enumerating values" later in this chapter.) This is convenient, but don't be misled: the values or keys aren't really an ordered list, and if you enumerate the same subkey twice in a row you could potentially get items back in a different order each time.

Enumeration strategies

When you enumerate keys or values, there are a few different strategies you can use to process all the enumerated keys. The easiest way is to call *RegQueryInfoKey* to find out how many subkeys or values exist, then use a simple loop to process every key or value. A small snippet implementing this tactic might look like this:

```
DWORD idx=0, keyCount = 0
LONG retVal = 0;

retVal = RegQueryInfoKey (inKey,
                    NULL, NULL,    // class & class size
                    NULL,          // reserved
                    &keyCount,     // # of subkeys
                    NULL,          // subkey length
                    NULL,          // class length
                    NULL,          // # of values
                    NULL, NULL, NULL, NULL);

for (idx=0; idx < keyCount; idx++)
{
    // get the idx'th key's name and length
    retVal = RegEnumKeyEx(interestingKey, idx, name, nameLen, NULL,
        NULL, NULL, NULL);
```

```
        // do something with it
    }
```

This approach has the advantage of being very simple to implement and understand; however, you may not want to process every key or value. Instead, if you
want to process only keys or values that meet some criterion, you can use a conventional **while** loop like this:

```
DWORD idx = 0;
bool keepGoing = true;
LONG retVal = 0;

while (keepGoing)
    {
        retVal = RegEnumKeyEx(interestingKey, idx++, name, &nameLen,
                        (unsigned long *)NULL, (char *)NULL, (unsigned
                        long *)NULL, (LPFILETIME)NULL);
        if (ERROR_SUCCESS == retVal)
        {
            // If we're interested in this key, we'd process it further;
            // we might also set keepGoing here if we only want one key
        }
        keepGoing = (keepGoing && retVal == ERROR_SUCCESS);
    }
```

With this approach, you don't have to know in advance how many keys or values
exist, and it's a simple matter to stop enumerating as soon as you find whatever it
is you're looking for.

Enumerating keys

You enumerate keys using the *RegEnumKeyEx* and *RegEnumKey* routines. They're
very similar; the primary difference is that *RegEnumKeyEx* allows you to retrieve
the modification time and class name for a subkey, while *RegEnumKey* doesn't. In
either case, you simply supply the **HKEY** you want enumerated and an index
value that indicates which subkey you want to see. The name (not the complete
path) of the corresponding subkey is returned, so you can open any subkey you
find by passing the name to *RegOpenKey* or *RegOpenKeyEx*.

```
LONG RegEnumKeyEx(hKey, dwIndex, lpName, lpcbName, lpReserved, lpClass,
    lpcbClass, lpftLastWriteTime);
```

HKEY	hKey	Handle to any open key or root key.
DWORD	dwIndex	Index, from 0 to the number of subkeys, indicating which key you want to fetch.
LPSTR	lpName	Points to an area that will receive the name of the enumerated key.

LPDWORD	lpcbName	Points to a DWORD containing the size of *lpName*; on return, contains the length of *lpName* in bytes, including the NULL terminator.
LPDWORD	lpReserved	Reserved; as always, must be NULL.
LPSTR	lpClass	Points to a buffer that will receive the subkey's class name; may be NULL if you don't care about this datum.
LPDWORD	lpcbClass	Points to a DWORD containing the size of *lpClass*; on return, contains the length of *lpClass* in bytes, including the NULL terminator. May be NULL only if *lpClass* is also NULL.
PFILETIME	lpftLastWriteTime	Points to a structure that will be filled in with the date and time of the last modification to the subkey; may be NULL if you're not interested.

RegEnumKey is identical in function, except for having fewer parameters.

```
LONG RegEnumKey(hKey, dwIndex, lpName, cbName);
```

HKEY	hKey	Handle to any open key or root key
DWORD	dwIndex	Index, from 0 to the number of subkeys, indicating which key you want to fetch
LPSTR	lpName	Points to an area that will receive the name of the enumerated key
LPDWORD	cbName	Points to a DWORD containing the size of *lpName*; on return, contains the length of *lpName* in bytes, including the NULL terminator

Enumerating values

Once you've located a key of interest, you might want to enumerate its values. Most Registry keys have at least one value; quite a few have many values whose number and contents vary from machine to machine. (HKCR is a good example, since it will differ depending on what classes and objects are registered on a machine.) You can accomplish this with *RegEnumValue:*[*]

```
LONG RegEnumValue(hKey, dwIndex, lpValueName, lpcbValueName, lpReserved,
    lpType, lpData, lpcbData);
```

HKEY	hKey	Handle to any open key or root key
DWORD	dwIndex	Ordinal index of the value you want to fetch; you'll usually start with 0 and move up until you either get ERROR_NO_MORE_ITEMS or hit the number of items returned by *RegQueryInfoKey*
LPSTR	lpValueName	Points to a buffer that, on return, contains the value's name

---

[*] Surprisingly, there's no *RegEnumValueEx*. The original function hasn't changed since its introduction, so Microsoft left it alone in Win32.

LPDWORD	lpcbValueName	On entry, points to the size of *lpValueName*; on return, points to length of string copied into *lpValue-Name, not* including the NULL terminator
LPDWORD	lpReserved	Reserved; must be NULL
LPDWORD	lpType	Points to a buffer that, on return, holds the type of the requested value (REG_DWORD, REG_SZ, etc.). May be NULL if you don't care what type the value is
LPBYTE	lpData	Points to a buffer into which the contents of the specified value are copied
LPDWORD	lpcbData	On entry, points to a DWORD containing the size of *lpData*; on return, contains the number of bytes written into *lpData*

To see *RegEnumValue* in action, check out Example 7-7 in "Example: Loading A Control with a Set Of Values" later in this chapter; the example illustrates the basic things you should do when enumerating a set of values:

- Call *RegQueryInfoKey* first to get the maximum subkey length, then use that to allocate any buffers you need to get the value name or contents.

- Make sure you either check for ERROR_NO_MORE_ITEMS or honor the number of values returned by *RegQueryInfoKey*.

- Open the parent key with KEY_READ or KEY_QUERY_VALUE access.

Getting Registry Data

Maybe you patiently enumerated a sequence or keys, or perhaps you already know just where the data you want is stored. Either way, at some point you'll want to actually retrieve a value stored under some Registry subkey. If you used *RegEnumValue*, you could have gotten the value's contents when you enumerated it, but if you just want to grab a single value whose path you know, there are better ways to do so.

Getting a single value

The first, and most useful, method of getting a single value's contents out of the Registry is the *RegQueryValueEx* function. As its name implies, it's a Win32 routine; you supply an open key and a value name, and it will return the value's data type, length, and contents.

```
LONG RegQueryValueEx(hKey, lpValueName, lpReserved, lpType, lpData,
    lpcbData);
```

| HKEY | hKey | Handle to any key or root key opened with KEY_READ or KEY_QUERY_VALUE access. |
| LPTSTR | lpValueName | Name of the value to query; if NULL or empty, queries default value. |

LPDWORD	lpReserved	Unused; must be NULL.
LPDWORD	lpType	On return, holds the data type of the value (REG_DWORD, REG_SZ, etc.). If you pass in NULL, no type data is returned.
LPBYTE	lpData	Points to the buffer that holds the value's contents on return. If you pass in NULL, no value data is returned but the *lpcbData* parameter holds the length of the contents.
LPDWORD	lpcbData	On input, points to the buffer that specifies the size of *lpData* buffer. On return, holds amount of data copied into *lpData*. You may pass in NULL if *lpData* is NULL also.

The most straightforward way to call *RegQueryValueEx* is just to get the value, like this (assuming I'm fetching a REG_DWORD value named "SomeValue" from a previously opened key):

```
nResult = RegQueryValueEx(hOpenKey, "SomeValue", NULL, NULL,
        (LPBYTE)&theValue, &valSize);
```

Since you always know how big a DWORD is, the size really isn't important. Things get a little more complex when querying for a string value named "Some-StringValue". At run time, I don't know the string's length, which means that I must either dynamically allocate a buffer or check to see whether there's more data available than my buffer can hold. *RegQueryValueEx* will return ERROR_MORE_DATA if the requested value has more data than can fit in the buffer length as specified by *lpcbData*.

```
DWORD bufSize = MAX_PATH;
char theBuf[MAX_PATH];

nResult = RegQueryValueEx(hOpenKey, "SomeStringValue", NULL, NULL,
        (LPBYTE)theBuf, &bufSize);
if (ERROR_MORE_DATA == nResult)
{
    // too much data for our buffer; fail, use another buffer, or do
    // something else
}
else if (ERROR_SUCCESS == nResult)
{
    // continue normally
}
```

Alternatively, you could find out how big the value is, then allocate the buffer for it. This approach requires an extra Registry query but lets you economize on memory by not allocating any more than you actually need:

```
DWORD bufSize = 0;
char *theBuf = NULL;

nResult = RegQueryValueEx(hOpenKey, "SomeStringValue", NULL, NULL,
                NULL, &bufSize);
```

```
        if (ERROR_SUCCESS == nResult)
        {
           theBuf = (char *)malloc(bufSize+1);  // allow extra byte for NULL
                                                // terminator
           if (theBuf)
           {
              nResult = RegQueryValueEx(hOpenKey, "SomeStringValue", NULL,
                                        NULL, (LPBYTE)theBuf, &bufSize);
              if (ERROR_SUCCESS == nResult)
                // do whatever with the value
              free(theBuf);
           }
        }
```

Notice that this code snippet added an extra byte to the buffer to allow for the
NULL terminator, which may be stored as part of the string. Also notice that I
didn't allocate extra space for a Unicode string: if you define UNICODE, the initial
call will return the string's Unicode length in *bufSize*, but if UNICODE isn't defined,
the string will be converted into ANSI, and *bufSize* will contain the ANSI string
length.

You can also use *RegQueryValue* to request a key's value, but it can only get the
default value (remember, that's the only value Win3.x supports, and *RegQuery-
Value* is a 3.x compatibility function).

```
LONG RegQueryValue(hKey, lpSubKey, lpValue, lpcbValue );
```

HKEY	hKey	Points to any currently open key or one of the root keys
LPCSTR	lpSubKey	Points to the subkey of *hKey* whose default value you want to get. If it's NULL, *RegQueryValue* will fetch the value of *hKey*
LPSTR	lpValue	Points to a buffer that will hold the value contents; may be NULL if you only want the contents' length
LPDWORD	lpcbValue	On entry, points to the length of *lpValue*; on return, indicates the actual length of the value's contents

Getting multiple values

You can retrieve multiple values from a key at once using *RegQueryMultipleValues,* but its interface can be a little confusing.

```
LONG RegQueryMultipleValues(hKey, valList, numVals, lpValueBuf,
    ldwTotalSize);
```

HKEY	hKey	Points to any currently open key or one of the root keys. The key must be opened with KEY_SET_VALUE or KEY_WRITE access.
PVALENT	valList	Array of VALENT structures (see below); each item holds the name of a value to retrieve on entry and holds the value's data on exit.
DWORD	NumVals	Number of elements in the *valList* array.

| LPTSTR | lpValueBuf | Points to the buffer which, at exit, will hold the retrieved values. |
| LPDWORD | ldwTotal-Size | On entry, points to the size (in bytes) of *lpValueBuf*, at exit, returns the number of bytes written to the buffer. |

To use this function, you fill out an array of VALENT structures; you put the value name youíre looking for in *ve_valuename*, and *RegQueryMultipleValues* will fill in the other fields for you.

```
typedef struct value_entA {
    LPSTR  ve_valuename;
    DWORD ve_valuelen;
    DWORD ve_valueptr;
    DWORD ve_type;
}VALENTA, FAR *PVALENTA;
```

On entry, *lpValueBuf* should point to a buffer big enough to hold all the value data youíre requesting. On return, you can iterate through *valList*; each itemís *ve_valueptr* member will point to the location *within lpValueBuf* where the value dataís actually stored. You can also call *RegQueryMultipleValues* with an *lpValueBuf* of NULL; when you do, *ldwTotalSize* will contain the buffer size required to hold all the requested values.

Adding and Modifying Values

Keys can signify things based on their presence or absence, but values are the best way to store persistent data in the Registry. The *RegSetValueEx* function does double duty; it can create new values or change the contents of existing ones.

```
LONG RegSetValueEx(hKey, lpValueName, Reserved, dwType, lpData, cbData);
```

HKEY	hKey	Points to any currently open key or one of the root keys. The key must be opened with KEY_SET_VALUE or KEY_WRITE access.
LPCSTR	lpValueName	Name of the value to set; if no value with the specified name exists, *RegSetValueEx* will create it. If *lpValueName* is empty or NULL, the supplied value is assigned to the key's default value.
DWORD	Reserved	Unused; must be 0.
DWORD	dwType	Type of the value you're adding or modifying; may be any of the types defined in Chapter 2.
CONST BYTE *	lpData	Data to load into the value.
DWORD	cbData	Length (in bytes) of the data pointed to by *lpData*. If the value contents are of type REG_SZ, REG_EXPAND_SZ, or REG_MULTI_SZ, *cbData* must reflect the length of the string plus the terminating NULL character.

If you call *RegSetValueEx* with the name of an existing value in *lpValueName*, its contents and type will be replaced by whatever you pass in. If no such value exists, it will be created with the contents and type you specify.

In addition to *RegSetValueEx*, there's also a second value-setting function you may use: *RegSetValue*. It was originally part of the Win 3.1 Registry API. You may remember from Chapter 1 that the Win 3.1 Registry only allowed a single value for each key. In keeping with that heritage, *RegSetValue* only allows you to set the default value for a key, and the value you set must be a REG_SZ. I present this function for completeness, but you should avoid it in favor of *RegSetValueEx*.

```
LONG RegSetValue(hKey,lpSubKey, dwType, lpData, cbData);
```

HKEY	hKey	Key to which the new value will be added; can be any currently open key or root key
LPCSTR	lpSubkey	Name of subkey that gets the value; if NULL, the value will be added to *hKey*
DWORD	dwType	Data type of new value; must be REG_SZ
LPCSTR	lpData	Pointer to string buffer containing new value's contents
DWORD	cbData	Length of *lpData*, not including its terminating NULL character

As with *RegSetValueEx*, if the key named in *lpSubkey* doesn't exist it will be created. In an additional twist, if the key named by *lpSubkey* doesn't exist, *RegSetValue* will create any keys necessary to construct a legal path, then add the default value to it. Note that if all you want to do is set the default value, you can do so by using *RegSetValueEx* and passing NULL for *lpValueName*.

Example 7-2 illustrates how *RegSetValueEx* works; the example sets the DiskSpaceThreshold value to the percentage of disk space you specify. This routine's used in a tool I wrote that configures new servers with the default settings we want on them before delivering them to customers or remote sites.

Example 7-2. SetDiskWarningThreshold

```
// This routine sets the DiskSpaceThreshold to the specified percentage.
// You should check all the system's disk volumes to figure out a reasonable
// percentage for the machine, then call this routine to set it.
long SetDiskWarningThreshold(const int inThreshold)
{
    char    lpName[MAX_PATH] = "System\\CurrentControlSet\\Services\\LanmanServer
                               \\Parameters";
    HKEY    hkResult = NULL;
    LONG    nResult = ERROR_SUCCESS;

    // preflight our arguments
    if (inThreshold < 1 || inThreshold > 99)
        return ERROR_INVALID_PARAMETER;
```

Example 7-2. SetDiskWarningThreshold (continued)

```
    // open the key with write access so we can set the value
    nResult = RegOpenKeyEx(HKEY_LOCAL_MACHINE, lpName, 0L, KEY_WRITE, &hkResult);
    if (ERROR_SUCCESS == nResult)
    {
        nResult = RegSetValueEx(hkResult, "DiskSpaceThreshold", 0L, REG_DWORD,
                                (unsigned char *)&inThreshold, sizeof(int));
        if (ERROR_SUCCESS == nResult)
            nResult = RegCloseKey(hkResult);
    }
    return nResult;
}
```

Deleting Keys and Values

You may find it necessary to delete keys or values from within your home-brewed Registry utilities. Since many of the lesser-known features of NT discussed in Chapter 9, *Registry Tweaks*, function based on the presence or absence of special trigger keys, turning these features on or off may require you to delete values, and there's no way to do so with a *.REG* file. You must be careful with your new-found destructive powers, though—accidentally deleting the wrong key or value can make your system stop working altogether.

Before you delete a key or value, you must have the parent key opened with adequate access. If you supply KEY_WRITE as the REGSAM value when you open the key, you'll be able to delete it. You can also request KEY_CREATE_SUB_KEY or KEY_SET_VALUE rights to gain delete access to keys and values respectively.

There's one other thing worth mentioning here: when you delete a key or a value, it's not actually deleted. Instead, the Registry subsystem marks the deleted items as deleted, but doesn't delete them until the next time Registry data is flushed (either explicitly with *RegFlushKey* or automatically). If you try to read, write, or enumerate a key or value that's been marked as deleted, you'll get ERROR_KEY_DELETED as a return value. You can always call *RegCloseKey* on a deleted key without getting an error, though.

Deleting a key

You delete individual keys with the *RegDeleteKey* routine. If you specify a valid key and subkey, the key will be immediately marked for deletion, even if other processes currently have the key open. This is different from the file metaphor used elsewhere in the Registry—if you try to delete an open file, the delete operation will fail, but not so with *RegDeleteKey*.

```
LONG RegDeleteKey(hKey, lpSubKey);
```

HKEY	hKey	Key pointing to parent of target value; may be a root key or a subkey
LPCSTR	lpSubkey	Name of the subkey to be deleted; if NULL or empty, the key specified by *hKey* will be deleted

You can't delete a root key, and you can't delete first-level subkeys of root keys. For example, you can't remove HKLM\SOFTWARE or HKCU\SOFTWARE, but you could remove HKLM\SOFTWARE\Microsoft (though I wouldn't recommend it). In addition, you may not delete a key that has subkeys; if you try to do so, you'll get an error. It's okay to delete keys that have values—the values will be deleted along with the key.

WARNING   Under Windows 95, *RegDeleteKey* will delete keys that have sub-keys. If your code depends on the NT behavior of failing when a targeted key has subkeys, it will work fine under Win9x!

Deleting a value

Deleting values is wonderfully straightforward (as long as you have KEY_WRITE or KEY_SET_VALUE access on the target key)! *RegDeleteValue* will remove the specified value from the key you provide.

```
LONG RegDeleteValue(hKey, lpValueName);
```

HKEY	hKey	Key pointing to parent of target value
LPCSTR	lpValueName	Name of the value to be deleted

If *lpValueName* is either NULL or contains an empty string, *RegDeleteValue* will delete the default value (you know, the one that appears as "<Default>" or "No Name" in Registry editors). Otherwise, *lpValueName* must contain the correct name of an existing value.

Using Registry Security Information

Under NT, every object in the entire system has security information attached to it. Registry keys are just objects, so they too can have access control lists. These ACLs control who may read, write, or delete the key and its values. Ordinarily, you won't need to control these ACLs at all; when you do, *RegEdt32* is probably the best tool for doing so. If you find it necessary or desirable to get a key's security data programmatically, though, you certainly can.

ACLs come in two types: system ACLs, or SACLs, are owned by (and can only be changed by) the system, while discretionary ACLs (DACLs for short) are controlled

What's in a Security Descriptor?

The short answer is "it depends." The long answer is, well, longer. A security descriptor, or SD, is really an opaque block of data that NT can parse into a set of security constraints. Every object in the system has an SD associated with it; a single SD will contain one or many sets of the following items:

- The security ID (SID) of the object's owner

- The SID of the object owner's primary group

- A discretionary ACL, which the object owner may freely modify

- A system ACL, which may only be modified by entities with system privileges

- Qualifiers, which specify whether the other items are self-contained or point to other SDs and ACLs

You can't directly modify (or even decipher) an SD's contents; instead, you have to use the security API routines, notably *InitializeSecurityDescriptor*, *GetSecurityDescriptorOwner*, *SetSecurityDescriptorDacl*, *SetSecurityDescriptorOwner*, and *SetSecurityDescriptorSacl*. With these, you can peel back the contents of a single SD and use the security data therein to verify or change who owns an object and who may access it with which permissions. Of course, your ability to do this depends entirely on whether your code has adequate permission itself when it runs!

by the owner of the object. As you might expect from security information, not just anyone can read either type of ACL. To read the DACL, the requesting process must have READ_CONTROL access on the key. To get this access, the requester must either own the key itself or the DACL must grant READ_CONTROL to the account under which the requester is running.

System ACLs are trickier. They can only be read by applications that have been granted the ACCESS_SYSTEM_SECURITY permission; in turn, the only way to get ACCESS_SYSTEM_SECURITY is for the calling process to ask for the SE_SECURITY_NAME privilege, open the key with a REGSAM value of ACCESS_SYSTEM_SECURITY, then turn off SE_SECURITY_NAME again.

To actually retrieve a key's security data (assuming you've fulfilled the access control requirements), you can use *RegGetKeySecurity*. Besides passing in the key whose information you want, you must also fill in the *SecurityInformation* field to indicate which data you want. If you have permission, *pSecurityDescriptor* will be filled with the ACL or ownership data on return, and *lpcbSecurityDescriptor* will contain the ACL size. ACLs vary in size, since they may contain one or many entries.

```
LONG RegGetKeySecurity (hKey, SecurityInformation, pSecurityDescriptor,
    lpcbSecurityDescriptor);
```

HKEY	hKey	Open Registry key whose security information you want
SECURITY_INFOR-MATION	SecurityInfor-mation	SECURITY_INFORMATION structure indicating what parts of the security descriptor you're asking for; may be any combination of items from Table 7-3.
PSECURITY_DESCRIPTOR	pSecurityDe-scriptor	Pointer to record to receive the security descriptor specified by *SecurityInformation*
LPDWORD	lpcbSecurityDe-scriptor	Points to a DWORD; on entry, it must hold the size of *pSecurityDescriptor*, and on return it contains the size, in bytes, of the returned security descriptor

If the buffer pointed to by *pSecurityDescriptor* is too small, *RegGetKeySecurity* returns ERROR_INSUFFICIENT_BUFFER and the *lpcbSecurityDescriptor* parameter contains the number of bytes required for the requested security descriptor. This makes it possible to efficiently allocate a buffer of the right size by calling it twice, like this:

```
long retVal = 0, aclSize = 0;
PSECURITY_DESCRIPTOR pWhat = NULL;

retVal = RegGetKeySecurity(theKey, DACL_SECURITY_INFORMATION, pWhat, &aclSize);
if (ERROR_INSUFFICIENT_BUFFER  != retVal)
    throw(retVal);
pWhat = malloc(aclSize);
retVal = RegGetKeySecurity(theKey, DACL_SECURITY_INFORMATION, pWhat, &aclSize);
if (ERROR_SUCCESS != retVal)
    throw(retVal);
```

Setting an item's security information

WARNING   If you're not thoroughly familiar with how NT's security system works, stay away from *RegSetKeySecurity* until you have a good set of Registry backups. Setting the wrong permissions on a key is much easier to do programmatically than through any of the GUI editing tools, so please be very careful.

Once you've gotten a security descriptor and modified it,* you can write it back to the key that owns it with *RegSetKeySecurity*.

```
LONG RegSetKeySecurity (hKey, SecurityInformation, pSecurityDescriptor);
```

HKEY	hKey	Open Registry key whose security descriptor you want to set
SECURITY_INFOR-MATION	SecurityInfor-mation	SECURITY_INFORMATION structure indicating what parts of the security descriptor you're changing
PSECURITY_DESCRIPTOR	pSecurityDe-scriptor	Pointer to security descriptor containing ACL data you want to apply to *hKey*

To ensure that your new security data gets written, you should call *RegCloseKey* on the modified key after successfully calling *RegSetKeySecurity*. This is true even if you've set security on one of the root keys; it won't actually be closed, but its cached security data will be updated.

Connecting to Remote Computers

In Chapters 4 and 5, you learned how to use *RegEdit* and *RegEdt32* to edit Registry data on remote computers. Adding this same functionality to your own programs is trivial: all you need to do is call *RegConnectRegistry* and use the HKEY it returns in any other calls you make to Registry API functions. When you're finished with the remote key, you call *RegCloseKey* on it as though it were a local key. The API function declaration looks like the following.

```
LONG RegConnectRegistry(lpMachineName, hKey, phkResult);
```

LPSTR	lpMachineName	Name of the remote machine you want to connect to; must not include the leading backslashes
HKEY	hKey	Root key you want to connect to: may be either HKLM or HKU
PHKEY	phkResult	Pointer to returned key in remote Registry

HasPackage (shown in Example 7-3) showcases *RegConnectRegistry* in action. You supply it with a machine name and a subkey; it checks the Registry on the specified machine to see whether it has a subkey of HKLM\SOFTWARE by the name you specify. The call to *RegConnectRegistry* and the corresponding *RegCloseKey* on the key it returns are the only changes needed to enable remote Registry connections in this small program.

Example 7-3. HasPackage

```
void main(int argc, char **argv)
{
```

---

* I'm not about to talk about how you actually create or modify ACLs; that's a book all by itself.

Example 7-3. HasPackage (continued)

```
char      lpName[MAX_PATH];
HKEY      hkRemoteKey = NULL, hkResult = NULL;
DWORD     dwIdx = 0;
LONG      nResult = ERROR_SUCCESS;
memset(lpName, 0x0, MAX_PATH);

// preflight our arguments
if (argc < 3)
    DoUsage(argv[0]);

nResult = RegConnectRegistry(argv[1], HKEY_LOCAL_MACHINE, &hkRemoteKey);
if (ERROR_SUCCESS == nResult)
{
    sprintf(lpName, "SOFTWARE\\%s", argv[2]);
    nResult = RegOpenKeyEx(hkRemoteKey, lpName, 0L, KEY_READ, &hkResult);
    if (ERROR_SUCCESS == nResult)
    {
        fprintf(stdout, "%s has a key for %s.\n", argv[1], argv[2]);
    }
    else
    {
        fprintf(stderr,
            "Error %d while opening SOFTWARE\\%s on remote machine %s\n",
            argv[2], argv[1]);
    }
    nResult = RegCloseKey(hkResult);
    nResult = RegCloseKey(hkRemoteKey);
}
else
{
    fprintf(stderr, "Error %d while opening remote registry on %s\n",
        nResult, argv[1]);
}

fflush(stdout);
}
```

Moving Keys To and From Hives

In Chapters 3, 4, and 5 you learned how to use the Registry editor functions that allow keys and values to be saved into hive files and later restored. You can do the same thing with your own code by using the routines discussed in this section.

Saving keys

The first step in moving hives around is to be able to create a hive; you can do this with *RegSaveKey.*

```
LONG RegSaveKey(hKey, lpFile, lpSecurityAttributes);
```

HKEY	hKey	Key to be saved; must be open. Everything below the specified key will be saved
LPCTSTR	lpFile	Full path of file to save in
LPSECURITY_ATTRIBUTES	lpSecurityAttributes	Pointer to SECURITY_ATTRIBUTES structure describing desired security on the new file; pass in NULL to use the process's default security descriptor

If the file you specify in *lpFile* already exists, *RegSaveKey* will fail with the ERROR_ALREADY_EXISTS error code. This prevents you from accidentally overwriting another hive file you'd previously saved. There's another subtlety involved with *lpFile*: if you don't specify a full path, the file will be created in the process's current directory if the key's from the local Registry, on return or *%systemroot%\ system32* for a key on a remote machine.

The created file will have the archive attribute set, and it will have whatever permissions are specified by *lpSecurityAttributes*. Instead of creating a brand-new security descriptor, you may pass NULL to have whatever security context applies to the process applied to the file.

Loading keys

Once you've saved keys into a hive file, the next thing you're likely to want to do is load them. You can do so in two distinct ways: you can load a hive as a new key, or you can replace the contents of an existing key with the hive's contents. Either approach requires the process that loads the keys to have the SE_RESTORE_NAME privilege.

RegLoadKey supports the former: you tell it what file to load and what to name the new subkey, and it will create the specified subkey and load the file into it. *RegLoadKey* will fail if the file doesn't exist or if the named subkey does exist.

```
LONG RegLoadKey(hKey, lpSubKey, lpFile);
```

HKEY	hKey	Open key under which the new subkey will be created; may be HKLM or HKU on a local machine, or a handle obtained by opening HKLM or HKU with *RegConnectRegistry*.
LPCTSTR	lpSubKey	Name of the subkey to create beneath *hKey*; the subkey must not currently exist.
LPCTSTR	lpFile	Full path name to the hive file you want to load into the new key. This file must have been created with *RegSaveKey* or *RegEdt32*'s Registry ➤ Save Key command.

TIP   Calling *RegCloseKey* on a key loaded with *RegLoadKey* will not
                   unload it; instead, you must call *RegUnloadKey* as described below.

If you want to overwrite an existing key that's part of one of the standard hives,
you can instead call *RegRestoreKey*. Like *RegLoadKey*, it takes a parent key and
the name of a file to load. However, in this case the parent key's subkeys will all
be replaced by the contents of the file. For example, if you open HKLM\SOFT-
WARE\Microsoft\Windows and pass that to *RegRestoreKey*, the key with that
name will persist, but every subkey and value beneath it will be deleted. After
RegRestoreKey returns, the victim key will contain whatever values and subkeys
were in the loaded file.

```
LONG RegRestoreKey(hKey, lpFile, dwFlags);
```

HKEY	hKey	Key whose values and subkeys you want to replace
LPCTSTR	lpFile	File (saved with *RegSaveKey* or *RegEdt32*) with the new contents you want loaded into *hKey*
DWORD	dwFlags	If you pass in 0 for this parameter, the entire *hKey* is replaced; if you pass in REG_WHOLE_HIVE_VOLATILE, *hKey* is replaced but the changes are not written to the Registry

Replacing a loaded key

Once you've loaded a hive file with *RegLoadKey*, you can replace the loaded key
with another hive file. This is a good way to dynamically swap between several
hives' worth of data. Changes don't take effect until the machine is restarted,
though.

```
LONG RegReplaceKey(hKey, lpSubKey, lpNewFile, lpOldFile);
```

HKEY	hKey	Open key that contains subkey you want to replace
LPCTSTR	lpSubKey	Contains the name of the subkey whose values and subkeys will be replaced by the newly loaded hive
LPCTSTR	lpNewFile	Contains full path to the hive file you want loaded; the file must be generated by *RegSaveKey* or *RegEdt32*
LPCTSTR	lpOldFile	Contains the name of a file to which NT will save a backup copy of the previously loaded hive file

Unloading a key

RegLoadKey allows you to load a stored hive file as a new hive under HKLM or
HKU. Once you've loaded a hive, it makes sense to have a way to unload it when
you're done, and *RegUnloadKey* provides that functionality.

```
LONG RegUnLoadKey(hKey, lpSubKey);
```

HKEY	hKey	Handle to an open key
LPCTSTR	lpSubKey	Full path to the subkey you want to unload

You may only unload keys you loaded yourself; this prevents you from unloading (accidentally or on purpose) an important key like HKLM\SOFTWARE. The process that calls *RegUnloadKey* must have the special SE_RESTORE_NAME privilege.

Getting Notification when Something Changes

If you wanted to write a program that would do something when a particular Registry key or value was changed, you could do it by sitting in an infinite loop and periodically checking the item of interest to see whether it had changed. This would be terribly inefficient, though, so it's a good thing there's another way to do it. The *RegNotifyChangeKeyValue* routine allows you to register your interest in a particular key or value, then go do something else. NT will notify you when the Registry key (or its attributes) changes; it won't, however, tell you if the key is deleted.

```
LONG RegNotifyChangeKeyValue (hKey, bWatchSubtree, dwNotifyFilter, hEvent
    fAsynchronous);
```

HKEY	hKey	Key you want to monitor for changes; may be a root key or any subkey.
BOOL	bWatchSubtree	When true, indicates that you want to watch all subkeys and values of *hKey*; when false, indicates that you want to watch *hKey* only.
DWORD	dwNotifyFilter	Flag specifying what events you're interested in; may be any combination of REG_NOTIFY_CHANGE_ NAME for renaming, addition, or deletion of a subkey, REG_NOTIFY_CHANGE_ATTRIBUTES for changes to any key attributes, REG_NOTIFY_ CHANGE_LAST_SET for changes to a value of a subkey, and REG_NOTIFY_CHANGE_SECURITY for changes to security.
HANDLE	hEvent	Event to post when a change is detected; ignored if *fAsynchronous* is false.
BOOL	fAsynchronous	When true, routine returns immediately and posts an event when a change takes place; when false, routine blocks until a change occurs

Flushing Registry Changes

The Registry uses a "lazy flusher" to propagate changes from memory to disk. The overall goal is to minimize the number of disk I/O operations, since they tend to be relatively expensive. The lazy flusher achieves this goal by not immediately writing every change out to disk as it occurs; instead, it aggregates changes and writes them when the system is mostly idle.

When you call *RegCloseKey*, whatever changes you've made are thus not immediately copied to disk. There can be an interlude of indeterminate length (Microsoft says "as long as several seconds" without elaborating) before your data actually hits the disk. For most applications, this is perfectly acceptable. However, if for some reason you really, really want to make sure your changes get written to disk, you can use the *RegFlushKey* routine to immediately force a Registry update:

```
LONG RegFlushKey (hKey);
```

Calling this routine will force the lazy flusher to buckle down and flush the specified key's data to its hive file; it may also cause other keys to be written as well. The Win32 SDK warns that this function is expensive, so you shouldn't call it often. *RegFlushKey* returns ERROR_SUCCESS when all goes well, or a standard NT error code for failed flush attempts.

Programming with C/C++

The API examples and documentation in earlier sections all present the Registry API in its native C/C++ form. Since many NT administrators are comfortable with C and/or C++, I'll start the programming examples by presenting three distinct uses for the Registry API routines I've already presented.

Example: Watching a Key for Changes

RegNotifyChangeKeyValue is a little-used, but very useful, routine. It's only present in NT, which perhaps accounts for its relative anonymity. If you need to be notified when a key or its values changes, it's the best tool for getting you that notification. *WatchKey*, shown in Example 7-4, is a small utility that takes advantage of *RegNotifyChangeKeyValue* to warn you when a key you specify has been changed.

How the code works

After a check of its initial command-line arguments, the code performs the following steps:

1. It identifies which root key "owns" the key you want to monitor; this is required because *RegOpenKeyEx* needs an already-open key (i.e., one of the roots) to open the target key. If it can't figure out which root the user specified, it prints an error and exits.

2. It captures the path name of the key to monitor and uses it, along with the root key, to call *RegOpenKeyEx*. The key is opened with KEY_READ access,

which includes **KEY_NOTIFY** access too. If the key can't be opened, we generate an error message and exit.

3. The target key is monitored with a call to *RegNotifyChangeKeyValue*. We pass **TRUE** for the *bWatchSubtree* parameter so that any change to a key or value beneath the target key will generate a notification. We pass all available event flags for the *dwNotifyFilter* parameter so that we'll be kept apprised of any changes. No event handle is passed in, and the *fAsynchronous* parameter is set to **TRUE** so that the process will block until a change occurs.

Example 7-4. The watchkey Utility

```c
// WatchKey.c
// Watches the key you specify until it changes, then displays the time and date
// when the change occurred.

#include <windows.h>
#include <stdio.h>
#include <time.h>


// error codes we generate
#define kBadParams    1
#define kNoRootKey    2
#define kCantOpenPath 3


static const HKEY hkRootList[5] = {HKEY_LOCAL_MACHINE, HKEY_CURRENT_USER, HKEY_
USERS, HKEY_CURRENT_CONFIG, HKEY_CLASSES_ROOT};
static const char *lpRootNames[5] = {"HKLM", "HKCU", "HKU", "HKCC", "HKCR"};

void DoUsage(const char *inName);


void DoUsage(const char *inName)
{
    printf("%s: improper command-line parameters\n", inName);
    printf("\tUsage: %s root path\n", inName);
    printf("\t\troot\tRoot key to monitor; may be HKLM, HKCC, HKCR,
        HKU, or HKCU\n");
    printf("\t\tpath\tFull path to subkey you want to monitor\n");
}


void main(int argc, char **argv)
{
    char     lpPath[MAX_PATH];
    HKEY     hkRoot = NULL, hkResult = NULL;
    DWORD    dwIdx = 0, dwRootIdx = 0;
    LONG     nResult = ERROR_SUCCESS;

    memset(lpPath, 0x0, MAX_PATH);
```

Example 7-4. The watchkey Utility (continued)

```
    // preflight our arguments
    if (3 != argc)
    {
        DoUsage(argv[0]);
        return;
    }

    // first argument must be the root key name
    while (5 > dwIdx && 0 == dwRootIdx)
    {
        if (0 == strcmp(lpRootNames[dwIdx], argv[1]))
            dwRootIdx = dwIdx;
        else
            dwIdx++;
    }
    if (0 == dwRootIdx)
    {
        DoUsage(argv[0]);
        fprintf(stderr, "!!! no root key named %s\n", argv[1]);
        return;
    }

    // get the path name
    strncpy(lpPath, argv[2], max(MAX_PATH, strlen(argv[2])));

    // open the corresponding key
    nResult = RegOpenKeyEx(hkRootList[dwRootIdx], lpPath, 0L, KEY_READ,
        &hkResult);
    if (ERROR_SUCCESS != nResult)
    {
        fprintf(stderr, "Error %d while opening %s\n", nResult, lpPath);
        fflush(stderr);
        return;
    }

    // watch it until something happens or the program's terminated
    fprintf(stderr, "Watching %s\\%s...\n", lpRootNames[dwRootIdx], lpPath);
    fflush(stderr);

    nResult = RegNotifyChangeKeyValue(hkResult,
                                      true,          // tell us if subkeys change
                                      REG_NOTIFY_CHANGE_NAME +
                                      REG_NOTIFY_CHANGE_ATTRIBUTES +
                                      REG_NOTIFY_CHANGE_LAST_SET +
                                      REG_NOTIFY_CHANGE_SECURITY,
                                      NULL,          // don't pass an event
                                      false          // wait; don't be
                                                     // asynchronous
                                      );
```

Example 7-4. The watchkey Utility (continued)

```
    if (ERROR_SUCCESS != nResult)
    {
        fprintf(stderr, "Error %d while monitoring %s\n", nResult, lpPath);
        fflush(stderr);
        return;
    }

    // if we're still here, that means the key was changed
    time_t now = time((long *)NULL);
    fprintf(stderr, "!!! Key %s\\%s changed at %s", lpRootNames[dwRootIdx],
            lpPath, ctime(&now));
    fflush(stderr);
}
```

Possible enhancements

WatchKey is a useful tool as it stands right now, but (as with almost every pro-gram ever written) it could be enhanced. Here are a few suggestions to get you thinking about how you could apply what you've learned:

- The first, and most obvious, improvement would be to let users specify val-ues for the *bWatchSubtree* and *dwFilterOptions* parameters, thus making the actual watching more flexible.

- Instead of just printing out the date and time when a modification occurred, you could generate an Event Log entry.

- Since *RegNotifyKeyValueChange* can function asynchronously, you could mod-ify the code in Example 7-4 so that it spawns a separate watcher thread for each key you want to monitor at one time; in conjunction with event logging, this would provide a low-overhead auditing mechanism that could be applied only to keys you're interested in.

Example: A Stack-Based Wrapper Class

Earlier in the chapter, I alluded to a neat C++ feature that is sadly underutilized. Whenever you create an C++ object, its constructor is called. When you're done with the object and are ready to delete it, you call a disposal method that calls the object's destructor. Calls to these methods are supposed to balance so that you never construct anything that doesn't get destroyed, and you don't destroy any object more than once. This may sound suspiciously like the rule for Registry keys: open them, use them, and always close them.

If you create automatic objects on the stack, the compiler will automatically call the objects' destructors when it's time to destroy them. This may happen because your code has finished executing the scope where the objects are, or it may be because a jump or exception caused the objects to go out of scope. Here's a very small example:

```
void test(void)
{
    anObject A;

    A.doSomething();
    if (A.IsEmpty())
        throw(kRanOutOfData);
    A.DoSomethingElse();
    if (A.IsFull())
        throw(kTooMuchData);
}
```

When this function starts up, *A* is allocated on the stack and its constructor is called. The destructor may potentially be called in three cases: when the function returns normally, when *kRanOutOfData* is thrown, or when *kTooMuchData* is thrown. No matter how we leave this function, *A*'s destructor will get a chance to clean up whatever the constructor did.

Example 7-5 shows the class definition for a stack-based Registry key class. The constructor opens the key you specify, and the destructor closes it again. In between, there are members for getting and setting individual values.

Example 7-5. The StKey Class Definition

```
class StKey
{
    public:
        StKey(HKEY inRoot, LPCTSTR inPath, REGSAM inAccess = KEY_READ);
        ~StKey();

        LONG GetDWORDValue(LPCTSTR inValName, DWORD &outCount);
        LONG GetStringValue(LPCTSTR inValName, LPSTR outValue, DWORD &ioBufSize);
        LONG GetValueCount(DWORD &outCount);

        LONG SetDWORDValue(LPCTSTR inValName, const DWORD inVal);
        LONG SetStringValue(LPCTSTR inValName, LPCTSTR inVal,
                        const DWORD inBufSize = 0, DWORD inType = REG_SZ);

        LONG AddDWORDValue(LPCTSTR inValName, const DWORD inVal);
        LONG AddStringValue(LPCTSTR inValName, LPCTSTR inVal,
                        const DWORD inBufSize = 0, DWORD inType = REG_SZ);

    private:
        HKEY mCurrKey;
};
```

How the code works

Example 7-6 shows the actual implementation of the *StKey* class.* The constructor and destructor are straightforward: they open and close the requested key, and that's it! Likewise, there's nothing magic about the *GetValueCount*, *GetDWORD-Value*, or *GetStringValue* members.

The most interesting piece is actually the *SetStringValue* member. It handles more than one type of Registry string; you probably remember that values may contain plain strings (**REG_SZ**), expandable strings (**REG_EXPAND_SZ**), or multiple strings (**REG_MULTI_SZ**). *SetStringValue* correctly creates values of all three types; in addition, it's smart enough to figure out the correct string length based on the input type.

Example 7-6. The StKey Class Implementation

```
StKey::StKey(HKEY inRoot, LPCTSTR inPath, REGSAM inAccess /* = KEY_READ */)
{
    long nResult = 0;
    mCurrKey = NULL;
    nResult = RegOpenKeyEx(inRoot, inPath, 0L, inAccess, &mCurrKey);
    if (ERROR_SUCCESS != nResult)
        mCurrKey = NULL;
}


StKey::~StKey()
{
    if (mCurrKey)
    {
        RegCloseKey(mCurrKey);
        mCurrKey = NULL;
    }
}


LONG StKey::GetValueCount(DWORD &outCount)
{
    return RegQueryInfoKey (mCurrKey,
                          NULL, NULL, NULL,
                          NULL, NULL, NULL,
                          &outCount,
                          NULL, NULL, NULL, NULL);
}


LONG StKey::GetDWORDValue(LPCTSTR inValName, DWORD &outValue)
{
```

---

* I omitted *AddDWORDValue* and *AddStringValue* from the example because they just call the corresponding *Set* routines.

Example 7-6. The StKey Class Implementation (continued)

```
    DWORD sz = sizeof(DWORD);
    return RegQueryValue(mCurrKey, inValName, (LPTSTR)&outValue, (long *)&sz);
}


LONG StKey::GetStringValue(LPCTSTR inValName, LPTSTR outValue, DWORD &ioBufSize)
{
    DWORD sz = sizeof(DWORD);
    return RegQueryValue(mCurrKey, inValName, outValue, (long *)&ioBufSize);
}


LONG StKey::SetDWORDValue(LPCTSTR inValName, const DWORD inVal)
{
    return RegSetValueEx(mCurrKey, inValName, 0L, REG_DWORD, (BYTE *)&inVal,
            sizeof(DWORD));
}


LONG StKey::SetStringValue(LPCTSTR inValName, LPCTSTR inVal,
            const DWORD inBufSize /* = 0*/,
            DWORD inType /*= REG_SZ*/)
{
    if (!IsValidStringType(inType))
        return ERROR_INVALID_PARAMETER;
    if (0 == inBufSize && REG_MULTI_SZ == inType)
        return ERROR_INVALID_PARAMETER;
    return RegSetValueEx(mCurrKey, inValName, 0L, inType, (BYTE *)inVal,
                    (inBufSize ? inBufSize : strlen(inVal)));
}


LONG StKey::AddDWORDValue(LPCTSTR inValName, const DWORD inVal)
{
    return SetDWORDValue(inValName, inVal);
}


LONG StKey::AddStringValue(LPCTSTR inValName, LPCTSTR inVal,
            const DWORD inBufSize /* = 0*/,
            DWORD inType /*= REG_SZ*/)
{
    return SetStringValue(inValName, inVal, inBufSize, inType);
}
```

Possible enhancements

You could easily extend this class to support a Standard Template Library-style iterator capability for value. This would make it easy to iterate through all values of a subkey in a structured, exception-safe manner. You could also make the constructor smarter, perhaps by allowing it to recognize and parse a fully qualified path like "\\enigma\HKLM\SOFTWARE\LJL\SMIME\Users" instead of requiring the root key and path to be separate. For a real treat, consider building a stack-based class that loads and unloads hive files!

Example: Loading A Control with a Set Of Values

If you store useful data as values attached to a subkey, at some point you'll want to get them out again. In writing an S/MIME-compliant electronic mail client, I found that I needed to get a list of stored user profiles (which we keep in HKLM\ SOFTWARE\LJL\SMIME\Users) and display them in a dropdown list so the user can efficiently pick a profile to use when logging in. The actual code that does so is in Example 7-7; it's fairly straightforward.

Example 7-7. Move the Values from a Key into a Windows Combo or List Box

```
#include <windows.h>

typedef enum {eCombo=0, eList} eBoxType;

HRESULT LoadBoxWithUsers(eBoxType inBoxType, HWND inControl, LPSTR inDefName,
                    int &outSelected)
{
    DWORD   nResult = ERROR_SUCCESS;
    HKEY    hkFirstKey;
    HRESULT retVal = 0;
    long idx = 0;
    DWORD dwValCount = 0;

    SendMessage(inControl, (eCombo ==
                inBoxType ? CB_RESETCONTENT : LB_RESETCONTENT),
                (WPARAM)0, (LPARAM)0);
    outSelected = 0;

    // try to open HKLM\SOFTWARE\SMAIL; if we succeed, enumerate
    // through its subkeys and return the first one
    nResult = RegOpenKeyEx(HKEY_LOCAL_MACHINE, "SOFTWARE\\LJL\\SMIME\\Users",
                    0L, KEY_READ, &hkFirstKey);
    if (ERROR_SUCCESS == nResult)
    {
        char *lpName = NULL;
        DWORD dwNameLen = 0;

        // find out what the longest subkey is and how many values exist
        nResult = RegQueryInfoKey (hkFirstKey,
                        NULL, NULL,   // class & class size
                        NULL,         // reserved
                        NULL,         // # of subkeys
                        NULL,         // longest subkey length
                        NULL,         // class length
                        &dwValCount,  // # of values
                        NULL, NULL,
```

Example 7-7. Move the Values from a Key into a Windows Combo or List Box (continued)

```
                              &dwNameLen,     // longest value contents
                              NULL);

        // allocate buffers based on what we just learned
        lpName = (char *)malloc(dwNameLen);

        for (idx = 0; idx <= dwValCount; idx++)
        {
            nResult = RegEnumValue(hkFirstKey, idx, lpName, &dwNameLen, NULL,
                            NULL, NULL, NULL);
            if (ERROR_NO_MORE_ITEMS != nResult)
                SendMessage(inControl, (eCombo == inBoxType ? CB_INSERTSTRING :
                        LB_INSERTSTRING), (WPARAM)-1, (LPARAM)lpName);

            // if this item matches the default, return it as a match
            if (inDefName && stricmp(lpName, inDefName) == 0)
                outSelected = idx;
            memset(lpName, 0x0, MAX_PATH); dwNameLen = MAX_PATH;
        }
        nResult = RegCloseKey(hkFirstKey);
      SendMessage(inControl, (eCombo == inBoxType ?CB_SETCURSEL :
                        LB_SETCURSEL),(WPARAM)outSelected, (LPARAM)0);
        free(lpName);
    }
    else
        retVal = E_NOT_FOUND;
    return retVal;
}
```

The first thing this code does is clear out the Windows list/combo box control; once that's done, it opens the key where the values I'm interested in are stored. If *RegOpenKeyEx* succeeds, a call to *RegQueryInfoKey* returns the length of the longest value and the number of values attached to the key.

With that information in hand, it's easy to iterate through the values by repeatedly calling *RegEnumValue*. As each value is retrieved, it's added to the combo box. If the caller specified a default value for the combo box, when that value is encountered its index is saved so I can preset the combo box's selection. This makes it possible to remember the user's last selection and have it appear as the selection when the program's next run.

Programming with Perl

Ahhh, Perl!* Once upon a time its power and entertainment value were reserved solely for Unix administrators. A long line of Windows programmers have labored

---

* Since this *is* an O'Reilly book, I was sternly admonished to talk about Perl.

to bring the Perl toolset to Win32; in doing so, they've added some nifty features not present in other platforms' Perl implementations. One of those features is surprisingly complete support for the Win32 Registry API. (To run any of the code in this section, you'll need Perl for Win32; it's available from *http://www.activestate.com/.)* Throughout the rest of this section, I'm going to assume that you're familiar with Perl syntax and semantics, particularly the Perl implementation of objects and modules. (If you're not, I highly recommend *Learning Perl On Win32 Systems* by Randal Schwartz, Erik Olson, and Tom Christiansen, O'Reilly & Associates, 1997.)

NOTE   Time for a disclaimer: I'm not much of a Perl hacker. Because There's More Than One Way To Do It, I welcome your suggestions for how the code in this section can be improved.

Perl for Win32 implements the Perl language and adds a huge wad of Win32-specific extensions; these extensions allow you to write Perl programs that use OLE Automation, the Registry, the NT accounts database, and many other Microsoft-specific features. If you don't use these extensions, you can write plain vanilla Perl and it will work fine, but the extensions let you use Perl's expressive power to make short work of tasks like creating batches of user accounts (as described in *Windows NT User Administration* by Timothy D. Ritchey and Ashley J. Meggitt; O'Reilly & Associates, 1997).

There are several ways to extend Perl for operating-system-specific functions. Perl for Win32 (which I'll just call Perl from now on) uses Perl modules; these modules add new definitions, keywords, and data types to the base language. The modules specify functionality; the actual implementation is usually done in external C or C++ code, wrapped as a DLL-like object called a PLL.

The Win32::RegXXX Functions

The Win32 Perl module includes definitions that correspond to each of the standard C function definitions described in "Programming with C/C++," earlier in this chapter. (Actually, *RegQueryMultipleValues* isn't implemented.) You can use them just like you'd use the C or Visual Basic equivalents; the one difference is that you should qualify the routine names by specifying that they come from the Win32 module. Example 7-8 shows what the program from Example 7-1 looks like when rewritten in Perl with the standard Win32 module's calls:.

Example 7-8. "Hello, World" from Example 7-1, Rewritten in Perl

```
require "NT.ph";
use Win32;
```

Example 7-8. "Hello, World" from Example 7-1, Rewritten in Perl (continued)

```
Win32::RegOpenKeyEx ( &HKEY_LOCAL_MACHINE,
        "SYSTEM\\CurrentControlSet\\Control\\ComputerName\\ActiveComputerName",
              &NULL, &KEY_READ, $theKey ) || die ("Couldn't open name key!");

Win32::RegQueryValueEx($theKey, 'ComputerName',
                        &NULL,             # our friend lpReserved
                        &NULL,             # type parameter
                        $who);
print "This computer is named $who\n";

Win32::RegCloseKey($theKey);
```

The first line imports a set of Win32 constant definitions; this is the rough equivalent of `#include <windows.h>` in a C program. The second line imports the Win32 module definitions themselves. The real fun starts with the call to *Win32::RegOpenKeyEx*. The most unusual feature of this call is that the constant parameters are passed by reference; other than that (and the call to `die`) it looks much like the C and Visual Basic calls discussed in other sections of this chapter.

Likewise, the call to *Win32::RegQueryValueEx* looks almost like the other languages' equivalents. One difference is that the value's returned in *$who*; since Perl doesn't need the length of the data in *$who,* there's no parameter for it. There is a parameter that can return the value's type, but in this case it's useless so I passed in `&NULL` instead of a variable reference.

Finally, once the computer name's been printed, *Win32::RegCloseKey* closes the key we opened. This is just as necessary in Perl as anywhere else; when you open an `HKEY`, NT needs to know when you're finished with it.

When to use them

If you're already comfortable with the C or Visual Basic interfaces, then the Win32 equivalents will seem familiar, because they are. In addition, the functions listed in Table 7-4 don't exist in the standard *Win32::Registry* distribution. If you're fluent in Perl, you can easily add routines you need (see "Shortcomings of registry.pm" later in this chapter for some hints on doing so), but you may find it less work to use the existing routines, perhaps intermixing them with calls to *Win32::Registry* methods.

Table 7-4. Some Registry Functions Are Only Available Through the Win32 Module

RegCreateKeyEx	RegEnumKey	RegEnumKeyEx
RegEnumValue	RegFlushKey	RegGetKeySecurity
RegNotifyChangeKeyValue	RegOpenKeyEx	RegQueryValueEx
RegReplaceKey	RegRestoreKey	RegRestoreKey
RegSetKeySecurity	RegUnLoadKey	ReqQueryInfoKey

The Win32::Registry Module

One of the big advances in Perl 5.x over its predecessors was the concept of a Perl object. Just like other object-oriented languages, Perl objects encapsulate both data and behavior; in addition, they follow the standard Perl practice of not requiring any kind of dynamic allocation to make them work. Compare the original Perl "Hello, world" program in Example 7-7 to the version shown in Example 7-9.

Example 7-9. Perl "Hello, World" Rewritten with the Win32::Registry Module

```
require "NT.ph";
use Win32::Registry;

$main::HKEY_LOCAL_MACHINE->Open( "SYSTEM\\CurrentControlSet\\Control\\
              ComputerName\\ActiveComputerName", $theKey )
   || die ("Couldn't open name key!");

$theKey->QueryValue('ComputerName',&NULL, $who);
print "This computer is named $who\n";

$theKey->Close();
```

To start with, instead of importing all of *Win32* we import only the Registry package (though we still need *NT.ph*). The big surprise starts on the next line: instead of calling *RegOpenKeyEx*, we call something named *$main::HKEY_LOCAL_ MACHINE->Open*. This is more sensible than perhaps it appears at first: in Perl, you can refer to any item anywhere in any Perl module by qualifying it with *$main*. It also helps if you know that the *Win32::Registry* module predefines objects for HKLM, HKU, HKCU, and HKCR, but they're named after the actual root keys. Just like C and C++, Perl uses the arrow operator (->) to indicate things that belong to an object, so *HKEY_LOCAL_MACHINE->Open()* is a call to a method defined as part of the *HKEY_LOCAL_MACHINE* object. Notice that the call to the *Open()* method looks much like *RegOpenKey*; it doesn't make any provision for the extra parameters present in *RegOpenKeyEx*, meaning that you can't request a particular set of permissions.

One more difference: instead of returning an HKEY, *Open()* returns another Perl object when it opens the key. *theKey* thus has all the same methods as the predefined root keys (or any other Registry object for that matter). Immediately after opening the new *theKey* object, we call its *QueryValue* method to get the value back. The second parameter would normally contain the value's type, which isn't useful in this example—passing &NULL forces *QueryValue* not to return any type data. When we're all done, we call *theKey*'s *Close()* method to close the key.

TIP   Internally, all the routines in *Win32::Registry* call the Win32 API rou-
                  tines, either directly or out of the *Win32* module. That means that
                  any limitations described earlier in "The Registry API" still pertain to
                  these calls, even though they're not completely identical to the origi-
                  nal routine definitions.

Opening and closing keys

Before you can do anything to a key or value, you must have an open key. These
are the most basic operations in Perl's Registry module, and they're pretty much
the same as they are everywhere else. You open keys with the *Open* method of
an already opened key (usually one of the root keys); it accepts the full path of
the key to be opened as an input and returns an object representing the newly
opened key:

```
$RegObj->Open( subkeyName, $SubKeyObj )
```

Once you're done manipulating a key, you should close it with the *Close* method:

```
$RegObj->Close( );
```

Creating keys

You can create a new subkey beneath an open key with the *Create* method. *Create* will create the requested key if it doesn't exist and return a reference to it; if
the key does exist, *Create* will open it for you.

```
$RegObj->Create( subkeyName, $subkeyOb j)
```

Unlike the original Win32 *RegCreateKeyEx*, this version won't create keys more
than one level below the original key. Since *Create* requires an open key to do its
magic, you may have to do something like this if you want to create a key that's
several levels down from one of the root keys:

```
# Create HKLM\SOFTWARE\LJL\SMIME\Users if it doesn't already exist
$main::HKEY_LOCAL_MACHINE->Open("SOFTWARE", $softwareKey )
    || die ("Couldn't open name key!");

$softwareKey->Create("LJL", $ljlKey);
$ljlKey->Create("SMIME", $smimeKey);
$smimeKey->Create("Users", $userKey);

# do something with userKey

$softwareKey->Close();
$ljlKey->Close();
$smimeKey->Close();
$userKey->Close();
```

The alternative is to extend *Create* to allow it to create nested keys, as described a little later in "Shortcomings of registry.pm." Furthermore, remember that this *Create* doesn't have a way for you to apply a security mask, so you may want to use *Win32::RegCreateKeyEx* instead.

Getting information about keys

You can query any key (not just an open one) to find out how many subkeys and values it has with the *QueryKey* method. This is mostly useful for satisfying your own curiosity, since you don't need to know how many keys or values a key has to get all the data (as you'll see in the next section).

```
$RegObj-> QueryKey( $keyToQuery, $subkeyCount, $valueCount )
```

Enumerating keys and values

Now it's time for a brief digression into Perl-land. (If you're already fluent, just skip down to the next paragraph.) Like practically every other computer language ever invented, Perl supports arrays. Perl also supports a data type called a *hash*. You may be familiar with the underlying concept under another name, like "associative array" or "dictionary list." A hash is just a data structure that maps a key to some data; it's like an array, but instead of being indexed by positive integers it's indexed by values.* *Win32::Registry* features two extremely useful routines that use arrays and hashes to grab large chunks of Registry data and prepare it for enumeration: *GetKeys* and *GetValues*:

```
$RegObj->GetKeys( @keyArray )
$RegObj->GetValues( %valueHashRef )
```

As you'd expect, *GetKeys* fills its array with the names of all subkeys of the requested key; it doesn't recurse down the tree, so the subkeys in its array represent only the first level beneath the requested key. When you call it, you must provide a reference to the array you want to store the keys in, and not the array itself. That means you have to add the \ reference operator in front of the array name.

GetValues is a little different. It retrieves a subkey's value list into a three-element hash. Each value has an entry; each entry contains the value's name, type, and contents. The name is used as the key, and the other values are stored "underneath" the key. *GetValues* also expects a reference, so you need the \ operator when calling it as well.

Example 7-10 illustrates one way you might put *GetKeys* and *GetValues* to use. After opening the key of interest, it calls *GetKeys* to get a list of the subject key's

---

* For much more on hashes, see Chapter 7 of *Learning Perl on Win32 Systems*, Chapter 5 of the original *Learning Perl*, or the heavy-duty *Programming Perl*.

subkeys. Once it has that list, it uses the **foreach** operator to print each key in the array. Next, a call to *GetValues* fills a hash with the names and contents of all the target key's values; another **foreach** statement prints those out too.

Example 7-10. Iterating Through Keys and Values with GetKeys and GetValues

```
use Win32::Registry;

$p = "System\\CurrentControlSet\\Services\\LanmanServer";
$main::HKEY_LOCAL_MACHINE->Open($p, $params) || die "Open: $!";

print "\nHere are the subkeys of $p:\n";
$params->GetKeys(\@subkeys);
foreach $k (@subkeys)
{
    print "\t$k\n";
}

print "\nHere are the values of $p:\n";
$params->GetValues(\%paramVals);
foreach $k (keys %paramVals)
{
    $key = $paramVals{$k};
    print "\t$$key[0]=$$key[2]\n";
}
```

This is different from the ordinary approach of getting one key or value at a time with the *RegEnum* functions; internally, both *GetKeys* and *GetValues* repeatedly call *RegEnumKeyEx* and *RegEnumValueEx*, but having all the keys or values collected into a single Perl data structure makes it much easier to process the collected elements than the corresponding code in C++ or Visual Basic.

Getting a single value

Win32::Registry only supports one function for getting a single value: *Query-Value*. Unfortunately, this works exactly like the standard *QueryValue* function—it only returns the value of the default or unnamed value entry, making it mostly useless. The solution is simple, though; you can easily extend *QueryValue* to properly retrieve values with names, too; the code in Example 7-9 depends on having this modification, which is included on the O'Reilly web site. See the section "Shortcomings of registry.pm" later in this chapter for details.

```
$regObj-> QueryValue( $valueToQuery, $type, $value )
```

Adding and modifying values

There are two different methods for setting a value in the Registry. Like the standard API, the *SetValue* method assigns contents to the default value. This is of limited use in most situations, but you may find a use for it in your own projects:

```
$regObj->SetValue( $valueName, $valType, $value )
```

When calling *SetValue*, the *valueName* and *valType* parameters are ignored.*

SetValueEx is much more useful; it can set the contents of any value, named or not. In addition, you can specify the type of the value you're storing, which is handy when you're working with something besides **REG_SZ** data.

```
$regObj->SetValueEx( $ valueName, $reserved, $valType, $value )
```

There's no practical difference between adding a new value and updating the contents of an existing one. Both *SetValue* and *SetValueEx* will create a value and set its contents if you call them for a key that doesn't have the named value.

Deleting keys and values

Deleting keys and values is pretty straightforward. The *DeleteKey* method removes the key you specify (which must be a subkey of the object you provide) and all its values. It won't remove the key if it has subkeys, though, so you'll have to delete any subkeys yourself.

```
$regObj->DeleteKey( $targetSubKey )
```

If you want to surgically remove a single value, *DeleteValue* is your best bet; it removes the value name you specify from its parent. This is identical to *RegDeleteValue*; like that function, you can only delete a value from its parent.

```
$regObj->DeleteValue( $targetValue )
```

Saving and loading keys

Win32::Registry includes functions for saving and loading Registry keys, but they're somewhat less flexible than the native API calls. *Save* saves a key and its subkeys and values to a filename you supply. If the file already exists, *Save* will fail. In addition, the account running your Perl program must have the **SE_RESTORE_NAME** privilege.

```
$regObj->Save( $filename )
```

What you save with *Save* can be reloaded with the *Load* function. It's equivalent to *RegLoadKey*, meaning that it will load the key you specify beneath the target subkey, just like *RegLoadKey* does.

```
$regObj->Load( $targetSubKey, $fileName )
```

---

* Many of the *Win32::Registry* routines include arguments that they don't use, all for compatibility with the original Win 3.x API. Old APIs never die...

Shortcomings of registry.pm

While writing this chapter I discovered that the Registry module included with build 313 of the ActiveState Perl distribution had some flaws. The first thing I noticed was that not all of the NT 4.x/5.x root keys are declared: HKCC and HKDD are missing. That was easy to fix. The next thing I noticed was that several useful Registry API routines didn't have counterparts in the module (see Table 7-4, earlier, for a full list of what's missing). For the most part, that's easy to fix too (for example, the *Connect* member for the Registry module is only about eight lines of Perl).

TIP   Philippe Le Berre (*leberre@bandol.grenoble.hp.com*) maintains an
               excellent page of *Win32::Registry* information at *http://www.inforoute.cgs.fr/
               leberre1/*. Many of the fixes discussed in this section came from his
               site.

More seriously, some of the provided routines have limitations or flaws that make them needlessly hard to use:

- *QueryValue* is basically useless as delivered, since it can only query a key's default value. There's no equivalent to *RegQueryValueEx*.

- *Create* can't create entire paths; it's limited to creating one sublevel at a time.

- None of the provided functions give any access to security or permission data. This makes it impossible to follow Microsoft's recommendation of only opening keys with the minimum access you need.

To address these limitations, and to roll in some bug fixes from various parts of the Perl community, I modified *registry.pm* and included it on the web site associated with this book. The changes have been submitted back to ActiveState, keeper of the Win32 Perl flame, and will hopefully be integrated into future builds.

Mixing Win32 and Win32::Registry

The *Win32::Registry* member functions all depend on having a Perl object to work with, and the standard *RegXXX* routines declared in the *Win32* module expect to get an HKEY instead of an object handle. Since every Registry object has a handle, it's fairly straightforward to call *RegXXX* routines from within code that uses the Registry module. The reverse isn't true, though, since the object-based methods can only be called by referencing an object—which the *RegXXX* routines don't have!

To get a key handle from a Registry object, just use it like this:

```
$regObj->('handle')
```

Example: Dumping Keys as Text

Perl excels at processing, formatting, searching, and generally handling textual information. Since the Registry is really one big binary blob, you might not think Perl would be a useful language for working with the Registry. However, as any true Perl hacker knows, Perl is useful for *everything*! Philippe Le Berre wrote a small Perl utility, *dumpreg.pl*, which dumps a specified key (and its subkeys and values) in a nice formatted list.

The main section of the code (shown in Example 7-11) gets the user's command-line input, validates it (filling in defaults where appropriate), connects to a remote machine if requested, opens the key to be traversed, and opens the output file. If any step fails, the program stops; if they all succeed, the *ProcessKey* routine gets called.

Example 7-11. The Main Section of dumpreg.pl

```perl
use Win32::Registry;
use Win32;

$Indent = "    ";

# Preflight: get the local machine name, file name, and key to traverse
$Node    = Win32::NodeName();
$File    = "Hive.key" unless $File = $ARGV[0];
$Key     = $ARGV[1] || exit Syntax();

# explode the key into its components
($Computer, $Root, $Key) = ($Key =~ /(\\\\.*?\\){0,1}(HKEY_[^\\]*){0,1}(.*)/i);
$Computer =~ s/\\$//;
($Path, $Key) = ($Key =~ /^\\?(.*)\\(.*?)$/);

# default to HKEY_LOCAL_MACHINE as root
if (!$Root)
{
    $Root = "HKEY_LOCAL_MACHINE";
}


print "Dumping:\n\t\"$Root\\$Path\\$Key\"\n";
print "\tfrom machine $Computer...\n" if ($Computer);
$RootKey = $$Root;


# Open the remote computer's Registry if we were asked to
if ($Computer)
{
    if (! $RootKey->RemoteConnect($Computer, $RootKey))
    {
        die "Could not connect to $Computer.\n";
    }
}
```

Example 7-11. The Main Section of dumpreg.pl (continued)

```
# Open the key, wherever it may be
$Temp = $RootKey->Open( "$Path\\$Key" , $TheKey);
if (!$Temp)
{
    die "failure.\nCan not open \"$Path\" -- $!\n";
}

# open the file and process the key
if ((open(FILE, ">$File")))
{
    print FILE "\\Registry\\Machine\\$Path\n";
        $KeyName = ProcessKey($TheKey,  1, $Key);
        $RootKey->Close();
        close(FILE);
}
else
{
    die "failure.\nCan not create file : $File -- $!\n";
}
```

ProcessKey itself is shown in Example 7-12. After printing a short status message to the standard output, it uses *GetValues* to load a hash with all values for the current key, then iterates through the values with **foreach** so it can print them all. The actual work of decoding the values and formatting them nicely is done by *ProcessString*, which is omitted here.

Example 7-12. ProcessKey Does All the Hard Work

```
sub ProcessKey
{
    my($SubKey, $iLevel, $Key) = @_;
    my(@SubKeys, %Values);
    my($NewKey, $Temp);


    $iTotal++;
    printf( "%03d)%s%s\n", $iTotal, $Indent x $iLevel, $Key);
    print FILE $Indent x $iLevel, "$Key\n";

    if ($iLevel)
    {
        # If we can get the key's values, dump them
        if ($SubKey->GetValues(\%Values))
        {
            $iLevel++;
            foreach $Temp (keys(%Values))
            {
                my($PreString) = $Indent x $iLevel . "$Values{$Temp}[0] = ";

                # ProcessString actually displays the data in the correct format
                ($Type, @Data) = ProcessString($Values{$Temp}[1],
```

Example 7-12. ProcessKey Does All the Hard Work (continued)

```
                                          $Values{$Temp}[2], $iLevel);
            print FILE "\n$PreString$Type",
                join( "\\\n" . " " x (length($PreString))));
        }
        $iLevel--;
        print FILE "\n";
    }
}

undef %Values;            # Clear the values hash to prevent stale data

# Recurse through any subkeys of the current key
if ($SubKey->GetKeys(\@SubKeys))
{
    foreach $Temp (@SubKeys)
    {
        if ($SubKey->Open($Temp, $NewKey))
        {
            ProcessKey($NewKey, $iLevel + 1, $Temp);
        }
    }
    $SubKey->Close();
}
}
```

Once the current key's values are all processed, *ProcessKey* calls *GetKeys* to get a list of subkeys for the current key. We see that **foreach** is brought to bear on the problem of processing the key list; each subkey of the current key is recursively fed to *ProcessKey* so that nested keys will be correctly processed.

Programming with Visual Basic

Visual Basic used to be regarded as a toy language, in large part because that's what it was. In true Microsoft tradition, though, it has been continually enhanced, revised, tweaked, and improved to the point where it's a real honest-to-goodness programming tool. While hard-core programmers may look down their noses at any language with "Basic" in its name, many administrators have come to know and love VB because it makes it extremely easy to construct robust applications with the full Windows look and feel.

Besides that, VB includes a wide range of components that allow it to easily connect to large databases, generate custom reports, and do a number of other things that are much more difficult to do in C++ (or even Perl, unless you're already fluent). A good friend of mine described VB by saying that its learning curve didn't reach as high as Visual C++, but it was a lot flatter at the bottom.

While you could use VB to write a tool whose purpose was to manipulate the Registry, it's more likely that you'll need to add Registry access to a VB program you already have (or are writing). Accordingly, in this section I'll focus on how to get data into and out of the Registry—that means opening and closing keys, enumerating keys and values, querying and setting values, and deleting keys and values. If you want to do anything else, you'll still be able to by using the API definitions discussed below.

NOTE   As in the sections on C++ and Perl above, I'm going to assume that you're already familiar with VB and how to use it. If you're really interested in learning lots more about Registry programming in any language—but particularly VB—I recommend Ron Petrusha's Nutshell Handbook *Inside the Windows 95 Registry* (O'Reilly & Associates, 1995).

Talking with the Outside World in VB

VB is arguably the most successful programming tool ever developed.[*] Its success is primarily because it's easy to write programs that actually accomplish something. This ease of use in turn comes from the ways that VB lets you extend its base functionality to add new features. First of all, you can write new procedures and functions in VB itself. This allows you to build up your own library of reusable pieces that you can apply to new programs as you write them.

That's nothing very new, though; almost all other languages offer some support for recycling code so it can be reused. VB also offers a sophisticated component model based on ActiveX controls—almost any functionality can be wrapped up into an ActiveX control so that other VB programmers can just drag-and-drop it into their own programs. This is part of the reason why so many VB programs sport sophisticated interfaces, with things like calendars, spreadsheet-style grids, and other frills. Since those elements can be packaged and reused, many programmers do just that. As a side effect of this componentization, there's a healthy market for selling VB components, and this acts as a further spur to component development.

DLL interfaces

Besides its component support, though, VB allows you to load any Windows DLL and call the routines it exports. Most of its support for Win32 API routines is actu-

---

[*] In terms of sales, anyway; let's not start any religious wars about what the One True Language is or should be.

ally implemented this way; there are function declarations that map a VB name to an exported routine in a DLL somewhere. Here's an example:

```
Declare Function RegOpenKey Lib "advapi32.dll" _
    Alias "RegOpenKeyA" _
    (ByVal hKey As Long, ByVal lpctstr As String, _
    phkey As Long) As Long
```

This tells VB that you're declaring a function named *RegOpenKey*. The actual implementation of the function lives in the *advapi32.dll* library, and the function in that DLL is actually named *RegOpenKeyA*. (Remember, all the Registry routines have both ANSI and Unicode variants, but VB usually uses the ANSI versions.) The rest of the function declaration contains the argument list. This particular function takes three parameters:

- *hKey* is declared as a `Long`, and the `ByVal` keyword tells VB to pass the value of the parameter, not its location in memory. This distinction is critical, since the DLL being called expects data to arrive in a particular format.

- *lpctstr* is declared as a `String`; because it's also declared with `ByVal`, its contents will be passed instead of its address. There's another reason why the string is declared with `ByVal`: VB uses its own string format, which the standard Win32 DLLs can't decipher. In this case, the `ByVal` keyword tells VB to convert the string into a standard ANSI string, with a `NULL` terminator, before passing it to the DLL.

- *phkey* is *not* passed by value; instead, its address is passed in to the DLL so that the DLL can return a handle to the newly opened key. When you don't use `ByVal`, VB assumes that you're passing parameters by reference. You can also use the `ByRef` keyword to explicitly declare that you want something passed by reference.

The last element in the declaration is the return type of the function. The Win32 API standard is that all functions return a long integer, which corresponds to VB's `Long` type—so that's what *RegOpenKey* returns.

A few more subtleties

The VB documentation includes an entire chapter on how to construct the correct VB function declaration for any C or C++ DLL routine. Even after reading this chapter several times, you may find the details confusing. Rather than send you back to read it again, let's see if I can boil the rules down to their essentials.

First of all, you've already seen the basic rule above: if you're passing in a variable that the API routine will fill in and return, you'll need to pass it by reference, not with `ByVal`. Strings are the exceptions to this—you'll always need to include

ByVal so that VB knows it should convert strings to and from its own funny format instead of passing them on to the unsuspecting Win32 DLLs.

The corollary to this rule is that you use ByVal when you're passing in a non-string parameter that the API routine can't modify. Examples include the HKEY you must pass in for all the Registry routines or the REGSAM and DWORD values you use with *RegCreateKeyEx*.

In C, C++, and Perl, you'll probably use NULL sometimes to indicate that you don't want to supply a value for a parameter. The Registry API routines allow this for most parameters, but you'll quickly run into trouble if you do something like the following:

```
Call RegCreateKeyEx(HKEY_CURRENT_USER, "SOFTWARE\LJL\ArmorMail\PFXLocation",
                0,                      'reserved
                0,                      'class -- but it's WRONG!
                0,                      'dwOptions
                KEY_READ,
                0,                      'security attributes -- WRONG AGAIN
                resultKey,
                disposition);
```

This seems perfectly legal; after all, it's a well-known fact that NULL is just a textual representation of 0. Unfortunately, the code above isn't passing a pointer whose value is NULL. Instead, you're passing a pointer that points to a NULL. This is like the difference between sending a letter to your spouse and sending a letter about your spouse—the consequences can be unintended and possibly severe.

Here's the correct way to call *RegCreateKeyEx*. The fix is to add ByVal to the two pointer parameters (*lpSecurityAttributes* and *lpClass*). This tells VB that you really want to pass NULL pointers instead of pointers *to* NULL.

```
Call RegCreateKeyEx(HKEY_CURRENT_USER, "SOFTWARE\LJL\ArmorMail\PFXLocation",
                0,                      'reserved
                ByVal 0,                'class
                0,                      'dwOptions
                KEY_READ,
                ByVal 0,                'security attributes
                resultKey,
                disposition);
```

Here's another bear trap that's waiting to snap shut on your ankle. Some of the Registry APIs accept raw data. For example, *RegSetValueEx* accepts the value contents you want to store as a block of type BYTE. Since it doesn't know whether you're storing a DWORD, a string, or something else, the function prototype doesn't specify a definite type. VB includes a rough equivalent, the As Any keyword. When you use it, you're telling VB not to check the data type of that parameter, which is tantamount to begging for trouble.

The solution recommended by Ron Petrusha in *Inside the Windows 95 Registry* is to declare aliases of functions that normally might use **As Any**. For example, this declaration adds an alias for *RegSetValueEx* that "knows" it's storing a string value.

```
Declare Function RegSetStringValue Lib "advapi32.dll" _
    Alias "RegSetValueExA" _
    (ByVal hKey As Long, ByVal lpValueName As String, _
    ByVal Reserved As Long, ByVal dwType As Long, _
    ByVal lpData As String, ByVal cbData As Long) As Long
```

This makes it possible to declare the *lpData* parameter as a string so the VB compiler can check it for correctness. You can also define similar aliases for setting DWORD, REG_MULTI_SZ, or REG_BINARY data.

Using the Registry with VB

Now that you know what to watch out for when calling the Registry API routines, it's time to move on to actually writing some Registry code in VB.

The VBA functions

VB includes a set of functions for accessing the Registry. Unfortunately, they are so limited as to be practically worthless:

- You may only access keys under HKCU\Software\VB and VBA Program Settings. Period. This is a severe limitation if you're writing programs that need to access keys that aren't under HKCU.

- The provided routines can only work with one level of keys, so if you open a key named HKCU\Software\VB and VBA Program Settings\MyStuff you can't access values under HKCU\Software\VB and VBA Program Settings\ MyStuff\CurrentVersion.

- You can only store and retrieve string values—no binary or DWORD data allowed.

These limitations came about because the built-in Registry routines were designed to be seamlessly compatible with Win3.x, Win95, and NT. This means that the functionality is restricted to the lowest common denominator. There's no reason to use them unless you really, really, really want your programs to run under Win3.x—not likely if you're reading this book. I won't talk about them any further.

Using WINREG.BAS

Even though the built-in VB functions are unsuitable for most uses, you still have another alternative: you can use the original Win32 API routines with suitable VB function declarations. If you follow the rules above, you could easily write your own set of VB function declarations for the Registry API, but doing so would be wasteful, because Andrew Schulman has already done so. *WINREG.BAS* (available from the O'Reilly web site at *http://www.oreilly.com/*) contains declarations for all the Registry API routines discussed in this chapter (except for *RegQueryMultipleValues*), plus some additional routines that you may find useful. You'll need this file to use the examples later in the chapter, and you'll probably want to use it in your own projects.

NOTE   You can also use a third-party VB control that encapsulates Registry functions into a higher-level set of routines. The Desaware Registry Control (*http://www.desaware.com/*) is one example, but there are others. The chief drawback to these controls is that they cost money, but they can save you time if you're not entirely comfortable with using the raw Registry routines.

Since all *WINREG.BAS* does is put a VB-compatible face on the API routines described earlier in the chapter, I'm not going to reiterate how those routines work or what their parameters are. Instead, let's see them in action.

Example: A RegEdit Clone

You may have noticed that *RegEdit* looks like a pretty simple program. For the most part, it is—it has to gather small amounts of data from the user, then pass that data on to one or another of the Registry API routines. In *Inside the Windows 95 Registry,* Ron Petrusha provided a *RegEdit* clone written in Visual Basic! It's not truly a clone; in fact, it doesn't do anything except display keys and values, but it does so with the familiar tree control, just like *RegEdit*. However, if you look at the clone in operation (see Figure 7-1), you'll be hard-pressed to tell the difference between the two.

Creating the initial tree

The first step in creating a *RegEdit* clone is to build the VB form definitions. Since that has nothing to do with the Registry, I won't talk about it here. (If you want to see the code, check out *http://oreilly.windows.com/registry.*) Instead, let's focus on the interesting stuff. The first block of interest is in the main form's Load method. It creates a new root key named "My Computer" in the tree list, then adds nodes for each root key.

```
Set nodRegTree = TreeView1.Nodes.Add("home", tvwChild, "HKCR", _
                          "HKEY_CLASSES_ROOT", "closed", "open")
Set nodRegTree = TreeView1.Nodes.Add("home", tvwChild, "HKCU", _
                          "HKEY_CURRENT_USER", "closed", "open")
Set nodRegTree = TreeView1.Nodes.Add("home", tvwChild, "HKLM", _
                          "HKEY_LOCAL_MACHINE", "closed", "open")
```

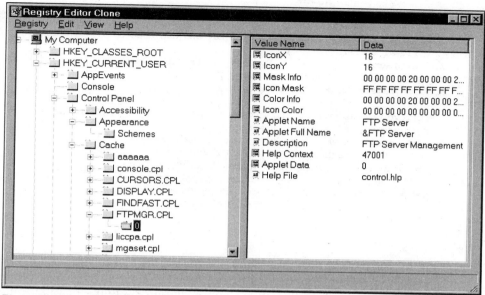

Figure 7-1. The RegEdit clone

```
Set nodRegTree = TreeView1.Nodes.Add("home", tvwChild, "HKU", "HKEY_USERS", _
                                "closed", "open")
If blnWinNT4 Then
    Set nodRegTree = TreeView1.Nodes.Add("home", tvwChild, "HKCC", _
                                "HKEY_CURRENT_CONFIG", "closed", "open")
    Set nodRegTree = TreeView1.Nodes.Add("home", tvwChild, "HKDD", _
                                "HKEY_DYN_DATA", "closed", "open")
End If
```

Once the tree view's set up, the next step is to make any root key that has sub-keys expandable. Part of this is making sure we have enough space to store the name of the longest subkey name that we might ever hit:

```
For intctr = 1 To TreeView1.Nodes.Count
    strNode = TreeView1.Nodes.Item(intctr).Key
    If strNode <> "home" Then
        ' Convert node abbreviation to handle
        Select Case strNode
            Case "HKCR"
                hKey = HKEY_CLASSES_ROOT
            Case "HKCU"
                hKey = HKEY_CURRENT_USER
            Case "HKLM"
                hKey = HKEY_LOCAL_MACHINE
            Case "HKU"
                hKey = HKEY_USERS
            Case "HKCC"
                hKey = HKEY_CURRENT_CONFIG
            Case "HKDD"
```

```
        hKey = HKEY_DYN_DATA
   End Select

   ' Get size of longest subkey for each key and use that to size the
   ' retrieval buffer
   Call RegQueryInfoKey(hKey, 0, 0, 0, 0, lngLenSubkeyName, 0, 0, 0, 0, 0, 0)
   lngLenSubkeyName = lngLenSubkeyName + 1
   strSubkeyName = String(lngLenSubkeyName + 1, 0)

   ' Retrieve one subkey; if that succeeds, get one subkey to find out if
   ' there are any subkeys for this node.
   If RegEnumKeyEx(hKey, 0, strSubkeyName, lngLenSubkeyName, 0&, _
               strClass, ByVal 0, ByVal 0&) = ERROR_SUCCESS Then
      strSubkeyName = Left(strSubkeyName, lngLenSubkeyName)
      'Add node to top-level key so icon appears with a "+"
      Set nodRegTree = TreeView1.Nodes.Add(strNode, tvwChild, _
               , strSubkeyName, "closed", "open")
   End If
 End If
Next
```

Notice the use of **ByVal** 0 to pass **NULL** pointers in the call to *RegEnumKeyEx*. There's another trick here, too: the call to *RegQueryInfoKey* gets the length of the longest subkey name, and that length is used to allocate the buffer that holds the subkey name returned by *RegEnumKeyEx*. This ensures that the buffer will always be long enough to hold the name, even if the longest name comes up first.

This code alone will display the initial tree, but it will be dead—users won't be able to expand or contract nodes in the tree as they can with *RegEdit*. Time for some additional code.

Expanding the tree

The next step is to allow users to expand tree nodes that have subkeys. The snippet in Example 7-13, taken from the tree view's **Expand** method, does just this. The code performs five basic operations:

1. If the user's trying to expand a subkey, we open it. This means we don't open any subkeys until the user explicitly asks us to, which is a big performance win.

2. It calls *RegQueryInfoKey* to find out how many subkeys there are. In addition, we get the length of the longest subkey name.

3. If the number of elements in this node doesn't match the number of subkeys, or if the node's **Tag** field tells us it was collapsed, we expand the tree by enumerating each subkey of the target and adding it as a node. In this step, the subkey count we got from step 2 is invaluable.

4. As we traverse subkeys of the expanded key, any of them that have at least one subkey themselves are marked as having children. This forces the tree

view control to mark them with the "+" icon so users know that node can be expanded.

5. If we opened a key in step 1, we close it again.

Example 7-13. Expanding a Node in the Registry Tree

```
' If we're expanding a subkey, open it. This allows us to only open a key
' when the user clicks on it.
If Len(Trim(strSubkey)) > 0 Then
    Call RegOpenKey(hRootKey, strSubkey, hKey)
    blnKeyOpen = True
Else
    hKey = hRootKey
End If

' Find out how many subkeys and values there are and their maximum name lengths
Call RegQueryInfoKey(hKey, 0, 0, 0, lngSubkeys, lngLenSubkeyName, _
                    0, lngValues, lngLenValueName, lngLenValueData, 0, 0)

' If the node isn't fully expanded, go ahead and expand it.
If (Val(Node.Tag)) <> 1 Or (Node.Children <> lngSubkeys) Then

    ' First, delete existing nodes
    lngChildren = Node.Children
    For intctr = 1 To lngChildren
        TreeView1.Nodes.Remove Node.Child.Index
    Next

    ' Enumerate all this key's subkeys, adding each one as a node.
    For lngIndex = 0 To lngSubkeys - 1
        lngLenSubkey = lngLenSubkeyName + 1
        strSubkey = String(lngLenSubkey, 0)

        ' get the lngIndex'th key
        Call RegEnumKeyEx(hKey, lngIndex, strSubkey, lngLenSubkey, 0&, 0, 0, 0)
        strSubkey = Left(strSubkey, lngLenSubkey)

        ' Add it as a tree node
        Set nodRegTree = TreeView1.Nodes.Add(Node.Index, tvwChild, , strSubkey, _
                                    "closed", "open")

        ' If this node has at least one subkey, add a child to it to enable it
        ' to be expanded too
        Call RegOpenKey(hKey, strSubkey, hChildKey)
        Call RegQueryInfoKey(hChildKey, 0, 0, 0, lngSubSubkeys, lngLenSubkey, _
                        0, 0, 0, 0, 0, 0)
        If lngSubSubkeys > 0 Then
            lngLenSubkey = lngLenSubkey + 1
            strSubkey = String(lngLenSubkey, 0)
            Call RegEnumKeyEx(hChildKey, 0, strSubkey, lngLenSubkey, 0&, 0, 0, 0)
            Call RegCloseKey(hChildKey)
            ' Add to most recent key
            lngNodeIndex = nodRegTree.Index
```

Example 7-13. Expanding a Node in the Registry Tree (continued)

```
    Set nodRegTree = TreeView1.Nodes.Add(lngNodeIndex, tvwChild, , _
                                         strSubkey, "closed", "open")
      End If
  Next
  Node.Tag = 1
End If


' If we opened a key earlier, close it
If blnKeyOpen Then Call RegCloseKey(hKey)
```

Displaying values

So now our clone can display the root keys and expand them when users request it—but what about displaying the values? To get value display capability, we need to do something when the user clicks on a tree node. That means adding a Node-Click event handler. After some setup and variable declarations (which I'm not showing here), our NodeClick routine starts by preflighting the value list and opening the requested key:

```
' Clear current contents of ListView control
ListView1.ListItems.Clear

' Open the registry key attached to this node
If Len(Trim(strPath)) > 0 Then
    Call RegOpenKey(hRootKey, strPath, hKey)
    blnOpenKey = True
Else
    hKey = hRootKey
End If
```

The next step is to find out how many values there are and how big the largest value name and contents are. Armed with that data, we can display a default value and stop if there aren't actually any values attached to this key:

```
' Get value count, max value name length, and max value contents length
Call RegQueryInfoKey(hKey, 0, 0, 0, 0, 0, 0, lngValues, _
                 lngMaxNameLen, lngMaxValueLen, 0, 0)

' Add default value entry if there aren't any real values present
If lngValues = 0 Then
    Set objLItem = ListView1.ListItems.Add(, , "<Default>", "string", "string")
    Exit Sub
End If
```

If there are real values, we know what the biggest value data block is, so we can size our data buffer accordingly:

```
' Redimension the byte array for value data using the max value contents length
ReDim bytValue(lngMaxValueLen)
```

Now the fun begins. We must enumerate over every value of this subkey, getting both its name and its contents. Each value has a type, and we want to display an appropriate icon in the left-most column of the value list, just like *RegEdit*:

```
' Enumerate all value entries of this subkey
For lngIndex = 0 To lngValues - 1
    lngNameLen = lngMaxNameLen + 1
    ' make sure our buffer's big enough
    strValueName = String(lngMaxNameLen, 0)
    lngValueLen = lngMaxValueLen
    Call RegEnumValue(hKey, lngIndex, strValueName, lngNameLen, 0, _
                    lngDataType, bytValue(0), lngValueLen)

    ' Determine icon type
    Select Case lngDataType
        Case REG_SZ, REG_MULTI_SZ, REG_EXPAND_SZ
            strIcon = "string"
        Case Else
            strIcon = "bin"
    End Select

    ' if it's empty, substitute "<Default>"; otherwise, use the name
    If lngNameLen = 0 Then
        strValueName = ""
        Set objLItem = ListView1.ListItems.Add(, , "< Default >", strIcon, strIcon)
    Else
        strValueName = Left(strValueName, lngNameLen)
        Set objLItem = ListView1.ListItems.Add(, , strValueName, strIcon, strIcon)
    End If
```

Users would hate our clone if it displayed everything in binary or hex, so we should neatly format and display the value data, no matter its type. In all cases, we do this with a call to *RegQueryValueEx*, combined with some formatting tweaking depending on the data type. Notice that for binary data there's no call to *RegQueryValueEx*; that's because the earlier call to *RegEnumValue* loaded the data directly into the *bytValue* array:

```
' Format and display data
Select Case lngDataType

    ' for a string, get the value and display it directly
    Case REG_SZ, REG_EXPAND_SZ
        strTemp = String(lngValueLen, 0)
        Call RegQueryValueEx(hKey, strValueName, 0, 0, ByVal strTemp, _
                        lngValueLen)
        objLItem.SubItems(1) = Left(strTemp, lngValueLen)

    ' for a multistring, get the value and pick it apart
    Case REG_MULTI_SZ
        strTemp = String(lngValueLen, 0)
        Call RegQueryValueEx(hKey, strValueName, 0, 0, ByVal strTemp, _
                        lngValueLen)
        strTemp = Left(strTemp, lngValueLen - 2)
```

```
            intPos = 1
            While intPos > 0
                intPos = InStr(1, strTemp, Chr(0))
                If intPos > 1 Then
                    strTemp = Left(strTemp, intPos - 1) & "|" & _
                                  Mid(strTemp, intPos + 1)
                End If
            Wend
            objLItem.SubItems(1) = strTemp

        ' for binary or BIG_ENDIAN values, display  in hex
        Case REG_BINARY, REG_DWORD_BIG_ENDIAN
            strTemp = ""
            For intctr = 0 To lngValueLen - 1
                strHex = Hex(bytValue(intctr))
                If Len(strHex) = 1 Then strHex = "0" & strHex
                strTemp = strTemp & strHex & " "
            Next
            objLItem.SubItems(1) = strTemp

        ' for a DWORD, display as a DWORD
        Case REG_DWORD
            lngLenDW = Len(lngTemp)
            Call RegQueryValueEx(hKey, strValueName, 0, 0, lngTemp, lngLenDW)
            objLItem.SubItems(1) = lngTemp
    End Select
Next
```

The last—but not least—step is to clean up any messes we may have made:

```
' Close the key if we opened it
If blnOpenKey Then Call RegCloseKey(hKey)
```

8

Administering the NT Registry

When you're responsible for administering computers—whether one or many—you quickly find that much of what you do on a daily basis is miscellanea. You create new accounts, remove old ones, figure out why your backup tape drive is dead, and so forth. It would be nice if your whole career could revolve around orderly, planned upgrades, maintenance, and migrations, but those little tasks are important too. This chapter will introduce you to several small tasks related to managing the NT Registry; while none of them is a full-time activity, all of them are worth doing.

Setting Defaults for New User Accounts

NT was designed from the start to support multiple user accounts sharing a single computer. Unlike DOS and Windows 3.x, NT provided a way (through the Registry, actually) to keep individual settings for each user. However, the original versions of NT didn't provide any way for these settings to be shared between computers, and there were no mechanisms for collecting all of a user's settings data in a single place.

NT 4.0 was the first version of NT to support the concept of *user profiles*. Like the profiles in Win95, NT 4.0 profiles capture a user's desktop environment, application settings, and other preferences. These profiles can roam from computer to computer, so that users can have their own personalized environment on every machine they log onto. In addition, administrators can configure these profiles to prevent users from changing all or part of the settings, thus making it easier to set up shared computer labs and other facilities where it's important to protect machines against tampering.

When you install NT on a machine, the system uses a default profile to provide settings for your user accounts. The first time a newly created account logs in, the default profile is copied into HKCU, thus making the new account inherit the default settings. Unfortunately, there's no direct way to change settings in this default profile. You can use the System Policy Editor (as described in Chapter 6, *Using the System Policy Editor*) to set policies for the "Default User" account, but if you want to change a setting that's not in one of the policy templates—say, the default currency format or the list of predefined URLs that Internet Explorer stores—you have two choices. You can create a new policy template that contains the new settings you want to apply, or you can edit the default user profile directly.

NT stores the default user profile in a file. On individual workstations and servers, the profile is stored in *%systemroot%\profiles\Default User*. You can also force the default profile to apply to all domain logons by putting it in the *NETLOGON* share of your domain controller.* When it's there, the file must be named *Ntuser.dat*. Whatever settings are in this file will be applied to new user accounts, but they won't affect existing accounts. *Ntuser.dat* is really just a Registry hive; when a new account logs on for the first time, NT copies the contents of the hive to HKCU, then writes the changes to the appropriate subkey of HKU. By changing what's in the initial hive, you affect what settings go into that user's HKCU when she logs on.

Because the default user profile is just a Registry hive, you can edit it with *RegEdt32*. Here's what to do:

1. Start *RegEdt32*. When it opens, open up the HKU window and select the HKU root key.

2. Use the **Registry ► Load Hive…** menu command to select the default user profile you want to edit. You can directly open *%systemroot%\profiles\Default User*, or you can edit *NTuser.man* if it's available.

3. When *RegEdt32* asks for a key name, make up any name that will remind you what the hive is for. I usually use "DefaultUserProfile." *RegEdt32* will import the hive and attach it under the name you supply.

---

* To do this, you'll need to use the "Copy To" button on the User Profiles tab of the System control panel to move the profile from your local machine to the domain controller's *NETLOGON* share.

4. Select the new hive key and use the **Security ➤ Permissions...** command to add `Everyone:Read` access to the key and its subkeys. This enables the profile sharing mechanism to copy keys from the default profile to users' HKCU.

5. Use *RegEdt32* to make the desired changes to subkeys of your new hive. As you make changes, they'll be transparently stored in the hive file.

6. Once you've finished editing all the hive keys, use the **Registry ➤ Unload Hive** command to detach the hive. Until you do this, no other computer or user can get access to the changes you've made.

Using Initialization File Mapping

In Chapter 1, *A Gentle Introduction to the NT Registry*, I described how the Registry evolved from its humble parentage of INI files. Many NT installations are still running 16-bit Win 3.1 applications that don't support the Registry, and a surprising number of 32-bit applications still rely on the old INI file structure—despite the fact that using the Registry is one of the requirements for getting the coveted "Designed for Windows 95" logo from Microsoft.

Since there's no way to upgrade skanky old 16-bit applications to use the Registry,* you might think that you're stuck forever with the mess of tracking, backing up, and protecting a mess of INI files. Not so! NT includes a feature called *initialization file mapping* (I'll call it just "mapping" from now on) that allows you to force Registry-unaware programs to load and save configuration data in the Registry instead of in an INI file.

NT already includes mappings for several system components, including the Windows clock desk accessory, the bundled 32-bit NT tape backup application, and even *RegEdt32*! Mappings aren't just for 16-bit applications; rather, they're for any application—16- or 32-bit—that doesn't include code to read and write Registry data.

Of course, mapping's not required; applications that depend on INI files can work just fine under NT without having the files mapped. In fact, unless you explicitly take action to map these files, they'll remain unmapped, and their normal INI file usage will continue without interruption.

---

* Chapter 5 of Ron Petrusha's *Inside the Windows 95 Registry* actually explains how to use the Win95 Registry from 16-bit and DOS apps, but there's no time machine that allows unmodified applications to do so.

How Does Mapping Work?

NT implements mapping by trapping the private profile API routines I mentioned in Chapter 1. Windows applications and components ordinarily use these calls to get and set data stored in INI files, but when there's a mapping entry, the NT kernel first checks for the presence of a mapping key. If one exists, and if it points to a key that contains data, that data is returned to the caller. If there's no mapping key, or if it points to an empty or non-existent Registry key, NT will go ahead and try to read the data from the INI file. The caller need never be aware that the data didn't come from the requested file.

Mapping only occurs when there's a mapping key in place. These keys are stored beneath the `HKLM\SOFTWARE\Microsoft\Windows NT\CurrentVersion\Ini-FileMapping` subkey. If you look there, you'll notice a number of subkeys with names like `Clock.INI`, `Win.INI`, and `SYSTEM.INI`. These keys tie sections of the old Win 3.1-style INI files to keys in the Registry so that old Windows 3.1 components like the Clock and the original media controller interface (MCI) will continue to find their settings.

Application programmers and administrators are free to create new mappings between any INI file and any key in the Registry. This allows you to move settings data to the Registry where it properly belongs; once it's there, you can edit, save, massage, and manage it using the skills you've learned throughout this book.

Time for a real-life story: a client had licensed several hundred seats for a popular email application. This app had a 32-bit version, but it didn't use the Registry. I created a mapping for the program's settings, then built a system policy template (see Chapter 6 for details) so they could centrally control how users set up their mail clients. Everyone walked away happy.

Setting Up Your Own Mappings

In an ideal world, all the applications on your computers would be 32-bit, Registry-aware, NT-native programs. Unfortunately, only people running NT on RISC-based machines that can't run Win95 or Win 3.x programs have that luxury. For the rest of us, though, it's easy to add mapping keys to force NT to use Registry keys instead of sections in an INI file; best of all, you can do so without any changes to the application that owns the INI file.

If you've ever opened an INI file, you know that it's divided into sections. Section names are enclosed by square brackets, and they contain name/value pairs. The whole arrangement looks like this sample from an imaginary data security package's INI file:

```
[Encryption]
DefaultSigAlgorithm=RSAWithSHA1
DefaultEncryptionAlgorithm=DES3-EDE-CBC
WipeFilesWhenDone=1
```

In this example, "Encryption" is the section name, and "DefaultSigAlgorithm," "DefaultEncryptionAlgorithm," and "WipeFilesWhenDone" are the value names.

Adding the mapping key

You may map any or all sections of any INI file to a Registry key. To do so, you must add a new subkey to HKLM\SOFTWARE\Microsoft\Windows NT\Current-Version\IniFileMapping. This subkey should have the same name as the INI file you're mapping; for example, to remap a file named *ccmail.ini* you'd add a new subkey with that name to the IniFileMapping key.

If you just add a new mapping key by itself, nothing will happen. This is because the named subkey just tells NT to watch for access to the INI file with the same name; it doesn't tell where the data are actually stored in the Registry. You specify the location (or locations) by creating values underneath the key. Each of these values should have a name that matches a section in the INI file. These section names are combined with the name of the parent key to help the profile API routines figure out what data you're requesting.

To map the key in the example above, you'd create a new key named HKLM\ SOFTWARE\Microsoft\Windows NT\CurrentVersion\IniFileMapping\ Crypto.INI. Under that key, you'd add a value named Encryption. The combination of these two values tells NT that any attempt to access the "Encryption" section of *crypto.ini* should instead look in the Registry.

The value you give to these section keys tells NT where the real data is stored in the Registry. Let's say that our data security program stores its data in HKLM\Soft-ware\Crypto\CurrentVersion\Settings. To complete the mapping we started in the previous paragraph, we'd specify this Registry key as the contents of the Encryption value. By doing so, we've given NT enough information to translate requests for data in an INI file to a Registry key.

Mapping key tricks

There are a couple of tricks that apply to building mapping key entries. First of all, you can specify a default value that will handle any sections that don't have explicit mappings. Going back to our data security program example, if you added an Encryption key, NT still wouldn't know how to map requests for data in the "Signature" section. However, by adding a default value (which appears as "<No Name>" or "Default") to the subkey, we can tell NT which key to use for any sections that don't have their own section keys defined.

There are also several special symbols that you may use in the values of section keys. Table 8-1 shows these symbols; you'll see them in action in the next section.

Table 8-1. Special Strings for Use in Initialization File Mappings

Symbol	What it means
SYS	Store data under a path relative to `HKLM\Software`; for example, `SYS:Netscape` expands to `HKLM\Software\Netscape`
USR	Store data under a path relative to `HKCU`; for example, `USR:Software\Qualcomm\Eudora` expands to `HKCU\Software\Qualcomm\Eudora`
!	Store data for this named section both in the Registry and the INI file; when data's written to one, it will be written to the other
@	Never read data from the INI file, even if no matching data is found in the Registry
#	When a new user logs in, copy the section's settings from the INI file into the specified Registry location

A mapping sample

The Entrust data security package from Entrust Technologies (*http://www.entrust.com/*) comes in both 16- and 32-bit versions, as well as versions that run under Unix and the MacOS. To preserve a consistent set of source code, the Entrust engineers decided to stick with INI files instead of using the Registry. Here's the process I followed to build a set of mappings to replace Entrust's INI files with Registry data.

1. I created a new subkey named `entrust.ini` under `HKLM\SOFTWARE\Microsoft\Windows NT\CurrentVersion\IniFileMapping`.

2. Since Entrust settings are user-specific, I created a new key, `HKCU\Software\Entrust`, to hold the settings data. I also added subkeys named `Other` and `EntrustSettings` to actually hold the data.

3. The interesting user-specific data in the Entrust INI file is all in the "Entrust Settings" section. To map it, I added a subkey named `Entrust Settings` under `entrust.ini` and gave it a default value of `@USR:Software\Entrust\EntrustSettings`. This makes NT map data stored in the "Entrust Settings" section to the key of the same name; the `@` prevents the mapping code from reading data from the INI file.

4. I gave the `entrust.ini` subkey a default value of `#USR:Software\Entrust\Other`. This forces NT to copy the INI file's data for new users and to store data for all other sections of `entrust.ini` in `HKCU\Software\Entrust\Other`.

The results of these steps are shown in Figure 8-1. As a finishing touch, I saved the mapping keys to a *.REG* file using *RegEdit* so I could quickly distribute them to users throughout our network.

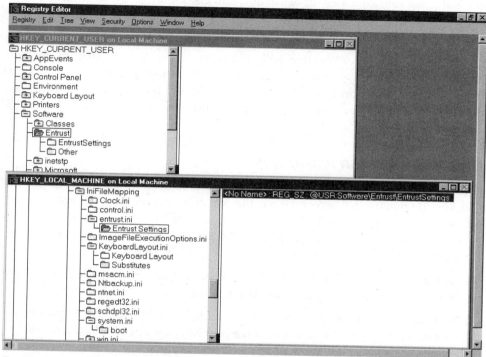

Figure 8-1. Adding INI file mappings

Limiting Remote Registry Access

In Windows NT 3.51 and earlier, any user could access the Registry on any machine over the network. From a security standpoint, this was much too liberal; NT 4.0 (and 3.51 with SP4 or SP5) defaults to allowing only members of the Administrators group to access the Registry remotely. This is considerably more secure than the original permissions.

However, this setting may not suit your environment. Sometimes allowing any member of Administrators access is still too permissive, since some high-value machines may warrant the added security of only allowing a single account or group to access their registries over the network. Conversely, you may want to proactively allow other users and groups to remotely connect to, and edit, Registry data on some machines.

You can control which users, groups, and services may access the Registry on a particular machine by setting the ACL for a single Registry key, namely `HKLM\SYS-TEM\CurrentControlSet\Control\SecurePipeServers\winreg`. The NT kernel will grant remote access to a machine's Registry only to those entities named in the access control list attached to the key.

Before proceeding, I should point out that this restriction key controls access to the Registry as a whole. You may still enforce more stringent controls on individual keys. For example, you might grant one group of users access to the Registry by setting the restriction key permissions accordingly, but if you put access controls on other keys that those users can see, the most restrictive set of controls will win out.

Creating the Restriction Key

Before you can take advantage of this restriction feature, you'll need the restriction key. By default, NT Server 4.0 has this key from the moment it's installed, but NT Workstation 4.0 doesn't. Neither do earlier versions of NT; if you want to restrict access, you'll have to manually add the restriction key to your Registry. Here's what to do if you don't already have this key available:

1. Log in as Administrator (or an account with administrator privileges) and run *RegEdt32*. Navigate to `HKLM\SYSTEM\CurrentControlSet\Control`.

2. Use the **Edit ➤ Add Key...** command to add a new key named `SecurePipe-Servers`, then select it and use **Edit ➤ Add Key...** again to add a new subkey named `winreg` to the `SecurePipeServers` key you just added.

3. Add a `REG_SZ` value named "Description" to the `winreg` subkey. Microsoft recommends that you give the description as "Registry server," but the exact contents are up to you.

Depending on your machine, you may find that you have some parts of the restriction key; for example, NT Workstation 4.0 with no service packs has the `HKLM\SYSTEM\CurrentControlSet\Control\SecurePipeServers` key itself, but it doesn't have the winreg subkey that's needed to actually make the restrictions work.

Setting Permissions on the Restriction Key

Once you've verified that the `winreg` key exists, you can use the **Security ➤ Permissions...** command to give it an access control list. The permissions applied to this key govern which users and groups can access your Registry via the network.

The Registry Key Permissions dialog (shown in Figure 8-2) allows you to change the users and groups that can access the key, as well as modify permissions for those users and groups that you choose to allow access. (If you need a refresher, see the section "Setting Registry Permissions" in Chapter 5, *Using RegEdt32.*)

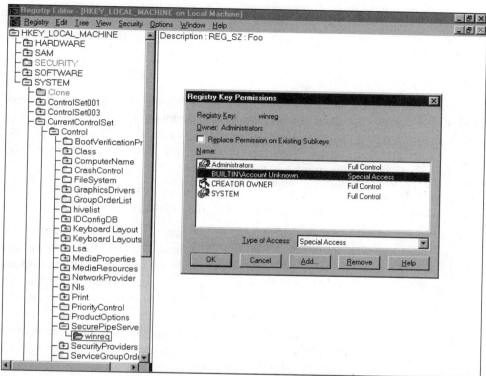

Figure 8-2. Setting Registry key permissions

NT 4.0 installations will by default have permissions like those shown in Figure 8-2: the Administrators or Domain Admins group will have Full Control rights, as will the system and the account that created the key. You can add new users and groups to this list and give them permissions commensurate with what you want them to be able to do; for example, you might grant read-only access to all domain users while restricting Full Control access to a single named account. Change whatever else you want, but leave the SYSTEM and CREATOR OWNER permissions alone; the kernel and Registry subsystem depend on these permissions to gain access to the key themselves.

WARNING   Some system services, like the directory replicator and the print
                 spooler, require remote access to the Registry. If you change the
                 access control entries on the winreg key, these services may stop
                 working. To avoid this problem, make sure that the accounts used
                 to run the replication service and the print spooler have explicit per-
                 missions in the ACL for the winreg key.

Allowing Exceptions

You may also choose to loosen the leash on your Registry a bit by allowing exceptions to the access control rules specified by the permissions on the winreg key.
These exceptions can be expressed in two ways: you can provide a list of keys
that are exempt from the access controls, or you may specify a list of users who
have free access to specific keys and their values.

Both methods are governed by values you add beneath HKLM\SYSTEM\Current-
ControlSet\Control\SecurePipeServers\winreg\AllowedPaths.

- The Machine value, of type REG_MULTI_SZ, accepts a list of Registry paths.
  Any path listed here will be visible to any machine on the network. By
  default, NT loads a set of paths that enable the replicator, print spooler, event
  logger, and kernel to function properly: System\CurrentControlSet\Con-
  trol\ProductOptions and Software\Microsoft\Windows NT\Current-
  Version for the kernel, System\CurrentControlSet\Control\Print\
  Printers for the print spooler, System\CurrentControlSet\Services\
  Eventlog for the event logging service, and System\CurrentControlSet\
  Services\Replicator for the directory replicator.

- The Users value (also a REG_MULTI_SZ) lists Registry paths that will be
  made available to any member of the Users or Domain Users group. This key
  is empty by default, and you should probably keep it that way unless you
  have a compelling reason to exempt individual users from the restriction key-
  imposed controls. In general, if you have a user who needs unusual access,
  it's better to put the user account into a group and assign the group a permission entry on the restriction key.

Access granted via either of these methods is still subordinate to permissions that
you've applied directly to individual keys. For example, if you use the
Security ➤ Permissions... command to apply Everyone:Read access to HKLM\Soft-
ware\Netscape\Netscape Navigator, then add that same path to the
Machine value, remote users won't be able to change the values under that subtree: the explicit ACL you've added overrides whatever access was granted by the
Machine entry.

Fixing Registry Security ACLs

Every key in the Registry has an ACL. Unfortunately, many of those ACLs are unnecessarily permissive. For example, by default the Everyone account token has write access to several keys that allow untrusted users to execute arbitrary programs—never a good idea. You can significantly improve your NT security posture by paying careful attention to a few simple steps.

First, a brief digression: every authenticated user is automatically a member of the Everyone group. On machines running NT 4.0 SP3 or later, these users are also members of the Authenticated Users group. Everyone also includes anonymous and guest accounts, though, so in general it's a wise idea to *never* grant Everyone:Full Control access to *anything* if you can prevent it.

On to the actual steps. First of all, apply the changes suggested earlier in the section "Limiting Remote Registry Access." Once you've done so, make sure that Everyone has only Read access on `HKLM\SYSTEM\CurrentControlSet\Control\SecurePipeServers\winreg\AllowedPaths`. This prevents an interloper from inserting her own allowed paths for anonymous access.

Next, follow Microsoft's suggestions from knowledge base article Q126713 and tighten the permissions on these three keys by limiting Everyone to Read access on them:

```
HKLM\SOFTWARE\Microsoft\Windows\CurrentVersion\Run
HKLM\SOFTWARE\Microsoft\Windows\CurrentVersion\RunOnce
HKLM\SOFTWARE\Microsoft\Windows\CurrentVersion\Uninstall
```

These keys specify programs to run when NT starts (`Run` and `RunOnce`) or when a program's uninstalled (`Uninstall`), so you don't want an attacker to be able to change them.

Likewise, you should remove the Server Operators group's Write permission on `HKLM\System\CurrentControlSet\Services\Schedule`. Normally, members of the Server Operators group have permission to schedule jobs, but these jobs can be run under the SYSTEM account—making it possible for a Server Operators member to gain Administrator privileges.[*] In the same vein, remove Server Operators' Write privilege on `HKLM\Software\Microsoft\WindowsNT\CurrentVersion\Winlogon` to prevent a similar attack on the `UserInit` and `BootVerificationProgram` values.

The next step is pretty open-ended: you should bolt down your Registry by restricting access wherever possible. The kicker is in knowing what's possible—

---

[*] Credit for uncovering these vulnerabilities goes to David LeBlanc of Internet Security Systems, Inc. (*http://www.iss.net*).

and that varies from application to application. For example, Office 97 requires Everyone:Read on its own keys under `HKLM\Software` and `HKCU\Software`. Remove that permission and some Office features stop working. The same is true for Internet Explorer 4.0 and a wide range of other products. As you make changes to Registry key ACLs, be sure to test the applications you need to run to ensure their correct function *before* rolling out your changes to the entire network.

A white paper written for Microsoft by Coopers & Lybrand* recommends changing `HKCR`, `HKLM\Software\Microsoft\RPC`, and `HKLM\Software\Microsoft\ Windows NT\CurrentVersion` to allow Everyone:Special Access. In particular, they recommend granting Everyone the Query Value, Enumerate Subkeys, Notify, and Read Control permissions. I'd extend that recommendation one notch further and suggest replacing Everyone with Authenticated Users. My first awareness of the vulnerability that prompted this change was Kirill Ermakov's security alert (*ekv@comp.chem.msu.su*). He noted that most keys under `HKLM\Software\ Microsoft` have Everyone:Delete and Everyone:Set Value access—making it possible for users to delete keys necessary for NT's proper operation. For example, you could easily delete the `LanmanWorkstation` and `LanmanServer` keys, which would stop you from offering or using SMB shares!

There's always the shotgun approach. David LeBlanc of ISS has written a tool called *everyone2user* (available at *ftp://ftp.iss.net/everyone2user.exe*) that recursively descends all six root keys of the Registry and changes access permission from the Everyone group to Domain Users or Users. This approach has generally proven safe in my experience, but it's always risky to make wholesale changes to your Registry. Make a good backup before using *everyone2user*.

Let me close on a cautionary note. Article Q139342 in the knowledge base warns of the consequences of setting improper permissions on `LanmanServer`. There are no articles (yet!) cautioning you about changing permissions on other keys, but that doesn't mean it's completely safe. Be careful, and keep good backups.

Encrypting HKLM\SAM with SYSKEY

Like Unix, NT doesn't store user or machine passwords. Instead, it takes the passwords and passes them through a scheme called a *one-way function*, or OWF. The OWF takes a password in and generates a new block of data that is related to, but doesn't contain, the password. The "OW" in OWF comes from the fact that it's infeasible to take the output of the OWF and "go backwards" to derive the original password. NT stores the OWF output instead of the password, so you can't steal an OWF and use it in place of a password.

---

* It's available online at *http://www.microsoft.com/ntserver/guide/cooperswp.asp*.

In the spring of 1997, an enterprising group of hackers from L0pht Heavy Industries (*http://www.l0pht.com*) publicized the fact that it was possible to get the OWF-generated password values out of an NT SAM database and feed them to a password-cracking tool. These types of attacks have been known for many years in the Unix community, but their appearance in the NT world generated a lot of headlines. In practical terms, the actual risk was fairly low, since only administrators have access to the SAM to get the OWFed passwords in the first place. Because administrators have essentially unlimited access to the system, they already can do things that make password cracking seem trivial.

However, Microsoft took a beating on the Internet and in the press for the perceived insecurity of the SAM password data. To provide a solution, Microsoft introduced a method of protecting the SAM data with strong encryption; the *SYSKEY* utility installs and controls this extra protective layer. *SYSKEY* is available with NT 4.0 SP3; it's also included as part of NT Server Enterprise Edition. Because NT 5.0 stores its user account data in the Active Directory, *SYSKEY* is neither included nor supported in NT 5.0.*

What SYSKEY Does

SYSKEY adds an extra layer of security to the password data stored in the SAM database by encrypting the hashed password data using a 128-bit *system key*. This key (Microsoft calls it the *password encryption key*, or PEK; so will I) is randomly generated when you install *SYSKEY*. Once your PEK is generated, NT uses it to encrypt and decrypt all password data (but not the ordinary account data) in the SAM. Because the data's encrypted, it's useless to any thief or cracker who might get it (and getting it still requires you to gain physical and administrative access to a domain controller). As a bonus, because the data is stored in encrypted form, it remains protected when it's backed up to an ERD or a tape.

Once the password data's encrypted, it's stored back into the SAM database, and services (including the local security authority, or LSA) that access the password data must depend on the kernel to decrypt it for them. For this to work, though, the kernel has to know what the PEK is at boot time: the SAM password information includes password data for system services that start when the machine's booted, in addition to the more mundane user password data.

To accomplish this, NT stores the PEK. You might wonder how storing the PEK could possibly increase security; it seems foolish to store the master password used to encrypt the data that's supposed to be protected! The answer is simple: *another* key is used to encrypt the PEK. This second key is the system key, after

---

* This is true as of NT 5 beta 1, but who knows whether that will change?

which *SYSKEY* is named. *SYSKEY* supports three options for storing the system key and making it available to the system when it's needed to decrypt the PEK.

The first, and most secure, option allows you to store the system key on a floppy. When the machine's booted, the floppy must be present so the kernel can retrieve the system key and use it to decrypt the PEK. Without the right floppy, the machine cannot be booted into the version of NT that's protected by that floppy.* This introduces a new single point of failure for your machines, so it's critical to keep backup copies of the floppy. In addition, the floppy serves as a token that allows access to the SAM data, so you must control who has access to it.

The next option is to store the system key encrypted with another key. This second key is generated from a passphrase you choose. Instead of inserting the system key floppy at boot time, a human must be present to type in the passphrase. The encrypted version of the system key is stored on the computer so that only the passphrase is required; there's no separate floppy or key disk involved.

Finally, you can choose to have the system key stored on the local machine. NT uses what Microsoft calls a "complex obfuscation algorithm" to hide the key. This is supposed to make it hard to compromise the system key. This reliance on "security through obscurity" offers considerably less security than the other available methods, but it has one saving grace: it allows unattended reboots, since the kernel can derive the PEK when needed without any human intervention. This is critical for some applications; only you can determine whether it's the best choice for your servers.

Before You Install SYSKEY

As with most other NT components, it's tempting to rush out and install *SYSKEY* now that you know how it can add security to your machines' Registry data. However, in this case it pays to be cautious and make sure you've adequately planned deploying *SYSKEY* on your network. It's important to understand what *SYSKEY* will protect you against and what additional problems it can potentially impose. Committing to using *SYSKEY* is not to be done lightly.

Every NT 4.0 workstation and server can run *SYSKEY*, and each machine can use any of the three system key storage options mentioned earlier. If you choose to use key floppies or passphrases, remember that the floppy or passphrase is just like an ERD: it's useful only on the machine where it was created, so you'll have

---

* Each NT installation gets its own unique PEK. If you have multiple versions of NT installed on a single computer, each has a unique PEK. If you have two NT installs on one machine and lose the system key disk for one of them, you can still boot the other one.

one disk or passphrase for every protected machine. (You can cheat and use the same passphrase on all machines, though.)

First of all, let's start with the scariest problem: *SYSKEY* can make your system more secure, but it's a one-way trip. Once you enable strong encryption of the SAM account database, there's no way to turn off encryption and go back to the old unencrypted version (though you can use an ERD, as described below). In practice, as long as you keep your ERDs up to date, you won't need to go back to the unencrypted version.

The next problem is what security experts call the "steel lock, balsa-wood door" problem. If you have multiple domain controllers for one domain, and one uses *SYSKEY* but the others don't, you haven't added any security to your network. One machine's SAM database is protected, but—since all the other controllers have replicated copies—the data you wanted to secure is still easy to grab. Ideally, you should implement *SYSKEY* on every machine that has an accounts database. That means all domain controllers and any NT workstation machine that has local accounts.

The final difficulty posed by *SYSKEY* is the fact that it adds security by encrypting the data on your machine. As long as you retain access to the system key, NT can decrypt the PEK and use it to access the stored passwords. If you choose to use a passphrase or key floppy, and you lose or forget it, you'll have to restore from an ERD. If the only ERD you have was made after the Registry was encrypted, you *still* won't be able to get in! It's critical to safeguard the key floppy and make backup copies of it so a bad floppy doesn't take you out of production—but since the key floppy is a security component, you have to keep careful watch over it.

"What I tell you three times is true"

Microsoft recommends making a total of three ERDs when installing *SYSKEY*: one before installing the *SYSKEY* hotfix or service pack, one after installing it but before enabling *SYSKEY*, and one after the first reboot after installing *SYSKEY*. While this may seem excessive, making all three of these disks maximizes the likelihood that you'll be able to recover your machine if it crashes in the future:

- The post-*SYSKEY* ERD contains the encrypted version of your accounts database. As you add and remove accounts, keep this ERD up to date. As long as you have the system key (either stored on the computer or on a floppy), you can restore the account database, and the rest of the Registry, from the ERD.

- The pre-*SYSKEY* ERD holds a complete record of your unencrypted Registry. If you ever need to recover the machine but don't have the system key, you have two choices: reinstall NT and lose all of your account data, or recover the Registry from this ERD and lose any changes made after *SYSKEY* was activated.

- The preinstall ERD protects you from problems with the hotfix or service pack. In general, you should *always* update your ERD just before installing any service pack or hotfix—this gives you an escape hatch if you need to back out of a fix that actually makes things worse on your machine.

Keep all three of these ERDs for each machine you might someday need to restore. At a minimum, that means you'll need them for every domain controller on your network, plus one set for any NT Workstation machine that has important local accounts.

Upgrading domain controllers

Microsoft also warns you about installing *SYSKEY* on your primary domain controller: if something goes wrong with the *SYSKEY* installation, or if you ever lose the system key for that one machine, no one will be able to log on to your domain! For domains with more than a few users, you should already have a backup domain controller anyway; if you don't, it's worth considering adding one.

The safest way to roll out *SYSKEY* in a multiple-domain or multiple-controller network is this:

1. Pick a domain. Make sure it has at least two domain controllers (one primary and one backup).

2. Demote the primary domain controller to backup status; this will automatically promote an available backup controller to the primary role. (If you need help doing this, see *Essential Windows NT System Administration* by Æleen Frisch.) This makes the newly promoted controller take charge of validating domain logon requests, and it also ensures that the new primary controller has a complete and correct copy of the domain account database.

3. Activate *SYSKEY* on the original primary domain controller. When you're satisfied that everything is working properly, demote the machine that got promoted in step 2. This will restore the original domain controller to primary status and leave your network as it was before you started.

4. Activate *SYSKEY* on the other domain controllers in the domain. If you have more than one domain on your network, go back to step 1 and pick another domain.

If you have domains with only one controller, it's probably okay to dispense with these steps and just activate *SYSKEY* on the controller, as long as you have the recommended set of three ERDs.

Turning On SYSKEY Protection

You control SAM database encryption with the *SYSKEY.EXE* executable. As you might expect, only administrators may turn on system key protection. The first time you run *SYSKEY*, you'll see the dialog shown in Figure 8-3. You'll note that the dialog warns you that encryption can't be disabled once you turn it on; you'll see that warning again after you first enable encryption. There are only five controls in the window: the Encryption Enabled and Encryption Disabled radio buttons show the current state of system key encryption on this machine. You can change from disabled to enabled, but not vice versa. The standard OK and Cancel buttons work like they do in every other dialog. The Update button allows you to change the key storage method later (you'll see how to do that in the next section, "Changing the key storage method").

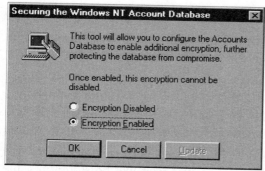

Figure 8-3. Initial SYSKEY dialog

The first step in activating *SYSKEY* is simple: click the Encryption Enabled radio button, then click the OK button. You'll see a warning dialog reminding you that this conversion can't be undone and suggesting that you ensure that you've got a current ERD before proceeding. When you click OK in that dialog, you'll see the Account Database Key dialog (see Figure 8-4), which you'll use to tell *SYSKEY* where you want the system key stored after it's generated:

- If you want to use a passphrase to unlock the system key, click the Password Startup button and type your password into the Password and Confirm fields. You may enter up to 128 characters for a passphrase, and longer phrases are better. Unfortunately, *SYSKEY* doesn't enforce any minimum length restrictions on the password. Microsoft recommends at least 12 characters, but it's easy to come up with a longer password than that: pick two easy-to-remember adjectives and a noun, then string them together with punctuation or special characters (like "exploding!friendly*holiday" or "galloping_sleepy#motor-home"). NT will feed the passphrase you enter to a special algorithm, which will generate a 128-bit key from it.

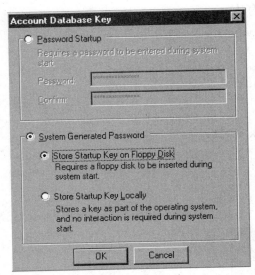

Figure 8-4. Specifying SYSKEY's location

- If you want the system to generate a password on its own, click the System Generated Password radio button. In this mode, NT will use its own pseudo-random number generator* to pick a random 128-bit system key. As you know, that key has to be stored somewhere. You get to choose where:

  — The Store Startup Key on Floppy Disk button instructs NT to keep the encrypted system key on a floppy. The key itself will be stored in a file named *StartKey.key*. When you choose this option, you'll need a floppy handy to hold the key. Although it may be temptingly close, *don't use your ERD* to store the key—doing so concentrates both pieces of data needed to steal passwords on a single floppy.

  — The Store Startup Key Locally button will store the obfuscated system key in `HKLM\SYSTEM`. When you choose this option, you'll be able to reboot the machine without having a human present.

Once you've selected the method you want to use, click the OK button. If you've chosen to store the key on a floppy, *SYSKEY* will prompt you to insert a floppy, and it will confirm that it's written the key to the disk. Otherwise, the key will be silently updated and *SYSKEY* will exit.

---

* The great mathematician and computer scientist John von Neumann once said that if you rely on software to generate random numbers you're living in a state of sin. However, cryptographically strong pseudorandom generators (like the one NT uses) are only a little sinful.

The next time you boot the machine, *SYSKEY* protection will be in effect. This means that unless you're storing the system key locally, you'll have to be at the machine every time it's rebooted to either type in the passphrase or stick in the key floppy.

TIP   If you're in a hurry, you can use the -1 flag with *SYSKEY*; this instructs it to silently generate a system key and store it on the local machine. This is a handy trick for use when setting up a new work-station or server; you can add the command to your ordinary setup scripts, then change the key storage method later when you have more time. This gives you immediate protection without any extra effort on your part.

Changing the key storage method

Once you've installed and activated *SYSKEY*, you're not bound to your initial choice of key storage. You can run *SYSKEY* again at any time and change from one method to another. When you change methods, *SYSKEY* generates a new system key and stores it instead of reusing the old key; this helps protect your password data against compromise.

To change the key storage method for a machine, run *SYSKEY* and click the Update button. The Account Database Key dialog (shown earlier in Figure 8-4) will appear; the radio button corresponding to the currently active storage method will be active. To change to a new method, just click one of the other radio buttons, filling in the password if necessary.

Because *SYSKEY* generates a new key when you change storage methods, you must supply the old key as part of the change process. This means that what happens after you click "OK" depends on what storage method you were *previously* using. If you changed from "Store Startup Key Locally" to something else, *SYSKEY* can get the old key from HKLM\SYSTEM, so you don't have to do anything. If you're changing from storing the password on a floppy or protected by a passphrase, *SYSKEY* will require you to provide the key disk or passphrase to continue. This prevents an attacker from changing the key, storing on a floppy, and stealing the floppy—thus rendering your machine unbootable.

Figure 8-5 shows the dialog that asks for the key disk, while Figure 8-6 shows the dialog requesting the current passphrase. If you supply the correct passphrase or floppy, *SYSKEY* will display a confirmation dialog to remind you that it's changed the system key, and the new key will be stored using the method you've chosen. If you don't supply the right information, *SYSKEY* won't change anything.

Figure 8-5. The key disk dialog

Figure 8-6. The password dialog

Restoring a SYSKEY-Protected Registry

Chapter 3, *In Case of Emergency,* described the mechanics of restoring a damaged Registry using an ERD. To restore a machine protected with *SYSKEY*, you follow this same basic procedure, but there are a few new subtleties introduced as a result of *SYSKEY*'s presence. The golden rule for restoring a *SYSKEY*-protected machine is simple: use the right ERD.

Restore SYSTEM and SAM hives

Even thought the actual encrypted account information is stored in the HKLM\SAM subtree, the actual PEK, as well as all the other data *SYSKEY* needs to tell where the system key is stored, lives in HKLM\SYSTEM. To recover an encrypted account database, you *must* restore both the SYSTEM and SAM hives at the same time—not just SAM. If you don't do this, NT won't be able to decrypt the Registry, either because it can't find the system key (if you don't restore SYSTEM) or because the key doesn't decrypt the data (if you don't restore SAM). Of course, you must restore these hives from the same ERD.

Get the right system components

If you got *SYSKEY* as the result of installing an NT 4.0 service pack, you may not have noticed that three existing system files were replaced as part of the update: *winlogon.exe, samsrv.dll*, and *samlib.dll*. These three files, along with *syskey.exe,* implement the account database protection. Their presence is required to enable the encrypted SAM data to be read and decrypted by system services that need it.

When you first install NT, it logs the versions of all the components you install in *system.log*. When you install service packs, hotfixes, or software like Internet Explorer that replaces one or more system files, the installer application is supposed to update the entries in *system.log* so that it always reflects the current version of all DLLs, drivers, and other operating system components.

What this means is that if you install *SYSKEY* as part of a hotfix or service pack, the *system.log* entries for *winlogon.exe, samsrv.dll,* and *samlib.dll* will reflect the versions installed with *SYSKEY*, not the original versions you installed. If you want to restore your machine to its pre-*SYSKEY* state, you'll need to use the NT setup application's "Repair system files" option to restore the original versions from your NT CD or file server. However, you must be sure to restore the SAM and SYSTEM hives from the pre-*SYSKEY* ERD: if you revert to the original system components but leave the encrypted Registry in place, nothing will work right.

WARNING   If you install *SYSKEY* but don't turn it on, the *winlogon.exe, sam-srv.dll,* and *samlib.dll* files won't match your original installation. When you install the new versions of these files, they change the Registry format even when encryption is off. If you use NT setup to restore these three files to their original state by using your pre-*SYS-KEY* ERD, you *must* also restore SAM and SYSTEM from the same ERD: if you don't, the old components won't be able to read the new Registry format.

Which ERD should I use?

Three ERDs is three more than most NT systems have, and so deciding which one to use may seem a little overwhelming. It's not hard, though: each ERD can put your system back into a particular state. Which one you use depends on what you want the restored system to have on it. Table 8-2 shows your options.

Miscellaneous Good Stuff

So far in this book, you've learned how to use a variety of tools to modify, back up, and restore the Registry. At this point, though, you might be wondering what you can actually *do* with some of these tools! There are some common and necessary administrative tasks involving the Registry; knowing how to perform them will help keep the machines under your care stable, secure, and safe.

Table 8-2. ERD Restoration Table

To revert to...	Use this ERD	Don't forget...
System as it was before installing *SYSKEY*	preinstall ERD	You may lose account database changes made since *SYSKEY* was installed.
		You must also choose "repair system files" in NT setup to restore the original versions of *winlogon.exe, samsrv.dll*, and *samlib.dll*.
		You can always fall back to this level, even without the system key.
System as it was after installing, but before activating, *SYSKEY*	pre-*SYSKEY* ERD	You may lose account database changes made since *SYSKEY* was installed.
		You can always fall back to this level, even without the system key.
		When using this ERD, *do not* "repair system files" from CD.
System as it was after activating *SYSKEY*	post-*SYSKEY* ERD	This preserves all account database changes since the ERD was updated.
		It requires presence of system key/passphrase on floppy or machine.
		When using this ERD, *do not* "repair system files" from CD.

Changing the Registry Size

Since the Registry is a collection of hives, most of which are actually disk files, you might not realize that NT actually maps the entire Registry into memory. Doing so makes it possible for Registry calls to perform efficiently; however, it means that as the Registry grows it takes up a larger proportion of the virtual memory space in your system. To prevent the Registry from sucking up too much space in the system's page file, NT maintains an internal parameter called the Registry Size Limit, or RSL. The RSL sets an upper bound on how much address space the Registry may occupy; however, as you add software and users to your machines, the Registry gets larger. If it gets so big that it starts to bump up against the RSL, problems will occur. (Go to the Microsoft knowledge base at *http://www.microsoft.com/kb/default.asp* and search for "Maximum Registry Size" to see a long list of such problems, most of which are reasonably obscure.)

By default, the RSL is set at about 20–25% of the total virtual memory allocation for the system. This limit is a maximum, not a guarantee, and the limit set by the RSL doesn't actually mean that that much space is reserved, just that the system can't use more than that. There's a complex relationship between the total size of the pool of available virtual memory and the RSL; in general, you should keep the RSL at 80% or less of the total virtual memory allocation. Failure to do so can result in impressive performance losses.

The Virtual Memory dialog (see Figure 8-7) shows you the current RSL *and* the current amount of space in use by the Registry. If the current size is more than 80% of the RSL, you should increase it. When choosing a new RSL, be sure to keep it below 80% of the total virtual memory size; in general, you shouldn't ever need to increase it above 33% of the virtual memory size. If you need more space even with an RSL 33% as big as your virtual memory stash, consider increasing the size of your virtual memory, *then* increase the RSL.

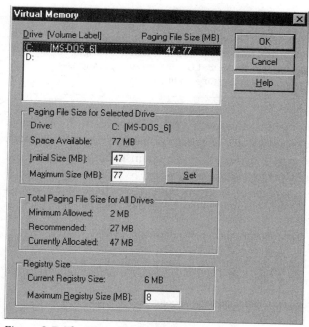

Figure 8-7. The Virtual Memory dialog

In NT 4.0, you adjust the RSL through the Virtual Memory dialog pictured in Figure 8-7. Here's how to change the RSL if you need to:

1. Open the System control panel and click on the Performance tab.

2. Click the Change button; the Virtual Memory dialog will appear.

3. Type a reasonable value into the Maximum Registry Size field.

4. Click OK, then close the Virtual Memory dialog, then close the System control panel. You'll be notified that your changes won't take effect until the next restart.

Auditing Registry Access

In "Auditing Registry Key Activity" in Chapter 5, you learned how to apply auditing controls to any key in the Registry. Since NT stores so much critical configuration data in the Registry, auditing some of it is a good idea—there are a number of keys you can audit to keep an eye on potential security problems or to catch users doing things they shouldn't be.

TIP   NT itself often determines whether a specific key is present by trying to read it and noting if the attempt fails. This is normal, and it's so common that I recommend you avoid auditing failed attempts on the Read, Query Value, or Enumerate Subkeys operations— doing so will generate lots of unnecessary audit log entries.

Once you turn on auditing, the events you specify will be stored in the system's event log. Since these files are your record of what auditable events have taken place, you need to make sure that they're protected against tampering too! Set their permissions to include Full Control for CreatorOwner, SYSTEM, and Administrators and Read for Everyone, then make sure no other users have write access to the log files.

Making sense of the audit log

When you enable auditing, NT will write an audit entry to the security event log whenever one of the conditions you specify comes true. Here's a sample entry:

```
12/2/97 11:27:19 PM Security Success Audit Object Access 560 Administrator
BOOMBOX
     Object Open:
     Object Server:    Security
     Object Type:      Key
     Object Name:      \REGISTRY\USER\S-1-5-21-34824712-245319459-1244863647-500
     New Handle ID:    240
     Operation ID:     {0,47947}
     Process ID: 2161664032
     Primary User Name: Administrator
     Primary Domain: BOOMBOX
     Primary Logon ID:    (0x0,0x1E35)
     Client User Name:    -
     Client Domain:  -
     Client Logon ID:     -
     Accesses          Create sub-key

     Privileges        -
```

I got this by turning on file/object access auditing in User Manager, then using *RegEdt32* to audit HKCU for successful Create Subkey access requests. Once I did, every time I created any subkey under HKCU I got a new audit record like the one above.

As you can see, this record tells me what key was the target of the request (the Object Name field), what user name made the attempt (along with that user's domain), and what access or privileges were requested. If you want to routinely scan your event logs for Registry accesses, I suggest using a tool like SomarSoft's *DumpEvt* (*http://www.somarsoft.com*), or writing your own Perl script to parse the Event Log using functions in the *Win32::EventLog* module.

Tracking software installations or reinstallations

Any software that uses the Registry (which means any package wearing the "Designed for Windows 95" or "Designed for Windows NT" logo, plus lots of others) will leave tracks in either HKLM\SOFTWARE or HKCU\SOFTWARE. Microsoft's recommendation is that software vendors create their own subkey of one of these two keys, so you'll see lots of entries like HKLM\SOFTWARE\NETSCAPE and HKLM\SOFTWARE\Qualcomm. You can audit these keys directly, or you can audit only specific subkeys of interest. For example, if you want to see an audit notice whenever someone adds new software to a machine, you could add an audit entry for "Create Subkey" on HKLM\SOFTWARE. If instead you wanted to know when someone installs only software made by Netscape, you could audit "Create Subkey" on HKLM\SOFTWARE\Netscape and HKCU\SOFTWARE\Netscape.

Guarding against Trojan horses

NT allows administrators to install one or more DLLs that validate passwords before passing them on to the logon subsystem. The NetWare gateway tools shipped with NT use such a DLL, and the documentation for what such a DLL should do is available from Microsoft. This opens the potential for a user to install a password-grabbing DLL that just stores the password in a file without changing it, then passes it on to the logon subsystem. NT keeps its list of these DLLs in HKLM\SYSTEM\CurrentControlSet\Control\Lsa\Notification Packages. I strongly recommend that you turn on auditing for this key.

Using the Resource Kit Utilities

Microsoft offers a separate package of NT tools, documentation, and utilities called the Windows NT Resource Kit. There are two versions: the NT Workstation Resource Kit contains tools pertinent to managing NT Workstation, and the NT Server Resource Kit includes server-specific material, plus everything from the Workstation edition. Even though some of the tools are only partly functional (like the "beta" telnet server that's been in beta for about two years now) and most are poorly documented, the Resource Kit is well worth the US$150 or so it costs, since many of its tools are unavailable from any other source.*

What's in the Resource Kit

The NT 4.0 Resource Kit CD has a wide variety of tools and documents on it. Table 8-3 summarizes items that have something to do with the Registry. Most of these tools originally shipped with the by-now-ancient NT 3.1 Resource Kit; in summer 1997, Microsoft issued an update to the resource kit (available from *ftp:// ftp.microsoft.com/bussys/winnt/winnt-public/reskit/nt40*), which adds a new tool, *reg.exe*. *reg* supersedes a number of other tools, even though they still appear on the resource kit CD. I've noted the superseded tools in the table so you'll know which ones you can safely skip over.

Table 8-3. Resource Kit Registry Tools

Tool	What it does	Notes
compreg.exe	Compares contents of two Registry values you specify—like *diff*.	See "Comparing Keys and Values" later in this chapter
reg.exe	Everything: add, remove, or change keys; load and unload hives, and lots more.	See "REG: The Swiss Army Knife" later in this chapter
regback.exe and *regrest.exe*	Backs up and restores Registry keys, values, and hives. Can be used to restore all or part of a damaged Registry.	Covered in Chapter 3
regchg.exe	Changes a single value from the command line.	Superseded by *reg.exe*
regdel.exe	Deletes the specified subkey of HKLM from the command line.	Superseded by *reg.exe*
regdir.exe	Provides a directory-style listing of a specified tree or subkey.	
regdmp.exe	Dumps the specified key, plus its subkeys and values, in text form.	
regentry.hlp	Documents many of NT's keys and values.	
regfind.exe	Searches the Registry for a specified value; works like *grep* or the search function in *RegEdit*.	See "Searching for Keys" later in this chapter
regini.exe	Adds, removes, or changes keys based on a command script you write.	

---

* Of course, you could argue that these tools should be included with NT itself. I'd agree with that, but then Microsoft would have to clean up, document, and test the tools, most of which are only of interest to support professionals, system admins, and the like.

Table 8-3. Resource Kit Registry Tools (continued)

Tool	What it does	Notes
regkey.exe	Offers a GUI to set several trivial parameters (auto-logon, number of cached user profiles, etc.).	Better to use system policies
regread.exe	Reads the specified subkey of HKLM and returns its values.	Superseded by *reg.exe*
regsec.exe	Sets security descriptors on a key and its subkeys; useful for undoing needlessly permissive default ACLs.	See "Fixing Registry Security ACLs" earlier in this chapter
restkey.exe	Restores a key saved by *SAVEKEY*.	Superseded by *reg.exe*
rktools.hlp	Gives a brief description of each tool in the Resource Kit.	
rregchg.exe	Changes a key's value on a remote machine.	Superseded by *reg.exe*
savekey.exe	Saves a key's values for later reloading.	Superseded by *reg.exe*

REG: The Swiss Army Knife

I have been heard to describe the *reg.exe* utility as "*RegEdt32* in a can." It does almost everything *RegEdt32* can do, but it allows you to do it from a command line.* Not only is this a boon when you want to quickly make a change without firing up *RegEdt32*; it also allows you to embed Registry operations in logon scripts and batch files. (Of course, you learned how to use the Registry from within Perl in Chapter 7, *Programming with the Registry*, but for the non-Perl-hackers among us *reg* is a welcome substitute.)

If you've ever used the *net* command, you'll immediately recognize how *reg* works. Like *net*, you use *reg* by giving it a command from a short list of options (query, add, update, delete, copy, save, backup, restore, load, and unload), followed by one or more optional parameters that the command you specify will interpret. Here's a short example in which *reg* gets the query command for a specified subkey of HKLM:

```
C:\ntreskit>reg query HKLM\Software\Qualcomm /s

Listing of [Software\Qualcomm]

[Eudora]
[Eudora\3.0.1]
```

---

* It's so useful that I've learned to overlook the many grammatical errors and misspellings in its prompts and error messages. Quality is job 1.1, right?

Querying keys

`reg query` allows you to query a single key for a single value, or a range of keys for all their values. This provides you with a quick way to check whether a key has the value you think it does, or in fact whether it has any values associated with it at all:

REG QUERY [*rootKey*\]*key* [*value*] [*machine*] [/S]

rootKey
> Optional; specifies which root key to use as base of query. May be HKLM, HKCU, HKCR, HKU, or HKCC. Defaults to HKLM if omitted.

key
> Specifies the full name of a key under the specified *rootKey*.

value
> Specifies a value under *key* to query. If omitted, all keys and values under *key* will be displayed.

machine
> Name of a remote machine to query; if omitted, defaults to local machine. You can only query HKLM and HKU on remote machines.

/s   Query all subkeys of *key*.

Adding new keys

`reg add` adds new keys and values to the Registry. You can add a value to an existing key, add a new key with no values, or create a new key and a value beneath it. If you try to add a key or value that already exists, *reg* will warn you.

REG ADD [*rootKey*\]*key* [*value=newValue*] [*machine*] [*dataType*]

rootKey
> Optional; specifies which root key to add new key under. May be HKLM, HKCU, HKCR, HKU, or HKCC. Defaults to HKLM if omitted.

key
> Specifies the full name of the key to add under the specified *rootKey*.

value
> Optionally specifies the name of a value to add under *key*. If omitted, the key will be created with no value.

newValue
> Contents of newly created value. String values may contain spaces and special characters, but must be enclosed in double quotes if they do.

machine
> Name of a remote machine to query; if omitted, defaults to local machine. You can only query HKLM and HKU on remote machines.

dataType

> Type of the new value to be added. May be REG_SZ, REG_MULTI_SZ, REG_ EXPAND_SZ, or REG_DWORD. If omitted, REG_SZ is the default. If you specify REG_DWORD, you must specify *newValue* as a decimal number.

For example, to add the value that disables Dial-Up Networking's "save password" checkbox, you could use this command:

```
reg add SYSTEM\CurrentControlSet\Services\
RasMan\Parameters\DisableSavePasswordValue=1
```

Updating existing keys

reg update updates a single value of an existing key. You can update any value where you have permission according to the parent key's ACL; if you're trying to modify a remote machine's Registry you must have access to it. *reg* will warn you if you try to modify a nonexistent value.

```
REG UPDATE [rootKey\]key [\value=newValue] [machine]
```

rootKey

> Optional; specifies which root key holds the targeted key. May be HKLM, HKCU, HKCR, HKU, or HKCC on local machine or HKLM or HKU on remote machine. Defaults to HKLM if omitted.

key

> Specifies the full name of the key to update under the specified *rootKey*.

value

> Specifies which value under *key* to update.

newValue

> Contents to use when replacing existing value. String values may contain spaces and special characters, but must be enclosed in double quotes if they do. DWORD values must be specified in decimal.

machine

> Name of a remote machine to query; if omitted, defaults to local machine. You can only query HKLM and HKU on remote machines.

Removing a key

reg delete removes a key or value. When removing a key, it will remove all subkeys and values beneath that key; however, it will ask you to confirm your intentions before it actually deletes anything. That notwithstanding, be careful when using this command. As with reg update, you can only delete keys where the ACLs (and/or the remote Registry settings) allow you access.

```
REG DELETE [rootKey\]key [\value] [machine]
```

rootKey

Optional; specifies which root key the targeted key lives under. May be HKLM, HKCU, HKCR, HKU, or HKCC on local machine or HKLM or HKU on remote machine. Defaults to HKLM if omitted.

key

Specifies the full name of the key to update under the specified *rootKey*.

value

Specifies which value under *key* to remove. If omitted, all keys and values under *key* will be deleted.

machine

Name of a remote machine to query; if omitted, defaults to local machine. You can only query HKLM and HKU on remote machines.

Copying keys and values

reg copy might be my favorite of all *reg*'s commands, if only because it greatly eases the process of copying settings from one place to another. You can use the command to copy a single value or an entire hive from its original location to another; the target location can be on the same machine as the source or on any other machine on the network! This command makes short work out of tasks like copying a standard set of file associations to new machines or tweaking one machine so its configuration matches another.

```
REG COPY [srcRootKey\]srcKey [\srcValue] [srcMachine] [destRootKey\]destKey
         [\destValue] [destMachine]
```

srcRootKey

Optional; specifies which root key holds the source key. May be HKLM, HKCU, HKCR, HKU, or HKCC. Defaults to HKLM if omitted.

srcKey

Specifies the full name of the source key.

srcValue

Optionally specifies a value under *srcKey* to copy. If omitted, all keys and values under *srcKey* are copied.

srcMachine

Name of a remote machine to act as copy source; if omitted, defaults to local machine. You can only use remote machines' HKLM and HKU as source roots.

destRootKey

Optional; specifies where copied key should be rooted. May be HKLM or HKU; defaults to HKLM if omitted.

destKey

Specifies the full name of the key to hold the copied data.

destValue

Optionally specifies name for a single copied value; ignored if no *srcValue* is specified.

destMachine

Name of a remote machine to serve as the copy target; if omitted, defaults to local machine.

When I installed a beta version of a popular Internet mail package, I (rightly, as it turned out) feared that the new version would damage the old version's Registry settings. A quick command saved the day:

```
reg copy software\qualcomm\eudora software\qualcomm\eudora-3.0
```

made a backup copy of my existing settings so I could install the new version, secure in the knowledge that I could easily revert back to a previous version if needed.

Saving and restoring keys

The *REGBACK* and *REGREST* utilities allow you to back up and restore entire hives, but *reg* offers a similar pair of functions that add the ability to save and reload individual keys, much like *RegEdt32*'s commands. To save a key and its values, you can use either **reg save** or **reg backup** (they're synonyms):

```
REG SAVE [rootKey\]key fileName [machine]
```

rootKey

Optional; specifies under which root key the key to save lives. May be HKLM, HKCU, HKCR, HKU, or HKCC on local machine or HKLM or HKU on remote machine. Defaults to HKLM if omitted.

key

Specifies the full name of the key to update under the specified *rootKey*. If omitted, all contents of *rootKey* are saved.

fileName

Names the file that will hold the saved data. *fileName* may not have an extension specified.

machine

Name of a remote machine to query; if omitted, defaults to local machine.

To quickly store a copy of all of your current settings, you could use this command:

```
reg save HKLM my-profile
```

then use it anywhere you can use a hive file.

You may also restore a saved hive with the **reg restore** command. This command overwrites an existing key with a new set of values, so you must be cautious when using it (*reg* will ask you to confirm your command before it overwrites anything, though):

```
REG RESTORE fileName [rootKey\]key [machine]
```

fileName

> Names the file that holds the data you want restored, with no extension.

rootKey

> Optional; specifies which root key the targeted key lives under. May be HKLM, HKCU, HKCR, HKU, or HKCC on local machine or HKLM or HKU on remote machine. Defaults to HKLM if omitted.

key

> Specifies the full name of the key whose subkeys and values will be replaced.

machine

> Name of a remote machine to query; if omitted, defaults to local machine. You can only query HKLM and HKU on remote machines.

Loading and unloading hives

The section "Saving and Loading Registry Keys" in Chapter 5 explains how you can use *RegEdt32* to load and unload saved keys as hives immediately beneath HKLM or HKU. The *reg* utility gives you the same ability, albeit with the same limitations.

To load a hive, you use the **reg load** command. Unlike **reg restore**, **reg load** loads the hive by adding it with the key name you specify instead of overwriting the key you specify. This makes it possible for you to use **reg load** to load a saved hive, edit it, and unload it again without making any changes to the rest of your Registry. (If you're wondering why you might want to do so, go back and reread the section "Setting Defaults for New User Accounts" at the beginning of the chapter.) Here's what the command looks like:

```
REG LOAD fileName [rootKey\]key [machine]
```

fileName

> Specifies the name of the hive file to load, with no extension. You may specify a full local or UNC path here.

rootKey

> Optionally specifies which root key the new hive should be created under. May be HKLM or HKU. Defaults to HKLM if omitted.

key

> Specifies the name of the key to receive the new hive; this key will be created and must not already exist. *key* must be an immediate subkey of HKLM or HKU.

machine

> Name of a remote machine to load the hive on.

For example, to load the *ntuser.dat* hive as suggested in "Setting Defaults for New User Accounts," just copy *ntuser.dat* to *ntuser-default*, then use this command:

```
reg load ntuser-default DefaultProfile
```

then modify the hive as needed.

Once you've finished working with a loaded hive, you may unload it with reg unload. Its command syntax is pretty simple:

```
REG UNLOAD [rootKey\]key [machine]
```

rootKey

> Optional; specifies which root key holds the hive to unload. May be HKLM, HKCU, HKCR, HKU, or HKCC on local machine or HKLM or HKU on remote machine. Defaults to HKLM if omitted.

key

> Specifies the full name of the key to unload. *key* must be an immediate subkey of HKLM or HKU.

machine

> Name of a remote machine on which to unload the hive; if omitted, defaults to local machine

Comparing Keys and Values

When you're trying to troubleshoot a configuration problem, it's often useful to examine the broken machine and one that works to discern what's different between the two. Without the resource kit, doing this with the Registry involves saving suspect portions of the Registry to a text file, then using a difference tool like *windiff* to highlight differences between the two files. The *compreg* tool, included for the first time in the NT 4.0 resource kit, provides a command-line tool for comparing differences in Registry keys. Here's how it works:

```
COMPREG key1 key2 [-v] [-r] [-e] [-d] [-q] [-n] [-h] [-?]
```

key1

> Specifies the full path to the first key to compare. This path can include a machine name (e.g., \\ENIGMA\HKEY_LOCAL_MACHINE\SOFTWARE\LJL). Instead of spelling out the Registry keys, you may abbreviate them by taking

the standard mnemonic we've used in this book and dropping the initial "HK"; for example, you could also specify a path of \\ENIGMA\lm\SOFT-WARE\LJL to save some typing. If no root is specified, HKCU is the default.

key2

> Specifies the full path to the second key to compare. This can be the same path as *key1* but on a different machine, or it can be a different path altogether. If you only specify a machine name, *compreg* uses the path from *key1* but looks for it on the computer specified in *key2*.

-*v* Verbose mode; prints both keys whose values differ and those that match.

-*r* Recurse into keys that only have a single subkey.

-*e* At exit, sets errorlevel to the last error encountered. This switch lets you test the return value of *compreg* when using it in scripts or batch files.

-*d* Suppresses printing the values of keys whose values differ; just prints the keys themselves.

-*n* Monochrome output (the default scheme uses multiple colors).

-*?* Displays a short help message.

The ability to find differences between two machines is extremely useful at times. While troubleshooting some of the entries in Chapter 9, *Registry Tweaks*, I wanted to clone an existing drive restriction and modify it. Unfortunately, after I modified it it didn't work, and I couldn't see what I had done wrong. A quick

```
compreg software\Microsoft\Windows\CurrentVersion\Policies\Explorer \\armory
```

showed me my error, and I was able to fix it without any further damage to my Registry or my self-esteem.

Searching for Keys

Sometimes there's no substitute for a little brute-force searching. If you've ever used *grep* or *findstr* (the Win32 equivalent) to find something you *knew* was somewhere on your disk, you'll love *regfind*. It's very flexible: it can search for value and key names or contents, it can search or search and replace, and it understands all of the common Registry data types. This flexibility makes it a bit more complex than some of the other reskit utilities, though:

```
REGFIND [-h hiveFile hiveRoot | -w win95Dir | -m \\machine]
        [-i tabStop] [-o outputWidth]
        [-p keyPath] [-z | -t dataType] [-b | -B] [-y] [-n]
        [searchString [-r replacementString]]
```

-*h hiveFile hiveRoot*

> Specifies the full path to a local hive file (generated with reg save or *RegEdt32*).

-w win95Dir

> Tells *regfind* to look for Windows 95 *user.dat* and *system.dat* hive files in the directory specified by *win95Dir*.

-m machine

> Specifies that *regfind* should search the NT machine named *machine*.

-i tabStop

> Sets the tabstop width; the default is 4.

-o outputWidth

> Tells *regfind* how wide to make its output. The default is the width of the console window, or 240 if the output's been redirected to a file.

-p keyPath

> Directs *regfind* to start looking in *keyPath*. You may specify one of HKEY_LOCAL_MACHINE, HKEY_USERS, HKEY_CURRENT_USER, or USER; since HKCR and HKCC are links into HKLM, this is not a big loss. If you omit this switch, *regfind* will search the entire Registry.

-z Searches for REG_MULTI_SZ or REG_EXPAND_SZ strings that are missing the required zero terminator or that have illegal lengths.

-t dataType

> Forces *regfind* to look only at values with the specified data type. You may specify any one of REG_SZ, REG_MULTI_SZ, REG_EXPAND_SZ, REG_DWORD, REG_BINARY, and REG_NONE. If no type is specified, *regfind* will look at all the SZ types.

-b Tells *regfind* to look for the specified search string inside of REG_BINARY values in addition to any SZ type specified with -t.

-B Same as -b, but also searches for ANSI strings in addition to Unicode.

-y When used during an SZ search, forces *regfind* to do a case-insensitive search. Ignored for REG_DWORD, REG_BINARY, and REG_NONE searches.

-n Searches key and value names, not just contents. -n and -t are mutually exclusive.

searchString

> String to search for. To search for strings with embedded spaces, brackets, etc., wrap it in double quotes. If no search string is specified, the search will find values of the specified type. When searching for a REG_DWORD, you may specify it in decimal or hex, with a leading 0x. When searching for a binary value, you must provide a length byte, optionally followed by a sequence of DWORDs containing the actual data to search for.

-r replacementString

> Replaces any occurrence of *searchString* with *replacementString*. *searchString* and *replacementString* must be of the same type, but their lengths may differ. There are several constraints that apply to the use of -r:
>
> — You may specify *replacementString* the same way as *searchString*. However, if your *searchString* is a REG_BINARY length only, you may not use -r.
>
> — If you specify -z and -r together, the replacement string will be ignored. Instead of replacing anything, *regfind* will fix any strings with missing terminators or bad lengths.
>
> — There's no confirmation option with -r, so it's a good idea to run *regfind* without it until you're sure that what will be replaced is what you want replaced.

Because this is a complicated command, an example may help to clarify how the command works. Let's try finding all the keys whose contents or names include the string "Mac":

```
C:\ntreskit>regfind -y -n Mac
Scanning \Registry registry tree
Case Insensitive Search for 'Mac'
Will match values of type: REG_SZ REG_EXPAND_SZ REG_MULTI_SZ
Search will include key or value names
\Registry
    Machine
        SOFTWARE
            Microsoft
                AsyncMac
                Exchange
                    Client
                        Mac File Types
                Shared Tools
                    Text Converters
                        Export
                            MSWordMac4
                            MSWordMac5
                            MSWordMac51
                        Import
                            MSWordMac
        SYSTEM
            ControlSet001
                Services
                    AsyncMac
                    AsyncMac2
                    EventLog
                        System
                            AsyncMac
            ControlSet003
                Services
                    AsyncMac
```

```
                    AsyncMac2
                    EventLog
                        System
                            AsyncMac
            Users
                S-1-5-21-1944135612-1199777195-24521265-500
                    Software
                        Microsoft
                            Ntbackup
                                Backup Engine
                                    Process Macintosh files = 1
                                    Machine Type = 0
                        Telnet
                            Machine1 = fly.hiwaay.net
                            LastMachine = hq
                            Machine2 = hq
```

The only real drawback to *regfind* is that it can't handle regular expressions or wildcards like *findstr* and *grep* can. Apart from that limitation, though, it's a valuable tool when you need to find a key whose value you know but whose path you don't.

Spying on the Registry with NTREGMON

Ask a private investigator what the best way to gather evidence is, and you're likely to get a simple answer: watch and wait. Unfortunately, trying to use *RegEdt32* or *RegEdit* to watch the registry as it changes is a difficult and unrewarding way to work. Unless you know ahead of time exactly which keys or values you want to watch, it's difficult to monitor individual changes, and there's no easy way to tell which application, process, or driver changed the setting you're trying to watch.

Mark Russinovich and Bryce Cogswell have solved this problem, to the delight of administrators and programmers everywhere. They wrote a utility called *NTREGMON* (available with source code from *http://www.ntinternals.com/*) that lets you spy on every Registry access made anywhere in the system. It can monitor reads, writes, and queries and record them in a log that you can peruse at will; it can also limit the Registry accesses it records based on filtering criteria that you supply. *NTREGMON* makes short work of figuring out who modified a particular key or value, and it's a great resource for watching what NT does with Registry data.

NTREGMON works by installing a small device driver when you run the application; this driver installs hooks to all the Registry API routines, so it can see what parameters callers pass in and what results the system returns. The *NTREGMON* application itself just opens the device driver and waits for it to send along the data it's captured.

Sneaking a Peek with RegEdt32

REGMON isn't the only way to spy on the Registry. Here's a handy trick that will allow you to see even the SAM and SECURITY hives (on NT 3.51 and NT 4 machines), which are normally inaccessible.

1. Enable the Scheduler service and have it log in as the SYSTEM account by selecting the "System Account" radio button in the Services dialog.

2. Once the Scheduler is running, open an NT command-line window and use the at command to schedule an invocation of *RegEdt32* in the near future. For example, if it's 1:35 P.M. when you start off, schedule *RegEdt32* to run at 1:36 P.M. like this:

   ```
   at 13:36 /interactive regedt32.exe
   ```

At the appointed time, *RegEdt32* will open, but it will be running under the SYSTEM account instead of your normal account. HKLM\SYSTEM and HKLM\SAM will be enabled, so you can open and inspect them. Don't expect to see much, since their contents are all binary data. *Don't edit anything in these hives.*

One extremely valuable thing you can do with this trick is to enable auditing on the SAM hive. This can give you an audit trail of attempted *and* successful misbehavior, including grabbing the password hashes or changing passwords on the Administrator account.

Learning the NTREGMON Interface

NTREGMON has an extremely simple interface. As you can see in Figure 8-8, it uses a single document window to display the Registry data it captures. The toolbar offers access to all six of the menu commands; the bulk of the window is devoted to the list of captured data. Each column of the list has its own header at the top of the list window; you can resize each column in the list by dragging the small vertical lines next to each header.

Each entry in the list displays six fields' worth of data:

- ID is a sequence number assigned by *NTREGMON*. The first thing it logs gets ID #1, and the ID is incremented from there. However, these IDs are assigned by the device driver. If events occur faster than *NTREGMON* can add them to its display list, you'll notice gaps in the numbering.

- Process shows the name of the process that made the request. Since DLLs are loaded into a process' address space, *NTREGMON* only shows the process name, not the name of the individual DLL making the request.

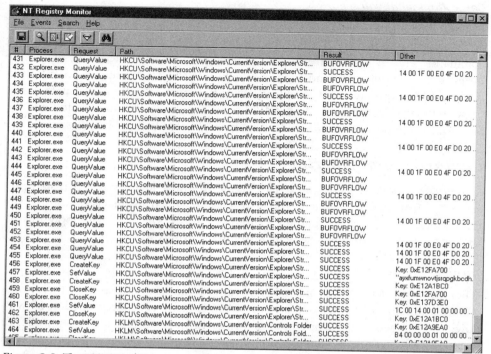

Figure 8-8. The NTREGMON main interface

- Request shows what action the requesting process asked for. Most often, you'll see QueryValue, OpenKey, CloseKey, and SetValue, but *NTREGMON* also reports enumerations, security changes, and all the other Registry services available through the Registry API documented in Chapter 7.

- Path shows the path supplied as part of the request. *NTREGMON* always shows the path including the topmost root key.

- Result shows the numeric result code returned by whatever Registry API routine was called. You'll see a lot of "SUCCESS" entries here, with an occasional "NOTFOUND." It's rare to see anything other than these two.

- Other is a catch-all field. For Registry calls that return data, *NTREGMON* will show the data here as a value of whatever type is appropriate. You'll see string values in quotes, but DWORDs, HKEYs, and other binary data will appear as a block of hex digits. It's up to you to interpret binary data and make sense out of it.

Controlling what you see

Besides dragging the column headers to resize each individual column, *NTREG-MON* doesn't offer much in the way of user interface. The **Events ➤ Clear Display** command erases the current list of logged Registry accesses, and the **Events ➤ Auto Scroll** command toggles whether *NTREGMON* attempts to automatically scroll the displayed list to always show the most recently added item. Apart from these two commands, *NTREGMON* is a vanilla application—it follows the Microsoft UI guidelines and doesn't offer any additional bells or whistles.

Capturing and Filtering

Using *NTREGMON* to figure out what's going on in the Registry is a two-step process. The first step is optional: you may choose which events you want to see (and which you don't) by building a capture filter. *NTREGMON* will apply this filter during the second step—the actual capture of events.

Turning capture on and off

When you first start *NTREGMON*, it's in capture mode. If you just sit there for a minute and let it run, you'll see an occasional Registry access recorded in its window; you can see many, many more if you switch to Explorer and open a file, or even click on an icon in your My Computer window. If you leave *NTREGMON* in capture mode, it's likely to capture an overwhelming amount of data, much of which won't bear any relation to the data you're actually looking for.

The best way to reduce this information overload is simple: turn off capture mode when you don't need it. The **Events ➤ Capture Events** command toggles capture mode off and on (as does the toolbar button).

Using capture filters

The **Events ➤ Filter…** command is the first command in the Events menu for a good reason: it's the most useful command in the whole program! The NTRegmon Filter dialog (see Figure 8-9) lets you specify in detail which events you want to see in the capture list and which you don't. Here are the filter criteria you may specify:

- Process filters by the name of the requesting process. In Figure 8-9, I've specified that I only want to see calls made by *spoolss.exe* and the DLLs it loads into its process space. You may use wildcards in this field, and case distinctions are ignored.

- Path Include and Path Exclude combine to allow you fairly fine control over what key paths are logged. The path, and its subkeys, you specify in Path Include will be monitored except for whatever paths you list in Path Exclude.

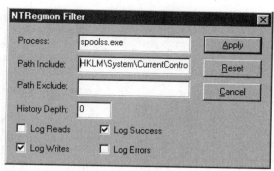

Figure 8-9. NTREGMON's filter dialog

For example, if you put HKLM\SOFTWARE in Path Include and HKLM\SOFT-WARE\Microsoft in Path Exclude, your log will show accesses to any keys in HKLM\SOFTWARE except keys under Microsoft. These paths may include wildcards, too.

- History Depth is mislabeled. It should say "Number of entries to keep" or something similar; it actually controls how many lines worth of data *NTREGMON* keeps before purging its internal list. The default value of 0 means that new data are just added at the end, but you can provide a specific value (say, "10" to have *NTREGMON* keep only the last 10 audited events).

- The Log checkboxes let you control what actions *NTREGMON* will log. By default, it will log reads, writes, successes, and errors, but you may adjust this to narrow down the breadth of the data you have to wade through.

Figure 8-9 shows a set of filter criteria, and Figure 8-10 shows the events captured by the filter criteria; I was trying to determine whether the printer spooler would write out all the printer properties if I changed just one of them.*

Saving your captured data

NTREGMON can save its logged data as a tab-delimited text file. There's no provision for saving part of a log—you can either save every logged event, or none. This is easy to work around, though; all you need to do is define an appropriate capture filter before you capture data, then there won't be any extraneous stuff in your capture log.

The **File ➤ Save**... and **File ➤ Save As**... commands let you save logged data to a file you specify. Unlike the Performance Monitor, there's no way to load a file of

---

* The answer: yes, it does. In fact, it even writes out data that are not part of this particular printer's property set.

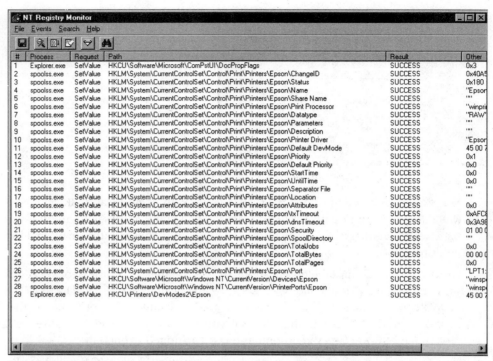

Figure 8-10. Filtered events

saved data for further review; you'll have to use a spreadsheet or text editor to
view the saved data if you need it later.

9

Registry Tweaks

In the preceding chapters, I showed you how to use the Registry tools and programming interfaces. As a sort of graduation exercise, this chapter contains a list of Registry settings you can use to change the way your computer behaves. I have deliberately not listed anything unsafe or dangerous here; as long as you follow the restrictions stated in each setting's explanatory text, these changes should be safe for you to make on any NT 4.0 machine.

If you carefully read Tables 6-1 through 6-4 in Chapter 6, *Using the System Policy Editor*, you may notice that some of these items are also editable through a system policy. That's on purpose; even if you're not using policies you may still want to make these changes. Of course, you can take any setting in this chapter and add it as a policy template file using the instructions in the section "Creating Your Own Policy Templates" in Chapter 6.

WARNING   Be careful to apply the correct capitalization to any values or keys you change. Some applications are smart enough to ignore case, but most aren't.

The actual mechanics of making these changes should be pretty obvious by now: use your favorite Registry editor to add or modify keys or values as described for each setting. Some of these tweaks require you to add a new key, while others may require you to add or change a specific value. In all cases, when I say something like "add the value `HKCU\Control Panel\Desktop\WindowMetrics\MinAnimate`," what that means is that you should add it if it doesn't already exist. If it does exist, change its value as suggested in the text.

User Interface Tweaks

The NT user interface is customizable in a lot of small ways. You can't easily change the standard way windows and menus work, for example, but you can change their colors. In that spirit, there are several adjustments you can make to change some basics of how you and NT interact with one another.

Add Your Own "Tip of the Day"

Microsoft Word for Windows introduced the "Tip of the Day" feature, which presents an ostensibly helpful tip every time you start a tip-enabled application. This feature made it into Windows 95, Office 95, NT 4.0, and a raft of third-party applications. Apart from disabling the feature altogether (which you can do with the "Don't show tips at startup" checkbox in the Tip of the Day dialog), you can add your own set of tips. This is particularly useful when you make this change as part of a system policy—you can build your own set of tips that are specific to your local environment, then remove the ability for users to turn the tips off. This is an easy, and cheap, way to disseminate information to your users. The list of tips is stored as a set of values under:

> HKLM\Software\Microsoft\Windows\CurrentVersion\Explorer\Tips.

The tip values are stored as sequentially named REG_SZ values; the first one is named "0", and the names go up from there. You can replace any of the existing tips included with NT by changing that tip's value; alternatively, you can replace all of them by removing all the values under Tips and replacing them with your own.

However, the tip list is only half of the necessary change. There's also a pair of REG_BINARY values that control whether tips are displayed and which tip comes next. These values are stored in HKCU, so they can be different for every individual user. Here's how they work:

HKCU\Software\Microsoft\Windows\CurrentVersion\Explorer\Tips\Show
> Controls whether tips are shown at startup or not. A value of 00000000 disables the tip display, while 01000000 enables it.

HKCU\Software\Microsoft\Windows\CurrentVersion\Explorer\Tips\Next
> Controls which tip appears next. Its value is a sequence number that must match the name of a value in the tips list. A value of 00000000 displays tip 0, 01000000 displays tip 1, 0c000000 displays tip 12, and so on. NT will automatically increment and update this value as each tip is displayed.

Disable Window Animations

NT 4.0 copies the Win95 habit of using animated rectangles to provide a "zooming" effect when windows are opened and closed. However, after the first few times you've seen this effect it can become annoying; it also causes a slight but perceptible slowdown as the system draws all the fancy rectangles instead of just closing the window directly.

If you want to disable this animation, you may do so by adding the REG_DWORD value HKCU\Control Panel\Desktop\WindowMetrics\MinAnimate and setting its value to 0. If you later decide that you like the animations after all, setting Min-Animate back to 1 will turn it back on again.

Speed Up the Taskbar

The NT 4.0 Taskbar is a useful addition to the standard user interface. When Apple was designing the Macintosh interface, their research found that a single menu bar at the top or bottom of the screen was the fastest menu system; instead of having to carefully guide the mouse to a particular area, you can just slam it down (or up) to the menu region without any need for precise control. The Taskbar's default location at the bottom of the screen satisfies this. One failing of the Taskbar, however, is the speed with which the Start menu (and other menus attached to Taskbar items) pops up. In a word, it's slow. Fortunately, the speed is adjustable via a Registry change.

To adjust the Taskbar popup speed, add a REG_SZ value named MenuShowDelay to HKCU\Control Panel\Desktop. This value determines the number of milliseconds the shell will pause before displaying the Taskbar. By default, it's set to "400," which is a 0.4 second delay. Adjust it to your taste, then reboot to make the change take effect.

Enable Tab for Filename Completion

If you're a Unix administrator or programmer, you'll love this one. Many Unix shells allow you to quickly complete filenames in the shell by using the Tab key. For example, if you type "ls -l aar" and hit the Tab key, the shell will look for files whose names start with "aar." If it finds one, it automatically expands what you typed into the full file or directory name. This is a lifesaver, especially since Unix allows you to have very long file and path names with embedded spaces—just like NT.

If you want to enable this behavior in NT 4.0 command windows, you can do it by adding a REG_DWORD named HKCU\Software\Microsoft\Command Processor\CompletionChar and setting its value to the hex value of the character you want to use for filename completion. (If you don't already have a Command Pro-cessor key you'll need to add it too.) To use the Tab key, set its value to 0x09. While you may use other characters, I'd stick with Tab, since nothing else in the command window uses it.

Run a Different Screen Saver While Waiting for a Logon

You probably know that you can use the "Screen Savers" tab of the Display con-trol panel to set a screen saver to be run after a specified period of inactivity. You can also choose which screen saver runs while an NT machine is waiting for a logon. The default choice displays the familiar "Press Ctrl+Alt+Del to log in" dia-log, complete with the three-fingered hand icon, but you can easily choose another.

WARNING   Some of NT's bundled screen savers are CPU hogs. If you're choos-ing a logon screen saver for an NT server, make sure you stick with the "blank screen" saver; otherwise, your server's valuable CPU cycles will be used to draw OpenGL objects or flying stars, robbing your server of the power it needs to handle your users.

If you want to use another screen saver while NT's waiting for someone to log on locally, you'll need to make three changes. First, add HKU\.DEFAULT\Control Panel\Desktop\ScreenSaveActive as a REG_DWORD; set its value to 1. This tells the system that when no one's logged in (e.g., when the .DEFAULT profile's being used) that you want a screen saver to run.

Next, edit the value of HKU\.DEFAULT\Control Panel\Desktop\SCRNSAVE.EXE to specify the full path of the screen saver you want to run. (If the screen saver you want is in the default location of *%systemroot%\system32*, you don't have to enter the full path.) For example, you might enter *sstars.scr* to run the "flying stars" screen saver.

Finally, edit the value of HKU\.DEFAULT\Control Panel\Desktop\Screen-SaveTimeOut and enter a value for the screen saver trigger time. This value, in seconds, specifies the amount of inactivity you're willing to allow before the screen saver kicks in.

Once you've made these changes, you must reboot the machine before they'll take effect.

Enable X Window-Style "Auto Raise"

The X Window system has a neat configuration setting called "auto-raise." When this setting's in effect, you don't have to click on a window to bring it to the front of the window stack. Instead, just passing the mouse over a window raises it. This takes a little getting used to, but once you've made the adjustment you'll find that it eliminates a lot of extra mouse clicks.

NT does something similar: it can automatically set the focus to a window when you put the mouse in it, but it won't raise that window to the top of the stack. This setting is off by default to avoid confusing people who haven't been exposed to auto-raise before. To turn it on, set the value of HKCU\Control Panel\Mouse\ ActiveWindowTracking to 1. You'll have to log out and log back on before the change takes effect.

Enable "Snap To Default Button"

Some X Window system implementations also have another handy feature: you can force the cursor to always jump to the default button of any dialog or alert that appears. This speeds the process of moving the cursor from wherever it happens to be to the dialog or alert, especially if you're using a high-resolution monitor or an input device that makes it hard to move the cursor quickly.

You can enable or disable this behavior by adjusting the value of HKCU\Control Panel\Mouse\SnapToDefaultButton. When this value is 0, as it is by default, no snapping occurs. Set it to 1, though, and the cursor will warp to the default button once you log out and log back on. Try it—you may like it.

Suppress Error Messages During Boot and Logon

During the NT boot process, it's not uncommon to see error dialogs reporting problems that occurred during startup. For example, you may see warnings telling you that a device driver couldn't be started, or that some other system component didn't do what it was supposed to do. You can suppress these error dialogs with a simple Registry change; the errors will still be logged on the system and application sections of the event log, but the dialogs won't interrupt or intrude on the boot and logon process.

The actual errors are displayed in two phases; their display is thus controlled by two separate Registry values. Messages that pop up as the result of errors in the boot phase are controlled by the value of HKCU\SOFTWARE\Microsoft\Windows NT\CurrentVersion\Windows\NoPopUpsOnBoot. Add this value as a REG_DWORD and give it a value of 1 to suppress boot errors, or 0 to allow the normal error dialog display.

Messages that appear as part of the post-boot startup phase (including messages produced by most device drivers and services) are controlled by a different value, `HKCU\SOFTWARE\Microsoft\Windows NT\CurrentVersion\Windows\Error-Mode`. Set this value to 0 to allow all system and application errors to display dialogs, 1 to display only application errors, or 2 to suppress all error dialogs. The default value is 0.

Filesystem Tweaks

The guts of NT's file system are mostly self-tuning. This is on purpose, following the theory that the file system can adjust its own caching and buffering better than you can. Whether this is true or not, there are still some changes you can make to control whether the file system does certain things. These changes apply to FAT, NTFS, and NTFS 5 file systems.

Change Low Disk Space Warning Threshold

Even though you may never have encountered it, NT can display an alert warning you that your disk is almost full. The threshold for these alerts is 90% disk usage; while this may seem generous, if you're using a large disk a 10% margin will result in you seeing these warnings even when the amount of space remaining is large in absolute terms. My local Internet service provider runs an NT news server with more than 80Gb of disk storage, so getting a warning that there's "only" 8Gb free is not very useful to them.

The `DiskSpaceThreshold` value controls when you see this alert; it sets the minimum amount of free space (as a percentage) that will trigger a warning. Add this value (it's a `REG_DWORD`) to `HKLM\System\CurrentControlSet\Services\LanmanServer\Parameters`; the value you specify should be the percentage of free space, from 0 to 99, which should trigger a warning. When the amount of free space on any volume falls below this value, you'll get a warning.

Use Longer File Extensions

Even though Win95 ostensibly supports long file names, there's an ugly secret involved: it really only supports three-character file extensions! That means that the names *medical.doc*, *medical.doctor*, and *medical.doctrine* all point to the same file. Since NTFS doesn't have that restriction, you can make it take advantage of the longer extensions instead of being stuck with the old-style three-character versions.

The value of `HKLM\System\CurrentControlSet\Control\FileSystem\Win95TruncatedExtensions` controls this behavior. By default, it's set to 0, which truncates extensions to the first three characters. Set it to 1 and reboot to take advantage of full-length extensions on NTFS volumes.

Turn Off CD-ROM AutoRun

Ahh, "AutoRun." While Microsoft undoubtedly did a favor for some users who like to automatically have CDs start running when they're inserted, many of the NT users I talk to don't like this feature. If, for example, you're loading the NT Resource Kit CD to copy a tool you need, do you really want to wait while the AutoRun-invoked setup tool loads, or would you rather just copy the file you need?

Happily, you can banish AutoRun from your machine with a simple change. Add a `REG_DWORD` value named `HKLM\SYSTEM\CurrentControlSet\Services\ Cdrom\Autorun` and set its value to 0, and you'll no longer be forced to wait for AutoRunning-CDs to do their stuff. You can later change the value to 1 if you want to re-enable AutoRun for CD-ROMs.

Suppress "Last Access" Timestamp on NTFS Volumes

NTFS volumes store a "last access" timestamp for every file and directory on the volume. The NTFS driver automatically updates this timestamp every time a file's accessed, whether for reading or writing. That means that every time you look at a directory listing, NT is busily updating the file timestamps. As you might guess, this is often a waste of CPU cycles and disk bandwidth that could better be used elsewhere. To prevent NT from maintaining the "last access" timestamp for NTFS volumes, add a `REG_DWORD` value named `NtfsDisableLastAccessUpdate` to `HKLM\System\CurrentControlSet\Control\FileSystem` and set its value to 1. Note that this change has no effect on the "last modified" timestamp.

Security Tweaks

WARNING   A surprising number of NT's security features are only accessible
through Registry tweaks. For the most part, these adjustments add
to your system's security; except as noted, you are not adding extra
risk by not making the changes discussed here. You should carefully note the security suggestions included in Chapter 8, *Administering the NT Registry*. They reflect changes that you *should* make to
preserve system security, while the items in this section are optional.

Clear the System Pagefile at Shutdown

The U.S. Government (in the form of the National Computer Security Center) has established a rating system for computer operating systems. This rating system, set forth in a document called the Orange Book, rates how secure operating systems are. To earn a particular rating, there are certain features that an OS must implement. One of these features is object reuse. Simply put, object reuse just means that objects (including disk blocks, memory, and other shared resources) are cleared out after use. This prevents any leakage of confidential data.

As shipped, however, NT doesn't implement reuse on the virtual memory's pagefile. A couple of publicized attacks[*] rely on the fact that NT's pagefile is left intact when the system shuts down; it can then be scanned for useful data. To prevent this, you can add the REG_DWORD value HKLM\System\CurrentControlSet\Control\Session Manager\Memory Management\ClearPageFileAtShutdown value and set it to 1; this forces NT to zero out the contents of the pagefile at system shutdown.

Prevent Caching of Logon Credentials

By default, NT workstations will cache the last ten sets of logon credentials received from a domain controller. This reduces the number of times a workstation has to contact a domain controller for verification of a logon request, and it often makes it possible to log on to a domain even when the domain controller isn't available on the network. If you want to prevent these credentials from being cached, as you might if you're running a high-security network, add a REG_DWORD value named Cached Logons Count beneath the HKLM\Software\Microsoft\Windows NT\CurrentVersion\winlogon key. Set its value to 0 to prevent any caching, or to the number of cached credential sets you're willing to allow.

Turn Off "Save Password" Option in Dial-Up Networking

The NT Dial-Up Networking (DUN) subsystem lets you maintain a separate user name and password for every entry in the Phonebook. You can also use the "Save this password" checkbox, which appears in the RAS Logon dialog; when you do, NT will store that account's password in the Registry. This is pretty insecure, especially when the machine using DUN is a laptop—if it's stolen, the thief has automatic access to your dial-up connection if the password's been saved.

---

[*] The attacks depend on application bugs; a well-written application won't leave any sensitive data in virtual memory, but a well-written OS won't expose it either.

You can force DUN not to store passwords by adding the REG_DWORD value Dis-ableSavePassword value to HKLM\SYSTEM\CurrentControlSet\Services\ RasMan\Parameters. If you set its value to 1, DUN won't display the "Save password" checkbox, and it will forget any passwords it has previously stored. This setting's a good candidate for inclusion in a policy template; that allows you to enforce the security setting you want applied.

Prevent Users from Changing Network Drive Mappings

Once you establish a set of drive mappings for your users (either as part of a logon script, a profile, or a persistent connection), you can protect them from changes by changing the permissions on HKCU\Network, and its subkeys, to remove the Delete and Create Subkey permissions. If you do this, users can still add or delete network connections, but the changes won't persist after they log out.

Do not remove the users' Set Value or Read access; if you do, connections won't be re-established when that user logs on again.

Control Who Can See Performance Monitor Data

NT's Performance Monitor is a nice addition to the system's basic toolset; it allows you to quickly gather and analyze performance data for local and remote machines. If you're like most network administrators or managers, though, you'd probably prefer that your servers' performance data be kept away from other network users, since there's no good reason for ordinary users to be monitoring a server's performance.

The permissions on the HKLM\Software\Microsoft\Windows NT\CurrentVer-sion\Perflib key control who may read a machine's performance data. By default, an ordinary NT 4.0 installation has Everyone:Read permission on this key. I suggest using *RegEdt32* to tighten those permissions: let Administrators have Full Control and remove Everyone altogether. If you want any user who's actually logged into the machine to have access, you can add Interactive Users:Read; doing so will keep network users from seeing the performance data while still allowing interactive users to monitor the machine if they need to do so.

Control Which Drives Are Visible Throughout the System

If you need to, you can hide drives on a machine so they don't appear in My Computer, Explorer, or the open and save dialog boxes. You might do this (in

conjunction with other access control measures like the "run only allowed applications" policy setting) to keep users from damaging their NT installations or installing unapproved software—hide the drives you don't want users to tamper with
and they won't see them. (Actually, hidden drives are accessible through the File
Manager and the NT command prompt. Solution? Turn those off with a policy.)
This hiding occurs on a per-user basis, too, so you have fairly fine control over
which volumes users can see.

Unlike every other value in this chapter, the value that controls drive hiding is
actually a bit mask. `HKCU\Software\Microsoft\Windows\CurrentVersion\`
`Policies\Explorer\NODRIVES` is a `REG_DWORD`, which makes it 32 bits long.
Since NT can only map 26 drives (*A:* through *Z:*), this mapping works out nicely.
The upper six bits of the value are ignored; the remaining 26 bits map to each
drive letter, with *A:* in the right-most position and *Z:* in the left-most, like this:

```
0 0 0 0 0 0 0 0 0 0 0 0 0 0 0 0 0 0 0 0 0 0 0 0 0 0 0 0 0 0 0 0
Z Y X           . . . . . . . . . . .                 C B A
```

To turn off drives A, B, C, and D, you'd end up with a mask value of
"00000000000000000000001111"; to turn off all drives, just use all 1 bits in the
mask. *RegEdt32* makes it easy to add new `DWORD` values as bitmasks or to edit
existing values as binary strings (see Chapter 5, *Using RegEdt32*, if you need more
details), so adding this restriction is easy to do. There's one caveat: if your drive
letters change—perhaps because you've added a new disk or removed an old
one—your `NODRIVES` values will be off, and you may suddenly lose sight of a
drive you wanted to keep visible.

Change When the Password Expiration Warning Appears

A good password policy is one of the cornerstones of network security. You start
by making users pick good passwords,* then follow up by setting a password
aging policy that forces users to change their passwords at reasonable intervals.†
NT will helpfully warn users that their password is going to expire two weeks, or
14 days, in advance. Since most users won't change their passwords when the
first warning appears (most, in fact, won't change until their password finally does
expire), why torture them with two weeks' worth of warnings?

Instead, add a `REG_DWORD` value named `PasswordExpiryWarning` to `HKLM\`
`SOFTWARE\Microsoft\Windows NT\CurrentVersion\Winlogon`. Set its value

---

* I can't explain it here, but there's an excellent discussion of what makes a password good or bad in
Windows NT Users Administration by Timothy D. Ritchey and Ashley J. Meggitt.

† You do this with the User Manager.

to the number of days you want to start the expiration warnings at; I recommend between three and seven days.

Allow Members of the Printer Operators Group to Add Printers

NT includes a number of built-in groups that allow you to assign limited administration privileges to people who need them. The Server Operators, Printer Operators, and Backup Operators groups allow a network administrator to grant greater-than-normal rights to these operators without making them members of the Administrators group.

Printer Operators can stop and restart the print spooler, route print jobs, and perform other printer-related administrative functions. However, they cannot add or modify printer ports, meaning that you can't delegate that responsibility to the people who should most likely have it. You may reverse this unhappy state of affairs by changing the permissions on a single Registry key. Here's what to do:

1. Open *RegEdt32* and select `HKLM\SYSTEM\CurrentControlSet\Control\ Print\Monitors`.

2. Use the **Security ➤ Permissions**… command to display the Registry Key Permissions dialog.

3. Click the Add button; when the Add Users and Groups dialog appears, select the Printer Operators group and give them Full Control access. Click OK; the Registry Key Permissions dialog will reappear with the new permissions.

4. Stop and restart the Spooler service, either with the Services control panel or by using the *net stop spooler* and *net start spooler* commands from an NT command window.

Set the Number of Authentication Retries for Dial-Up Connections

You may adjust the number of authentication attempts DUN will allow before it decides the remote user is bogus and hangs up the phone. By default, DUN allows two unsuccessful retries; you can adjust this value from zero to 10 by editing the `HKLM\System\CurrentControlSet\Services\RemoteAccess\Parameters\AuthenticateRetries` value. A value of zero tells DUN to hang up at the first failure, which may be too restrictive for users who must type in passwords manually—I habitually set the value to 1 so that users can make one mistake before they have to start over again.

Keep Users from Changing Video Resolutions

Being able to change screen resolution and color depth on the fly is a terrific NT feature—until your users start changing settings when you don't want them to. You can prevent this by changing the permissions on the settings key for the video card. The exact location of this key varies depending on the number and type of video cards installed in a particular computer, and it will vary between machines that have different video card types.

The key to change permissions on is located at:

```
HKLM\System\CurrentControlSet\Hardware Profiles\Current\System\
CurrentControlSet\Services\devicename\DeviceX
```

where *devicename* is the name of your video adapter driver (mine is "S3," but you should be able to deduce the right value for your computers depending on what type of card you have). The proper value for *DeviceX* will vary too, but if you only have one video card it will always be "Device0."

Set the Authentication Timeout for Dial-Up Connections

In addition to setting the number of authentication retries you'll allow, you can also specify how long each attempt may take before the system counts it as a failed attempt. By default, DUN allows connecting users 120 seconds to either authenticate successfully or have their attempt deemed a failure. Edit the value named HKLM\System\CurrentControlSet\Services\RemoteAccess\Parameters\AuthenticateTime to adjust the timeout period; you can set any value you like from 20 seconds all the way up to 10 minutes (or 600 seconds; the value must be specified in seconds).

Keep Remote Users from Sharing a Mounted CD-ROM or Floppy

By default, NT automatically creates an administrative share for every disk or CD-ROM volume. This share, which is named by the drive letter plus a dollar sign, is invisible, so it doesn't appear in Network Neighborhood—but a savvy user can find it anyway. There may be times when you don't want anyone but the locally logged-in user to access a CD-ROM; for example, many reference CD-ROMs have strict licensing limits that promise big trouble if you share the CD-ROM across the network.

Remember the brief discussion about object reuse? It applies to other shared resources, too, including CD-ROMs and floppies. In its quest to gain C2 security certification for NT, Microsoft added two Registry keys that cause the CD-ROM and floppy drives to be allocated to the currently logged-in user. When this allocation occurs, other users can't access the drives *or* the media in them; when no one's logged in, the drives are unallocated and may be shared.

Two keys under `HKLM\Software\Microsoft\WindowsNT\CurrentVersion\Winlogon` implement these settings: `AllocateFloppies` and `AllocateCDRoms`. Both are of type `REG_SZ`. To force allocation of either device type during logon, set the appropriate key's value to 1; to turn allocation off, set the key's value to 0.

Keep Users from Customizing "My Computer"

There's no policy setting that prevents users from changing the name or icon of the My Computer icon on the desktop. If you've ever had to administer a lab full of computers, you've probably had at least one incidence of finding a machine's My Computer icon renamed to "Beavis & Butthead" or something even worse. To nip these changes in the bud, change the access permissions on

    HKLM\Software\Classes\CLSID\20D04FE0-3AEA-1069-08002B30309D

Remove Everyone:Full Control on this key and change it to Authenticated Users:Read.

Performance Tweaks

When it comes to computers—particularly those running NT—you can never have too much speed. The least expensive performance upgrade for NT machines is usually just additional RAM, since NT can productively use as much as you can stuff into your computers. Failing that, you can make a few small changes to improve both your computers' speed and their availability.

Automatically Delete Cached User Profiles

User profiles make it easy to centralize and distribute user-specific settings. This enables users to have their same desktop settings follow them as they wander around your network. However, these profiles take up space; if you have many users who interactively log onto a particular machine, their cached profiles will slowly accumulate, stealing your disk space as they build up.

The Resource Kit's *delprof* tool manually removes profiles, but you can tell NT to automatically delete cached profiles when they're no longer needed. When a user logs on, if her profile isn't on the local machine, NT will fetch it and keep it there until it's removed or updated (in which case the updated version is downloaded into the cache). This makes it possible to log on and get profile information even when the domain controller(s) aren't answering profile requests. If you enable automatic removal, NT will delete the cached profile when the user logs out. The good news is that this approach saves disk space at a small cost in extra profile downloads; the bad news is that users may not be able to log on when your domain controllers are unavailable—there won't be a cached profile on the machine for them to use when logging on.

If you want cached profiles to be deleted automatically, add a REG_DWORD value named `DeleteRoamingCache` to HKLM\SOFTWARE\Microsoft\WindowsNT\CurrentVersion\Winlogon. Give it a value of 1 to enable removal, or 0 to allow cached profiles to stay around.

Enable Automatic Reboot After a Crash

Normally when an NT machine crashes, it produces a "Blue Screen of Death" (BSOD), which indicates the cause of the crash and gives some information about the system's state when the crash happened. The problem with this approach is that the server will sit there, BSOD proudly displayed, until a human comes along and reboots it. This is not ideal for most server applications—if no one is able to get to the machine to reboot it, none of its users can use it. Imagine having your Exchange server go down while you're on vacation, with users unable to get mail until you can find someone in the office to go reboot it for you!

You can force NT to automatically reboot after a crash by setting the value of HKLM\SYSTEM\CurrentControlSet\CrashControl\AutoReboot to 1; this forces the system to automatically reboot after writing out the crash log file.

Record Evidence of a Crash

Besides the standard crash dump file, you can also tell NT to record the occurrence of a crash in two ways. First, the kernel can send an administrative alert to another machine; this alert may provide the first warning you get of a fresh crash. Second, the kernel can record a crash message in the event log. If you've turned on the automatic reboot option as discussed above, having a message in the event log gives you positive confirmation of the time when the crash occurred.

Both of these capabilities are controlled by values under the HKLM\SYSTEM\CurrentControlSet\CrashControl key. To turn on alert broadcasting, set the SendAlert value to 1 instead of its default of 0. To turn on event log messages, set the LogEvent value to 1 as well.

TIP	All of the values under the `CrashControlkey` can be set through the Startup/Shutdown tab of the System control panel. Better still, you can control them by writing a policy template file so you can automatically install the settings you want on all machines in your domain.

Enabling Automatic Logon After Boot

My local library has a batch of PCs running an electronic library catalog application. These machines are basically single-function kiosks; the librarians don't want people using them for anything else. To get the machines set up to run with as little intervention as possible, the catalog software's installed as part of the Startup group; that way, it runs when Windows 95 starts. An NT-based kiosk system would allow the library to keep their computers more secure and administer them with less hassle; they can even get the automatic logon feature that Windows 95 offers.

WARNING	Never, never, never enable auto-logon with an account that has administrative privileges. If you ever leave your machine unattended, an office prankster (or determined attacker) can have the run of your network right from your machine. Good security practice dictates that you only log in with an administrative account when you need to do something that requires the extra privileges.

To enable automatic logons, you have to make a total of four changes to values under `HKLM\Software\Microsoft\Windows NT\Current Version\Winlogon`:

1. Set the `DefaultDomainName` value to the name of the domain you want to automatically log into. Of course, instead of a domain you may specify the name of the computer itself.

2. Set `DefaultUserName` to the user account name you want to use when logging on.

3. Add a `REG_SZ` named `AutoAdminLogon` and set its to value to 1.

4. Add a `REG_SZ` named `DefaultPassword` and set its contents to the password for the account you specified in `DefaultUserName`. If you leave this value blank, automatic logon will be turned off (actually, `AutoAdminLogon` will be set back to its default value of 0).

Once you make these changes, the next reboot will automatically log on the account you specified. If you want to log on as a different user, hold down the

Shift key as you log off the machine; NT will allow you to use the standard logon dialog to log on as another user.

Power Off at Shutdown

Most laptops, many workstations, and even a few servers have smart power management hardware that lets the operating system actually turn off the hardware when the system is shut down. While not all machines can take advantage of this, it's nice to have the "Shut Down" command do just that instead of requiring an extra trip to the power button.

The `HKLM\Softwate\Microsoft\WindowsNT\CurrentVersion\Winlogon\PowerdownAfterShutdown` value enables this feature; add it as a `REG_SZ` and set its value to 1, and your computer will actually turn itself off when you tell NT to shut down—if your hardware supports this feature. If it doesn't, no harm will come to it, but the feature won't work. Reset `PowerdownAfterShutdown` back to 0 to restore normal operation.

Force Hung Tasks to End When Logging Off

When you log off of or shut down an NT machine, the system scheduler will attempt to stop any running tasks. In addition to shutting down any drivers or services started by the system, NT must shut down the 16-bit Windows subsystem and any applications you've started yourself. Most well-behaved Win32 applications will honor a system shutdown request,* but it's unfortunately common to see hung tasks in the VDM prevent the entire system from shutting down.

NT's normal response to this problem is to display a dialog that asks whether you want to cancel the shutdown or logoff, wait for the recalcitrant task to stop by itself, or kill off the task. You can automate this process by specifying that you always want NT to go ahead and kill tasks that don't listen to shutdown requests; this finally makes it possible for you to tell your machine to reboot and go get a diet Coke while it does, secure in the knowledge that it won't be still waiting for you to end a task when you return.

To force this shutdown, add a `REG_SZ` value named `AutoEndTasks` to `HKEY_USER\<SID>\Control Panel\Desktop`. Set it to 1 to forcibly kill off unresponsive tasks. You may also want to add the same value to `HKU\.DEFAULT` so that new accounts inherit it; you can also add it to a policy template.

---

* Oddly, Microsoft's own Visual Studio product insists on having you answer a "save changes" dialog before it will honor such requests.

Set a Time Limit for Shutting Down Tasks

You now know how to force an automatic end to tasks that won't stop when they get a shutdown request, but did you know you can also tell NT how long to wait before deciding an application isn't answering? If you add a REG_SZ value named WaitToKillAppTimeout to HKEY_USER\<SID>\Control Panel\Desktop, you can specify the interval (in milliseconds again) that NT will wait before deciding that an application is ignoring the shutdown request. The default is a generous 20 seconds; if, like me, you're impatient you can whittle this down to 10 seconds or even less. If the user process doesn't answer the shutdown request and terminate within this time period, and AutoEndTasks is defined, the NT scheduler will kill off the task.

Speed Up System Shutdowns

When you boot an NT machine, part of the boot phase involves starting up all the system's drivers and services. Conversely, part of the shutdown process requires that all of these services be shut down so they can write out any data they've got cached. This is particularly important when you consider that Exchange Server, SQL Server, and several other BackOffice server products depend on NT services.

However, waiting for system shutdown can take a long time, depending on the service load you have running. Part of the problem is the generous default time-out value: when NT shuts down, it gives each service up to 20 seconds to shut down before the system kills it. If you have many services running, this time can add up.

The HKLM\SYSTEM\CurrentControlSet\Control\WaitToKillServiceTime-out value specifies how long NT should wait before killing a service; the value is a REG_SZ expressed in microseconds (1000 microseconds make one second). You can adjust this value as low, or high, as you'd like.

Note that WaitToKillAppTimeout and WaitToKillServiceTimeout are two different values! The former controls the timeout period for system tasks, while the latter only applies to NT services.

It's critical to leave services enough time to clean up after themselves and write out any cached data they may be maintaining internally. If you don't, you may lose all or part of the data maintained by the service; since the DHCP, DNS, WINS, Exchange, and SQL servers are all services, this poses a real risk to your data—you probably shouldn't adjust this value on machines that run any of these services.

Automatically Try to Detect Slow Network Connections

Face it: not all network connections are as fast as you'd like. In fact, if your network includes sites that are linked by a WAN, you may find they're much, much slower than you'd like. In a domain environment, NT will normally attempt to fetch a user's profile from the domain controller. In a typical enterprise network, not every WAN-connected site will have its own domain controller—meaning that logon requests from Huntsville may have to go to a domain controller in Chicago. With more than a few users, you'll quickly wish there was a way to encourage NT to use cached user profiles whenever possible.

Good news: you can do exactly that. The first step is to set a time limit for deciding whether a connection is "slow" or not. NT makes this decision by pinging the domain controller and waiting for a response. If the response takes longer than a threshold you specify, the link is considered "slow." You can set this threshold by adding a `REG_DWORD` value named `HKLM\Software\Microsoft\Windows NT\CurrentVersion\Winlogon\SlowLinkTimeOut` and setting it to the number of milliseconds (remember, 1000 milliseconds make one second) to wait for a ping response. The default value of 2000 means that NT will wait 2 seconds for a response; if you're really desperate, you may adjust this value all the way up to 120,000 milliseconds (or 2 minutes).

The other required change is to add a `REG_DWORD` named `SlowLinkDetectEnabled` to `HKLM\Software\Microsoft\Windows NT\CurrentVersion\Winlogon`. This value controls whether or not NT pays attention to `SlowLinkTimeOut`. When `SlowLinkDetectEnabled` is 0, NT won't attempt to detect a slow link. When it's 1, the system will wait for the amount of time specified in `SlowLinkTimeOut`; if that amount of time passes, the user may select a locally cached profile instead of continuing to wait.

Don't Automatically Create 8.3 Names on NTFS Volumes

For backwards compatibility with DOS, Windows for Workgroups, and other OSes that don't understand long file names, NTFS automatically creates standard 8.3 filenames and stores them along with the NTFS long name. For example, this chapter's full name is *Chapter 9 draft.doc*, but its 8.3 name is *CHAPTE~1.DOC*. If you don't care whether older OSes and software can read your file names, you can turn off the process that automatically creates short names for long-named files. If you depend on DOS or Win3.x programs on your computers, this probably isn't a good idea, as they depend on 8.3 names; however, if you're only running 32-bit applications you should be in good shape.

To accomplish this, add a new REG_DWORD value named NtfsDisable8dot3-NameCreation to HKLM\System\CurrentControlSet\Control\FileSystem and give it a value of 1. After you reboot, the system will no longer create 8.3 names for new files (but it won't delete the old ones).

WARNING   You may be surprised to find out that many allegedly 32-bit applications rely on 8.3 filenames to work properly. Don't apply this tweak until you've made a full backup of all NTFS volumes on your machine, and be prepared to use that backup to restore from if things don't work properly.

Disable the Printer Browse Thread

When you create a new printer share, the print spooler service starts a new thread whose job is to broadcast announcements of the share's presence. Print servers and clients can receive these announcements and automatically add the new printer to their lists of known resources. To ensure that print servers have consistent resource lists, each print server *also* broadcasts its list of known shares. This enables other servers to be sure that their resource lists are complete. The combination of these two broadcasts can cause unneeded broadcast traffic, since once a printer's established and the servers have all seen it, there's little need to keep retransmitting the data.

You may disable the printer browse thread on each machine that shares a printer with the network; you may also wish to disable the thread on any centralized print servers on your network. Once you do, remember that when you add new printers they won't show up in browse lists until you re-enable the browse thread on *all* machines where you've disabled it.

To stop the browse thread, add a new REG_DWORD value named DisableServer-Thread to HKLM\SYSTEM\CurrentControlSet\Control\Print. Give it a value of 1 to disable the thread or 0 to re-enable it, then restart the computer to make the change effective. Since printer browsers share information, it may take as long as one hour for all the print servers on your network to make themselves known again by broadcasting.

Forcibly Recover a Crashed PDC

If your domain's PDC crashes or becomes unavailable before you have the chance to promote a BDC, the key that controls the server's role won't be changed to reflect that the PDC isn't a PDC anymore. When you recover and reboot the PDC, it thinks it's still a PDC, but when it discovers the newly promoted PDC on the network the original PDC petulantly stops its *netlogon* service.

The recommended way to fix this is to edit the default or "<No Name>" value of
`HKLM\Security\Policy\PolSrvRo`. Its value will be 0x03000000 for a PDC and
0x02000000 for a BDC. To turn the PDC into a BDC, change the value to
0x02000000, then reboot.

TIP　　　　This tip and the one that follows appear courtesy of the NT*Pro user
group newsletter. Membership in NT*Pro is free, and you can learn
an astounding amount from the newsletter. Visit http://
www.ntpro.org and have a look around.

To accomplish this fix, you'll have to allow the Administrators group Full Control
permissions on `HKLM\Security\Policy\PolSrvRo`. Make sure to restore the permissions back to their original state after making the change.

Getting the Most from Your Cache

By default, the NT HAL tries to recognize the amount of L2 cache on your motherboard. Sometimes it succeeds, and sometimes it fails. You can make sure that the
HAL knows how much cache you have installed by checking the value of the
`SecondLevelDataCache REG_DWORD` value under the `HKLM\System\Current-`
`ControlSet\Control\Session Manager\Memory Management` key.

When this value is 0, that tells the HAL that you have 256Kb of L2 cache. If you
have a different amount installed, set `SecondLevelDataCache` to the amount, in
Kb, of cache you've actually got. For example, if you have a 512Kb cache, set the
value to be a *decimal* value of 512 or a *hex* value of 0x400. If you get this wrong,
your machine may be unstable, so make sure to enter the right value in the right
base.

Hiding Servers from Network Computers

There may be times when you want to keep human browsers from seeing a particular server on your network. You may hide the server from Network Neighborhood and other browsing tools while still allowing users who know what share
they want to access it. To hide a server (or workstation, for that matter), you'll
have to add a new value to `HKLM\SYSTEM\CurrentControlSet\Services\Lan-`
`manServer\Parameters`. Name the new value `HIDDEN` and give it a type of `REG_`
`DWORD` and a value of 1 (to hide it) or 0 (to make it visible). You'll have to restart
the computer to make it stop broadcasting its presence; in addition, it can take an
hour or two for the newly hidden machine to drop out of sight on other machines
on your network.

Network Tweaks

NT's networking subsystem is pretty flexible. Most of the things you can change are exposed through the Network control panel and its various tabs, subdialogs, and property pages. However, there are some things you can change on your own that will smooth your network operations.

Create a Shared Favorites Folder for All Network Users

A standard NT installation gives every user her own Favorites folder. Since Internet Explorer and Microsoft Office both use this folder extensively, you might find it useful to build a shared Favorites folder containing IE shortcuts or Office documents that you want to make available to all your users.

Building a shared Favorites folder is pretty easy. The first step is to build the folder itself: on one of your file servers, share the directory you want to use as the shared Favorites folder. It can be an existing directory, or you may create a new one. Be sure to set appropriate share and NTFS permissions.

Next, on each machine you want to use the shared folder, you'll need to change the value of `HKCU\Software\Microsoft\Windows\CurrentVersion\Explorer\ User Shell Folders\Favorites` from its existing setting to the path to the new folder. For example, if your shared folder is on a machine named *armageddon* in a share named *favorites*, your new Favorites value would read `\\armageddon\ favorites`. You can make this change as part of a system policy by adding a new policy template; you may also put it in `HKU\.DEFAULT` so that newly created accounts inherit the setting.

Automatically Use Dial-Up Networking to Log On

You can force NT to always use DUN to log onto your selected domain. Normally, when you have DUN installed and active you'll see a checkbox in the logon dialog that allows you to use DUN to establish a connection to your network for logon; setting this value forces the checkbox to stay on permanently. You might do this on a laptop or other computer that can only connect to your LAN via DUN.

To force this change, add a new `REG_SZ` value named `RasForce` to `HKLM\SOFT-WARE\Microsoft\WindowsNT\CurrentVersion\Winlogon` and set its value to 1. After you reboot, the "Logon using Dial-up networking" checkbox will be permanently selected, and you won't be able to deselect it. This means that if you can't access your remote network, you can't log on! (As a workaround, you can restore from an ERD or edit the Registry using *RegEdt32*'s network connection function.)

Enable the WINS Proxy Agent

NT machines can act as Windows Internet Name Service (WINS) proxies; these proxies answer name resolution requests from machines (like Macintoshes or Unix machines) that don't speak the WINS protocol. In NT 4.0, the only way to enable this proxy mode is via a Registry change (in earlier versions, there was a checkbox in the TCP/IP control panel).

To turn a machine into a WINS proxy, add a new `REG_DWORD` value named `HKLM\System\CurrentControlSet\Services\Netbt\Parameters\EnableProxy` and give it a value of 1. This will enable the target machine to route WINS resolution requests to an available WINS server.

Set the Number of Rings for Answering Incoming Dial-Up Networking Calls

If you're using a TAPI or Unimodem-based device to answer incoming DUN calls, you may have noticed that the standard method of adjusting the *modem.inf* file to control how many times incoming calls may ring before the modem answers them doesn't work. This is by design, but it's not well-documented. The solution is to add a new Registry value to indicate the number of rings you want to allow. Add `HKLM\CurrentControlSet\Services\RasMan\Parameters\NumberOfRings` as a `REG_DWORD`, then set its value to the number of rings you want to use (between 1 and 20). Once you reboot your computer, DUN will answer only after the specified number of rings have occurred. Note that if you're not using a TAPI/Unimodem modem, this value will be completely ignored.

Turn On Logging for Dial-Up Networking

You can enable logging for Dial-Up Networking connections by changing the value of `HKLM\System\CurrentControlSet\Services\RasMan\Parameters\Logging` from its default of 0 to 1. When you do, DUN will log details of the initial connection in *%systemroot%\system32\ras\device.log*; this log will reveal what data DUN sends to the remote device and what responses come back. This log is invaluable when you're trying to troubleshoot DUN connections that fail at initial establishment.

Keep a Dial-Up Networking Connection Up After You Log Out

NT 4.0 automatically terminates DUN connections when you log off. This is a sensible feature (even though it's a change from previous versions), since it keeps you from inadvertently running up big connection or long-distance bills during a time when you're not even logged on to your machine. However, there may be times when you want the connection to stay up even when no one's logged on. For example, keeping the connection open when no one's logged on enables the DUN-connected machine to share files and printers with other network users.

To keep DUN connections active even when the user who started them has logged out, add `HKLM\Software\Microsoft\Windows NT\CurrentVersion\Winlogon KeepRasConnections` as `REG_SZ`. Set it to 1 and connections will stay connected when users log out; set it back to 0 to enable the standard NT 4.0 behavior of automatically disconnecting DUN.

Set the Dial-Up Networking Automatic Disconnect Timer

You can reset the deadman timer that causes DUN connections to hang up after a certain period of inactivity. The default value hangs up idle connections after 20 minutes, but you may change the value to any period between 1 minute and 1000—enough of a range for most uses. To effect this change, edit the `REG_DWORD` value named `HKLM\System\CurrentControlSet\Services\RemoteAccess\Parameters\AutoDisconnect` and set it to the number of idle minutes you're willing to tolerate before hanging up the connection. If you want the connection to always stay up until manually disconnected, set `AutoDisconnect` to zero.

Printing Tweaks

The paperless office is not yet upon us, and may never be. Until it finally arrives, you'll need to keep printing things, and if you're using NT you can improve your printing experience with some minor Registry changes.

Keep the Print Spool Service from Popping Up Dialogs

The print spooler has an annoying "feature" that causes it to display alerts telling you when a print job has been submitted. I was delighted to find that you can stop it from doing so by adding a new `REG_DWORD` named `NetPopup` to `HKLM\SYSTEM\CurrentControlSet\Control\Print\Providers`. Give it a value of 0 to suppress the alerts, or 1 to re-enable them. After making this change, you'll need to reboot, but you'll be free of print status messages forevermore.

Change the Print Spool Directory

NT defaults to putting its print spool directories on the system disk. If you have a small number of print jobs, or a large disk, this may work out fine; for disk space or performance reasons, though, it may make more sense to move your print spool directories to another volume. For example, networks that include high-resolution color printers like the Epson Stylus 1520 (which can print 11"x17" pages in 24-bit color—each page takes several tens of megabytes of spool space!) can quickly overwhelm the free space on a typical NT system disk. Unfortunately, there's no user interface for changing the spool locations; fortunately, you're probably comfortable enough with the Registry so that you don't *need* a user interface!

If you want to change the spool directory for a single printer, you'll need to add a new value to `HKLM\SYSTEM\CurrentControlSet\Control\Print\Printers\` `<PrinterName>`, where `PrinterName` is the name you gave the printer when you created its spooler entry. Name the new value `SpoolDirectory` and make it a `REG_SZ`. For this item's value, supply the full local path to the spool directory. The spool directory can't be a UNC path, and it must exist.

If you want to change the default spool used for any printer that doesn't specify its own spool directory, you should add a `REG_SZ` value named `HKLM\SYSTEM\` `CurrentControlSet\Control\Print\Printers\DefaultSpoolDirectory`. As with `SpoolDirectory`, the path you specify here must be a fully qualified local path, and it must exist before you make the change.

If you add either of these values, you'll need to stop and restart the Spooler service. To avoid losing any queued print jobs, it's best to make these changes only when your print queues are empty; that keeps users from having to resubmit their jobs to get them into the new spool directory.

Stop Print Job Logging In Event Log

Normally NT logs every print job processed by a server in that machine's application event log. Since for the most part these logs fall into the category of "data no one will ever look at," you can configure the spooler service to not make these log entries in the first place.

To suppress print job event log entries, add a new `REG_DWORD` value named `HKLM\SYSTEM\CurrentControlSet\Control\Print\Providers\EventLog` and give it a value of 0. As with all the other printing tweaks, this change won't take effect until you stop and restart the Spooler service.

10

The Registry Documented

Documenting the Registry is like building a cathedral in the Middle Ages: it's a task that spans generations,* with many collaborators each doing a small piece of the work. Powerful forces come to bear; some help the work, while others hinder it. In the end, the result is overwhelming: massive, imposing, yet open to all comers. (One major difference: cathedrals are spiritually uplifting. Try as I might, I just can't get that same feeling from the Registry. If you do, drop me a note.)

What's Here and What's Not

Because the Registry is so dynamic, there's no possible way to capture the meaning of every key in a single document. As I write this, Microsoft is preparing to release new versions of Exchange Server, Internet Information Server, Windows 98, Windows NT 5.0, and a host of other products, each of which will have its own set of Registry keys and values. Quite apart from the proliferation of versions is the problem of what configuration a particular machine has. What software's on it? Which NT service pack? Is it part of a network? Does it run any server products?

As if Microsoft products alone weren't enough of a problem, there's an ongoing flood of third-party products running on Win32—web servers, Usenet news servers, CAD tools, office applications—and they all have their *own* keys.

So, the first confession I have to make is that this chapter's incomplete. By design, it doesn't include information about any keys that aren't part of the core NT 4.x operating system: no BackOffice components, no Netscape servers, no nothing. Instead, it covers only the most interesting keys found in an ordinary networked installation of NT Server 4.0.

---

* Generations of operating systems, anyway.

The good news is that the pages you're looking at now represent a small subset of what's documented about the Registry. Because of space and time limitations, I had to choose the most important keys and document them here. The online Registry database, maintained at *http://oreilly.windows.com/registry*, is more complete. Instead of shoveling a bunch of stuff onto a CD, knowing it would be obsolete by the time this book hit the shelves, I've chosen to focus on building a living archive of knowledge about what's in the Registry. As time goes by, this archive can be enhanced and expanded in ways that an ordinary paper document can't.

This chapter, then, is like a traveler's foreign-language phrase book. It won't teach you every word of the language, but it will teach you the most important words and phrases. (I wonder what the Registry equivalent of "Where is the bathroom?" would be?)

Building the Perfect Beast

Remember the phrase about "many collaborators" in the first paragraph of this chapter? That's where you come in. One of the most striking things about the extremely popular Linux is that it has been built, one piece at a time, by a vast army of programmers, admins, and users, each contributing according to her skills. I want the online Registry database to be the same way. Accordingly, it's designed so that you can add new keys and values to the database when you discover them.

The point behind this approach is twofold: first of all, it distributes the workload of maintaining such a large dataset. More important, though, it makes everyone who submits an entry part of the documentation process. Think of it as giving something back to the net community that has given us all so much.

HKLM\HARDWARE

HKLM\HARDWARE is the odd man out in the Registry for two reasons. First of all, all its keys are volatile, meaning that they're never stored on disk. This is because when NT boots, it can interrogate the system to find out what hardware's present, but it needs to keep track of that information before any device drivers have actually been loaded. Since there's no requirement that Registry hives actually be stored in a hive file[*] (instead of in RAM), loading HARDWARE into RAM as a volatile hive makes it accessible to boot-time components *and* the driver loading phase. Because its contents are volatile, changes you make to this hive won't be stored on disk.

---

[*] There may as well be such a rule, though; HARDWARE's the only volatile hive.

The second odd thing about this subkey is that almost all of its values are stored as REG_BINARY values. This makes it difficult to edit values in this tree. That's actually a *good* thing, because doing so can suddenly render your machine inoperable. Since NT creates this tree from scratch each time it boots, there won't be any permanent damage, but you should still treat this tree as read-only.

HARDWARE\DESCRIPTION

The DESCRIPTION subkey stores data to represent what actual physical hardware is present when the NT executive first starts up. This list may have items on it that don't appear in the DEVICEMAP or RESOURCEMAP subkeys; for example, a SCSI adapter that fails to initialize will be in DESCRIPTION but may not appear in either of the others.

The data in DESCRIPTION comes from the hardware recognizer. On non-x86 machines, this task is handled by the ARC firmware. x86 machines use the familiar *ntdetect.com*. In either case, the recognizer gathers data about the configuration of the system's buses, serial, parallel, mouse, and keyboard ports, SCSI and video adapters, and floppy drives. Notice that network adapters, PCMCIA cards, and external devices like printers aren't included on this list; they're not automatically detected in NT 4.0.

Each bus controller (ISA, PCI, EISA, etc.) gets its own subkey under MultifunctionAdapter; in turn, each of these keys has subkeys for each device found on that bus. For example, HARDWARE\DESCRIPTION\System\Multifunc-tionAdapter\3\DiskController\0 points to the first disk controller on my desktop machine's motherboard bus. If I had a secondary controller, it would appear as DiskController\1.

Any device in the DESCRIPTION tree may optionally have values named Compo-nentInformation and ConfigurationData. These values, both of which are of type REG_BINARY, store information about the device; the exact contents vary by device type, and frankly I don't know the details.

HARDWARE\DEVICEMAP

DEVICEMAP links devices in the DESCRIPTION subtree with device drivers in HKLM\SYSTEM\ControlSetX\Services. Each device that requires a driver will have an entry that points to a driver in one of the control sets. During the two driver start phases, the kernel can consult entries in DEVICEMAP to find the matching entry in the Services subkey; that data specifies what driver should be loaded, what phase it should be loaded in, and what configuration data it requires. (See the section "SYSTEM\CurrentControlSet\Control" later in this chapter for details on the Services subkey.)

HARDWARE\RESOURCEMAP

DEVICEMAP ties hardware entries to device drivers; RESOURCEMAP ties those same device drivers to physical machine resources like DMA address ranges and IRQs. Since there is a finite number of these hardware resources, and since conflicts between multiple devices can render them *all* inoperable, this subkey is an important part of NT's load phase.

Each class of device has its own subkey under RESOURCEMAP; for example, RESOURCEMAP\ScsiAdapter is the device class key for (you guessed it) SCSI adapters. Every device in that class gets its own subkey under its class key. That means that a machine with two SCSI adapters will have two entries, the names of which will correspond to the device driver names in the Services subkey.

The contents of RESOURCEMAP come from the device drivers themselves. When a device driver starts, it claims whatever resources it needs for its hardware device and updates its entry in RESOURCEMAP to indicate what it used.

HKLM\SOFTWARE

HKLM\SOFTWARE is the motherlode of software configuration information. Any configuration data that an application or system component needs may be stored here; settings that are specific to an individual user belong in that user's HKU\SOFTWARE key. For example, the SOFTWARE\Microsoft\Windows NT Current-Version\Winlogon key stores settings that apply to the *winlogon* program. These settings apply to all users on the machine, so they belong under HKLM. On the other hand, an individual user's choices for which tools to use to view certain types of web content properly belong to that user, so they should go under HKCU (e.g., Software\Netscape\Netscape Navigator\Viewers).

SOFTWARE\Classes\CLSID

This key is the root under which all of the machine-wide class definitions are registered. In NT 5.0, classes may also be registered under HKCU\Software\Classes. This might happen if a user installed an application for private use; in that case, the application's installer is supposed to be smart enough not to pollute HKCR with classes that can only be used by that application. See the section "HKCR\CLSID" for details on the format of this key's subkeys and values.

SOFTWARE\Microsoft

This key is the root location for parameters and settings for all Microsoft products installed on a machine. As you might expect, such a key covers a multitude of sins.

Microsoft\ActiveSetup

ActiveSetup is Microsoft's name for its "new and improved" setup system. ActiveSetup records which components have been installed on a machine in the Installed Components subkey. Each installed component has its own class ID subkey under Installed Components where it can store its own settings; for example, Internet Explorer's data is located at HKLM\SOFTWARE\Microsoft\Active Setup\Installed Components\{89820200-ECBD-11cf-8B85-00AA005B4383}.

Microsoft\Cryptography

NT 4.0 introduced Microsoft's Cryptographic Application Programming Interface, better known as CryptoAPI. CryptoAPI provides OS-level services for signing, verifying, and encrypting data, as well as for using digital certificates for access control and authentication. Complete documentation for CryptoAPI is available online at *http://www.microsoft.com/msdn/*.

CertificateStore

This subkey contains the store of X.509 certificates currently loaded onto a particular machine. As new certificates arrive, CryptoAPI applications can read and verify them, then store them here if desired.

CertificateStore\CertificateAuxiliaryInfo

Each stored certificate can have arbitrary data associated with it. Microsoft calls this data "tags"; applications may add tags to certificates, but don't have to. This subkey will usually be empty.

CertificateStore\Certificates

The default value of this subkey contains the number of certificates as a REG_SZ, plus one named value for each certificate. For example, if three certificates are present, they'll be stored in values named "1," "2," and "3," and the default value will contain "3." Each certificate's value contents consist of a binary chunk of data that actually contains the certificate itself.

Microsoft\NtBackup

The bundled Windows NT backup tool stores its settings here. Interestingly, this key is remapped by HKLM\SOFTWARE\Microsoft\Windows NT\CurrentVersion\IniFileMapping\Ntbackup.ini, meaning that the backup program (bless its ancient little heart) thinks it's using an INI file to store its settings in.

Microsoft\RAS

The Dial-Up Networking service was originally known as RAS. Sometimes Microsoft calls it RAS, sometimes DUN; in this case, its Registry settings all have

"RAS" in the name somewhere. The values in this key control the Remote Access Service, which clients can use to dial into an NT machine.

CurrentVersion

This subkey looks very much like the CurrentVersion\Network Cards keys you'll meet in the section by the same name. That's not surprising, since RAS is really just a virtual NIC. CurrentVersion's values specify the setup info file name (Infname), major and minor software versions, and the path where RAS parts are stored (PathName). In addition, the CurrentVersion\ NetRules subkey specifies the rest of the information gathered when RAS was first installed.

Protocols

This subkey contains a set of REG_DWORD flags that govern what protocols are selected and which may be used. For example, the fTcpIpSelected and fTcpIpAllowed flags indicate whether the server supports TCP/IP RAS connections or not.

Each installed RAS protocol has its own subkey; for example, TCP/IP-specific settings are stored in Microsoft\RAS\Protocols\IP. These subkeys contain values and flags specific to the protocol.

TAPI DEVICES

This subkey holds a list of any Telephony API (TAPI)-compliant devices known to the RAS service, including any Unimodem devices.

SOFTWARE\Microsoft\Windows NT

This subkey contains configuration settings that are specific to Windows NT; this key doesn't include settings for the shell or Explorer. The CurrentVersion subkey contains a number of interesting pieces of data, as well as some subkeys that merit their own mentions:

RegisteredOwner and RegisteredOrganization

These REG_SZ values store whatever values you entered into the name and company fields of NT's installation dialogs. You can freely change them if need be.

CurrentVersion and CurrentBuildNumber

Together these two REG_SZ values identify what core version of NT you're running. A stock 4.0 installation will have a version of "4.0" and a build number of "1381"; later versions will obviously have different values.

SystemRoot

This value points to the system directory. If you ever need to migrate your NT installation to a different volume, be sure to update this as part of the process.

SourcePath

This REG_SZ points to the source from which NT was originally installed. For example, on several of my machines this value contains "\\\\armory\\NTS4\ \i386" because it was installed from a share on *\\armory\NTS4*. Note that the stored value uses two backslashes to represent each actual backslash character. If you change it you should do the same.

ProductId

This string holds the Microsoft "product ID," which is nothing more than a magic number combined with your CD key. If you ever forget your CD key, it starts in the fifth digit of this string's value (i.e., if the value is "0382410434935404931," the CD key is 410-4349354).

CSDVersion

This value indicates what service pack, if any, is installed. The boot loader uses this (along with CurrentVersion and CurrentBuildNumber) to display the blue-screen boot-time message that tells you what you're booting (mine currently says "Build 1381; Service Pack 3").

CurrentVersion\AeDebug

This subkey tells the system what debugging application to use (if any) when a program crashes.

Debugger

Specifies the program to run when an application crashes. The value may include the full path and any arguments (for example, Visual C++ 5.0 installs *d:\\Program Files\\DevStudio\\SharedIDE\\BIN\\msdev.exe -p %ld -e %ld* as this value).

Auto

REG_SZ specifying whether the debugger should just be run ("1") or whether the user should be prompted to choose between starting the debugger and killing off the errant app ("0", the default).

UserDebuggerHotKey

REG_DWORD that, when set, specifies a key code that will instantly start the debugger when pressed. Leave this alone.

Multimedia driver stuff

The installed list of multimedia device drivers is stored in three subkeys of CurrentVersion: Drivers32, DriverDesc, and DriverList. They're pretty self-explanatory; each device class has a mapping that specifies what DLL handles its requests and what its human-readable name is.

CurrentVersion\Network Cards

This subkey contains one entry for each installed network adapter card or wrapper. For example, a machine with one network card and Dial-Up Networking installed will have two entries: one for the NIC and one for DUN. The first entry is stored in a subkey named "1" (or CurrentVersion\Network Cards\1 if you prefer), and subsequent cards count up from there. These keys each have several values, but the most important ones are ServiceName (which specifies which driver runs the card) and Title (which determines the name that appears in the Network control panel).

Each network adapter subkey can in turn have a subkey named NetRules. This key contains values that specify what kind of adapter it is (type), what setup information file was used to install it (InfName), and what kind of device it actually is (class and block).

CurrentVersion\ProfileList

The list of cached profiles on a particular machine lives here. Each profile has a subkey whose name is its SID; these subkeys contain a path that points to the actual hive containing the profile (ProfileImagePath), some flags that NT uses to control profile loading (Flags and State), and a second copy of the SID that owns the profile (Sid).

CurrentVersion\Shutdown

There are two interesting values stored under this key: LogoffSetting and ShutdownSetting. Both are DWORD values that may range from 0-3. They control what button is selected by default in the Logoff and Shutdown dialogs; you can preset the choice you want to use as a default by adjusting their contents. Table 10-1 lists the available values.

Table 10-1. CurrentVersion\Shutdown Controls the Default Logoff and Shutdown Buttons

Value	What it means
0	Make the "Logoff" button the default
1	Make the "Shutdown" button the default
2	Make the "Shutdown and Restart" button the default
3	Make the "Shutdown and Power Off" button the default; ignored unless the computer has power-management support

CurrentVersion\Winlogon

The *Winlogon* service provides a graphical interface that allows you to log onto or off of the console of a Windows NT computer. The values under the Winlogon subkey let you change some aspects of how the logon process works.

TIP   Most of these values are here for you to customize. The System Policy Editor provides an easy way to set these values to meet your
needs, even on many machines. See Chapter 6, *Using the System Policy Editor*, for details.

AutoAdminLogon

Signals whether the computer should automatically log on with a stored
account name and password. When this REG_SZ is set to 1, the values of
DefaultUserName, DefaultDomainName, and DefaultPassword will be
used to attempt a logon. This value must be manually added.

AutoRestartShell

REG_DWORD that controls whether Explorer (or whatever other shell program's
specified) should be restarted if it crashes. The default, 0x01, means yes.

DebugServerCommand

Microsoft describes this as a command used for internal debugging of
winlogon at Microsoft. Its default value is "no"; I have no idea what other values might mean. If you know, please tell me.

DefaultDomainName

winlogon stores the name of the domain (or machine) that hosted the last successful logon here.

DefaultPassword

When AutoAdminLogon is set to 1, this password (which must be the password for the account given in DefaultUserName) will be used in the logon
attempt.

DefaultUserName

winlogon stores the name of the last account that successfully logged on in
this value. You may change it and set the AutoAdminLogon value to force an
automatic logon to a particular account.

DeleteRoamingCache

When this REG_DWORD value is set to 1, cached copies of roaming profiles will
be deleted when each user logs off. You must add this value manually.

DontDisplayLastUserName

NT normally displays the name of the last account to log on in the Welcome
dialog. Set this REG_SZ value to 1 to keep this space blank, or 0 (the default)
to allow the last account to be displayed.

LegalNoticeCaption

NT can display a warning dialog immediately after the logon dialog is dismissed; this makes it possible for you to display a warning message, as recom-

mended by the Computer Emergency Response Team, to warn intruders that they are in fact intruding. NT uses the `REG_SZ` value you put in `LegalNoticeCaption` to title the warning dialog. By default in NT 4.0, this value exists but is empty.

LegalNoticeText

The warning text displayed in the post-logon warning dialog comes from the `LegalNoticeText` value, which is also blank by default.

ParseAutoexec

`REG_SZ` that specifies whether *autoexec.bat* should be parsed at logon time or not. If the value is set to 1, *autoexec.bat* is interpreted when you log on.

PowerdownAfterShutdown

`REG_SZ` that controls whether NT will attempt to power down the computer when it's shut down. 0 means no, 1 means yes. This value has no effect on machines without power management support.

ProfileDlgTimeOut

If a user logs in but can't get a copy of their current logon profile, NT will display a dialog asking what the user wants done to fix the problem. This `REG_DWORD` value sets the timeout (in seconds, from 0–600) after which any user profile dialog boxes will be automatically dismissed.

ReportBootOk

When NT boots, it saves the boot configuration as the "last known good" control set. Ordinarily, this `REG_SZ` is set to 1, which tells the system to automatically update the control set when booting finishes. If this `REG_SZ` value is set to 0, the system won't automatically update the last known good set. This value must be "0" if you supply alternate values in the `BootVerification` or `BootVerificationProgram` keys.

RunLogonScriptSync

Specifies whether logon scripts should be run synchronously (so the desktop doesn't appear until the script completes) or asynchronously (so the script runs while the desktop is being activated). This is a `REG_SZ`; set it to 1 to force the script to run synchronously.

Shell

This value tells NT what program to run as the system shell. By default, *explorer.exe* is the preferred shell. You may change it, but doing so may have unpredictable results.

ShutdownWithoutLogon

As an administrator, you may choose whether or not to allow users to shut down their workstations or servers without being logged in. A `REG_SZ` value of 1 in this value will add a Shutdown button to the standard logon dialog, while a value of 0 will remove it. By default, this button is on for NTW 4.0 and off for NTS 4.0.

SlowLinkDetectEnabled

When set to on (the default), *winlogon* will automatically detect slow network connections and flag them as such. When off, no such detection will occur.

SlowLinkTimeOut

This REG_DWORD sets the timeout value, in milliseconds, after which a link is marked slow when SlowLinkDetectEnabled is on.

System

This value specifies which programs are trusted to run in the system context. Changing it may open a security hole, since untrusted programs can run with high privileges. The default is *lsass.exe;* don't change it. In NT 4.0 pre-SP3, the default also includes *spoolss.exe.*

Taskman

Specifies the path to an executable to be used for the system task manager. If this value is missing or empty, *taskman.exe* will be used by default.

Userinit

This value specifies which programs should automatically be started when a user successfully logs on. The default value is userinit,nddeagnt.exe; *userinit* specifies that the shell named in Shell should be run, and *nndeagnt.exe* starts the NetDDE service process.

VmApplet

The default contents of this value are rundll32 shell32,Control_RunDLL\ "sysdm.cpl\", but I don't know what it means.

HKLM\SYSTEM

HKLM\SYSTEM is where NT keeps its crown jewels—the configuration settings used to boot the current incarnation of the machine, as well as a number of ancillary settings that govern pretty much everything the OS and kernel services do.

There are three subkeys of interest directly beneath HKLM\SYSTEM:

Disk

This subkey stores information about the physical and logical disk volumes on your machine. When you run the Disk Administrator utility for the first time, this key's created; subsequent runs of Disk Administrator update the key's data, which is then used to keep track of how your disks are configured.

Select

Ever wonder how NT keeps track of which control set is the "last known good" set? Here's the answer! Each of the four values is a REG_DWORD that contains the ordinal index of a *ControlSetXXX* entry under HKLM\SYSTEM:

Current

Contains the ID of the control set currently in use; this set is the one linked to HKLM\SYSTEM\CurrentControlSet.

Default

Contains the ID of the control set that will be used to boot the machine next time, unless you manually intervene during the boot process.

LastKnownGood

Contains the ID of the "last known good" set; this ID will only change when a boot fails.

Failed

Contains the ID of the control set in force the last time a boot failed.

Setup

This key holds settings that NT's setup installer uses to figure out which installation phases have been completed and where the installation is currently.

WARNING   Experimenting with the Setup key may bring you a visit from the Blue Screen of Death with a fault code of SYSTEM_LICENSE_VIOLATION.

SetupType

Indicates whether the setup program's running in GUI mode, in text mode, or not at all.

SystemSetupInProgress

This REG_DWORD will be 1 if the system is in the middle of a setup, and 0 otherwise. NT uses this value to figure out what to do after a reboot; that's how it knows what to do when you reboot partway through setup.

SystemPartition

Contains the ARC path (e.g., *Device**Harddisk0**Partition1*) to the system partition.

OsLoaderPath

Points to the path (relative to SystemPartition) where the NT boot loader lives. On x86 machines, this will usually be "\\", but on Alpha, PPC, or even MIPS machines it may point elsewhere.

NetcardDlls

This REG_MULTI_SZ stores the names of the DLLs needed for the network cards detected in the final phase of NT's setup operation.

SYSTEM\CurrentControlSet\Hardware Profiles

Hardware profiles let you establish multiple "personalities" for a single machine that may have different configurations. For example, my desktop box has a Bus-Logic SCSI card that runs the boot disk and some additional external hardware. I occasionally need to add a second SCSI controller. If I left the second card's driver permanently installed, it would fail to start at boot time and NT would complain about a driver failure. Instead, I create a new hardware profile and enable the card driver for that profile only.

By default, CurrentControlSet\Hardware Profiles will always have two subkeys: 0001 (the first profile on the machine) and CurrentProfile, which links to one of the available profiles. When you add a new profile in the System control panel's Hardware Profiles tab, NT creates a new subkey of Hardware Profiles for you. You can then customize the profile with the System control panel or by using the Devices and Services control panels.*

The actual contents of the hardware profile keys are pretty sparse: they consist of small subtrees of HKLM\SOFTWARE and HKLM\SYSTEM\CurrentControlSet. The profiles only include flags that have been changed from the base hardware profile; for example, the only difference in my one-SCSI and two-SCSI profiles is that the one-SCSI profile has an entry for the second card's driver that tells the driver it's disabled.

SYSTEM\CurrentControlSet\Control

This key's named Control for a good reason: its subkeys and values control much of the kernel's functionality.

Control\BootVerificationProgram

The BootVerificationProgram specifies a program that will be run by the NT service loader at boot time. This program's job is to judge whether a boot was successful or not; if not, the machine can be rebooted using the last known good control set instead. Writing a boot verification program isn't that hard: you need to check whatever conditions make a boot successful and call NT's NotifyBootConfigStatus() function with either TRUE or FALSE. The latter forces the system to reboot using the last known good control set.

---

* For lots more on hardware profiles, see *Windows NT in a Nutshell*.

The only value under this key is ImagePath, which you use to specify the full path to the boot verification program you want to run.

Control\Class

The Control\Class key lists instances of devices like mice, SCSI controllers, and sound cards. Each class of device has a subkey, named with the CLSID class identifier. These CLSID keys may in turn have subkeys; for example, the modem key (whose CLSID is the unpronounceable "{4D36E96D-E325-11CE-BFC1-08002BE10318}") has one subkey for each installed modem, and each of these subkeys in turn has its own parameters stored as subkeys and values.

Control\CrashControl

Much as Microsoft would like to pretend otherwise, NT machines crash just like any other kind. What happens when a crash occurs depends on the values set in the CrashControl key. You normally adjust these values in the Startup/Shutdown tab of the System control panel, but setting them directly in the Registry (or via the Policy Editor) gives you an easy way to control what happens during a crash.

LogEvent

When this REG_DWORD is set to 1, a crash generates an entry in the system event log. When it's 0, as it is by default, no event log entry is created.

SendAlert

This REG_DWORD causes an administrative alert message to be broadcast when it's set to 1; its default value is 0.

CrashDumpEnabled

NT may or may not generate its equivalent of a core file when a crash occurs. You decide which it is by setting this REG_DWORD to 0 (don't generate a dump file) or 1 (do generate one). These files can be loaded by a variety of post-mortem debuggers that you can use to isolate the cause of a particular or persistent crash. The default is 0.

AutoReboot

You can have a crashed machine reboot itself automatically by changing this REG_DWORD value from its default of 0 to 1.

DumpFile

This REG_EXPAND_SZ specifies where the crash dump should go. By default, it ends up in the NT system directory with a name of *memory.dmp*.

Overwrite

When this REG_DWORD is 1, the crash dump file will be overwritten when a new crash occurs; when it's 0, the dump file will be preserved and a new one created.

Control\Enum

Subkeys of this key contain information about every driver, device, or service that might potentially be attached to the machine. For example, Control\Enum will contain entries for the ATAPI driver even on machines with no ATAPI interface. These keys are used by the system to map devices and services with their drivers and configuration data.

Control\FileSystem

These values control the NT file system's naming behavior. The file system itself is self-tuning and doesn't store any parameters out in the open where they can be tweaked, so you'll have to content yourself with these.

Win31FileSystem

If you set this REG_DWORD to 1, any FAT volumes will suddenly start acting like old-style Win3.x volumes: neither long file names nor access/modification times will be created or updated. By default, this option is off, but you may need to turn it on if you're using Win3.x or DOS applications that can't handle even a hint of long file names.

NtfsDisable8dot3NameCreation

By default (i.e., when this value's set to 0) NTFS creates 8.3 names for long file names. This slows things down. Set this value to 1 to prevent NTFS from creating 8.3 names; this means that DOS applications and computers using different languages than your own may not be able to access files on an NTFS share.

NtfsDisableLastAccessUpdate

NTFS keeps track of when each file and directory was last accessed. This timestamp's even updated when you get a directory listing or otherwise traverse a directory; as you might expect, this imposes a performance penalty. Set this REG_DWORD to 0 to turn the last-access timestamp off, or to 1 (the default) to turn it on.

NtfsAllowExtendedCharacterIn8dot3Name

This DWORD controls whether characters outside the standard printable ASCII set (including characters from languages other than the system language) may be used in 8.3 names on NTFS volumes. If the value is 0 (the default), 8.3 names can only contain legal ASCII characters; if it's 1, any non-reserved character may be used.

Win95TruncatedExtensions

Win95 only honors the first three characters of file extensions. By default, this REG_DWORD is set to 0, which forces NT to truncate extensions to the first three characters. Set it to 1 and reboot to take advantage of full-length extensions on NTFS volumes.

Control\Hivelist

This subkey holds the locations of the system's hive files. See Chapter 2, *NT Registry Nuts and Bolts,* for a discussion of hive files. It's very important to leave these values alone; if you don't, you can prevent the system from finding one or more necessary hive files, which will probably render your machine unbootable.

Control\LSA

The Local Security Authority, or LSA, is the NT security component charged with enforcing access controls on local objects. For the most part it does an admirable job; however, there's one significant security problem that this key *causes.*

The Notification Packages value contains a list of DLLs that will be notified any time a user changes an account password. This is supposed to allow seamless synchronization of NetWare and NT passwords; the default value for this entry is "FPNWCLNT," which is the name of the File and Print Services for NetWare DLL. However, if you're not running the NetWare module an attacker can load her own *FPNWCLNT.DLL* and use it to steal passwords.

To guard against this, set the Registry ACL on this key to limit any non-administrator access. If you're not running the NetWare services, remove FPNWCLNT from this value. If you are, set a file ACL on the *FPNWCLNT.DLL* file so it can't be removed or replaced.

Control\Print

Control\Print, rather unsurprisingly, contains configuration and settings data for the NT printing subsystem. One handy feature of the NT print mechanism is that it supports remote printer drivers, meaning that you can install drivers for Win95, Win3.x, and various flavors of NT on a central server and feed them to clients as needed. These drivers are registered in the Environments subkey of this key; there are also some useful values directly beneath Control\Print:

MajorVersion and MinorVersion

These two REG_DWORD values specify the major and minor version of the printer subsystem.

DisableServerThread

This value controls whether printer shares advertise themselves over the network. You have to manually add this REG_DWORD value and set it to 1 to turn off the thread; if it doesn't exist, or if its value is 0, the thread will remain active.

SchedulerThreadPriority

This value raises or lowers the priority of the printer scheduling thread. It's a REG_DWORD, and its default value of 0 means "leave the thread at normal priority." You can set this value to either +1 (which raises the thread's priority) or -1 (which lowers it).

BeepEnabled

If you want notification when a remote print job fails, set this REG_DWORD to 1 and NT will beep every 10 seconds when a remote print job error occurs. The default value of 0 prevents any unnerving beeping from disturbing you while working.

NoRemotePrinterDrivers

You might find it desirable to tell NT *not* to serve remote drivers for some devices. The default value of this REG_SZ is "Windows NT Fax Driver," meaning that that particular driver won't ever be offered to remote clients.

Control\SecurePipeServers

This key allows you to restrict remote access to the Registry, which I strongly recommend you do. See the section "Limiting Remote Registry Access" in Chapter 8, *Administering the NT Registry*.

Control\Session Manager

The Session Manager key contains a group of private configuration parameters that NT uses for internal housekeeping. Except for the values listed below, you should avoid editing any of these values.

ObjectDirectories

This REG_MULTI_SZ names the object directories that NT will create at boot time. Do not edit them at the risk of rendering your machine unbootable.

BootExecute

This REG_SZ value specifies a program to run at boot time. Normally, this value's empty. After a crash it's set to run *CHKDSK*, and after you convert a FAT volume to NTFS it's set to autocheck autoconv \DosDevices\x: / FS:NTFS.

ProcessorControl

> I don't know what this is for, but it's a DWORD whose default value on NTW is 2 even on a uniprocessor machine.

RegisteredProcessors

> This REG_DWORD controls how many processors NT will attempt to use. It may reflect the number of processors you actually have, or it may be substantially larger—up to 32 on some NT Server installations.* If you want to dumb down a multiprocessor machine for testing or to play a nasty prank on someone, adjust this value to 1. NT will only use as many processors as this value tells it to.

LicensedProcessors

> This value specifies how many processors this version of NT is licensed to handle. On an NT workstation, it will be set to 2, while it will be 4 for a server. Editing it may cause a blue-screen crash with SYSTEM_LICENSE_VIO-LATION.

Control\Session Manager\Memory Management

This key deserves its own section even though most NT machines won't ever have it. One alleged advantage of NT over some Unix variants is that NT self-tunes its virtual memory system for maximum performance. Part of this tuning is calculating how big a pagefile to use and how much physical RAM to reserve as a sort of rainy-day fund. The algorithm that actually performs the tuning takes into account how much physical RAM your machine has. Article Q126402 in the Microsoft knowledge base provides a complicated formula that you can use to approximate what this algorithm does.

The reason why the Memory Management key usually isn't present is because NT will do its own tuning unless you add two values to the key. The PagedPool-Size and NonPagedPoolSize values, if present, will override the self-tuning mechanism; if their values are 0, the self-tuning goes back into effect. I strongly recommend leaving these values alone unless you see a knowledge base article or other reliable suggestion to do otherwise.

SYSTEM\CurrentControlSet\Services

Many NT components are implemented as services, which are roughly equivalent to Unix daemons or NetWare NLMs—small faceless programs that run in the background, even when no users are logged in. Services can be device drivers, applica-

---

* As far as I can tell, the exact value depends on which HAL your machine uses.

tion servers, or any other kind of background task, and they can run in the local system context or be bound to run under a particular account.

By convention, NT's system services store their parameters under the **Services** subkey of the current control set. Third-party services may store their settings here, or they may choose to use **HKLM\SOFTWARE**.

All of the services whose settings live in **SYSTEM\CurrentControlSet\Services** have some combination of the following values attached to them:

DependOnGroup

> This **REG_MULTI_SZ** names all the prerequisite groups for this service. For example, a SCSI PC Card reader might name "SCSIMiniport" here to indicate that its service shouldn't be started until at least one service in the "SCSIMiniport" group has been successfully started.

DependOnService

> Like **DependOnGroup**, this **REG_MULTI_SZ** contains a list of prerequisites for a service; the difference is that this value contains names of services that must be started first, not entire groups.

ImagePath

> This **REG_EXPAND_SZ** specifies where the actual executable for this service is located. Device drivers usually don't have this value, but standalone services like the DHCP, DNS, and WINS servers usually do.

PlugPlayServiceType

> I don't know what this does.

DisplayName

> Some services include a "friendly" name suitable for display in the Services control panel. Those that do store it here as a **REG_SZ**.

ObjectName

> Background services may be run under a particular account. By default, services always run as *LocalSystem*; some services (like the printer spooler, scheduler, and Services for Macintosh package) are usually run under their own account. **ObjectName** stores the name of the account under which the service is run, if any. For kernel drivers, this value specifies which kernel object will be used to load the driver.

Type

> This **REG_DWORD** specifies the kind of service or driver this is; it must always be one of the values in Table 10-2. At boot time, the system loads drivers

according to their type: kernel-mode drivers first, then filesystem drivers, and on down the list.

Table 10-2. The Type Value Specifies the Service Type

Value	What it means
0x01	This item is a kernel-mode device driver.
0x02	This item is a kernel-mode device driver that implements file system services.
0x04	This item is a bundle of arguments used by a network adapter.
0x10	This item is a Win32 service and should be run as a standalone process.
0x20	This item is a Win32 service that can share address space with other services of the same type.

Start

This REG_DWORD specifies when the subject service should actually be started. When you open a service in the Services control panel, you can assign the start type with a set of five radio buttons whose labels correspond to the "Start Type" column in Table 10-3.

Table 10-3. The Start Value Controls when Services Are Loaded

Value	Start Type	What it means
0x00	Boot	The kernel loader will load this driver first because it's required to utilize the boot volume device.
0x01	System	This service should be loaded by the I/O subsystem when the kernel is brought up.
0x02	Autoload	This service should always be loaded and run, no matter what.
0x03	Manual	This service should be loaded, but the user must start it manually from a control panel or the command line.
0x04	Disabled	This service should be loaded but may not be started by the system or the user.

Group

Birds of a feather flock together, and so do NT services. Any items with the same value in their Group key are considered to belong to the same group; when it's time to start services within a group, group members' Tag values are used to decide which group members should be loaded first.

Tag

The REG_DWORD Tag value specifies the load order within a single group. For example, if there are five devices in the "SCSI Miniport" group, the one with the lowest Tag value will be loaded first, then the next highest, and so on.

ErrorControl

Some services are more important than others. The `ErrorControl` value is proof, since it lets critical services be marked as such. If a service fails to load, or fails during startup, what happens next is governed by that service's `ErrorControl` value. Possible values are listed in Table 10-4.

Table 10-4. ErrorControl Governs what Happens on a Failure

Value	What it means
0x00	If this driver can't be loaded or started, don't worry; ignore the failure and don't display any warnings.
0x01	Act normally. If this driver fails during startup, produce a warning message but proceed with the boot process.
0x02	Be afraid. If the startup process is currently using the last known good control set, continue on; if it's not, switch to the last known good set.
0x03	Play "Taps." Record the current startup as a failure. If this startup is using the last known good set, run a diagnostic. If not, switch to the last known good set and reboot.

There are also four subkeys commonly found beneath subkeys of `Services`:

Linkage

Network adapters can be bound to multiple protocols and services. Every network card driver will have a `Linkage` subkey, which stores the bindings data for that particular card. Disabled bindings are stored in `Linkage\Disabled`. None of the binding subkeys or values are directly editable; you should only change them via the Network control panel.

Parameters

`Parameters` is a catch-all subkey used to let drivers and services store their private settings. Some components store their settings in `HKLM\SOFTWARE`. Device drivers (particularly those for network cards) can store hardware-specific settings like their preferred IRQ and DMA ranges; other drivers and services can store whatever they want to here.

Performance

Services that offer Performance Monitor counters advertise them by creating a `Performance` key. Beneath this key, there are several values that tell the Performance Monitor which DLL to load to activate the counters and what routines the service offers for collecting performance data.

Security

The format of this key's values is undocumented and unknown to me, but it must have something to do with security!

Of course, any individual service is free to store additional values either as part of its key or in subkeys added to the ones listed above.

Services\Browser

The Browser service controls NetBIOS browsing, including acting as a master browser when requested. (For a complete description of how NetBIOS browsing actually works, see article Q102878 in the Microsoft knowledge base.) The `Services\Browser\Parameters` subkey contains five particularly interesting values:

MaintainServerList

> This `REG_SZ` can assume three values: "Auto" (the default), "Yes," and "No." When it's "No," the system doesn't cache the list of browser announcements it hears, so it can't become a browse server. When it's "Auto," the list is cached, and the computer may force an election (which it can win) for a new master browser when necessary. When it's "Yes," the computer always acts as a browse server.

BackupPeriodicity

> `REG_DWORD` value, in seconds (legal values range from 300-4294967, or about 48 days), which specifies how often a backup browse server should contact the master browser for an update.

MasterPeriodicity

> Like `BackupPeriodicity`, except that it controls how often a master browser should contact the domain master browser.

IsDomainMaster

> `IsDomainMaster` is just what its name implies: a `REG_SZ` that indicates whether this computer is, or is not, a domain master browser. Legal values are TRUE and FALSE.

QueryDriverFrequency

> This `REG_DWORD` value represents the interval (0–900, in seconds) after which a browser will decide that its name cache is invalid and will request a new copy of the available server list. Increasing this value speeds up browsing at the cost of keeping stale data in the cache longer; conversely, decreasing it keeps data fresher at the expense of bandwidth.

Services\DHCP

The Dynamic Host Configuration Protocol, or DHCP, is becoming more and more widespread because it offers an easy way to manage TCP/IP networks. NT Server includes a DHCP server that can serve any client that follows RFC 1533. The DHCP server's parameters are stored under its `Parameters` key:

BackupDatabasePath

> The DHCP server keeps a backup copy of its database. This `REG_SZ` value lets you specify where it's kept. By default, it will go in a subdirectory under the master database directory. You should edit this to move the backup data-

base to another volume on the same machine so you'll be protected from disk failures.*

BackupInterval

This REG_DWORD specifies the interval in minutes at which DHCP backs up its database. By default, backups happen every 60 minutes, but you may specify any interval.

DatabaseCleanupInterval

DHCP leases and reservations expire. Good housekeeping practices dictate that these old records be scavenged from the DHCP database; Database-CleanupInterval (a REG_DWORD whose default value is also 60) specifies how many minutes should pass between scavenging runs.

DatabaseLoggingFlag

Performance will suffer, but you can log DHCP transactions if you feel it necessary. A value of 1 in this REG_DWORD enables logging, while 0 turns it off.

DatabasePath and DatabaseName

By default, these two REG_SZ values combine to point to a file named *dhcp.mdb* in *%systemroot%\system32\dhcp*. If you need to, you can edit these values to put the DHCP database somewhere else.

RestoreFlag

When you want to restore the DHCP database from the backup copy, just stop the service, set this REG_DWORD to 1, and start the service again. Doing so triggers the automatic restore function of the DHCP server. When it's done, it will reset this value back to 0.

Besides these parameters, you can instruct the DHCP server which TCP/IP configuration parameters to deliver to clients. Once you do this (using the **DHCP Options ➤ Scope** command in the DHCP server manager), one or more subkeys under DHCP\Parameters\Options will appear—one subkey per option, each named after the option number. These new keys tell the server where to get the values that are being broadcast to the client machines. Don't edit them.

Services\EventLog

The Event Logger service has three subkeys under Services\EventLog: one for the application log, one for the system log, and one for the security log. These subkeys are named after their respective logs and each contain four values, all of which are editable via the Event Viewer application:

---

* And you should keep a backup copy as well, since depending on software to keep good backups of its own configuration data is risky at best.

File

This `REG_EXPAND_SZ` supplies the full path to the event file. If you want to store your event logs on a secure partition, you can edit this value to do so.

MaxSize

Specifies the maximum size, in kilobytes, that the log can grow to before it's marked as full.

Retention

This `REG_DWORD` represents the number of seconds entries will be retained before they may be overwritten. The default is 7 days (or, more exactly, 604,800 seconds).

Sources

Each system component that logs event messages can supply its own message file. This makes it possible for logged messages to be very specific, since the component that generated them has extensive knowledge about why the entry was logged. This `REG_MULTI_SZ` holds a list of names. Each name is interpreted as a subkey of `EventLog\Application`, `EventLog\Security`, or `EventLog\System`. Each of these subkeys in turn contains two values that specify which message file to use for that named component.

Services\LanmanServer

The Server service actually does all the hard work of sharing files and printers under NT. Its parameters live under `Services\LanmanServer`, and there certainly are a lot of them! Most parameters are automatically tuned by NT based on the server load, but some must be tweaked manually. Here they are:

AutoDisconnect

You can automatically force idle clients to disconnect by setting this `REG_DWORD` value to the number of minutes of idle time you're willing to allow. Clients who have open files or searches on a connection won't be disconnected, but completely idle clients will be.

AutoShareServer and AutoShareWks

NT will ordinarily create administrative shares of your local disks on NT Workstation, and can be made to do so on NT Server. These two values are both `REG_DWORD`s. When set to 1, the default, any local drive on your server will be mapped to a hidden share. When these values are 0, no such shares will be created.

Comment

This `REG_SZ` holds the comment displayed next to this machine's name when users browse the network.

DiskSpaceThreshold

The `DiskSpaceThreshold` value controls when NT reports that a disk is low on space. The value represents a minimum percentage of free space; when the space available drops below that percentage, a warning alert is generated. This value's a `REG_DWORD` and can range from 1–99%. The default value is 10.

Hidden

If you want to hide a server or workstation from network browsers, set this `REG_BINARY` value to 1 and it will disappear. Clients who know it's there can still access it, but it won't show up in Explorer or any of the other browsing tools.

RestrictNullSessionAccess

LAN Manager, NT's ancient ancestor, allowed users to connect with a *NULL session*[*] to get some types of information from a server, including a list of available shares and account names. Because this is a security vulnerability, Microsoft now offers a way to deny NULL session access to network resources—this value. Set it to 0 if you want to allow NULL session access (not recommended), or 1 if you want to deny it. When set to 1, the shares and pipes specified in `NullSessionShares` and `NullSessionPipes` can still use NULL sessions.

NullSessionShares and NullSessionPipes

These two `REG_SZ` values list any file shares and/or pipes that NULL session-using clients may access. By default, they're both empty, meaning that no one can use NULL sessions when `RestrictNullSessionAccess` is enabled.

Users

This `REG_DWORD` controls how many users may simultaneously log on to your server. Its legal range is from 1 to 0xFFFFFFFF. As a practical matter, you should probably set this to some value less than or equal to the number of actual licenses you have for your server, although being able to say "my server handles 4 billion users" will probably impress your non-system-admin friends.

Services\NetBt

You can run the NetBIOS protocol over a TCP/IP connection; this combination is called NBT or (occasionally) NetBT. NBT makes NetBIOS traffic routable, which works better on multi-segment networks than plain NetBIOS. It can also provide a performance boost, and with the advent of the Internet it makes it possible to offer NetBIOS services over an Internet or PPTP connection. The NetBT service

---

[*] So named because instead of supplying a valid username and password you open a null session with an empty username and password.

handles encapsulating NetBIOS data into TCP/IP packets, and its Parameters key contains several values that govern the overall operation of the NetBT service:

DhcpXXX

There are several values whose names begin with Dhcp. These are set automatically by the DHCP client service. Any Dhcp value can be overridden by its non-DHCP counterpart: for example, DhcpScopeID is overridden by ScopeID. Don't change any of the Dhcp values or DHCP will stop working properly.

EnableDNS

This REG_DWORD indicates whether DNS name resolution is enabled. When it's 1, the default, NetBT will use DNS to resolve names that can't be resolved via WINS, *lmhosts*, or broadcast queries; when it's 0, DNS won't be used. Microsoft warns against changing this value in the Registry; instead, you should use the Network control panel.

EnableLMHOSTS

This REG_DWORD value indicates whether *lmhosts* will be used to resolve names that can't be resolved via WINS or broadcast queries. Like EnableDNS, you shouldn't modify it directly.

EnableProxy

This DWORD controls whether this computer will answer WINS proxy requests; these proxy requests come from computers not running WINS and allows connections across subnets. Don't change this value directly either.

LmhostsTimeout

You can control the timeout period for DNS and *lmhosts* name queries by adjusting this REG_DWORD value. It represents the timeout period in milliseconds; the default value of 6000 allows a 6-second timeout, but you can adjust it from 1000–0xFFFFFFFF. Tweaking this value lets you accommodate slow DNS servers, so it might make a good system policy entry.

NameSrvQueryCount

"If at first you don't succeed, try, try again" applies to name resolution, too. By default, NetBT will issue three WINS queries for a name before deciding that the name can't be resolved. You can change this REG_DWORD's value to anything between 0 and 65,535 to change the number of requests.

NameSrvQueryTimeout

A single WINS query will either be answered or not. This REG_DWORD controls the number of milliseconds after which a query is judged to have timed out. Its default value of 1500 allows for a 1.5-second timeout, but you may use any value from 1000–0xFFFFFFFF. The maximum time it can take to decide a name can't be resolved via WINS is thus equal to `NameSrvQueryCount` multiplied by `NameSrvQueryTimeout`.

WinsDownTimeout

If no WINS servers can be contacted, the system can automatically wait a prescribed period before trying to contact a WINS server again. The length of this period is controlled by `WinsDownTimeout`, which is a `REG_DWORD` number of milliseconds. By default, the system will wait 15 seconds after failing to catch a WINS server before it tries again, but you can modify this interval to any value between 1000 and 0xFFFFFFFF milliseconds.

In addition to these settings, each adapter card to which NetBT is bound has its own adapter-specific settings, which may supplement or override the ones in `Services\NetBt\Parameters`. These settings are stored under the `Services\NetBt\Adapters` subkey; each adapter has a subkey named after its driver. These keys have the same `DhcpXXX` values as the `Services\NetBt\Parameters` key. In addition, their `NameServer` and `NameServerBackup` values specify the IP addresses of the primary and backup WINS servers *for that adapter*. If present and non-blank, these values are used instead of the corresponding system-wide entries.

Services\Netlogon

The Netlogon service handles communications between an NT machine (whether it's a workstation or a server) and its domain controllers. On networks with more than one NT 3.x/NT 4 domain controller, Netlogon is also in charge of synchronizing the domain accounts database between the primary and backup controllers. There are eight significant values in `Services\Netlogon\Parameters`:

DisablePasswordChange

To secure conversations between domain controllers and domain computers, each computer in the domain uses a unique, randomly-generated password to log on to the domain. This password is regenerated every seven days. Normally, you'd leave this alone, but there are two cases where you might want to force NT *not* to change the password. The first is if you're dual-booting more than one copy (or version) of NT on a single machine. Keeping the account password unchanged ensures that each copy of NT can be a member of the domain without anyone changing the domain password behind its back. The other, more common, reason is that every password change represents a change to the domain SAM database. In large domains, these changes can force replication to occur more often than you may find desirable. Turning off the automatic updates will eliminate these changes.

By default, this REG_DWORD is set to 0, meaning that password changes will be allowed. Setting it to 1 on a machine will prevent *that one machine* from asking for a new password, but you must do it on every machine in your domain for it to be effective.

RefusePasswordChange

As an alternative to setting DisablePasswordChange on lots of machines, you can set the REG_DWORD RefusePasswordChange value to 1 on all domain controllers in the domain. This forces the DC to refuse any password change request from NT 4 clients. It doesn't stop the clients from trying, however. See article Q154501 in Microsoft's knowledge base for a full explanation of this parameter and its ramifications.

Pulse

This REG_DWORD controls how often replication pulses are sent. All the changes occurring between pulses are collected together; when the pulse interval expires, the changes are sent to any domain controller that needs an update. Up-to-date domain controllers don't get a pulse. The default interval is 300 seconds. but you may specify any number of seconds from 60 to 48 hours' worth (172,800).

PulseConcurrency

When a PDC has updates, it sends pulses to each BDC that needs the update. The BDC responds by asking for the updated data. The number of pulses a PDC can queue at one time is controlled by this REG_DWORD; the default value of 20 means that 20 BDCs can be pulsed—thus the PDC may have to deal with 20 update requests at one time. You can specify any value from 1 to 500; the bigger the number, the more load may be placed on the PDC.

PulseMaximum

Specifies a maximum interval after which a BDC will be sent an update pulse, even if it doesn't need an update. The default value is 7200 seconds, or two hours, but you may specify any interval in seconds, from 60 to 172,800.

PulseTimeout1 and PulseTimeout2

These two values control how long a PDC waits when pulsing a BDC before it considers the BDC unresponsive. PulseTimeout1 regulates how long the BDC has to answer a pulse; it can be anywhere from 1–120 seconds. PulseTimeout2 specifies how long the PDC will wait for the BDC to finish absorbing the update data once it's sent, from 1–300 seconds.

ReplicationGovernor

Under ordinary circumstances, *Netlogon* uses a 128Kb buffer for copying the SAM database, and it replicates the database whenever a preset number of changes accumulate. For domain controllers on a WAN or slow local link, these settings can consume a significant amount of your bandwidth. The REG_

`DWORD ReplicationGovernor` value can range from 0 to 100; its value represents a percentage of both the buffer size and the amount of time an outstanding replication request may be in progress. For example, a `ReplicationGovernor` value of 25 specifies that a BDC should use a 32Kb buffer (25% of 128Kb) and that a replication request can be on the Net no more than 25% of the time. You must make this setting on every BDC you want to affect; it has no effect on the PDC. Do not set this value to zero! If you do, the PDC will never synchronize with the affected BDC.

Scripts

This `REG_SZ` value specifies the full path to the directory where logon scripts are kept.

Update

Ordinarily, the SAM database will be synchronized only after a certain number of changes have accumulated. You can force *Netlogon* to completely synchronize the database when the service starts by setting this `REG_SZ` value to "Yes." The default value, "No," allows synchronization to happen when needed.

Services\RasMan

The Dial-Up Networking (née RAS) subsystem lets you dial into remote computers and communicate using Microsoft's protocols, IPX, or TCP/IP. The RasMan service is the component that actually handles making over-the-modem network connections on outbound calls. There are only two significant values for this service's **Parameters** subkey:

DisableSavedPasswords

Normally, each user may choose whether she wants DUN to save her passwords or not. You can compel DUN not to cache these passwords by adding this `REG_DWORD` value and setting its value to 1. When you do, DUN won't display the "Save password" checkbox, and it will forget any passwords it has previously stored.

Logging

When this `REG_DWORD` is 1, the DUN dialup component logs its interaction with whatever serial device it's using. This is a great way to troubleshoot connection problems; DUN will log to the *%systemroot%\system32\ras\device.log* file until a connection is established. The log file is cleared when you stop and restart DUN components or when its size exceeds about 100Kb.

The `Services\RasMan\PPP` key has all the really useful DUN settings, including these:

NegotiateTime
> Time, in seconds, that the PPP module will allow for a successful connection negotiation. If the two sides can't complete negotiation in this period, the connection fails. The default value is 150 seconds, but you may set it to any `DWORD` value. A value of 0 means the connection will never fail.

Logging
> When this `REG_DWORD` is set to 1, each PPP connect, disconnect, or failure event is logged to \%*systemroot*%*system32**ras**ppp.log.*

ForceEncryptedPassword
> PPP servers may specify what types of authentication they support. The `ForceEncryptedPassword` value forces an NT RAS server to request CHAP authentication from its clients instead of the less secure PAP. Set this `REG_DWORD` to 1 to force CHAP authentication or 0 to allow PAP. This value has no effect on computers that aren't RAS servers.

Services\Replicator

The Directory Replicator service (usually called just "the replicator") can mirror directories on one server in a domain to other workstations and servers. Any machine may import replicated directories, and any server may export them. What gets replicated and when is controlled by values under the `Services\Replicator` key. First of all, the `Exports` and `Imports` keys contain one value entry for each exported or imported directory. You manage these lists with the Directory Replication dialog in the NT Server Manager.

The `Parameters` subkey contains parameters (also settable through the Server Manager) that control how the replication process actually runs:

ExportPath
> This `REG_SZ` contains the full path to the directory being exported. Any given machine may only export a single directory; on domain controllers, this is almost always the directory where logon scripts are stored, but it can be anything.

GuardTime
> `GuardTime` tells the replicator service how long to wait after the last file change before sending a new change notice. Its value can range from 0 (send changes immediately) to half of the value of `Interval`. This value has no effect unless you specify that the export files should be "Stabilized" in the Server Manager.

ImportPath

Specifies the full path to the directory where imported files and directories are stored on the local machine.

Interval

This REG_DWORD value specifies how often an export computer should check its export directory for changes. The default is 5 minutes, but the value may range from 1 to 60 minutes.

Pulse

Pulse controls when the export computer will rebroadcast change notices. These change notices are sent even when no changes occur so that importers know whether they missed any updates due to network outages. The value of Pulse may range from 1 to 10; it's used as a multiplier of Interval. A Pulse value of 3 (the default) combined with an Interval of 60 (minutes) means that redundant change notices will be sent every 3 hours.

Replicate

This REG_DWORD controls what replication role this machine plays. A value of 1 means this machine exports files; a value of 2 means it imports from other exporters, and a value of 3 (the default) means it can do both.

Services\Tcpip

TCP/IP is a complicated protocol, so it's not surprising that there are a large number of values in Services\Tcpip\Parameters. In keeping with Microsoft's hands-off approach, most parameters that affect how the TCP/IP stack allocates resources are self-adjusting, and I haven't documented them here because there's really no reason to ever adjust them.

TIP It may be tempting to adjust some of these parameters on all your machines by building a policy file—but it's a better idea to use DHCP, which is designed specifically for this task. As a side bonus, DHCP works with non-Windows computers too.

DataBasePath

This REG_SZ contains the path where the TCP/IP stack should look for its *hosts*, *lmhosts*, *networks*, and *protocols* files. By default it points to *%systemroot%\system32\drivers\etc*.

DefaultTTL

The Time-To-Live (TTL) value determines how many hops a single packet may take as it's routed. Each router along the way decrements the TTL; when it reaches zero the packet's dropped. By default, NT marks its packets with a

TTL of 32, but this may be too short for some applications. It's a REG_DWORD, so you can adjust it up to 255 if necessary.

Domain

This REG_SZ contains the domain name for the machine that you entered in the TCP/IP Properties dialog.

Hostname

This REG_SZ contains the hostname you entered in the TCP/IP Properties dialog.

NameServer

This single REG_SZ contains a list of IP addresses (with a space between each address) indicating which DNS servers you've configured for DNS-based address resolution. This value, if any, overrides the name server list provided via DHCP.

IPEnableRouter

This REG_DWORD corresponds to the "Enable IP Forwarding" checkbox on the Routing tab of the TCP/IP Properties dialog. When this DWORD is 1, the system will attempt to route IP packets between the subnets attached to its network adapter cards; when it's 0 (or when you only have one NIC) no routing takes place.

SearchList

This REG_SZ value contains a space-separated list of domain names to append to any hostname that's missing a suffix and can't be resolved.

EnableSecurityFilters

When set to 1, this REG_DWORD enables the TCP/IP stack to filter incoming connections according to the ports specified in TcpAllowedPorts and UdpAllowedPorts below.

PersistentRoutes

Starting with NT 3.51, you could add persistent static routes with the *route add* command. Should you do so, each route is stored as a REG_SZ value under the Services\Tcpip\PersistentRoutes subkey. Each route has its own value entry, constructed as a REG_SZ:

destinationAddr, subnetMask, routeGateway, routeMetric

The entries' names contain all the useful data; their contents are empty.

In addition to these parameters, each network adapter card to which TCP/IP is bound has its own individual set of parameters stored in the card's key under HKLM\SYSTEM\CurrentControlSet\Services\adapter\Parameters\Tcpip.

IPAddress

> This REG_MULTI_SZ contains the actual IP addresses assigned to the physical adapter card. If the first address in the list is "0.0.0.0," the address will be assigned by a DHCP server. You can add multiple addresses to a single adapter card by adding them here.

DefaultGateway

> This REG_MULTI_SZ specifies a default target for packets that aren't destined for one of the addresses on the IPAddress list.

DontAddDefaultGateway

> This REG_DWORD (which doesn't get created automatically) can be either 0 or 1. When it's 1, NT won't use a default gateway entry for this adapter. Microsoft warns that "PPTP users must add this Registry entry for each adapter that is not connected to the Internet" to prevent accidentally routing unintended traffic across a PPTP link.

EnableDHCP

> If this REG_DWORD is 1, NT will ask the DHCP client service to configure the first IP address on this adapter.

SubnetMask

> Since IPAddress allows multiple addresses, SubnetMask is a REG_MULTI_SZ too—it needs to accommodate one subnet mask per IP address! If the first mask is "0.0.0.0," all the mask data will be retrieved from DHCP. You should have one subnet mask for every IP address specified in IPAddress.

TcpAllowedPorts and UdpAllowedPorts

> These two REG_MULTI_SZ values allow you to specify a set of ports on which connections will be accepted. When EnableSecurityFilters equals 0, these values are ignored; when it equals 1, connections from these ports will be allowed, but connections from all other ports will be rejected.

HKU

The "U" in HKU stands for "user." That's appropriate, since HKU's subkeys store settings that vary from user to user. Every time a user logs in, one of two things happens. If the user's never logged in before, the system makes a new copy of the contents of HKU\.DEFAULT and stores it in a new subkey whose name matches the user's SID. If the user has logged in before, her subkey under HKU is mapped to HKCU and the logon process continues. There are some subtleties to this process; for example, if the network's using profiles, the system may have to fetch the user's profile from a server if it's not locally cached.

HKU\.DEFAULT

The settings in this hive are used as a baseline for new users when they log in. The section "Setting Defaults for New User Accounts" in Chapter 8 discusses how you can modify these defaults so that all new users will automatically get the defaults you set when their HKU subkeys are created.

HKU\sid

Each user account has a unique SID; this SID is used to identify that account's settings under HKU. For a detailed description of what keys and values are stored under HKU*sid*, see the section "HKCU" later in this chapter.

HKCR

HKCR is the backbone of the OLE/ActiveX subsystem. The shell, the Explorer, and many applications depend on the data stored here for prosaic tasks like deciding which icon to display with a file or what to do when the user double-clicks a file. OLE applications need this data to determine what servers to start when a user embeds or links a foreign object into a document, and the Distributed OLE and DCOM systems need it too.

HKCR\ext

The original Win3.x scheme for linking a file with the application that created it was to associate the file's extension with the name of an executable. With the introduction of OLE, though, it became necessary to associate file contents with DLLs, since an OLE server might be a DLL instead of a standalone application. The Win 3.x File and Program Managers were primitive at best, and to improve them Microsoft needed a lot more information about files, their creators, and their types.

The starting point for these improvements is the set of *filename-extension keys* that live under HKCR. These keys are named after file extensions: HKCR\.txt, HKCR\.html, and so on. The default value of each of these keys contains a string called the *application identifier* like "textfile" or "htmlfile." This value is used to look up an HKCR subkey of the same name.

While it's possible to add other values to file association keys, no part of the system will use them, and they're subject to being overwritten, so don't count on your values being available if you keep them here.

HKCR\fileType

For each file association key, there will usually be a single key whose name matches the application identifier. These keys are called *class-definition keys*. Continuing the example above, let's say there's a key named HKCR\htmlfile. To figure out what to do with a file when the user double-clicks it, the shell follows three steps:

1. Strip the extension from the file and use it to find a file association key like HKCR\.doc or HKCR\.pl.

2. Open the file association key and get its default value, then use that value to look for a key with the same name. For example, if HKCR\.pl's default value is "Perl script," the shell will look for HKCR\Perl script and try to open it. This subkey is called the application identifier key.

3. The application identifier key contains values that the shell parses to figure out how to open or edit a file, or to create a new copy of a particular file type or object.

Each application identifier key can have a number of values and subkeys. Which ones a particular application's key has varies. Here are the most common subkeys you'll encounter:

CLSID

This subkey's default value contains the *class ID*, or CLSID, assigned to an OLE object. OLE applications (including Explorer and the shell) can use this CLSID to keep track of a file or object's type.

DefaultIcon

The default value of this subkey contains the path to an executable or DLL and a resource ID. When it needs the icon for a file, the Explorer will look up the application's class-definition key, get the DefaultIcon value if it exists, and load that icon. By changing this value you can alter the icons displayed for a particular file type.

Shell\Edit, Shell\Open, and Shell\Print

These subkeys each have a further subkey: Command. When the system sees one of the Shell\XXX keys, it knows that this class type can be opened, printed, or edited. The value of the Command subkey gives the actual command that will perform the requested action.

shellex

The shellex subkey makes it possible for clever programmers to add items to the Properties dialog for a particular file type. The value of the shellex\PropertySheetHandlers value can specify a CLSID; when the shell looks up the CLSID's key it can figure out which property sheet or dialog to open for that item.

HKCR\CLSID

This subkey contains all of the CLSIDs for classes installed on the system. Each CLSID key contains a value that provides a human-readable name for the class (which appears in the Insert Object dialog of most OLE-compatible applications). There are a variety of other subkeys that can be attached to a particular entry under HKCR\CLSID\clsid. The most important ones are `InprocServer32` and `InprocServer`. These specify which DLL implements the code to create or edit objects of this CLSID's type.

HKCU

We all like to customize our environments. We do it at home, at work, in our cars, and pretty much anywhere else we can get away with it. When you customize your NT environment and applications, the changes end up in subkeys of HKCU, which is actually a link to your SID's subkey under HKU. Only a currently logged-in user has access to HKCU. It can't be opened remotely with *RegEdit* or *RegEdt32*, nor can a SID key under HKU be edited while someone with a different SID is logged in.

The contents of HKCU vary more than any of the other root keys because applications store their user-specific settings here too. If Ellen and Joe share a computer, their respective HKCU subkeys can end up looking very different—Ellen might install and use Netscape, Visual Studio, and BoundsChecker, while Joe might stick with Office 97 and Internet Explorer. Accordingly, in this section I'll confine my discussion to the most important subkeys of HKCU.

HKCU\AppEvents

For better or worse, Microsoft included the capability in NT 4.0 (and Win95, too) to associate sounds with system events like opening or closing windows, logging out, and so on. This feature certainly falls into the customization arena, and application developers can add their own event classes. For example, if you install Microsoft's Visual DevStudio you can get audio alerts when your compilation succeeds, when the debugger hits a breakpoint, and so on.

The event-to-noise mappings are stored in HKCU\AppEvents. Each event that has a sound associated with it will have the name of the *.wav* file to play as the con-

HKCU 333

tent of its default value. For a fun prank, write a small Perl script that randomly assigns *.wav* files from *%systemroot%\media* to random events.*

HKCU\Console

MS-DOS's command-line interface is, to put it politely, extremely limited. If you're used to a powerful Unix shell like *bash*, *zsh*, or *tcsh*, using NT's command line is only slightly better. The really weak spot, though, is the appearance and behavior of the console window—after all, you can always write command scripts in Perl, KixStart, or REXX, but you're stuck looking at them through that old throwback 80x24 white-on-black ugly-font DOS window!

Fortunately, the NT console is customizable, so you don't have to suffer any longer. The customization settings all live under `HKCU\Console`, and they're so self-explanatory (guess what `FontSize` does) I won't cover them here.

HKCU\Control Panels

Each installed control panel may have its own subkey and settings beneath `HKCU\ Control Panels`. `HKU\.DEFAULT` has default settings for all of the control panels, so `HKCU\Control Panels` may not contain as many values as you'd expect. Additionally, many control panels (notably Network and Multimedia) store their settings in other parts of the Registry.

HKCU\Environment

The `Environment` key contains whatever environment variables are set in the "User Variables" list of the System control panel's Environment tab. They're stored as name-value pairs. For some reason, some variables are stored as `REG_SZ` entries, while others are stored as `REG_EXPAND_SZ`. It doesn't seem to matter what's *in* the value, either; some non-expandable strings are still tagged as `REG_EXPAND_SZ`. Weird.

HKCU\Printers

The system stores information about printers the current user may use in `HKCU\ Printers`. Each printer gets its own value entry directly under `HKCU\Printers`. This entry specifies what the default printer for this particular user is. The printer settings themselves (for all printers, not just the default one) are actually stored in `HKLM\SYSTEM\CurrentControlSet\Services\Print\Printers`.

---

* The publisher and I jointly disclaim any liability arising from you doing this to your boss, spouse, or co-workers.

HKCU\Software\Microsoft

As you've no doubt inferred from the name, user-specific settings for Microsoft components are stored under this key. Until you install Internet Explorer and/or Microsoft Office on a machine, though, there are relatively few of these keys; most NT settings are stored under HKLM, and there aren't that many settings to hold here.

Microsoft\NtBackup

The bundled NT Backup application has a fairly large number of settings in it. All of these settings can be manipulated using the program's standard user interface, but you may be interested in setting some of them via system policies—for example, the NtBackup\UserInterface\UsePassword flag can be set to require that backup tapes be password-protected. There are six subkeys under Microsoft\ NtBackup:[*]

Backup Engine

   The values under this subkey control the actual backup process: how many buffers should be reserved for the tape drive, whether Mac files on an NTFS volume should be backed up, and so forth.

Debug

   If you're having problems getting a backup device to work, you can configure debug logging through the values in this key.

Display

   These settings store your choices of font size, window position, and other display parameters.

Hardware

   The settings you choose for whatever type of tape hardware your system has are stored here.

Logging

   You can turn on logging for individual backup jobs through the *ntbackup* user interface. When you do, these values are used to figure out whether the log file should be printed and what the root of its filename should be.

User Interface

   The catch-all key, this holds values that don't have a place anywhere else, like whether the tape should be ejected when the backup completes or whether the backup should be automatically verified when it's done.

---

[*] And *ntbackup* doesn't even know it—it's using an INI file remapped to this key.

For a more complete explanation of the ins and outs of *ntbackup*, see *Windows NT Backup and Restore* by Jody Leber (O'Reilly & Associates, 1998).

Microsoft\RAS Autodial

The Dial-Up Networking autodialer's settings are stored under this key, which retains its name for backward compatibility.

Addresses

Each time you establish an autodialed connection, DUN stores the address that caused the dialing in a value under **Addresses**. The IP address or DNS name serves as the value name for each entry. Entries under **Addresses** have three values: **Tag**, **LastModified**, and **Network**.

Control

This subkey is where the actual control settings for the autodialer live. There are only three of them:

DisabledAddresses

This **REG_MULTI_SZ** stores a list of IP addresses or DNS names for which an autodialed connection will never be established. You can use this list as an extremely low-rent blocking proxy by filling it with addresses of sites you don't want to connect to.

LoginSessionDisable

I have no idea what this is for. It appears to be set by the **RasGetAutodialParm()** API routine. If you know what this does, I'd love to hear.

DisableConnectionQuery

Ordinarily, DUN will pop up a little dialog asking you for permission to start a connection when it needs one. This is annoying because if you start something that requires a connection, you have to stay there to answer the dialog—its default action button is "No, don't dial." You can subdue this annoyance by setting **DisableConnectionQuery** (a **REG_DWORD**) to 1. This will force DUN to always start a dialup connection when one is required.

Locations

There's one subkey of **Locations** for each dialing location you have defined.

Entries

Likewise, there will be one subkey under **Entries** for each phonebook entry you've used. The value for an entry will be of the form **NetworkX**, where X is some small integer. This indicates which DUN dialup adapter you used to make this connection.

Networks

This key has subkeys named after the values of `Entries'` subkeys: `Network0`, `Network1`, and so on. Each of these entries in turn has a value named "1" which points back to an entry under `Entries`.

Microsoft\RAS Monitor

The `RAS Monitor` key stores settings for the Dial-Up Networking monitor. Nine of the fourteen values stored here track the window size and position of various monitor windows; the other five are flag and setting values whose structure isn't documented.

Microsoft\RAS Phonebook

The system-wide set of DUN phonebook entries is stored in *%systemroot%\ system32\ras\rasphone.pbk*. This file (or the personal phonebook files you can create and use instead) holds the phone numbers, network settings, and login credentials for each entry in your phonebook.* These settings can differ widely between entries; you might have one entry for your ISP that tells DUN to use server-supplied values for everything and another for dialing in to your office intranet that uses a fixed set of IP, DNS, and gateway addresses.

The values beneath `Microsoft\RAS Phonebook` control DUN dialing for all entries in the phonebook. As you can see, they provide a fairly rich set of options.

AllowLogonLocationEdits *and* AllowLogonPhonebookEdits

These two `REG_DWORD`s control whether users may change their dialing location or phonebook entry during login. They're only effective if you've enabled the option to allow logging on via DUN. Note that when you change these parameters in the Appearance tab of the Logon Properties dialog from within *rasphone*, these values are actually changed in `HKU\.DEFAULT\Soft-ware\Microsoft\RAS Phonebook`, not in `HKCU`.

AlternatePhonebookPath

If you specify an alternate phonebook in the User Preferences dialog's Phonebook tab, the path to that phonebook will appear here.

AreaCodes

In the Basic tab of the Edit Phonebook Entry dialog, you can specify whether you want to use the TAPI dialing properties or not. If you do, you can enter an area code for the phonebook number. This `REG_MULTI_SZ` tracks the area codes you've entered in the phonebook.

---

* *.pbk* files are plain text, so you can inspect and edit them to your heart's content. You can also copy them from one NT 4 machine to another; this is an easy way to get a consistent set of phonebook entries for a group of machines.

CallbackMode

DUN supports three callback modes via this value. They only apply if the remote server offers to perform a callback. The first option, set if this REG_ DWORD is 0, tells the DUN client to refuse callback requests. A value of 1 (the default) specifies that DUN should ask you whether you want to accept it or not, and a value of 3 means "yes, always accept a callback if requested."

CloseOnDial

When it's set to 1, as it is by default, this REG_DWORD tells DUN to close the phonebook application when it's finished. Set this value to 0 to keep the phonebook application open after dialing completes.

DefaultEntry

This REG_SZ specifies which phonebook entry appears as the default entry when you open the Dial-Up Networking phonebook. Adjust it to make a particular entry appear.

ExpandAutoDialQuery

Before DUN autodials for you, it may ask you to confirm that you really want to dial (unless you have "Always prompt before auto-dialing" unchecked in the Appearance tab of the User Preferences dialog). When it does ask for confirmation, the "Settings" button in the confirmation dialog shows additional controls for choosing a location and turning off the confirmation requests in the future. Setting ExpandAutoDialQuery to 1, its default, makes these extra controls immediately visible. Setting it to 0 requires users to hit the Settings button to see them.

IdleHangUpSeconds

This value specifies the number of seconds a DUN connection may be idle before the client hangs it up. Note that this isn't the same as the timeout value specified by the RAS (or PPP) server. The value should be in seconds; a value of 0 tells DUN to never hang up.

LastCallbackByCaller

I don't know what this is for either.

NewEntryWizard

As with so many other NT components, the DUN phonebook features a wizard that will ostensibly help you create new entries. The Appearance tab of the User Preferences dialog features a checkbox that lets you specify whether you want to use the wizard or not; this REG_DWORD reflects that value.

OperatorDial

You can toggle a DUN setting that tells it not to dial because you'll be dialing manually. This REG_DWORD value reflects that option; when it's 1, that means that the system will wait for you to dial before attempting to connect.

PersonalPhonebookFile

Besides the alternate phonebook file, you may specify an individual phone-book file for your own use (after all, this is HKCU!). If you specify a personal phonebook in the User Preferences dialog's Phonebook tab, the path to that phonebook will appear here.

PhonebookMode

This REG_DWORD specifies which phonebook DUN will use. The default value of 0 means that *%systemroot%\system32\ras\rasphone.pbk* will be used; a value of 1 means that the user's personal phonebook will be used, and a 3 means that the value in **AlternatePhonebookPath** will be used.

Phonebooks

This REG_MULTI_SZ keeps a list of all the phonebooks you've ever specified in **AlternatePhonebookPath** so it can build a combo box listing them for your later reference.

Prefixes

This REG_MULTI_SZ contains a list of all the prefixes you've ever specified for phone entries in your phonebook. This allows DUN to present a nice combo box listing your previous choices.

PreviewPhoneNumber

This REG_DWORD reflects the setting of the "Preview Phone Number" check-box in the Appearance tab of the Edit Phonebook Entry dialog. When it's set to 1, users may edit the phonebook entry's number before it's dialed.

RedialAttempts

By default, if a connection doesn't happen on the first attempt, DUN will quit trying. This happens because the default value of **RedialAttempts** is 0. You can enable as many retries as you'd like, and DUN will patiently keep trying until it connects or makes the specified number of attempts.

RedialOnLinkFailure

This value (a REG_DWORD) specifies whether DUN should automatically resur-rect a failed connection. Sometimes a connection will drop for no good rea-son; setting this value to 1 will cause DUN to redial and restart the connection if it fails.

RedialSeconds

This value specifies the number of seconds (15 is the default) to wait between redial attempts, assuming you've set **RedialAttempts** to greater than 0.

ShowConnectStatus

This REG_DWORD has two possible values: 1 (the default) displays a connec-tion progress dialog that indicates what's happening on the connection, and 0 will suppress the dialog (useful when you're making connections via command-line scripts).

ShowLights

In a nod to the Win95 way of doing things, NT's DUN can display some little blinking lights in the system tray to duplicate the front-panel LEDs of most external modems. The Dial-Up Networking Monitor is in charge of this vital function. By default, this REG_DWORD's value is 1, meaning that the DUN Monitor will be started before the connection is—therefore, the lights will be present. If you don't enjoy seeing them (or, more likely, if you're not paying any attention to the system tray), you can set this value to 0 to hide them.

SkipConnectComplete

Until you tell it otherwise, DUN displays a dialog telling you that you've successfully connected. One of the options in this dialog is a checkbox that says "Don't show this dialog again." That checkbox controls the value of SkipConnectComplete: when it's 1, that tells DUN to omit the dialog. By default, its value is 0, so you'll see this dialog until you manually turn it off.

Suffixes

Like Prefixes, this value's a REG_MULTI_SZ. Its purpose is to store a list of any suffixes you've ever specified for a DUN phone number.

UseLocation

By default, you can select any of the installed TAPI locations when making a DUN connection. This is especially useful if you have a machine that frequently moves between different area codes or countries. However, if you want to keep users from changing their location from the DUN phonebook, just set this REG_DWORD to 0 instead of its default value of 1. (Note that users can still use the Modems control panel to change locations.)

UseAreaAndCountry

I haven't been able to identify what this does.

WindowX and WindowY

These values specify the (x,y) location of the upper-left corner of the DUN phonebook window.

Besides this cornucopia of values, Microsoft\RAS Phonebook has an additional subkey, Callback. Every installed modem device on the system will have its own subkey under Callback, named after the device (e.g., Callback\Standard Modem (COM2)). If you set the callback mode to "always call me back at this number," the number you supply for that device will go in the subkey's Number value. This provides a convenient way to preset a callback number, perhaps as part of a mass laptop installation.

Microsoft\Windows\CurrentVersion

A surprising amount of code originally developed for Win95 has found its way into NT 4.0. In fact, Microsoft's eventual goal is to unify the Win9x and NT lines until what's left is a nice Win9x interface over the security, performance, and scalability of NT. To facilitate this merging, Microsoft included a compatibility key: `Microsoft\Windows\CurrentVersion`. Software, like Explorer or Internet Explorer, which expects to find Registry settings under this key, would be sorely disappointed to learn that under NT this key doesn't exist. To prevent having to modify all their applications, they instead added this key. Besides the shell, Explorer, and IE, no other applications write to it, but Win95 applications running under NT may read from it if they're not NT-savvy.

HKCU\Microsoft\Windows NT\CurrentVersion

This key is pretty much a mixed bag: it holds user-specific settings that have no home elsewhere. For example, NT's Server Manager applications store their settings in a subkey of `Windows NT\CurrentVersion\Network` even though they might more properly live under `HKCU\Software\Microsoft\ServerManager` or somesuch.

Devices

The `Devices` subkey contains one value entry for each installed printer on a system. Apart from that, it doesn't seem to do anything else.

Network

The Event Viewer, Server Manager, and User Manager all keep their small sets of user-specific settings here. The only other interesting item is the `PersistentConnections` subkey, which contains a list of shares that NT should reconnect when the user logs in again.

Program Manager

The entries under this key are retained for older applications that expect to find things here.

Windows

Just as with `Program Manager`, this key primarily exists for backward compatibility, especially with the WOW subsystem.

Winlogon

Alone among the subkeys of `Windows NT\CurrentVersion`, `Winlogon` actually has three useful values beneath it. They duplicate similar entries in `HKLM\SOFTWARE\Microsoft\Windows NT\CurrentVersion\Winlogon`, but these entries apply only to the currently logged in user.

ParseAutoexec

This `REG_DWORD` specifies whether to parse *autoexec.bat* when the user logs in. 1 (the default) means yes; 0 means no.

ProfileType

Specifies the profile type of the current user's profile. A 1 means it's a local profile; other values indicate a cached, roaming, or mandatory roaming profile.

RunLoginScriptSync

If this `REG_DWORD` is set to 1, any logon script for this user will be run before the desktop and shell are started. This is the default. Setting the value to 0 allows the logon script process to run in parallel with the shell as it starts.

HKCC

HKCC is just a pointer that links to the current hardware profile at `HKLM\SYSTEM\ Hardware Profiles\Current`. Under Win9x, HKCC is dynamically generated and filled with the list of VxDs and other drivers that are currently active. Since NT has no comparable way to load such a list, HKCC exists as a compatibility aid.

HKDD

HKDD exists primarily as a convenience for software developers whose programs were originally designed for Win95. NT-based applications, notably the Performance Monitor, don't get data out of HKDD. However, Win95 code that uses subkeys of HKDD will still work, since NT remaps HKDD data into the appropriate subkeys elsewhere in the Registry.

Index

S

/s swtich (ERDisk), 64
/s switch (RDISK), 60
/s- switch (RDISK), 60
SACLs (system ACLs), 192
SAM key, 43
    encrypting with SKS, 33
    encrypting with SYSKEY, 242–251
    restoring from ERDs, 250
Save method (Perl), 215
"Save Password" option, 280
saving
    captured Registry data
        (NTREGMON), 271
    logon credentials, 280
    monitoring system cache, 292
    Registry keys, 196, 215
    Registry keys in files, 116–119
    Registry keys with reg.exe, 261
SchedulerThreadPriority key, 313
scheduling regular backups, 52
Schulman, Andrew, 76, 105
screen saver during logon, 276
Scripts key, 325
SDs (security descriptors), 193
searching (for) keys and values, 89–91,
        115–116, 264–267
SearchList key, 328
SecondLevelDataCache key, 292
SecurePipeServers key, 313
security, 31–33, 126–134
    ACLs (see ACLs)
    API routines for, 192–195
    auditing Registry access, 254–255
    auditing Registry activity, 17, 129–133
    bug fixes, 34
    cryptography, 301
    customizing, 279–285
    DACs (discretionary access
        controls), 127
    editing Registry, warning about, 18–19,
        55–57
    emergency repair disks (see ERDs)
    encrypting SECURITY\SAM, 242–251
    HKLM\SECURITY key, 43
    key ownership, 17, 133–134
    limiting remote Windows NT
        access, 237–240
    LSA (Local Security Authority), 312

password expiration warnings, 282
permissions (see permissions)
policies (see system policies)
Registry and, 16
Registry backups (see backups of
        Registry)
Registry key permissions, 32
removing crash evidence, 286
restriction (winreg) key, 238–240
safeguarding data, 52–57
SKS (System Key Security), 32–33
SYSKEY protection, 56
Trojan horses, 255
Win32 API data types for, 172–175
Windows NT model, 6
Security Account Manager (SAM), 43
    encrypting key for, 242–251
    encrypting Registry data on, 33
SECURITY_ATTRIBUTES data type, 174
SECURITY_DESCRIPTOR data type, 174
security descriptors (SDs), 193
security IDs (SIDs) for HKU subkeys, 25
SECURITY_INFORMATION data type, 174
SECURITY key, 33, 43
Security key, 317
Select key, 44, 308
SendAlert key, 310
Server service, 320
servers, hiding from network
        computers, 292
service packs (SPs), 34
services
    configuration settings, 314–329
Services for Macintosh (SFM) package, 102
Services key, 45, 314–329
    adapter\Parameters\Tcpip subkey, 329
Session Manager key, 313
Set Value permission, 16, 126
SetDiskWarningThreshold utility
        (example), 190
settings
    system policy, applying, 139–141,
        152–155
Settings key, 47
Setup key, 44, 308
setup program, WinNT, 65
SetupType key, 308
SetValue method (Perl), 214
SFM (Services for Macintosh) package, 102

About the Author

Paul Robichaux is an experienced software developer and author. He's worked on Unix, Macintosh, and Win32 development projects over the past six years, including a stint on Intergraph's OLE team. He is the author of the *Windows NT Server Administrator's Guide.*

Colophon

The animal featured on the cover of *Managing the Windows NT Registry* is a female or a juvenile orangutan. The word "orangutan" comes from the Malayan for "man of the woods." Ancient legend has it that orangutans have the ability to speak, but choose not to because they are afraid that if humans find out, they will put the orangutans to work.

Orangutans are native to the forests of Borneo and Sumatra. Male adults have long beards and mustaches, and highly developed cheek pads and throat pouches. The throat pouches are used as resonators for mating calls and calls to mark territory. Human males have a similar throat pouch, called the "Morgagnitic pouch," but it is very small in most men. It becomes well developed in trumpet players, bass singers, and Muslim prayer callers.

These great apes are almost completely arboreal. They move by swinging from one tree branch to the next, and descend to the ground only when there is no branch to swing to, and occasionally to gather branches for building sleeping nests. Because of the orangutans' method of locomotion, their arms are very strong and long, measuring up to 7.8 feet when outspread and reaching to the ankles when standing upright. Their legs, in contrast, are relatively weak. They eat primarily fruit, but will also eat bark, leaves, flowers, and eggs. They get their drinking water by scooping it out of holes in the trees.

Orangutans mate while swinging from tree branches. Infants weigh approximately 3.5 pounds at birth. For about the first year the infant is completely dependent on its mother, and clings to her by entwining its fingers in her fur. If orangutan babies are orphaned they need to be given a substitute to cling to, and they usually display great affection for their surrogate "mothers." Development in the first year is similar to that of human babies.

Other than humans, orangutans have no natural enemies. However, as a result of hunting and habitat destruction, they are in danger of becoming extinct.

Edie Freedman designed the cover of this book, using a 19th-century engraving from the Dover Pictorial Archive. The cover layout was produced by Kathleen Wilson with Quark XPress 3.3 using the ITC Garamond font. Whenever possible, our books use Rep-Kover™, a durable and flexible lay-flat binding. If the page count exceeds Rep-Kover's limit, perfect binding is used.

The inside layout was designed by Nancy Priest and implemented in FrameMaker by Mike Sierra. The text and heading fonts are ITC Garamond Light and Garamond Book. The illustrations that appear in the book were created in Macromedia Freehand 7.0 and screen shots were created in Adobe Photoshop 4.0 by Robert Romano. This colophon was written by Clairemarie Fisher O'Leary.

 # *More Titles from O'Reilly*

Windows NT Administration

Windows NT in a Nutshell

By Eric Pearce
1st Edition June 1997
364 pages, ISBN 1-56592-251-4

Anyone who installs Windows NT, creates a user, or adds a printer is an NT system administrator (whether they realize it or not). This book features a new tagged callout approach to documenting the 4.0 GUI as well as real-life examples of command usage and strategies for problem solving, with an emphasis on networking. Windows NT in a Nutshell will be as useful to the single-system home user as it will be to the administrator of a 1,000-node corporate network.

Windows NT User Administration

By Ashley J. Meggitt & Timothy D. Ritchey
1st Edition November 1997
218 pages, ISBN 1-56592-301-4

Many Windows NT books introduce you to a range of topics, but seldom do they give you enough information to master any one thing. This book (like other O'Reilly animal books) is different. *Windows NT User Administration* makes you an expert at creating users efficiently, controlling what they can do, limiting the damage they can cause, and monitoring their activities on your system. Don't simply react to problems; use the techniques in this book to anticipate and prevent them.

Windows NT SNMP

By James D. Murray
1st Edition February 1998
464 pages, Includes CD-ROM
ISBN 1-56592-338-3

This book describes the implementation of SNMP (the Simple Network Management Protocol) on Windows NT 3.51 and 4.0 (with a look ahead to NT 5.0) and Windows 95 systems. It covers SNMP and network basics and detailed information on developing SNMP management applications and extension agents. The book comes with a CD-ROM containing a wealth of additional information: standards documents, sample code from the book, and many third-party, SNMP-related software tools, libraries, and demos.

Essential Windows NT System Administration

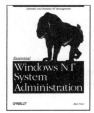

By Æleen Frisch
1st Edition February 1998
486 pages, ISBN 1-56592-274-3

This book combines practical experience with technical expertise to help you manage Windows NT systems as productively as possible. It covers the standard utilities offered with the Windows NT operating system and from the Resource Kit, as well as important commercial and free third-party tools. By the author of O'Reilly's bestselling book, *Essential System Administration*.

Windows NT Backup & Restore

By Jody Leber
1st Edition May 1998 (est.)
250 pages (est.), ISBN 1-56592-272-7

Beginning with the need for a workable recovery policy and ways to translate that policy into requirements, *Windows NT Backup & Restore* presents the reader with practical guidelines for setting up an effective backup system in both small and large environments. It covers the native NT utilities as well as major third-party hardware and software.

Windows NT Server 4.0 for NetWare Administrators

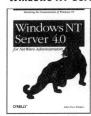

By Robert Bruce Thompson
1st Edition November 1997
756 pages, ISBN 1-56592-280-8

This book provides a fast-track means for experienced NetWare administrators to build on their knowledge and master the fundamentals of using the Microsoft Windows NT Server. The broad coverage of many aspects of Windows NT Server is balanced by a tightly focused approach of comparison, contrast, and differentiation between NetWare and NT features and methodologies.

O'REILLY™

TO ORDER: **800-998-9938** • **order@oreilly.com** • **http://www.oreilly.com/**
OUR PRODUCTS ARE AVAILABLE AT A BOOKSTORE OR SOFTWARE STORE NEAR YOU.
FOR INFORMATION: **800-998-9938** • **707-829-0515** • **info@oreilly.com**

Windows NT Administration

Windows NT Desktop Reference

By Æleen Frisch
1st Edition January 1998
64 pages, ISBN 1-56592-437-1

A hip-pocket quick reference to Windows NT commands, as well as the most useful commands from the Resource Kits. Commands are arranged ingroups related to their purpose and function. Covers Windows NT 4.0.

MCSE: The Core Exams in a Nutshell

By Michael Moncur
1st Edition May 1998 (est.)
300 pages (est.), ISBN 1-56592-376-6

MCSE: The Core Exams in a Nutshell is a detailed quick reference for administrators with Windows NT experience or experience administering a different platform, such as UNIX, who want to learn what is necessary to pass the MCSE required exam portion of the MCSE certification. While no book is a substitute for real-world experience, this book will help you codify your knowledge and prepare for the exams.

MCSE: The Electives in a Nutshell

By Michael Moncur
1st Edition June 1998 (est.)
550 pages (est.), ISBN: 1-56592-482-7

A companion volume to *MCSE: The Core Exams in a Nutshell, MCSE: The Electives in a Nutshell* is a comprehensive study guide that covers the elective exams for the MCSE as well as the Internet requirements and electives for the MCSE+Internet. This detailed reference is aimed at sophisticated users who need a bridge between real-world experience and the MCSE exam requirements.

Managing the Windows NT Registry

By Paul Robichaux
1st Edition April 1998
470 pages, ISBN 1-56592-378-2

The Windows NT Registry is the repository for all hardware, software, and application configuration settings. This is the system administrator's guide to maintaining, monitoring, and updating the Registry database. A "must-have" for every NT system manager or administrator, it covers what the Registry is and where it lives on disk, available tools, Registry access from programs, and Registry content.

Learning Perl on Win32 Systems

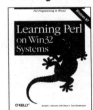

By Randal L. Schwartz, Erik Olson &
Tom Christiansen
1st Edition August 1997
306 pages, ISBN 1-56592-324-3

In this carefully paced course, leading Perl trainers and a Windows NT practitioner teach you to program in the language that promises to emerge as the scripting language of choice on NT. Based on the "llama" book, this book features tips for PC users and new, NT-specific examples, along with a foreword by Larry Wall, the creator of Perl, and Dick Hardt, the creator of Perl for Win32.

Perl

Perl

Learning Perl, 2nd Edition

By Randal L. Schwartz & Tom Christiansen
Foreword by Larry Wall
2nd Edition July 1997
302 pages, ISBN 1-56592-284-0

In this update of a bestseller, two leading Perl trainers teach you to use the most universal scripting language in the age of the World Wide Web. With a foreword by Larry Wall, the creator of Perl, this smooth, carefully paced book is the "official" guide for both formal (classroom) and informal learning. It is now current for Perl version 5.004.

Learning Perl is a hands-on tutorial designed to get you writing useful Perl scripts as quickly as possible. Exercises (with complete solutions) accompany each chapter. A lengthy, new chapter in this edition introduces you to CGI programming, while touching also on the use of library modules, references, and Perl's object-oriented constructs.

Perl is a language for easily manipulating text, files, and processes. It comes standard on most UNIX platforms and is available free of charge on all other important operating systems. Perl technical support is informally available—often within minutes—from a pool of experts who monitor a USENET newsgroup (*comp.lang.perl.misc*) with tens of thousands of readers.

Contents include:

- A quick tutorial stroll through Perl basics
- Systematic, topic-by-topic coverage of Perl's broad capabilities
- Lots of brief code examples
- Programming exercises for each topic, with fully worked-out answers
- How to execute system commands from your Perl program
- How to manage DBM databases using Perl
- An introduction to CGI programming for the Web

The Perl Cookbook

By Tom Christiansen & Nathan Torkington
1st Edition June 1998 (est.)
600 pages (est.), ISBN 1-56592-243-3

The Perl Cookbook is a collection of hundreds of problems and their solutions (with examples) for anyone programming in Perl. The topics range from beginner questions to techniques that even the most experienced Perl programmers might learn from.

Advanced Perl Programming

By Sriram Srinivasan
1st Edition August 1997
434 pages, ISBN 1-56592-220-4

This book covers complex techniques for managing production-ready Perl programs and explains methods for manipulating data and objects that may have looked like magic before. It gives you necessary background for dealing with networks, databases, and GUIs, and includes a discussion of internals to help you program more efficiently and embed Perl within C or C within Perl.

Learning Perl on Win32 Systems

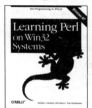

By Randal L. Schwartz, Erik Olson & Tom Christiansen
1st Edition August 1997
306 pages, ISBN 1-56592-324-3

In this carefully paced course, leading Perl trainers and a Windows NT practitioner teach you to program in the language that promises to emerge as the scripting language of choice on NT. Based on the "llama" book, this book features tips for PC users and new, NT-specific examples, along with a foreword by Larry Wall, the creator of Perl, and Dick Hardt, the creator of Perl for Win32.

Mastering Regular Expressions

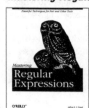

By Jeffrey E. F. Friedl
1st Edition January 1997
368 pages, ISBN 1-56592-257-3

Regular expressions, a powerful tool for manipulating text and data, are found in scripting languages, editors, programming environments, and specialized tools. In this book, author Jeffrey Friedl leads you through the steps of crafting a regular expression that gets the job done. He examines a variety of tools and uses them in an extensive array of examples, with a major focus on Perl.

Annoyances

Windows Annoyances

By David A. Karp
1st Edition June 1997
300 pages, ISBN 1-56592-266-2

Windows Annoyances, a comprehensive resource for intermediate to advanced users of Windows 95 and NT 4.0, details step-by-step how to customize your Win95/NT operating system through an extensive collection of tips, tricks, and workarounds. You'll learn how to customize every aspect of these systems, far beyond the intentions of Microsoft. This book shows you how to customize your PC through methods of backing up, repairing, compressing, and transferring portions of the Registry. Win95 users will discover how Plug and Play, the technology that makes Win95 so compatible, can save time and improve the way you interact with your computer. You'll also learn how to benefit from the new 32-bit software and hardware drivers that support such features as improved multitasking and long filenames.

Word 97 Annoyances

By Woody Leonhard, Lee Hudspeth & T.J. Lee
1st Edition August 1997
356 pages, ISBN 1-56592-308-1

Word 97 contains hundreds of annoying idiosyncrasies that can be either eliminated or worked around. Whether it's the Find Fast feature that takes over your machine every once in awhile, or the way Word automatically selects an entire word as you struggle to highlight only a portion of it, *Word 97 Annoyances* will show you how to solve the problem. It's filled with tips and customizations, and takes an in-depth look at what makes Word 97 tick—mainly character and paragraph formatting, styles, and templates.

This informative, yet humorous, book shows you how to use and modify Word 97 to meet your needs, transforming the software into a powerful tool customized to the way *you* use Word. You'll learn how to:

- Customize the toolbar so it works the way you want it to
- Reduce your stress level by understanding how Word defines sections or formats paragraphs and accepting some apparent annoyances that are built into Word
- Write simple VBA programs to eliminate your own personal annoyances

Excel 97 Annoyances

By Woody Leonhard, Lee Hudspeth & T.J. Lee
1st Edition September 1997
336 pages, ISBN 1-56592-309-X

Learn how to shape Excel 97 in a way that will not only make it most effective, but will give you a sense of enjoyment as you analyze data with ease. Excel 97, which ships with Office 97, has many new features that may be overwhelming. All of the various toolbars, packed with what seems to be an unending array of buttons, might seem a bit intimidating, not to mention annoying, to the average user. *Excel 97 Annoyances* is a guide that will help create some order among the available options by providing customizations that require only a few simple clicks of the mouse button.

This book uncovers Excel 97's hard-to-find features and tells how to eliminate the annoyances of data analysis. It shows how to easily retrieve data from the Web, details step-by-step construction of a perfect toolbar, includes tips for working around the most annoying gotchas of auditing, and shows how to use VBA to control Excel in powerful ways.

Office 97 Annoyances

By Woody Leonhard, Lee Hudspeth & T.J. Lee
1st Edition October 1997
396 pages, ISBN 1-56592-310-3

Despite marked improvements from version to version, much in Office 97 remains annoying. Two dozen shortcuts are scattered on the Start menu in no apparent order; the Shortcut Bar is filled with an overwhelming number of applications; and many hidden gems are tucked away in various places on the Office 97 CD. *Office 97 Annoyances* illustrates step-by-step how to get control over the chaotic settings of Office 97 and shows how to turn the vast array of applications into a simplified list of customized tools ready to execute whatever task they've been designed for.

This book shows you how to:

- Configure the Office Shortcut Bar to provide an effective tool for accessing Office applications and documents
- Customize the toolbar of each Office application except Outlook
- Use Visual Basic for Applications (VBA) as a macro language to control the behavior of the individual Office components
- Control pan-Office "sticky" settings
- Manage shortcomings in the Office Binder, an integration utility developed to address shortcomings in Office integration

How to stay in touch with O'Reilly

1. Visit Our Award-Winning Web Site

http://www.oreilly.com/

★ "Top 100 Sites on the Web" —*PC Magazine*
★ "Top 5% Web sites" —*Point Communications*
★ "3-Star site" —*The McKinley Group*

Our web site contains a library of comprehensiveproduct information (including book excerpts and tables of contents), downloadable software, background articles, interviews with technology leaders, links to relevant sites, book cover art, and more. File us in your Bookmarks or Hotlist!

2. Join Our Email Mailing Lists

New Product Releases

To receive automatic email with brief descriptions of all new O'Reilly products as they are released, send email to:
listproc@online.oreilly.com
Put the following information in the first line of your message (*not* in the Subject field):
subscribe oreilly-news

O'Reilly Events

If you'd also like us to send information about trade show events, special promotions, and other O'Reilly events, send email to:
listproc@online.oreilly.com
Put the following information in the first line of your message (*not* in the Subject field):
subscribe oreilly-events

3. Get Examples from Our Books via FTP

There are two ways to access an archive of example files from our books:

Regular FTP

- ftp to:
  ftp.oreilly.com
  (login: anonymous
  password: your email address)
- Point your web browser to:
  ftp://ftp.oreilly.com/

FTPMAIL

- Send an email message to:
  ftpmail@online.oreilly.com
  (Write "help" in the message body)

4. Contact Us via Email

order@oreilly.com
To place a book or software order online. Good for North American and international customers.

subscriptions@oreilly.com
To place an order for any of our newsletters or periodicals.

books@oreilly.com
General questions about any of our books.

software@oreilly.com
For general questions and product information about our software. Check out O'Reilly Software Online at **http://software.oreilly.com/** for software and technical support information. Registered O'Reilly software users send your questions to: **website-support@oreilly.com**

cs@oreilly.com
For answers to problems regarding your order or our products.

booktech@oreilly.com
For book content technical questions or corrections.

proposals@oreilly.com
To submit new book or software proposals to our editors and product managers.

international@oreilly.com
For information about our international distributors or translation queries. For a list of our distributors outside of North America check out:
http://www.oreilly.com/www/order/country.html

O'Reilly & Associates, Inc.
101 Morris Street, Sebastopol, CA 95472 USA
TEL   707-829-0515 or 800-998-9938
          (6am to 5pm PST)
FAX   707-829-0104

O'REILLY™

TO ORDER: **800-998-9938** • **order@oreilly.com** • **http://www.oreilly.com/**
OUR PRODUCTS ARE AVAILABLE AT A BOOKSTORE OR SOFTWARE STORE NEAR YOU.
FOR INFORMATION: **800-998-9938** • **707-829-0515** • **info@oreilly.com**

Titles from O'Reilly

Please note that upcoming titles are displayed in italic.

WEB PROGRAMMING

Apache: The Definitive Guide
Building Your Own Web Conferences
Building Your Own Website
CGI Programming for the World Wide Web
Designing for the Web
HTML: The Definitive Guide, 2nd Ed.
JavaScript: The Definitive Guide, 2nd Ed.
Learning Perl
Programming Perl, 2nd Ed.
Mastering Regular Expressions
WebMaster in a Nutshell
Web Security & Commerce
Web Client Programming with Perl
World Wide Web Journal

USING THE INTERNET

Smileys
The Future Does Not Compute
The Whole Internet User's Guide & Catalog
The Whole Internet for Win 95
Using Email Effectively
Bandits on the Information Superhighway

JAVA SERIES

Exploring Java
Java AWT Reference
Java Fundamental Classes Reference
Java in a Nutshell
Java Language Reference, 2nd Edition
Java Network Programming
Java Threads
Java Virtual Machine

SOFTWARE

WebSite™ 1.1
WebSite Professional™
Building Your Own Web Conferences
WebBoard™
PolyForm™
Statisphere™

SONGLINE GUIDES

NetActivism   NetResearch
Net Law   NetSuccess
NetLearning   NetTravel
Net Lessons

SYSTEM ADMINISTRATION

Building Internet Firewalls
Computer Crime: A Crimefighter's Handbook
Computer Security Basics
DNS and BIND, 2nd Ed.
Essential System Administration, 2nd Ed.
Getting Connected: The Internet at 56K and Up
Linux Network Administrator's Guide
Managing Internet Information Services
Managing NFS and NIS
Networking Personal Computers with TCP/IP
Practical UNIX & Internet Security, 2nd Ed.
PGP: Pretty Good Privacy
sendmail, 2nd Ed.
sendmail Desktop Reference
System Performance Tuning
TCP/IP Network Administration
termcap & terminfo
Using & Managing UUCP
Volume 8: X Window System Administrator's Guide
Web Security & Commerce

UNIX

Exploring Expect
Learning VBScript
Learning GNU Emacs, 2nd Ed.
Learning the bash Shell
Learning the Korn Shell
Learning the UNIX Operating System
Learning the vi Editor
Linux in a Nutshell
Making TeX Work
Linux Multimedia Guide
Running Linux, 2nd Ed.
SCO UNIX in a Nutshell
sed & awk, 2nd Edition
Tcl/Tk Tools
UNIX in a Nutshell: System V Edition
UNIX Power Tools
Using csh & tsch
When You Can't Find Your UNIX System Administrator
Writing GNU Emacs Extensions

WEB REVIEW STUDIO SERIES

Gif Animation Studio
Shockwave Studio

WINDOWS

Dictionary of PC Hardware and Data Communications Terms
Inside the Windows 95 Registry
Inside the Windows 95 File System
Windows Annoyances
Windows NT File System Internals
Windows NT in a Nutshell

PROGRAMMING

Advanced Oracle PL/SQL Programming
Applying RCS and SCCS
C++: The Core Language
Checking C Programs with lint
DCE Security Programming
Distributing Applications Across DCE & Windows NT
Encyclopedia of Graphics File Formats, 2nd Ed.
Guide to Writing DCE Applications
lex & yacc
Managing Projects with make
Mastering Oracle Power Objects
Oracle Design: The Definitive Guide
Oracle Performance Tuning, 2nd Ed.
Oracle PL/SQL Programming
Porting UNIX Software
POSIX Programmer's Guide
POSIX.4: Programming for the Real World
Power Programming with RPC
Practical C Programming
Practical C++ Programming
Programming Python
Programming with curses
Programming with GNU Software
Pthreads Programming
Software Portability with imake, 2nd Ed.
Understanding DCE
Understanding Japanese Information Processing
UNIX Systems Programming for SVR4

BERKELEY 4.4 SOFTWARE DISTRIBUTION

4.4BSD System Manager's Manual
4.4BSD User's Reference Manual
4.4BSD User's Supplementary Documents
4.4BSD Programmer's Reference Manual
4.4BSD Programmer's Supplementary Documents
X Programming
Vol. 0: X Protocol Reference Manual
Vol. 1: Xlib Programming Manual
Vol. 2: Xlib Reference Manual
Vol. 3M: X Window System User's Guide, Motif Edition
Vol. 4M: X Toolkit Intrinsics Programming Manual, Motif Edition
Vol. 5: X Toolkit Intrinsics Reference Manual
Vol. 6A: Motif Programming Manual
Vol. 6B: Motif Reference Manual
Vol. 6C: Motif Tools
Vol. 8 : X Window System Administrator's Guide
Programmer's Supplement for Release 6
X User Tools
The X Window System in a Nutshell

CAREER & BUSINESS

Building a Successful Software Business
The Computer User's Survival Guide
Love Your Job!
Electronic Publishing on CD-ROM

TRAVEL

Travelers' Tales: Brazil
Travelers' Tales: Food
Travelers' Tales: France
Travelers' Tales: Gutsy Women
Travelers' Tales: India
Travelers' Tales: Mexico
Travelers' Tales: Paris
Travelers' Tales: San Francisco
Travelers' Tales: Spain
Travelers' Tales: Thailand
Travelers' Tales: A Woman's World

O'REILLY™

TO ORDER: **800-998-9938** • **order@oreilly.com** • **http://www.oreilly.com/**
OUR PRODUCTS ARE AVAILABLE AT A BOOKSTORE OR SOFTWARE STORE NEAR YOU.
FOR INFORMATION: **800-998-9938** • **707-829-0515** • **info@oreilly.com**

International Distributors

UK, EUROPE, MIDDLE EAST AND NORTHERN AFRICA (EXCEPT FRANCE, GERMANY, SWITZERLAND, & AUSTRIA)

INQUIRIES
International Thomson Publishing Europe
Berkshire House
168-173 High Holborn
London WC1V 7AA
United Kingdom
Telephone: 44-171-497-1422
Fax: 44-171-497-1426
Email: itpint@itps.co.uk

ORDERS
International Thomson Publishing Services, Ltd.
Cheriton House, North Way
Andover, Hampshire SP10 5BE
United Kingdom
Telephone: 44-264-342-832 (UK)
Telephone: 44-264-342-806 (outside UK)
Fax: 44-264-364418 (UK)
Fax: 44-264-342761 (outside UK)
UK & Eire orders: itpuk@itps.co.uk
International orders: itpint@itps.co.uk

FRANCE
Editions Eyrolles
61 bd Saint-Germain
75240 Paris Cedex 05
France
Fax: 33-01-44-41-11-44

FRENCH LANGUAGE BOOKS
All countries except Canada
Telephone: 33-01-44-41-46-16
Email: geodif@eyrolles.com
English language books
Telephone: 33-01-44-41-11-87
Email: distribution@eyrolles.com

GERMANY, SWITZERLAND, AND AUSTRIA

INQUIRIES
O'Reilly Verlag
Balthasarstr. 81
D-50670 Köln
Germany
Telephone: 49-221-97-31-60-0
Fax: 49-221-97-31-60-8
Email: anfragen@oreilly.de

ORDERS
International Thomson Publishing
Königswinterer Straße 418
53227 Bonn, Germany
Telephone: 49-228-97024 0
Fax: 49-228-441342
Email: order@oreilly.de

JAPAN
O'Reilly Japan, Inc.
Kiyoshige Building 2F
12-Banchi, Sanei-cho
Shinjuku-ku
Tokyo 160-0008 Japan
Telephone: 81-3-3356-5227
Fax: 81-3-3356-5261
Email: kenji@oreilly.com

INDIA
Computer Bookshop (India) PVT. Ltd.
190 Dr. D.N. Road, Fort
Bombay 400 001 India
Telephone: 91-22-207-0989
Fax: 91-22-262-3551
Email: cbsbom@giasbm01.vsnl.net.in

HONG KONG
City Discount Subscription Service Ltd.
Unit D, 3rd Floor, Yan's Tower
27 Wong Chuk Hang Road
Aberdeen, Hong Kong
Telephone: 852-2580-3539
Fax: 852-2580-6463
Email: citydis@ppn.com.hk

KOREA
Hanbit Media, Inc.
Sonyoung Bldg. 202
Yeksam-dong 736-36
Kangnam-ku
Seoul, Korea
Telephone: 822-554-9610
Fax: 822-556-0363
Email: hant93@chollian.dacom.co.kr

SINGAPORE, MALAYSIA, AND THAILAND
Addison Wesley Longman Singapore PTE Ltd.
25 First Lok Yang Road
Singapore 629734
Telephone: 65-268-2666
Fax: 65-268-7023
Email: daniel@longman.com.sg

PHILIPPINES
Mutual Books, Inc.
429-D Shaw Boulevard
Mandaluyong City, Metro Manila, Philippines
Telephone: 632-725-7538
Fax: 632-721-3056
Email: mbikikog@mnl.sequel.net

CHINA
Ron's DataCom Co., Ltd.
79 Dongwu Avenue
Dongxihu District
Wuhan 430040
China
Telephone: 86-27-3892568
Fax: 86-27-3222108
Email: hongfeng@public.wh.hb.cn

ALL OTHER ASIAN COUNTRIES
O'Reilly & Associates, Inc.
101 Morris Street
Sebastopol, CA 95472 USA
Telephone: 707-829-0515
Fax: 707-829-0104
Email: order@oreilly.com

AUSTRALIA
WoodsLane Pty. Ltd.
7/5 Vuko Place, Warriewood NSW 2102
P.O. Box 935
Mona Vale NSW 2103
Australia
Telephone: 61-2-9970-5111
Fax: 61-2-9970-5002
Email: info@woodslane.com.au

NEW ZEALAND
Woodslane New Zealand Ltd.
21 Cooks Street (P.O. Box 575)
Waganui, New Zealand
Telephone: 64-6-347-6543
Fax: 64-6-345-4840
Email: info@woodslane.com.au

THE AMERICAS
McGraw-Hill Interamericana Editores, S.A. de C.V.
Cedro No. 512
Col. Atlampa 06450
Mexico, D.F.
Telephone: 52-5-541-3155
Fax: 52-5-541-4913
Email: mcgraw-hill@infosel.net.mx

SOUTH AFRICA
International Thomson Publishing South Africa
Building 18, Constantia Park
138 Sixteenth Road
P.O. Box 2459
Halfway House, 1685 South Africa
Telephone: 27-11-805-4819
Fax: 27-11-805-3648

O'REILLY™

O'Reilly & Associates, Inc.
101 Morris Street
Sebastopol, CA 95472-9902
1-800-998-9938

Visit us online at:
http://www.ora.com/
orders@ora.com

O'REILLY WOULD LIKE TO HEAR FROM YOU

Which book did this card come from?

_____

Where did you buy this book?
- ❏ Bookstore
- ❏ Direct from O'Reilly
- ❏ Bundled with hardware/software
- ❏ Other _____

- ❏ Computer Store
- ❏ Class/seminar

What operating system do you use?
- ❏ UNIX
- ❏ Windows NT
- ❏ Other _____

- ❏ Macintosh
- ❏ PC(Windows/DOS)

What is your job description?
- ❏ System Administrator
- ❏ Network Administrator
- ❏ Web Developer
- ❏ Other _____

- ❏ Programmer
- ❏ Educator/Teacher

❏ Please send me O'Reilly's catalog, containing a complete listing of O'Reilly books and software.

Name _____   Company/Organization _____

Address _____

City _____   State _____   Zip/Postal Code _____   Country _____

Telephone _____   Internet or other email address (specify network)

Nineteenth century wood engraving
of a bear from the O'Reilly &
Associates Nutshell Handbook®
Using & Managing UUCP.

BUSINESS REPLY MAIL
FIRST CLASS MAIL   PERMIT NO. 80   SEBASTOPOL, CA

Postage will be paid by addressee

O'Reilly & Associates, Inc.
101 Morris Street
Sebastopol, CA 95472-9902